GLADSTONE AND IRELAND

GLADSTONE AND IRELAND

THE IRISH POLICY OF PARLIAMENT FROM 1850–1894

BY

LORD EVERSLEY

AUTHOR OF "PEEL AND O'CONNELL," "AGRARIAN TENURES,"
AND "COMMONS AND FORESTS"

GREENWOOD PRESS, PUBLISHERS
WESTPORT, CONNECTICUT

Originally published in 1912
by Methuen & Co., Ltd., London

Reprinted from an original copy in the collections
of the Brooklyn Public Library

First Greenwood Reprinting 1971

Library of Congress Catalogue Card Number 74-114520

SBN 8371-4795-6

Printed in the United States of America

PREFACE

I N 1887, after the rejection of the first Home Rule Bill, at the suggestion of Mr. Gladstone, I published, under the title of *Peel and O'Connell*, a review of the Irish policy of Parliament, from the Act of Union, in 1800, to the death of Sir Robert Peel, in 1850. I did not carry it further, as most of the chief actors in the period which followed, including Mr. Gladstone, were still alive, and it was not possible to write with the same freedom as on the earlier period. There is no longer this difficulty ; with a few exceptions the chief actors have passed away. I have therefore continued the story for nearly another half century, till the retirement of Mr. Gladstone from political life, in 1894, which marked the close of an epoch, of which he was the principal figure.

As in the earlier work, I have not attempted to write a full history of Ireland during this period. My object has been to explain the action of Parliament in respect of Irish affairs, to show its sequence and to point the conclusions from it. I have adverted to events in Ireland only so far as was necessary for this purpose. In the same view I have referred to my personal visits to Ireland in 1877–8, 1881–2, and 1887–8, and have included some passages from two journals of them which I published in 1887–8.

I need not add that I have made great use of Lord Morley's monumental work *The Life of Mr. Gladstone*, and of Mr. Barry O'Brien's most interesting *Life of Parnell*. There are also the works of Sir C. Gavan Duffy, Mr. A. M. Sullivan, Mr. T. P. O'Connor, Mr. Justin McCarthy, Mr. William

O'Brien, Mr. Michael Davitt, and Mr. F. H. O'Donnell, which deal with the same period, largely from an auto-biographical point of view. The Lives of Archbishop Tait, Mr. W. E. Forster, and the Duke of Devonshire also throw much light on parts of this period. The summaries of debates in Parliament in the *Annual Register* are in many cases as good as can be. After comparing them with the full records of debates in *Hansard*, I have made more or less use of them.

I must also express my grateful thanks to Lady Byles for the assistance she has most kindly rendered to me.

ABBOTSWORTHY HOUSE, WINCHESTER
February 20, 1912

CONTENTS

GLADSTONE AND IRELAND

CHAPTER I

IRELAND AFTER THE FAMINE

FOR nearly twenty years after the famine of 1846–7 there was little of interest in Irish affairs in the House of Commons. The schism which had occurred after the death of O'Connell between the main party of the Repeal Association and the Young Irelanders caused the withdrawal of popular support in Ireland from the former. The latter lost many of their leaders by the conviction and transportation of Smith O'Brien, Mitchel, Meagher, and Martin. Others narrowly escaped the same fate by flight and expatriation. Gavan Duffy, almost alone, remained of prominent leaders. He was twice put on trial, but in spite of every effort to pack juries for his conviction, some jurymen stood out for his acquittal, and the prosecutions failed. Duffy was editor of the *Nation*, and did his best, in that paper, to keep alive the spirit of the Young Irelanders. He was not a revolutionist, like Mitchel; he was a statesman, and an ardent land reformer. He protested against the practice of Irish Members using their influence in the House of Commons to obtain appointments for themselves, or for their friends and supporters. He urged in his paper that they should give a pledge not to accept office, and should hold themselves independent of the two main political parties in Parliament. This had been one of the main causes of difference between O'Connell and Young Ireland.

In O'Connell's opinion, it was a grave cause of complaint to Ireland that long after victory had been achieved for the cause of Catholic emancipation, all offices under the Government, whether of the higher class such as Judges, Stipendiary

Magistrates and others, or of the lower class, consisting of Postmasters, Excise and Customs Officers, and the like, were still conferred only on adherents of the old ascendancy party, and that Catholics were practically excluded. He saw nothing wrong, but rather the reverse, in his followers taking appointments, as the reward of Parliamentary support, or obtaining them for their friends and constituents. What better could they do? On the other hand the Young Irelanders maintained that such action, on the part of the representatives of Ireland, made it impossible for them, by legitimate pressure, to obtain any legislation which Ireland required.

At a meeting of the National Confederation Gavan Duffy carried a resolution in favour of an independent opposition, but it found no favour with the officers of the Repeal Association, and was disregarded. It is certain that in the years which followed the death of O'Connell, during the Governments of Russell, Aberdeen, and Palmerston, the Irish Members lost caste and influence in the House of Commons by their greed for appointments. The Whips of the Liberal Party, by promises or expectations held out to them and their supporters, could rely on most of them in party divisions.

Meanwhile in Ireland the process of clearing estates of their tenants, by wholesale evictions, was in full swing. The recent famine had made it impossible for vast numbers of these tenants to pay any rent at all for two or three years. The arrears of rent, thus accumulated, hung round their necks, and put them completely at the mercy of their landlords. The Encumbered Estates Act also gave an impetus to evictions in two ways. It became the interest of the owners of properties, listed for sale under the Act, to clear the estates of tenants, in order to increase their saleable value; and the introduction, after the sales, of a new class of owners, who came into possession without any of the traditions of the estates, or knowledge of the tenants, and who were bent only on making the best of their bargains, resulted in the same policy of clearance being pursued. In the years which followed the famine many wide districts in the west and elsewhere in Ireland were turned into grazing farms by the wholesale eviction of tenants.

This led to a great popular movement throughout Ireland in favour of a legal recognition of tenant right and security of tenure. In August, 1850, a Tenant Right Convention was held in Dublin, presided over by Dr. Gray (later Sir John Gray), the owner and editor of *The Freeman's Journal*. It was attended by a great array of delegates of tenant farmers from every part of Ireland, including Ulster. Resolutions were carried unanimously in favour of what were later known as the "three Fs," Fair Rent, Fixity of Tenure, and Free Sale of the tenants' interest—principles which were only conceded to tenants in Ireland in 1881, after more than thirty years of agitation, and of suffering from the harshness of the existing law.

Gavan Duffy joined in the movement and became its practical leader. Unfortunately for the success of the cause another storm broke out in the political world which roused the passions of the Catholics in Ireland, and distracted the attention of great numbers from the grievances of tenant farmers. It afforded the excuse for many who did not really sympathize with them, or whose personal interests were adverse to them, to ride off on another question.

Very shortly after the Tenant Right Convention a Papal rescript was issued, recognizing the Catholic hierarchy in Great Britain, and conferring territorial titles, drawn from English and Scotch cities in the dioceses, on Archbishops and Bishops, previously dignified only by foreign titles. The pastoral letter of Cardinal Wiseman, in which this Papal rescript was made public, was undoubtedly of a very contentious character, and such as was certain to rouse opposition. The scheme of the Papal Court was regarded in religious circles in Great Britain as an aggressive action, on the part of the head of the Church of Rome, full of menace to the Protestant cause. It created a panic in the minds of vast numbers of good people. Lord John Russell apparently sympathized personally with this view. At all events he gave way to this religious frenzy, and fanned it into a still stronger flame of fury, by a violent letter to the Bishop of Durham, in which he denounced the Papal rescript in the strongest terms. He did so as the head of the Government, but without concert with his colleagues in the Cabinet. This gave rise to a counter storm of indignation on the part of Roman Catholics, especially those in Ireland.

In the following year (1851) Lord John Russell introduced

in the House of Commons a Bill making the assumption of
titles by Roman Catholic Bishops illegal and punishable by
heavy penalties. This was supported by an overwhelming
majority of Members of both parties. In vain did some of the
ablest men in the House of Commons—such as Mr. Gladstone,
Mr. Bright, Sir James Graham, Mr. Roebuck, Mr. Sidney
Herbert, and others, endeavour to stem the tide of intolerance.
In vain they pointed out the futility of the measure, and the
certainty that it would prove a dead letter. The Irish Catholic
Members did their utmost to oppose the Bill, and strained the
forms of the House by obstructing it in Committee. The whole
Session was wasted in passing the Bill through the House
of Commons. It passed the House of Lords with little
difficulty, not, however, without some dignified protests by
Lord Aberdeen and others.

Chief among the Irish opponents of the Bill in the House of
Commons was William Keogh, a lawyer of small repute in his
profession, but a most powerful and persuasive speaker on the
public platform, who had already gained the ear of the
Nationalist Party in Ireland by his eloquence and force. He
was supported by John Sadleir, a financier who had founded
the Tipperary Bank, and had induced thousands of farmers, in
the south of Ireland, to deposit their savings in it, and who was
believed at that time to be a man of great wealth and financial
credit. With his relatives, Scully and Keatinge, and a few other
adherents, a small band was formed in the House of Commons,
who, by the violence of their opposition to the Ecclesiastical
Titles Bill, acquired the name of the " Pope's brass band."
Their action gained for them great applause in Ireland.
Subsequent events showed that these men were pursuing only
their own interests. They were glad to have the opportunity
of dishing the movement in favour of the tenant farmers.
They felt that the obligation imposed by the Tenants' League
of independent opposition in the House of Commons would
be fatal to their interests. They had no wish to commit themselves to a course, where they would be bound to refuse the
emoluments of office. The agitation against the Ecclesiastical
Titles Bill involved no such obligation. They were hoping for
office, Keogh in order to retrieve his finances, which were at
a very low ebb, and Sadleir and his friends to strengthen
their position in the financial world. The leaders of the

Tenants' League already distrusted these men. Gavan Duffy in *The Nation*, and Dr. Gray in *The Freeman's Journal*, made no secret of their hostility. They felt that the cause of the tenants was endangered by this rival agitation against the Ecclesiastical Titles Bill. The Tenants' League was supported by men of all religious opinions, by Protestants from Ulster, equally with Catholics from other parts of Ireland. A new great issue between Catholics and Protestants might drive a dangerous wedge between them, which would have a serious effect on the Tenant Right cause.

Early in 1852, the Government of Lord John Russell was unexpectedly defeated in the House of Commons on their Militia Bill. Resignation followed, and Lord Derby formed a new Government. Parliament was dissolved in July, and a General Election took place. As the result of it, the two main parties of Whigs and Tories were very evenly divided, so far as Great Britain was concerned. In Ireland the elections turned mainly on the Catholic and Tenant Right questions, with the result that sixty-two representatives were returned in the Catholic interest, and forty-three in favour of the Government. The majority, therefore, of the Irish members held the balance between the two main parties in the new Parliament. They were masters of the political position, and might make or mar a ministry.

The majority from Ireland consisted of three groups. There was the Whig section, including not a few landowners, moneyed men, and lawyers. There was the group of Keogh and Sadleir and his relatives and friends, who had violently opposed the Ecclesiastical Bill. Its numbers were increased by the result of the elections. There was also the group of staunch Tenant Righters, which had also added to its number. Gavan Duffy was returned, for the first time, by New Ross, Lucas by the County of Meath, and Maguire for Dungarvan—a great accession of debating strength. Isaac Butt also was first returned for an Irish constituency as a Protestant and Tory.

With rare exceptions all the sixty-two Members, consisting of the above three groups, had pledged themselves, in their elections, to support the programme of the Tenants' League. There was therefore a great opportunity for an Irish Party to insist upon its land policy. A Liberal Government could not be formed against their opposition. Nor could the

Tory Government have remained in office without their support.

In repeated speeches before and during the election Keogh had promised that he would maintain the independence of the Irish Party and would not take office unless their demands were acceded to

" I know," he said, " that the road I take does not lead to preferment. I do not belong to the Whigs. I never will belong to them. I do not belong to the Tories. I never will have anything to do with them."

At one of the meetings held in Cork, on behalf of the candidature of Mr. Scully, Keogh was attacked by Mr. McCarthy Downing and accused of insincerity to the tenants' cause. Keogh defended himself in a speech of great eloquence, which completely carried away his audience.

In the course of it he said:

" I have declared myself in the presence of the Bishops of Ireland and of my colleagues in Parliament, that the Minister of the day, be he whom he may—let him be the Earl of Derby, let him be Sir James Graham or Lord John Russell—it is all the same to me, so help me God. No matter who the Minister may, no matter who the party in power may be, I will neither support the Ministry nor that party, unless they come into power prepared to carry the popular measures which Ireland demands."

Immediately after the General Election, on September 8th, a Tenant Right Conference was held at Dublin, attended by forty of the newly elected Irish Members. A resolution was proposed at this meeting by Keogh, seconded by Mr. Roche (afterwards Lord Fermoy), pledging the Irish Members to hold themselves perfectly independent of, and in opposition to all Governments, which did not make it part of their policy to give to the tenants of Ireland a measure embodying the principles of Tenant Right and security of tenure.

When Parliament met it was still uncertain what course the Irish members would take. In the evenly balanced condition of the two main parties, they were masters of the position. The issue between the Whigs and the Tories was deferred, for a short time, till the Budget of Mr. Disraeli was before the House. In the meantime the leaders of the Liberals had time to compose their differences, and to present a united front to the enemy. The Irish vote was still trembling in the balance.

It has been asserted by Gavan Duffy that, at this juncture, negotiations took place between him and Mr. Disraeli for the support of the Irish members to Lord Derby's Government. He demanded on their behalf, as the price of their support, the adoption by the Government of a Tenants' Right Bill, which would be satisfactory to them. He said that Mr. Disraeli, who was Leader of the Government in the House of Commons, and therefore almost equal in authority to the Prime Minister, was willing to assent to this. But the secret of the negotiations leaked out, and came to the knowledge of the landlord party in Ireland. A question was put, on their behalf, in the House of Lords, to the Prime Minister by Lord Roden. Lord Derby, who was himself the owner of a great estate in the south of Ireland, and doubtless sympathized with the land-owning class, replied in unmistakable terms that nothing would induce him to support such a measure, which he agreed would be inconsistent with the rights of property.

The Irish members no longer hesitated. They felt assured that they had nothing to hope from Lord Derby's Ministry. They voted against the Budget. Their votes turned the scale. It was rejected by a majority of nineteen only, the exact number by which the Irish Liberals exceeded the Tory Members in that country. Lord Derby's Ministry came to an end. A new Government was formed by a combination of the Liberals and Peelites, with Lord Aberdeen as Prime Minister, and Lord John Russell as Leader in the House of Commons, without a portfolio, and Lord Palmerston as Home Secretary. All Ireland was in suspense. What would their members do in this crisis ? The new Government would be dependent on them. What was to be the condition of the support of the Irish members ? It soon transpired that the Irish Brigade had sold itself to Lord Aberdeen. Its leading members took office. Sadleir became Lord of the Treasury, William Keogh was Irish Solicitor-General, Edmond O'Flaherty was Commissioner of Income Tax, and so on.

On taking office, these men made no condition whatever as regards legislation for Ireland. The tenant farmers, and their claim for Tenant Right, were flung overboard. Nothing in the whole range of political history of Ireland ever caused more supreme and lasting disgust and loathing than this treacherous betrayal of its cause by Keogh and Sadleir, and their band of adherents. It is now well known that Keogh was, at that time, in the gravest financial difficulties. He was at the end of his resources. He was encumbered with debt. His professional income at the Bar was insignificant. The emoluments of office were essential to him. The position of Law Officer was the certain stepping-stone to a judgeship, which was the goal of his ambition. His election at Athlone had only been secured by the grossest bribery of the few electors there, at prices for votes which overcame every patriotic motive. His re-election, on taking office, was opposed by the Tenants' League, but in vain. The electors greedily swallowed again the great sums paid for their votes. The cost of this re-election added to Keogh's embarrassments. Sadleir was also at this time on the down grade, as regards his great financial operations. While every one in Ireland believed that he was a millionaire banker, of unimpeachable credit; while thousands of tenant farmers, in the south of Ireland, had entrusted him with their little hoards of savings, he had misused their trust, and had lost immense sums in wild speculations, and was already in the gravest difficulties. Office in the new Government might do much to restore his credit, though the salary was not large enough to make much difference. The Tenants' League successfully opposed him on re-election at Carlow. Later he found a seat at Sligo, another of the small and corrupt boroughs, which were the scandal of Irish Parliamentary representation. It is said that he bribed even the members of the Committee of his opponent to vote for him. He was elected by a small majority. In an action at law, arising out of a scandalous proceeding in this election, he perjured himself in the witness-box, and the jury found a verdict against him. As a result he was compelled, in January, 1854, to resign his office as Lord of the Treasury. Already there were rumours that his bank was in financial peril. This was averted for the time; but two years later the crash came. The bills of the Tipperary Bank were dishonoured by its agents in London. It was discovered that Sadleir had been raising money by forging bonds and other securities. He anticipated the public announcement of his crime and his arrest, by committing suicide. He was found dead early one morning on Hampstead Heath, with a tankard beside him smelling strongly of prussic acid. When the news reached Tipperary Sadleir's Bank closed its doors. Mad scenes occurred among its ruined depositors. Revelations were made of fraud, forgery, and robbery. The total of these defalcations reached to over a million.

O'Flaherty had already fled the country, leaving behind him bills to the amount of £15,000, bearing the name of Keogh among the rest, which was said to be forged. Later James Sadleir, the brother of the dead banker, was expelled the House of Commons for having fled the country under charge of fraud.

Keogh survived the ruin of his associates. In 1855, on the accession of Palmerston to the position of Prime Minister, in place of Aberdeen, he was promoted to the post of Attorney-General. In the following year he was raised to the Bench, in spite of the vehement and repeated protests of the Irish National Press.

Gavan Duffy in despair, finding that there was no prospect of Parliament doing anything for the cause he had at heart, determined to emigrate. He gave up the editorship of *The Nation*, and his seat in the House of Commons, in 1855. He emigrated to Australia, where he carved out a new and distinguished career for himself, and eventually became Prime Minister of the Colony of Victoria. Lucas, than whom the tenants in Ireland had no better friend and supporter, though he was not a native of that country, died about this time when on a mission to Rome. The Irish Parliamentary Party—so far as their leaders and men of influence and eloquence were concerned—were almost extinguished. During the Ministries of Aberdeen, Palmerston, and Russell, down to 1866, they gave no trouble. They hardly counted as a Parliamentary force. They were kept in order by the Liberal Whips—not without suggestion of corruption in some quarters, and at all events by the profuse distribution of patronage in the lower branches of the Civil Service. The defection of the Irish Party caused by the betrayal of their cause by the Keogh-Sadleir group had its effect in three following General Elections. In 1857 the Tories returned 48 out of the 103 Irish Members ; 55, or a majority, in 1859 ; and 48 again in 1865.

It was during Palmerston's last Ministry that the story

was told that some one pointed out to the Tory Whip that an Irish Member was taking notes, with the intention of speaking for the Government. " Are you sure it was not gold ? " the Whip replied.

During these twelve years no legislation of any value whatever was obtained by the Irish tenants from Parliament. Tenant Right Bills were introduced, in successive Sessions, by Mr. Sharman Crawford and others, but they were invariably rejected by overwhelming majorities.

In 1860 Mr. Cardwell, when Irish Secretary, endeavoured to deal with the question from a purely English point of view. He carried two measures through Parliament—the one enabling tenants for life of entailed estates to grant leases to farm tenants, but on terms so strictly limited that no one ever took advantage of it, and the measure was a total failure. The other measure, known as the Deasy Act, named after his Attorney-General, aimed at making tenancies in Ireland the subject of contract only, in destruction of any custom or common law claim to compensation for improvements. It declared that no tenant should be entitled to claim compensation for improvements, except under the terms of an express contract with his landlord. By what process of reasoning Mr. Cardwell could have persuaded himself that such a measure could possibly content the Irish tenants, as a settlement of their claims, it is difficult to conceive.

In 1865, when Mr. Maguire moved for a Committee to inquire into the working of Mr. Cardwell's Act of 1860, while agreeing to the motion, Lord Palmerston said that " for his part he could not see the justice or advantage of giving to one man the right of determining what should be done with another man's property." The Government was represented on the Committee by Mr. Cardwell, Mr. Lowe, and the then Chief Secretary for Ireland, Sir Robert Peel. At their instance the Committee, after hearing much evidence on behalf of the tenants, reported that the principle that compensation should only be secured upon improvements made with consent of the landlord ought to be maintained. This negatived completely any claim for retrospective improvements, and rejected the contention that tenants had any permanent interest in their holdings. From 1852 to 1866 the position of the Irish tenants in the British Parliament was absolutely hopeless.

Meanwhile, many landlords, in the south and west of Ireland, proceeded to put in force the full powers, which the English law, as interpreted by Irish judges, and supported by the Irish Executive, gave to them. They cleared their estates wholesale of tenants, without any compensation for their improvements, making cattle ranches of the land, or converting it into large tillage farms, and compelling the former tenants and their families to emigrate.

This process was commended to them by the rigid political economist of that period, as one which was justified by the laws of progress. They contended that it was in the interests of the Irish people that Ireland should be converted into a purely pastoral country, by the clearance of small tenants, and their forced emigration, and by the substitution of Scotch farmers familiar with large tillage farms.

These wholesale clearances had their effect, not only on the country districts immediately concerned, but on the neighbouring small towns, which had supplied the wants of the people thus dispossessed. Their trade was greatly reduced, while the population of the towns was often increased by a pauperized class of the evicted families, who were unable to afford the cost of emigration. The returns of emigrants from Ireland show that between 1849 and 1860 they numbered 1,551,000 and between 1860 and 1870 867,000. There were in addition the number of Irishmen and their families, who transferred themselves to the slums of the great towns in England, and those who crowded into the smaller towns of Ireland, or became agricultural labourers, without any land out of which to eke the miserable wages which the farmers could afford to pay.

CHAPTER II

ABOUT the year 1858 a revolutionary movement commenced in Ireland, and among the Irish, in the United States, under the name of Fenianism. It simmered unnoticed for a few years, and burst into flames in 1865–7. Historians concur with statesmen, such as Mr. Gladstone and Mr. Bright, in attributing this movement to the long neglect of Parliament to apply remedies for the undoubted grievances of Ireland, and to the wholesale evictions, and the clearance of estates, resulting in the enforced emigration of such vast numbers of Irish families, carrying with them the recollection of injustice and wrong.

The interior history of this Fenian conspiracy, and whence came the funds which financed it, is still very obscure. We know, however, that it had its origin in the United States, among the Irish who had emigrated from their native country, and that an Association was there formed which spread very widely through the country. It was based on extreme hostility to the British Government. The oath taken by its members bound them to make war against England when called on to do so. Its head centre was James Stephens, who had been implicated in Smith O'Brien's abortive outbreak, in 1848, and had escaped after many adventures. In 1858 he revisited Ireland, and founded in Dublin the Fenian organization known as the Irish Republican Brotherhood. It made preparations for a rising under promises of armed assistance from America.

The movement received no support whatever from the Bishops and clergy of the Catholic Church in Ireland, who had always objected to secret societies. Mr. A. M. Sullivan, the able owner and editor of *The Nation*, did his utmost to prevent the spread of the movement. In spite of this, the organization made rapid strides. It was claimed that many thousands of Irish soldiers in the British Army became members of it. Many Fenians enlisted for the purpose of inducing soldiers to join. Later, the conclusion of the Civil War in America set free great numbers of Irishmen, who had fought for the maintenance of the Union, and who were now ready, with Hibernian humour, to fight for the disruption of the British Empire. Many of them returned to Ireland for the purpose, and were engaged in secretly drilling the Fenian recruits. In 1863, in a Convention at Chicago, it was decided to make every preparation for a rising in Ireland. For two years the Fenian organ, *The Irish People*, preached treason in Ireland in the most open way. But in 1865, an informer, Pierce Nagle, gave full information to the authorities at Dublin Castle of the designs of the revolutionary party, and their personnel. Lord Wodehouse, the Lord Lieutenant (later and better known as Lord Kimberley), acted upon this information with great promptitude and vigour. He determined to anticipate a rising, and to crush the movement before it had the opportunity of making headway. On September 15th, 1865, the police broke into the office of *The Irish People* and suppressed its issue, and took into custody all concerned in it. O'Donovan Rossa, Luby, Kickham, O'Leary, and later James Stephens were arrested. The latter, however, effected his escape from Richmond Bridewell, with the connivance of some minor official, and, after being some weeks concealed in Dublin, fled to France. Rossa, Luby, Kickham, and O'Leary were tried for high treason by a special commission, over which, to the indignation of the Irish Party, Judge Keogh was selected to preside, and, on the evidence of Pierce Nagle, were convicted and sentenced to long terms of penal servitude.

This did not have the effect of suppressing the conspiracy. The American emissaries were still active in most parts of Ireland, and secret drillings continued. Early in the following year (1866) Lord Wodehouse applied to the Government in London for greater powers to deal with this revolutionary movement. The escape of Stephens, he said, had given fresh energy to it. Depôts and manufactories of arms had been discovered in various parts of Ireland, and large numbers of Irish-American emissaries were known to be dispersed throughout the country, swearing in members, endeavouring to seduce the troops from their allegiance, and holding out false hopes of the intervention of the United States Government. More than five hundred emissaries from America were known to the police, and their numbers were continually augmented from England and Scotland. The Government thereupon applied to Parliament, early in the Session of 1866, for a suspension of the Habeas Corpus Act, and for power to arrest on suspicion, and to detain in prison for six months, without trial, any persons who they had reason to believe were engaged in this conspiracy. A measure to this effect was carried through Parliament in a single day, and received the Queen's Assent on the following day.

Rapid as was the passage of this Coercion Bill through the House of Commons, it led to one very important speech being delivered, which had great influence on public opinion in England. Mr. Bright, while not opposing the measure, made one of his best and most impressive speeches on the state of Ireland. He expressed the shame and humiliation which he felt at being called upon, for a second time, in a Parliamentary career of twenty-two years, to suspend the constitutional rights of the people of Ireland. He traced the causes of the chronic discontent to the neglect of the Imperial Parliament, which since the Union had passed many Coercion Bills, but few good measures for Ireland. He pointed out that the fact of Fenianism having to some extent a foreign origin, aggravated the difficulty, and he asked why Englishmen and Scotchmen, when they emigrated, did not, like Irishmen, carry with them an inveterate hatred to the Government and institutions of their birth ? He declared that it was not in human nature to live content under such institutions as existed in Ireland, and when this insurrection was suppressed, there would still remain the seeds of another crop of disaffection. He believed there was a mode of making Ireland loyal, and he threw the responsibility of discovering it on the Government and on the Imperial Parliament. Mr. John Stuart Mill, the eminent philosopher, then Member for Westminster, supported Mr. Bright, and expressed the hope that if these extraordinary, but no doubt necessary, powers were granted, Parliament would not go to sleep for another eighteen years over the grievances of Ireland.

The measure was supported by Mr. Disraeli on behalf of the Conservative Opposition. Only six members voted against it. The new Act was put in force on the very day it passed through Parliament. Great numbers of arrests were made in Ireland. This led to the hurried departure of numerous emissaries from America. The country appeared outwardly to subside into its usual state of tranquillity. The Fenians in America, however, still maintained the belief that an armed rising in Ireland was possible. Stephens publicly pledged himself that it would take place in 1866. The year went by and no great insurrection occurred. Sporadic attempts, however, were made in many parts of the country. Men assembled at the instance of some central association, and met at specified places, but they found no arms ready for them ; they were easily dispersed.

Another series of State trials took place at which the chief promoters of the movement were sentenced to penal servitude. The movement was apparently extinguished by these measures. At all events disaffection was driven below the surface. Two incidents, however, occurred, which exercised a great influence in succeeding years.

The first of these was the forcible release from a prison van at Manchester, in 1867, by an armed body of Fenians, of Colonel Kelly, who was being conveyed to prison. Colonel Kelly had succeeded Stephens as the head of the Fenian movement in Ireland. He had crossed the Channel for the purpose of attending a Fenian meeting at Manchester, and was arrested there with a companion, Captain Deasy, by the police, in ignorance of their identity and under the suspicion that they were engaged in a burglary. Thirty armed Fenians attacked the van on its way to the prison, and dispersed the drivers and guards. They called on Sergeant Brett, the policeman who was inside the van with the prisoners, to open the door and release Kelly and Deasy. On his refusal to do so, one of them fired a shot from a pistol through the keyhole of the door, with the object of forcing it open. The shot struck Sergeant Brett and killed him. A female prisoner in the van then took the key from Brett's pocket, opened the door, and released Kelly and Deasy. They made their escape and were not recaptured. Meanwhile a large body of policemen made their appearance on the scene, and after a fierce struggle with the body of men engaged in the attack, succeeded in capturing twenty-six of them.

A Special Commission of two judges was appointed to try these men. Five of them were found guilty of murder, and seven others of riot and assault. Subsequent inquiries proved that one of the five was present only as a spectator, and that he had no part in the conspiracy. He was accordingly pardoned. Another of the five was reprieved on the ground that he had not been armed. The remaining three — Allen, Larkin, and O'Brien (*alias* Gould)—were hanged. The seven convicted of riot were sentenced to penal servitude.

Mr. Justice Blackburn, who with Mr. Justice Mellor tried these cases, laid down as law that if the jury were satisfied that the accused had a common design, that dangerous violence was used in furtherance of that design, and that death resulted from it, the crime was murder. This was undoubtedly sound law. Subsequent events, however, in Ireland showed that it was a grave error on the part of the Government to inflict capital punishment on these men. There was much doubt from the evidence whether the three men were more responsible for what occurred than any of the others engaged in the affair, or whether any one of the three had actually fired the fatal shot.

On being found guilty, these men, while disclaiming any intention to kill Brett, claimed that their complicity in the attack was in the nature of a political offence. They made a dramatic appeal from the dock to Irish opinion by joining in the exclamation, " God save Ireland," a phrase which became a watchword with the Irish people. Irish opinion was profoundly roused on their behalf. It was believed that they had been unjustly condemned and hanged. They became martyrs in the eyes of the Nationalists. Multitudes of people in every part of Ireland made demonstrations, by processions through the streets, to testify their grief. Mr. A. M. Sullivan took part in one of these processions at Dublin, and condemned the execution of these men in his paper. He was prosecuted with others for attending an unlawful assembly, but the jury did not convict. In further proceedings, however, he was convicted of seditious libel, and was sentenced to six months' imprisonment, in spite of the fact that he had done his best to discourage Fenianism.

A monument was later erected by public subscription to the memory of the Manchester martyrs, as they were called, in the centrè of the town of Ennis (County Clare), without hindrance by the Government.

The other case was that known as the Clerkenwell explosion. It came to the knowledge of the Irish Fenians in London that one of their leaders, General Burke, was imprisoned in Clerkenwell jail. An attempt was made to effect his release in December, 1867. A barrel of gunpowder was placed against the wall of the prison, in a narrow street. On this being exploded the wall of the jail was blown down for some length. The prisoner, fortunately for him, was not in that part of the prison. If he had been there, he would have been blown to pieces by the action of his friends. The result of this reckless proceeding was that twelve harmless persons, living in houses on the opposite side of the street, were killed, and a hundred and twenty were wounded. For this most wanton attack a man named Barrett was convicted of murder, and was hanged at Newgate, without causing any demonstrations of sympathy on his behalf in Ireland.

These two violent acts for a time greatly exasperated public opinion in England against the Irish. They had, however, the effect of bringing home to the English people the depth of discontent among Irishmen, and the necessity for probing its causes, and finding some remedy which should alleviate it. The best evidence of this is to be found in a passage of a speech delivered by Mr. Gladstone two years later, when speaking in the course of the debate on the Disestablishment of the Irish Church.

" In my opinion, and in the opinion of many with whom I communicated, the Fenian conspiracy has had an important influence with respect to Irish policy. . . . The influence of Fenianism was this—that when the Habeas Corpus Act was suspended, when all the consequent proceedings occurred, when the tranquillity of the great city of Manchester was disturbed, when the metropolis itself was shocked and horrified by an inhuman outrage, when a sense of insecurity went abroad far and wide . . . then it was when these phenomena came home to the popular mind, and produced that attitude of attention and preparedness on the part of the whole population of this country which qualified them to embrace in a manner foreign to their habits in other times, the vast importance of the Irish question."[1]

Reverting to 1866; it is to be noted that in the debate on the Address at the commencement of the Session, Mr. Gladstone, as Leader of the House, made his first important pronouncement on Irish policy. An amendment was moved by The O'Donoghue expressing regret at the widespread disaffection in Ireland, and representing that it was the duty of the Government to examine and remove the causes of it. Mr. Gladstone, in reply, while opposing the motion, said that the law must be vindicated, and that being done, inquiry into the existence of disaffection became an obligation which no Government could resist. The Fenian conspiracy, instead of releasing the Government from the obligation to improve the conditions of Ireland, raised it higher, and he appealed to the House to judge the Government by their conduct on the various measures which would be brought forward. The principle on which they would frame their measures was that of consideration for Irish opinion on purely Irish questions. The amendment was supported by only twenty-five Members.

Among the few able and independent men at that time representing the Irish Party in the House of Commons were Sir John Gray and Mr. Maguire. The former had been a follower of O'Connell in the repeal agitation. He had been put on trial with his chief in 1844. He had been Lord Mayor of Dublin and was greatly distinguished as a municipal reformer. He was the owner and editor of *The Freeman's Journal*, the most important of the organs of the more moderate branch of the Irish Party. He had recently been one of the founders of the Tenants' League. He had also, on behalf of his paper, instituted an inquiry into the condition and funds of the Established Church, the report of which had produced a great effect on public opinion in Ireland. On April 10th, 1866, he made a motion in the House of Commons to the effect " that the position of the Established Church in Ireland is a just cause of dissatisfaction to the people of that country and urgently demands the consideration of Parliament." He contended that the Establishment had failed polemically and politically, and had accomplished no object for which it was imported into the country. It had neither succeeded as a missionary

[1] *Hansard;* May 31st, 1869.

Church in winning over the Roman Catholic population nor had even held its own.

He disclaimed any wish or intention to transfer one shilling from the Protestant Church to the Roman Catholic priesthood. He concluded by pointing out the great importance of removing the feeling of religious inequality, produced by the ascendancy of one Church over the others, and alleged that this question lay at the root of all Irish grievances.

The Irish Secretary, Mr. Chichester Fortescue, replied that though personally regarding the resolution with cordial concurrence, it was impossible for the Government to accept it, unless they were prepared to follow it up by immediate action, and he maintained that Irish opinion was not yet sufficiently clear, strong, and matured to call upon them for that. The opposition, therefore, of the Government, at the present moment, would be founded not on any grounds of equity or of permanent policy, but simply on considerations of time and circumstances. Mr. Whiteside, an eminent lawyer, representing Dublin University, speaking on behalf of the Opposition, vehemently opposed the motion. He denied that Ireland was a Roman Catholic country. He contended that the intelligence, wealth, and industry of Ireland were Protestant. He stigmatized the motion as an attack on property and on the Protestant religion, prompted by the Roman hierarchy. The debate was adjourned before coming to a decision on the motion, but it was of great importance as indicating the drift of opinion of the Government.

Later in the same Session the Irish Secretary dealt with another thorny subject. He introduced a Bill for giving effect to Mr. Cardwell's Land Act of 1860, which had proved to be a dead letter. He proposed that where tenants in the future effected permanent improvements, they should be entitled, if dispossessed by their landlords, to a lump sum equivalent to the increased letting value of their holdings.

This Bill was violently opposed by the Conservative Party in the House of Commons. Lord Naas (later Lord Mayo) moved a resolution condemning it as injurious to the holders of small farms, and affirming the principle that compensation should only be granted for improvements made with the consent of the landlord. The debate which followed was of the more interest as it led to speeches by Mr. Lowe (later Lord

Sherbrooke) and Mr. John Stuart Mill, each stating with great force the opposite views of two schools of political economy on the subject of Irish Land Tenure.

Mr. Lowe pointed out that the introduction of a compulsory term into voluntary contracts was a blunder and a solecism ; for if both parties knew of it, provision would be made against it, and if one of the two was ignorant, a fraud would be committed against him. He warned the House against dealing with this question on sentimental grounds, maintaining that in legislating for Ireland it was the duty of Parliament not to deviate from the strict principles of political economy. The object of the Bill, he said, was to perpetuate small holdings. These contracts should be regulated by supply and demand. Emigration, if left alone, by reducing competition would in time put the tenants in a position to get better terms. Concession, he warned the House, would not end there ; fixity of tenure must follow, and ultimately a permanent settlement like that of Bengal.

Mr. Mill made a closely reasoned speech in reply. The measure, he said, was a fulfilment of the promise of the Government, made by Mr. Gladstone early in the Session, to legislate for Ireland according to Irish exigencies and not according to English routine. It had been said that what would do for England might do for Ireland. In this application of the same laws to England and Ireland, not only did they not know the people of whom they were talking, but they did not know themselves. The fact was that Ireland was not an exceptional country. It was England that was exceptional. Was there any other country in the world where, as a general rule, the land was held in large farms, and was cultivated by capitalists, at rents fixed by contract, while the mass of the people were entirely detached from it, and simply received their day's wages ? In this respect Ireland resembled the rest of the world. It was England that was peculiar. Was it therefore right to look to England's experience to meet Ireland's exceptional case ? They ought rather to look to continental experience, for it was there where the similarity to Ireland could be found to exist. What did continental experience tell them as a matter of historical fact ? It told them that wherever a system of agricultural economy, like that in Ireland, had been found consistent with good cultivation and the good condition of its peasants, rents had not been fixed as in Ireland by contract, but the occupier had the protection of fixed usage, the custom of the country, and had secured to him permanence of tenure so long as he pleased to possess it. He maintained that the right of the improver of the land to the value of his improvement, so far from infringing on the rights of property, was of itself a right of the same description as those of property.[1] The speech pointed to a much wider remedy than that in the Bill—to some form of security of tenure and judicial determination of rents.

The debate on the Bill was adjourned, and it did not come on for discussion again. Within a short time the Government of Lord Russell was defeated in Committee on the Bill for extension of the Parliamentary franchise in England and Wales —on an amendment moved by Lord Dunkellin, son of Lord Clanricarde—an Irish Whig Member. Lord Russell resigned, and Lord Derby formed a new Government in which Lord Mayo became Irish Secretary. His first task was to introduce a Bill for the renewal of the Act for suspending the Habeas Corpus Act. Mr. Maguire opposed the renewal of the Act on the ground that the ordinary tribunals had sufficiently vindicated the law, and that measures of repressing unaccompanied by those of a remedial nature tended rather to aggravate than lessen discontent and disaffection. No case, he said, had been made out for continuing despotic government.

Mr. Gladstone, on behalf of the Opposition, supported the Government. He did not think that it would be proper, when a new Government had entered on office, to anticipate their policy towards Ireland. If the late Ministry had been in office it would have been their duty to apply for a renewal of the Act. The second reading of the Bill was carried by 108 to 31.

In the Session of 1868, during Lord Derby's administration, and while the Reform Bills for Scotland and Ireland were still under discussion, a most important debate took place on the state of Ireland, spread over four days. It was one of the rare debates which are the turning-points in political history, and in which the policies of the two great parties in the State are definitely pronounced, and the issue between them fairly laid before the country.

[1] *Hansard*, May 17th, 1866.

Mr. Maguire, on the part of the Irish Members, opened the discussion, alleging that the discontent in Ireland, which was the cause of the Fenian conspiracy, had its origin in the land question, and in the existence of the Established Church. The former had led to the exodus of vast numbers of the Irish people, and to the planting in America of implacable enemies to British rule and power ; while the latter was a scandal and a monstrous anomaly, which Englishmen, if it applied to themselves, would not tolerate for a single hour. He repudiated on the part of the Catholics any desire to participate in the spoil of the Protestant Establishment. The Catholic Bishops and clergy, he said, had declared over and over again that they would not touch a farthing of the funds of the Established Church, although derived from lands once the property of the Catholics. They could not accept any payment from the State, for they well knew, if they were to accept it, they would lose all spiritual influence over their flocks, and would become either the spies or the stipendiaries of the State. Lord Mayo, the Irish Secretary, replied on behalf of the Government. While not denying that much disaffection and disloyalty existed in Ireland, he claimed that it was among a much lower class of persons than in previous cases, that all landowners or traders, of whatever religion, were strenuous opponents of Fenianism, that the Catholic Bishops and clergy were also opposed to it, and that the real strength of the movement was in the United States.

While denying that the creation of a peasant proprietary, such as had been advocated by Mr. Bright, Mr. Mill, and Sir John Gray, would be beneficial to Ireland and would have a conservative effect, alleging that it would only lead to the old system of subdivision of property, he intimated that the Government would introduce a Bill for giving greater facilities to limited owners to grant leases. They also proposed to confer a charter on a new Catholic University. With regard to the Established Church, nothing could be done until a Royal Commission had reported, but the indication was that the Government were inclined to a policy of levelling up, in the sense of endowing the Catholic clergy out of State funds, or out of the superfluous property of the Established Church.

The announcement of this policy gave no satisfaction to the Irish Party in the House of Commons. Mr. Mill and Mr. Lowe renewed their duel on the subject of agrarian legislation, the former defending a proposal he had recently launched in a pamphlet, for buying out the landlords in Ireland and turning the tenants into peasant proprietors. The most important speech in the debate was that of Mr. Gladstone, who boldly announced an Irish policy far in advance of anything he had done in the past. The Church as a state institution, he said, must cease to exist. He condemned the proposal to effect religious equality by levelling up, and redividing the revenues of the Church among the clergy of other denominations, or by endowment out of State funds. As regards land legislation he asserted the real grievance of Ireland had been acknowledged by the Devon Commission. The improvements effected by the tenants should be admitted by law to be their property. He thought that the full recognition of this would obviate the necessity for any fixity of tenure. As regards the University question he admitted that the Irish had a grievance, but he threw cold water on the proposal for creating a purely Catholic University. The scheme of the Government was an idea only which was dead before it had lived. It will be seen that this momentous speech of the statesman, to whom Lord Russell had recently surrendered the leadership of the Liberal Party, foreshadowed the policy pursued by Mr. Gladstone with enormous vigour during the next few years.

Later, with the object of pledging the party to the policy of disestablishing and disendowing the Irish Church, Mr. Gladstone moved in the House of Commons a series of resolutions ; the first and most important of them to the effect " that it is necessary that the Established Church of Ireland should cease to exist, due regard being had to all personal interests and to all individual rights of property." The resolution was framed so as to pledge the House to the policy of disendowing the Church as well as disestablishing it. It led to a debate spread over eleven days. The resolution was carried by a majority of fifty-six after negativing a dilatory motion of Lord Stanley on behalf of the Government.

This was followed up by a Bill for suspending new appointments in the Irish Church. It was carried through all its stages in the House of Commons, by majorities of about the same as that for the resolution. In the House of Lords the Bill was rejected, on the motion for its second reading, after a long debate, by a majority of 93—192 to 99. The speeches of Lord Derby, on behalf of the Government, and of Lord Salisbury, who had lately left the Government on account of their Reform Bill, were especially violent. They described the policy indicated by it as complete spoliation. Lord Derby denied that the Catholics of Ireland had any grievance. They had everything they wanted except their neighbour's goods. The Queen was to be called upon to act in direct opposition to her Coronation oath. The policy was inconsistent with the Union. Ireland would gain nothing, and would suffer by being deprived of a class of resident gentry. It would be dangerous to England and fatal to Ireland. Lord Salisbury appealed on the highest ground, that of justice to the Irish Church, and to the Irish Protestants, who had always been loyal, and whose loyalty might not be proof against such ungenerous treatment. He called on the House to reject so crude, violent, and objectless a measure. These violent speeches paled beside the fiery discourse of the Archbishop of Armagh.

"If your Lordships," he said, "overthrow the Irish Established Church, you will put to the Irish Protestants the choice between apostasy and expatriation, and every man among them who has money or position, when he sees his Church go, will leave the country. If you do that, you will find Ireland so difficult to manage that you will have to depend on the gibbet and the sword." [1]

On the first defeat of the Government, in the House of Commons, on the resolutions respecting the Irish Church, Mr. Disraeli tendered their resignation to the Queen, but it was ultimately decided that they should remain in office until after the dissolution of Parliament, which was to be expedited so as to take place in the autumn. This seems to have been the best course, for an immediate dissolution was practically impossible. It was necessary to complete the Reform Bills for Scotland and Ireland, and to give time for the registration of new voters there and in England. The Irish Reform Bill need alone concern us. The existing franchises in Ireland were nominally wider than in England, but practically much more restricted. For the Counties in Ireland the franchise was an occupation of £12 in value, and for Boroughs £8 in value, as

[1] *Hansard*, June 26th, 1868.

compared with £50 and £10 in England. But the numbers of voters were relatively much fewer in Ireland owing to the general average of wealth being so much less.

The Irish Reform Act was a very small measure. It left the County franchise as it was. It established a £4 rate of franchise for Boroughs in lieu of the household suffrage in England. The Government resisted any extension of it and was supported by small majorities of the House. The result was that while in England the Reform Act of 1868 gave an immense extension of the suffrage, both in the Counties and in the Boroughs, and was accompanied by a considerable, though insufficient, redistribution of seats, that in Ireland was almost a nullity, leaving the electoral franchise much as it was, and preserving the numerous corrupt little Boroughs. It was not till 1884 that Ireland was dealt with, as regards the franchise and the distribution of seats, in a manner which gave a fair Parliamentary representation to its people.

CHAPTER III

THE IRISH CHURCH

LATE in the year 1868, after the settlement of the Reform question, Parliament was dissolved and a General Election took place. The issue before the constituencies turned almost wholly on the Irish Church. The very great extension of the Borough franchise in Great Britain, giving to the working classes a great preponderance of electoral power, did not result in any immediate demand affecting the interests of labour. Justice and religious equality to Ireland were the main topics, conceived on the part of the new electors in a lofty and unselfish public spirit. The credit of inspiring this generous policy was mainly due to Mr. Gladstone. For the first time in his career, in a series of great meetings in his candidature in South-West Lancashire, he developed fully his remarkable powers on the public platform. His speeches, most cogent in their argument, and persuasive in form, appealed to the higher instincts of his audiences, and of the electors of the whole country through the Press. They concentrated the attention of the Liberal Party in Great Britain on his Irish policy.

The Disestablishment and Disendowment of the Irish Church may seem to us now a task easy of accomplishment ; but the risks at the time to the Liberal Party and to the position of its leader were great. The Church of England was very strong, especially in Lancashire. It feared that its own fate might be involved in that of its sister establishment in Ireland. It put forth its full strength. Mr. Gladstone's closely reasoned speeches were the main cause of success at the elections. As a result of them, the Liberal Party improved its position by the gain of twenty-eight seats. It obtained a majority of 112 in the three countries. The votes of the newly enfranchised working men in the Boroughs of Great Britain were mainly responsible for this. In the English Counties the Liberal Party suffered many losses. Mr. Gladstone himself was defeated by Mr. Cross (later Lord Cross) in South-West Lancashire. He was indebted for a seat in the new Parliament to the Borough of Greenwich, which had elected him, without putting him to the labour of personal intervention in the contest. Lord Hartington, Mr. Bruce (later Lord Aberdare), Mr. Milner Gibson, Mr. Roebuck, Mr. Horsman, Mr. Bernal Osborne, and Mr. Frederick Peel, all of them conspicuous members of the Liberal Party, were among the slain. Mr. Mill was defeated in the contest for Westminster, a most serious loss to the House of Commons.

In Ireland, Liberals, Tenant Righters, and even Fenians united to support candidates pledged to Mr. Gladstone's policy. It was the last occasion on which there was a straight issue in that country between the two historic parties. Seven seats were won, on the balance, mainly by Whig candidates, and as the result of the election forty-two supporters only of the Government were returned and sixty-three of the various sections of the Opposition. Of these about half consisted of pure Whigs. But they had, for the most part, pledged themselves to support the principle of Tenant Right.

Mr. Disraeli did not wait for the meeting of Parliament. He made a new precedent by resigning office, after the elections were over, admitting that the verdict of the country was against him. Mr. Gladstone was then commissioned by the Queen to form a Ministry. On receiving an intimation to this effect at Hawarden, when engaged in felling a tree, he is reported to have said gravely, " My mission is to pacify Ireland."

The Cabinet, which Mr. Gladstone then formed, was undoubtedly, so far as its personnel was concerned, the ablest and best of his four Ministries, and the most homogeneous—a great element of strength. It was also the Government which made the most mark in legislation of any in the nineteenth century. It was most earnestly desirous of pacifying Ireland by measures of justice and equality. Only a single Irishman, however, was a member of the new Cabinet, Mr. Chichester Fortescue, afterwards Lord Carlingford, a Whig of detached and independent views, who was more advanced on the question of Land

Reform than almost any of his colleagues. He was appointed Irish Secretary. Mr. O'Hagan, who had been a Young Irelander in his early days, became Lord Chancellor of Ireland with a peerage, and Serjeant Sullivan, a lawyer of eminence and of subtle intellect, was the Irish Attorney-General. The Government, therefore, was well manned for dealing with Irish questions. Mr. Bright, as President of the Board of Trade,[1] was the only Radical in the new Cabinet

On the meeting of the new Parliament, the Coercion Act of the previous year was allowed to expire, and Mr. Gladstone lost no time in presenting a Bill for dealing with the Irish Church. He introduced it, on March 1st, 1869, in a speech three and a half hours in length, and of remarkable perspicuity, without a redundant sentence, as generously admitted by his opponent Mr. Disraeli, enlivened here and there by passages of great eloquence. His great and complex scheme was the product of his own brain and invention. No one of his colleagues in the Government had any share in it. It bore the impress of his financial genius. There was no other man in the country who could have worked it out with the same completeness and thoroughness in detail, and with the same tender regard for the permanent interests of the religious body he was dealing with. No other statesman could have given a popular explanation of it, so as to make its underlying principles, and its method of achieving them, intelligible and acceptable to the whole body of the supporters of the Government, and impervious to the attacks of his opponents. Its object was to sever, at once and for ever, all connection between the Episcopal Protestant Church of Ireland and the State, and, by disendowing it of its temporalities, to remove every vestige of grievance on the part of the great majority of the people of Ireland, in respect of the inequality of treatment of religious bodies ; at the same time to do so in a manner which would fully respect all vested rights of individuals, and would set up the severed Church as a voluntary association, and give it the best chance of maintaining itself in the future.

Provision was made in the Bill for the constitution of a new Church Body or Synod, in which all the churches and parsonage houses, and all endowments given to the Church since the

---

[1] The writer was associated with Mr Bright as Secretary to the Board of Trade.

Reformation, were to be vested. A temporary Commission was also to be created, to whom all the other property of the Church, its tithes, and the landed property of the Episcopal and other bodies, and ancient endowments of all lands, were to be transferred, with instructions to wind them up by sale or otherwise, and to pay for life to the existing holders of all benefices or offices, under the Church, their present stipends, subject, however, to the condition that they were to continue to perform their accustomed services and duties, while in receipt of their salaries, under the control of the new Church Synod. The Church Commission was empowered to agree to commutations of the life salaries of the Bishops and clergy, on the demand of a certain proportion of the clergy of each diocese, and to hand over the commutation money to the new Synod. The annual vote of £25,000 to the Catholic College for Priests at Maynooth was to be capitalized at the rate of fourteen years' purchase; and the capital sum was to be handed over to the governors of that College. The life interests of the Nonconformist ministers in Ulster, who were the recipients of the Regium Donum grant of £35,000 a year, were to be respected in the same way as those of the Disestablished Church, and the grant was thenceforward to cease.

The total value of the Church property of all kinds was estimated at about 16 millions, of which 9 millions represented the value of the tithe rent charges, and $6\frac{1}{2}$ millions the value of the landed and other property. The estimated commutation of the stipends of the clergy was £5,700,000. The capital sum for extinguishing the grant to Maynooth and the Regium Donum was £1,100,000 and the compensation to the owners of advowsons £900,000. Other charges and expenses made up a total of about $8\frac{1}{2}$ millions, leaving an estimated surplus, after the process of winding up was completed, of about $7\frac{1}{2}$ millions. It was proposed in the Bill to devote this to the relief of unavoidable calamity in Ireland. Specific appropriations were proposed for lunatic asylums and county infirmaries. The preamble of the Bill laid down the important principle that no part of the surplus was to be devoted to the support of any religious bodies—thus negativing the principle of concurrent endowment of other religious bodies.

In propounding this scheme Mr. Gladstone, over and over

again, insisted that it was in the permanent interest of the Church itself. " I believe," he said, " it will be favourable to religion." " It is essential to those principles of right on which any religion must rest." " The establishment cannot continue to exist with advantage to itself or without mischief to the country." " The measure must be prompt and final— the grievance must be put out of sight, out of hearing, out of mind. The Church must not be inflicted with the pain of a lingering death. Every means should be taken of softening the transaction." " The proposed commutation would be favourable to the Church by enabling the Church body and individual incumbents to adjust their relations, and make a more economical application of their resources, than would be possible by the maintenance of the original annuities." [1]

When we look at the results of the scheme, since it passed into law, we shall see how enormously important this principle of commutation has been in saving for the newly constituted Church a large part of its endowment. Looking back, we may surmise that Mr. Gladstone foresaw this, but abstained from explaining it more fully, lest he should alienate some of his supporters among the Catholics of Ireland, and the Noncon- formists of England, by showing how favourable the scheme would be to the Disestablished Church, and what large endowments would remain to it, on the assumption that the Church people did their best to meet the new position.

Mr. Disraeli moved the rejection of the Bill on the second reading, in a speech which, even at this distance of time, is worth reading for its literary merit, although its substance was unsound, and none of his gloomy prophecies have been verified. He strongly opposed Disestablishment on principle. " It is," he said, " because there is an Established Church that we have obtained religious liberty, and enjoy religious toleration, and without the union of Church and State, I do not see what security there would be for religious liberty or toleration."

On the subject of Disendowment he was most emphatic, and his speech was loaded with expressions of " confiscation," " plunder," " robbery," and " sacrilegious spoliation." " In a certain number of years," he said, " the Protestant Church will not have left to them a shilling of property, while they

[1] *Hansard*, March 1st, 1869.

will see a richly endowed Roman Catholic clergy and a comfortable Presbyterian body, and both provided for out of their property."

Mr. Disraeli's speech, though carefully prepared and laboured, and not without its passages of eloquent attacks, did not leave the impression of real earnestness and conviction, or of belief in successful opposition. These elements were supplied in the debate by Dr. Ball, Member for the University of Dublin, a lawyer of eminence, and a most eloquent champion of the Irish Church, and Mr. Gathorne Hardy, representing Oxford University, who expressed in passionate language the opinions of the great majority of the clergy of the Church of England. They presented the case against the Bill as well as it could be. The point on which both of them most relied was that the Bill, if passed, would be a virtual repeal of the Act of Union of 1801, by doing away with an essential part of it, which declared that the Protestant Church of Ireland was to continue, and that it was to be one as regards doctrine, discipline, and government with the Church of England. Dr. Ball inveighed against the harshness and unrelenting rigour with which the Bill had been framed. The inevitable result of it, he said, would be general discontent—of the clergy, because the sources of their endowment would be taken from them, of the laity because new and additional burthens would be imposed on them. Religious animosities would be increased and great bitterness of feeling would result. He had doubts whether the new Episcopal body of the Church of Ireland could ever be formed. In any case, the Bill was no presage of peace and conciliation. It would be a precedent for organic changes of a more dangerous character. Mr. Gathorne Hardy followed in the same strain. In an impassioned peroration he said : " When I find that endowments, which I believe are sacred to the service of Almighty God, are given to purposes for which they were never intended, and taken from those who have done no wrong . . . when also I find that Protestants, left without clergy to look after them, will be absorbed in the Roman Catholic body, to the best of my judgment and to the best light of my conscience the Bill is alike wrong in the sight of God, and against the interests of my country. I do not hesitate to denounce and oppose this sacrilegious measure."

It cannot be said that Mr. Gladstone was much aided by

any speeches from Irish Members, or from his Nonconformist supporters. They were effaced by his own complete defence of the Bill. The most conspicuous speech in support of the Bill was that of Mr. Bright, who dealt with the subject in a lofty spirit—one of his greatest efforts in the House of Commons —his only speech of real distinction while a member of the Government.

The Bill was read a second time by a majority of 118. It passed through the Committee stages unscathed, after long discussions. Here again Mr. Gladstone was supreme. He defended his scheme against all opponents, and completely silenced them in debate, by his infinite superiority of knowledge of the subject. The only assistance he needed and received was that of the Irish Attorney-General, who on legal points showed great skill in debate. The Government was supported by unfailing majorities. The measure, with a very few minor concessions, passed a third reading by a majority of 124.

In the House of Lords the fate of the Bill long hung in the balance. The position of the Liberal Government there was not then so hopelessly impotent, as it has been in later years. During Lord Palmerston's Ministries, the two parties had been almost evenly divided in the House of Lords. In 1869, the normal majority of the Tory Party was believed to be about forty. It was known that some of the Tory Peers would vote for the Bill, but it was quite uncertain, up to the last moment, which way the balance would lie.

We now know, from the published letters of Queen Victoria and Archbishop Tait, that the Queen, though much disapproving the policy of the Irish Bill, and regretting that it had been thought necessary by Mr. Gladstone to introduce it, was most anxious to avoid a conflict between the two Houses of Parliament, and regarded with the greatest alarm the result of a hostile vote on the Bill by the Lords. In letters to the Archbishop the Queen urged him to use his influence in favour of the second reading of the Bill.[1] This fell in with the Archbishop's own views. He was not influenced in the opposite direction by a letter from Mr. Disraeli, who had so recently elevated him to his high position, urging that the Lords should be " brave, firm, and unfaltering."

[1] *Life of Archbishop Tait*, II, 24.

The Archbishop was more than an exemplary prelate of the Church ; he was a most sagacious and independent statesman. He recognized that the Church of Ireland, as it existed, was indefensible.

The Bill was introduced by Lord Granville. He was supported in debate by Lord Salisbury and Lord Carnarvon, who, two years previously, had resigned their posts in Lord Derby's Government and who, in 1868, had spoken and voted against the Suspensory Bill ; also by Lord Grey and by the veteran Lord Russell.

The Conservative Party in the Lords was then led by Lord Cairns, who had been Lord Chancellor in Mr. Disraeli's short Government, on the retirement of Lord Derby. He was an Irishman from Ulster, sharing in the strong anti-national views and the narrow prejudices of the Protestants of that province. He spoke in the strongest terms against the Bill, and advised its rejection. He was supported by Lord Derby in this last, but not the least effective, of his many eloquent and polished speeches. Lord Derby had resigned office in the Liberal Government of 1834, sooner than agree to the very limited proposal to appropriate a small part of the revenues of the Irish Church to secular purposes, a measure which in three successive years was rejected by the House of Lords, and was finally dropped. It is conceivable that if concessions had then been made, the Irish Church might have been saved from the present wider attack on it. Lord Derby was unchanged and unchangeable. He asserted that the Bill was opposed to the Act of Union and to the Coronation Act of the Sovereign ; that it was as impolitic as it was immoral. The speech of the debate, however, for the Opposition was that of Dr. Magee, Bishop of Peterborough, who had recently been promoted to this See from an Irish Deanery. He represented with extraordinary force and eloquence, which electrified the usually torpid House, the repugnance of Irish Protestants to the Bill. He attacked the Bill mainly on its general policy, as an act of injustice, cruel, harsh, and niggardly. He denied that the verdict of the electors had been given on any such scheme. He was supported in this view by Dr. Alexander, the Bishop of Derry—later Archbishop of Armagh, whose speech is worthy of notice, if only for the purpose of showing that Bishops are not endowed with the gift of prophecy. He affirmed that voluntaryism was quite unsuited to Ireland. The Bill, he said, would leave the Irish Church unprovided for after the death of the existing clergy. It would bring about in Ireland "an atheistical nation, under the redominion of a Papal Legate, and stamped with undying hostility to the Protestant religion."

Throughout all the speeches of the opponents of the Bill there was the same misconception as to its effects. There was an incapacity to understand how the Irish Church could be reconstituted under the new scheme, and how its clergy and its services could be maintained. There was also a strong desire among many Peers to appropriate the surplus, resulting from winding up the property of the Church, to the provision of residences and glebes for the Roman Catholic and Presbyterian clergy.

Archbishop Tait, while recommending the Peers not to reject the Bill, on the second reading, and himself abstaining from voting, attacked its details. There can be little doubt that the Archbishop averted the defeat of the Bill at this stage. Had he thrown his influence against it the Lords would have rejected it. He did not indeed persuade his episcopal brethren. Fifteen of them voted solid against the Bill. The Archbishop of York and the Bishop of Oxford (Wilberforce) abstained from voting. Alone the Bishop of St. Davids (Thirlwall) voted for it after a most powerful speech, in which he completely disposed of the episcopal argument against it that it was sacrilege. The result of the division was uncertain up to the last minute, but when the tellers came to the table it appeared that the second reading had been carried by a majority of 33—179 to 146.

As often happened in the House of Lords, the acceptance of the principle of the Bill, on the second reading, was only a prelude to an attempted destruction of it in detail in Committee. The Conservative lords fell upon the clauses, and wrought havoc on them. They struck out of the preamble the important words excluding the application of any part of the surplus funds of the Disestablished Church to religious purposes. Later, they introduced a clause, on the motion of Lord Stanhope, enabling the purchase of residences for Catholic and Presbyterian clergy. This was strongly opposed by Lord Cairns, but was carried against the Government by a small majority. They then proceeded to deal with the finance of the Bill, increasing in a number of different ways the amount to be left in the hands of the intended Church body, so as to form a new endowment for the Church. Of the seven millions, estimated as the surplus, five millions were to be appropriated in this way. The Government made some concessions. They agreed to give half a million in lieu of private endowments acquired by the Church, since 1660, about double their estimated amount. They agreed to an addition of 7 per cent to the commutation money, on the plea that the lives of the clergy were of longer duration than the average of ordinary persons, according to the usual tables of mortality, an estimate which turned out to be incorrect. These concessions in no way conciliated the Opposition, but rather whetted their appetite for more, in their seven nights' struggle in Committee on the Bill.

The mutilated Bill returned to the House of Commons. Mr. Gladstone made short work of the Lords' amendments. He affirmed that they practically destroyed the Bill. Instead of disendowing the Church, the Bill, as altered, would leave it a highly endowed body, free from any State control. Those who had proposed these changes had been living in a balloon. The House of Commons supported Mr. Gladstone by majorities as great as those which had passed the Bill. It returned the Bill to the House of Lords in its original form, with the exception of the concessions already referred to, and a few minor amendments. The House of Lords met again, on July 20th, to consider whether to insist on their amendments. Meanwhile the Queen had again been active in urging conciliation. A letter to the Archbishop said: " The Queen cannot view without alarm the possible consequence of another year of agitation, which would be likely to result in worse, rather than better, terms for the Church. Concessions will have to be made on either side." [1]

On taking up the Bill again, the Lords seemed to be ready for battle, and prepared to face the consequences of the defeat of the Bill. The first question for them was their amendment to the preamble. By a large majority, they insisted on the exclusion of the words forbidding the application of the funds to any religious purposes. Thereupon Lord Granville moved

[1] *Life of Archbishop Tait,* II, p. 36.

the adjournment of the House, intimating that the Government could no longer be responsible for the conduct of the Bill. A short delay occurred before the House met again. This was availed of by the Queen and the Archbishop for further negotiations. Dr. Tait was for giving way still further, and so also Mr. Disraeli appears to have been.

A conference finally took place between Lord Granville and Lord Cairns. The latter took upon himself to come to terms, which practically surrendered the claims of the House of Lords, subject to a very few concessions on the part of the Government. The proposed provision of residences for Catholic and Presbyterian clergy was abandoned. The Government agreed to leave the distribution of the surplus funds to a future Parliament, and to give up their scheme for applying part of it to lunatic asylums. The final demands of the Lords were reduced to very slender proportions. The Government agreed to add another 5 per cent to the commutation money when effected through the Church body. When the Lords met again the crisis was over. Lord Cairns justified the course he had taken, on his own initiative, of agreeing to these terms. No exception was publicly taken by the party behind him. But Lord Derby immediately rose from his seat and left the House in great dudgeon.[1] There can be little doubt that the final arrangement was due mainly to the influence of the Queen and to the Archbishop. In his journal the Archbishop wrote :

" We have made the best terms we could, and thanks to the Queen, a collision between the Houses has been avoided ; but a great occasion has been poorly used, and the Irish Church has been greatly injured, without any benefit to the Roman Catholics."[2]

The sequel has not justified the Archbishop's verdict on the transaction.

It remains to state briefly the results to the Protestant Episcopal Church of Ireland of the great measure, so much dreaded by its members. Forty-three years have elapsed since it became law. With very rare exceptions, all the Bishops and clergy then existing, and whose life interests in their stipends were respected and provided for by the Act, have

---

[1] Lord Derby never entered the House again. He died three months later. [2] *Life of Archbishop Tait*, II, p. 42.

passed away, and a new generation of clergy has grown up, under completely altered conditions, no longer connected with the State, or provided for out of State endowments. It is now certain that not one of the gloomy predictions of the Irish and English prelates in the House of Lords, or of opposing politicians in both Houses of Parliament, has been verified. Everything has occurred in the interval, in the manner provided under the Act, and in the order and with the fortunate results expected and promised by Mr. Gladstone. The Church reconstituted and reorganized itself immediately after the Act without any difficulty. A governing Church body was formed, and was sanctioned by Charter from the Crown, consisting of Bishops and clergy and of lay members in equal numbers, and with the addition of a certain number of co-opted members, of whom a majority were laymen. This representative body tackled the difficulties of the new position with courage, and with the greatest financial ability and prevision.

They wisely determined to avail themselves of the scheme which had been foreshadowed by Mr. Gladstone, and rendered possible by his Act. By their advice, the Bishops and clergy, with rare exceptions, agreed to the commutation of their emoluments and salaries on the terms of the Act, and the payment of the aggregate of these commutations to the Church body, to whom they looked in the future for the payment of their existing stipends, and to whom they were bound to render their services as ministers. The Commission appointed, under the Act, to wind up the affairs of the Church, paid over to the new Church body, in respect of 1282 Bishops and incumbents, the sum of £5,818,000, the actuarial value of their interests in those endowments, with the addition of 12 per cent conceded by Parliament, and in respect of 900 curates the sum of £1,700,000. They also paid the sum of £500,000 for private endowments created since the Reformation. The Church body therefore found itself in possession of a capital sum of about £8,000,000, with the obligation to pay their existing stipends to the Bishops and clergy.

The Church body then appealed to the members of their Church in Ireland, and to churchmen in England, for immediate support in subscriptions and donations for the maintenance of their Church. The appeal met with a generous response in Ireland, and a somewhat niggardly one in England.

In the two or three years after the Act subscriptions and donations were made to them, at the rate of £220,000 a year, and for the whole forty years they have averaged £165,000, and have amounted to an aggregate of over 6 millions.

The Church body then set to work to reduce the redundant members of their clergy. They were able to effect this by offering to the clergy favourable terms of release from the obligation of continued service during their lives. Those of the age of thirty-five were allowed to go free, on accepting one-third of the commutation money secured to them by the Act, and those of the age of sixty-five were allowed two-thirds of the same, with proportional increases or reductions for inter-mediate ages. Upwards of 1000 of the 2380 clergy compounded on these terms and were freed from further service. The resulting profit to the Church body of these compounding clergy amounted to no less than £1,300,000. The number of the clergy for the future establishment was greatly reduced by the amalgamation of parishes where Churchmen were few in number, with the result that the total number now employed is 1535, compared with 2380 before 1869. The present aggre-gate of stipends of the Bishops and clergy is £314,000 exclusive of their residences and glebes, as compared with £590,000 a year inclusive of residences and glebes at the time when the commutations were fixed. For ten of the Bishops alone the stipends are now £18,000 a year, compared with £48,800 a year under the old conditions.

The result of all these operations has been that the Church body is now in possession of all the churches, of all the resi-dences of the Bishops and clergy, of glebes for the rural clergy not exceeding in each case ten acres, for which they have paid £587,000, and of invested funds valued at slightly over 9 millions, the interest of which is more than sufficient to pay the stipends as now fixed of its Bishops and clergy. The Church body is further in receipt of annual subscriptions and donations which for the last five years have averaged £165,000 a year, of which £100,000 a year is provided by parochial assessments voluntarily paid, and the remainder by donations to the Church body itself.

It is stated on good authority that the total number of persons of all ages who are members of the Church is 580,000, of whom 209,000 are in the Diocese of Down. It may be doubted whether any religious body in the United Kingdom, not connected with the State, is so well provided with a staff of clergy, receiving better income, or has a larger endowment in proportion to its members.

The position of the disestablished Church as a religious community is not less satisfactory. Its Synod, freed from control of the Legislature, has been able to make what changes it desired in its ritual.

The most striking testimony to the good effect of the great Act in giving vitality to the Church was that of Lord Plunket, late Archbishop of Dublin, who had been Bishop of Meath in 1869, and had strongly opposed the passing of the measure. In his episcopal charge, in 1892, after twenty-three years' experience of the working of the new order, he said :

" When I count up the advantages which followed Disestablishment, when I think of the renewed strength and vitality which our Chuich has derived from the admission of the laity, and responsible participation in the councils, in the disposition of patronage, and in the financial departments of her work, when I observe the spirit of unity and mutual respect which has been engendered by the ordeal of our common adversity, and the increased loyalty and love which are being daily shown to their Mother Church by those who have had to make some sacrifice on her behalf, when I remember too the freedom from agrarian complications, which our disconnection with all questions of tithe and the tithe rent charge has brought about, and the more favourable attitude, as regards our influence on the surrounding population, which we occupy because of our severance from any State connection, when I remember all the counterpart of advantages which we enjoy in our new and independent position, and when I try to hold the balance evenly and weigh the losses and the gains of the whole, I say, boldly and without reserve, that in my opinion at least the gain outweighs the loss."

Not less conspicuous have been the political results of the great Act of 1869. It has completely removed every vestige of grievance in Ireland of religious inequality. There is no suggestion of jealousy on the part of other religious bodies of the large endowments remaining to the Protestant Episcopal Church. It is recognized that the present favourable position is due to the efforts of its clergy and laity, during

the time when the life interests of the clergy were running
out.

The eventual surplus, after winding up the property of the
Church, was in close accord with the original estimate of Mr.
Gladstone. He expected a surplus of 7½ millions. Concessions
during the passing of the Bill reduced this by about one
million. The actual surplus has proved to be about 7 millions. It has been disposed of by successive Acts of Parliament as follows : (1) Intermediate Education, £1,000,000 ;
(2) the Royal University, £600,000 ; (3) Pensions to
National School Teachers, £1,300,000 ; (4) the Congested
Districts Board, £1,500,000 ; (5) Distress Works, £1,271,000 ;
(6) Arrears of Rent (1882), £1,950,000 ; (7) Sea Fisheries,
£250,000.

The great success—financial, religious, and political—of the
Act of 1869 is a striking tribute to Mr. Gladstone's constructive
power, and to his energy, ability, and enthusiasm in carrying
the scheme. Of all the men of his generation there was no
one who had such a grasp of principle, and such a mastery
of detail, by the combination of which such a great operation
was carried through.

CHAPTER IV

THE LAND ACT OF 1870

NO sooner was the Session of 1869 at an end, and its great achievement, the Irish Church Disestablishment Bill, safely landed, than Mr. Gladstone turned his almost superhuman energies to the even more complex and difficult subject of Irish Land Tenure. Through many months of the recess he was engaged in studying the past literature of the question, and in corresponding with his colleagues in the Cabinet, in the endeavour to bring them into harmony for legislation in the coming Session.

The subject was new to him. He had never previously taken part in the debates on Irish Tenant Right Bills. It did not call into play his great genius for finance. It bristled rather with legal difficulties of great complexity and subtlety. The scheme which ultimately resulted from his labours was not, like that dealing with the Irish Church, his own sole invention. It appears to have been largely, if not mainly, the product of his two Irish advisers, Mr. Chichester Fortescue and Sir Edward Sullivan. To the latter, perhaps, must be mainly attributed the important feature of the Bill, which commended itself to Mr. Gladstone, and which was ultimately, by his persuasion, adopted by the Cabinet, namely the concession to the Irish tenants of something more than compensation for improvements effected by them, and which took the form of payment for goodwill, on eviction by their landlords.

In order to understand the principle involved, and its bearing on subsequent legislation, it is necessary to point out that the great bulk of the Irish tenants, large and small, held their farms under yearly tenancies, liable to eviction after six months' notice to quit. By the law, as it then stood, the tenant, on giving up his holding, was not entitled, apart from any specific covenant, to compensation for any improvements effected by himself and his predecessors. With the rarest exceptions, however, all the improvements, including the houses and farm buildings and everything which added to the original and prairie value of the land, had been effected by the tenants. The landowners as a rule had done nothing to improve the land. They were not expected, as English landowners were, to erect and maintain the buildings or to drain, fence, or otherwise improve the land. This state of the law applied equally to Ulster as to the rest of Ireland ; but a well-defined and universally admitted custom in that province, not sanctioned by the law, mitigated its hardships. Under this custom the tenant, on giving up his holding, was entitled to claim either from the incoming tenant or from the landlord, not merely the value of the improvements, but a money payment beyond, which represented the goodwill in the farm. It was well understood also that a tenant, once in possession, was entitled to remain there, so long as he paid his rent, and also that the rent would not be increased to a point when it would impair the customary tenant right ; and further that a tenant had the right to sell his interest in the holding to an incoming solvent tenant, to whom the landowner could make no valid objection. This custom existed throughout the whole of the Province of Ulster, varying, however, as to the amount payable for good-will. Though not recognized by law, it was practically enforced by combinations of tenants, and was acquiesced in by landlords. It was well understood that there would be no scruple, on the part of tenants, in resorting to an agrarian vendetta, if any serious breach of the custom was committed by a landowner ; and some of the most determined murders and outrages had occurred in that province, in the rare cases when the custom was violated by the landlord.

Analogous customs existed in some other parts of Ireland. Whether recognized by landowners or not, payments were generally made by incoming to outgoing tenants. The essence of the new scheme, incorporated by Mr. Gladstone in his Irish Land Bill, was the legal recognition of the Ulster custom, so far as concerned the payment of the customary tenant right to an outgoing tenant, including not merely compensation for improvement, but also a payment for goodwill, and its extension to the rest of Ireland by an analogous provision.

A scale of payments to the outgoing or evicted tenant was laid down, varying from seven times the rent in the case of holdings under £10 a year in value, to twice the rent in respect of holdings of £100 a year. It was provided, however, in respect of this statutory compensation, that it was not to be paid, in the event of eviction for refusal or neglect to pay rent, unless the judge authorizing the eviction should hold that, under the special circumstances of the case, it ought to be paid. This, if adopted, would have enabled the Court to deal with cases where the non-payment of rent was due to its exorbitant amount, or to the failure of crops, or to a great fall of prices, or to other exceptional circumstances.

It is clear from the correspondence referred to by Lord Morley that Mr. Gladstone had great difficulty in bringing his colleagues into line on this scheme. There was a section of his Cabinet, including the Duke of Argyll, Lord Clarendon, Mr. Lowe, and Mr. Cardwell, who were political economists of the older type, far removed from the school of Mill, and who stood by the English principles of landownership. There was Mr. Bright, who recognized fully the evils of the existing state of things in Ireland, but who believed that they could only be cured by multiplying small ownerships of land. He urged a scheme for effecting this, by gradually converting tenants into owners, with the aid of State loans. The sterner economists objected to this scheme almost as much as they did to the interference with freedom of contract. It was also no immediate remedy, for it could only be given effect to gradually, as estates came into the market, and it would leave the great bulk of the tenantry without any protection.

There was, lastly, Mr. Fortescue, the only member of the Cabinet who had any knowledge of Irish tenancy, who recognized that the tenants of Ireland were not the product of free contracts, but were in the nature of hereditary holders of the land, with a qualified, customary, but legally unrecognized right of occupancy, for which it was necessary to provide protection against arbitrary eviction. Mr. Fortescue prevailed with his chief and through him with the Cabinet, and the economists ultimately gave way ; while Mr. Bright was appeased by the promise of clauses, which would give effect to his views as to the conversion of tenants into owners, by the advance of two-thirds of the purchase money by the State on favourable terms of interest and repayment of principal spread over a term of years.

It may seem strange to us now when looking back at these proceedings, by the light of subsequent events, that no effort was made to ascertain what would satisfy the Irish tenants themselves, through their representatives in the House of Commons, or through their organs in the Press, such as *The Freeman's Journal.* No negotiations appear to have been undertaken in these directions. The demands of the tenants, as formulated in many Tenant Right Associations and at public meetings, were for fixity of tenure, at rents to be fixed by law or arbitration, and for the right of free sale. The scheme of the Government was very far short of this. There was to be no interference with the amount of rent. The landlords were to retain power to raise their rents, subject to the right of the tenants to give up their holdings, and to claim the compensation provided in the Bill. There were no means of compelling a reduction of rent however exorbitant, or however much it might expropriate the admitted interest of the tenant. There was no fixity of tenure, and no right of sale by an outgoing to an incoming tenant. The Ulster custom, therefore, was not legalized so far as its most important features were concerned. Still less was protection given to tenants in other parts of Ireland against rack-renting landlords.

The principle and the policy of the measure have never been more tersely and clearly explained than in a letter of Mr. Gladstone's to Archbishop Manning, quoted by Lord Morley : " The Bill," he wrote, " is intended to prevent the Irish landlord from using the terrible weapon of arbitrary and unjust eviction, by so framing the handle that it shall cut his own hands with the sharp edge of pecuniary damages. The man evicted without any fault, and suffering the usual loss by it, will recover whatever the custom of the country gives, and where there is no custom, according to a scale, besides whatever he can claim for permanent buildings or reclamation of land. Wanton eviction will, as I hope, be extinguished by provisions like these. And if they extinguish wanton eviction, they will also extinguish those demands for unjust augmentations of rent, which are only formidable to the occupier because the power of wanton or arbitrary eviction is behind them."[1]

The letter is important, for it shows that Mr. Gladstone was aware that one of the main subjects of complaint of the Irish tenants was the unjust increases of rent which expropriated their interest in their holdings. There was nothing, however, in his speech on introducing his measure to indicate his opinion on this most important point.

Mr. Gladstone explained his great and complex measure in a masterly speech of three and a half hours in length. He dealt fully with the history of Irish Land Tenure. He disclaimed any interference with the freedom of contract, more than was absolutely necessary. He referred to the demand made in some quarters for a right of continued occupancy subject to payment of rent, for which the tenant was liable, or to such rent as should be settled from time to time by fair valuation, and a right to sell his interest to a solvent tenant, to whom the landlord could not make reasonable objection, only to disclaim any such intention. " Will the Irish people," he said, " follow such disastrous leadership ? I believe not. I hold that each successive act of justice develops feelings of content and loyalty, and narrows the circle of disaffection." " There is in Ireland—do not let us conceal it from ourselves —not only a reckless, but a demoralized and demoralizing agency, which is now at work, for the twofold purpose of disturbing the country through agrarian crimes, and making peaceful legislation impossible."

The measure was not opposed in principle by the Tory Party in either House of Parliament. In the House of Commons, on the second reading, Mr. Disraeli, as Leader of the Opposition, admitted the necessity of some such measure, but he disapproved of many of its details. He protested against the interference with freedom of contract, which he regarded as " one of the greatest sanctions for the progress of civilization." Dr. Ball took the same line in stronger language. More serious opposition came from a small section of the Irish Members representing the interests of the tenant farmers, from Sir John Gray, the owner of *The Freeman's Journal*, Mr. Bryan, Mr. Moore, and a few others. They contended that nothing would satisfy the Irish tenants short of fixity

[1] Morley, *Life of Gladstone*, II, p. 294.

of tenure and the arbitration of rents. " I do not depreciate the Bill," said Sir John Gray. " It is a great and solid and, I will add, a noble and generous advance. But the interests of the people must be considered in a full settlement. The Irish tenants do not require a Bill of pains and penalties against their landlords. They ask for a Bill of rights for themselves." On the other hand Mr. Maguire and The O'Donoghue, representing another advanced section of the Irish Members, warmly supported the Bill—the latter describing the opposition to it as the " gambols of excited patriots." Sir Roundell Palmer, the most eminent member of the English Bar, who had refused the post of Lord Chancellor in Mr. Gladstone's Cabinet, on account of his objection to disendowing the Irish Church, supported the Land Bill as a " humiliating necessity "; but he insisted on the absolute and imperative obligation to put down the disturbances in Ireland which had caused this necessity. " It would be a mockery to talk of justice and of redress of wrongs if you allow the rights, which in the Bill are solemnly asserted, to remain at the mercy of secret associations and of bands of conspirators."

The Bill was read a second time by a majority of 442 to 11. Of the minority of 13, including the tellers, three were English Members. It followed that only 10 Irish Members out of 103 were of opinion that the measure was so deficient as to be unworthy of acceptance. It was debated in Committee for three and a half months. Upwards of 300 amendments were moved. Mr. Gladstone bore almost alone the burden of this protracted debate. He had lost the support of Sir Edward Sullivan, who had been elevated to the Bench in Ireland. Mr. Bright was ill, and Mr. Lowe gave him no moral support. Mr. Chichester Fortescue had no debating power. In one of his letters Mr. Gladstone said, " I feel that when I have spoken I have not a shot left in my locker." At times most important clauses were in peril. Mr. Disraeli moved an amendment limiting compensation to the value of past improvements. This was defeated by a majority of 76; much less than the ordinary party majority. It fell to 32, a dangerously low figure, on a motion of Mr. Fowler, a Liberal banker, proposing to restrict the compensation for disturbance to holdings under the value of £50 a year. It was supported by Sir Roundell Palmer, who was also one of the severest critics on other details. Mr. Gladstone said of him in his correspondence that " he knew no more of Irish Land Tenure than he did of tenures in the moon." " With his legal mind, legal point of view, legal aptitudes and inaptitudes, he comes and stirs the susceptibilities of Members to such a point that he is always near bringing us to grief."[1] The Bill, however, with some few concessions escaped these rocks and quicksands, and finally passed a third reading, without opposition and without substantial alteration.

In the House of Lords the Bill was read a second time without a division. The Tory Party there was led by the Duke of Richmond, who had recently succeeded Lord Cairns in this position. He was a man of plain common sense representing about the average opinion of their Lordships. He advised them to accept the Bill in principle, but to amend it greatly in Committee. It was subjected to most hostile criticism in debate. There was not a single peer there representing the majority of the Irish people, not one possessing any sympathy with Irish tenants, not one who had any real knowledge of Irish tenure, except those interested as landlords in the opposite camp.

In Committee on the Bill the Lords proceeded, after their usual fashion with Irish measures, to wreck it in detail. Amendments were carried against the Government which entirely altered its character, and which would have deprived it of all healing grace. Lord Granville piloted the Bill with consummate tact and skill. Many of the amendments were withdrawn at a later stage, and others were reduced to harmless dimensions in deference to some concessions offered by the Government. What remained were rejected by the House of Commons, or were conceded in part, or were later the subject of compromise. One, however, most serious amendment was insisted upon by the Lords, which later had the most unfortunate effect.

It has already been shown that in the Bill, as introduced, compensation for the disturbance of a tenant was not to be paid, if the tenant was evicted for non-payment of rent, with the qualification, however, " unless the Court should be of opinion that on special grounds it shall be paid."

The House of Lords, on the motion of Lord Cairns, struck

---

[1] Morley, *Life of Gladstone*, II, p. 295.

out this proviso. " The purpose of the Bill," he said, " was
that the right to compensation should be correlative with the
performance of the contract, and that the tenant who had
broken his contract, and had been removed on that account,
should not be allowed to say that he had been capriciously
evicted." " The proviso in the clause, however, would enable
any one of the thirty-three Assistant Barristers in Ireland to
decide upon special grounds that eviction for non-payment of
rent was a disturbance, entitling the evicted tenant to compensation. The Assistant Barrister might say, Parliament has
left it to me to determine what are special grounds. Well,
this is a bad year, and I will decide that to be a special
ground."

The clause went back to the House of Commons and, after
it had been bandied about between the two Houses, the
Government, finding that the Lords were inexorable on this
point, gave way rather than risk the loss of the Bill. But they
succeeded in inducing the Lords to apply the qualification to
holdings valued at less than £25 a year " if the Court should be
of opinion that the non-payment of rent is owing to its being
exorbitant " ; and in this form the clause finally passed into
law.

Mr. Gladstone in agreeing to this said : " The Government
attached great value to the clause. They had done all in their
power and exerted their utmost influence with their supporters
to avoid conflict, and to wash their hands of the responsibility
of a confirmed difference of opinion between the two Houses.
They made the concession with the greatest pain and reluctance, because it was against their conviction of what the Bill
ought to accomplish." [1]

In this mutilated state the Bill passed into law. It will be
shown later how serious this action of the Lords proved to be,
when, after a disastrous season, large masses of small tenants
in Ireland were unable to pay their rents, and when many bad
landlords resorted to their old game of wholesale evictions.

In review of this Land Act and of the long discussion upon
it in the two Houses, we must now, by the light of subsequent
experience, admit that it was not successful. It did not prove
to be a remedy for the evils which it was hoped to cure. It was
the first Act only of a great agrarian reform in Ireland, spread

[1] *Hansard*, July 21st, 1870.

over a long period of years, of which we have not yet quite seen the end.

Mr. Gladstone had warning that it would not be a final settlement of the question. Lord Morley says that, while the Bill was under discussion, Mr. Gladstone received, through Archbishop Manning, a memorial from the Irish Catholic Bishops to the effect that it would fail to give content, and that no measure short of one conceding fixity of tenure and arbitration of rents would have the desired effect.

Already there were ominous signs that discontent in Ireland was by no means appeased by the two great measures affecting the Church and the land. At the end of the Session of 1870 a vacancy occurred in the county of Tipperary. The electors returned O'Donovan Rossa, who had been convicted of high treason in the Fenian prosecutions, and it became the duty of Mr. Gladstone to move that the election should be set aside, on the ground that a convicted felon was incapable of sitting in the House. The motion was carried by a majority of 293, only 10 Irish Members voting against it.

Between the second reading and the Committee stage of the Land Bill, the Government found itself under the necessity of introducing and carrying a Coercion Act for Ireland, moderate indeed in its provisions, as compared with many previous and subsequent Acts of the same kind, but yet giving exceptional powers to the Executive in Ireland, in respect of the possession of firearms, and in regard to the press in proclaimed districts. It also enabled Grand Juries, with the approval of the Judge and Court, to levy rates for compensation to families of persons subjected to serious outrages. The Bill, unlike others of that ilk, passed the House of Commons without difficulty, only fifteen Irish Members voting against it. It must be presumed that Mr. Gladstone very unwillingly assented to the measure. Lord Morley says that he pressed the Irish Government the other way. " What we have to do is to defy Fenianism, to rely on public sentiment and to provide (as we are doing) the practical measures that place public sentiment on our side ; an operation which I think is retarded by any semblance of severity to those whose offences we admit among ourselves to have been the ultimate result of our misgovernment of the country." The Irish Government, however, was able to get its way. It had been too accustomed to the use of coercive acts to believe in governing without them. Probably also there were men in the Cabinet who agreed with Sir Roundell Palmer in insisting on remedial measures being accompanied by exceptional measures to put down agrarian crime, and who did not believe in the efficacy of the former. In the same spirit of conciliation, and in the hope of favourably striking the imagination of the Irish people, Mr. Gladstone pressed on his Cabinet, early in 1870, the importance of giving an amnesty to the Fenians still detained at Portland as convicts. He failed to get their consent till the end of the year. It was even then coupled with the condition that the men, thus released, should be banished from the United Kingdom—a provision which, in the opinion of many in England, and of the majority in Ireland, deprived the act of much of its grace.

Whatever the defects of the Land Act, it had the effect of putting an end to the arbitrary and wholesale eviction of tenants in ordinary times. Agrarian outrages were consequently reduced in the few years which followed. It was not till the bad seasons of 1878–9 that the defects of the Act became apparent, and agitation of a far more formidable character was renewed.

CHAPTER V

THE IRISH UNIVERSITY BILL

IN the Session of 1873 Mr. Gladstone made another valiant effort to deal with an Irish grievance, the third branch of the Upas Tree, as he called it, that of University Education. The grievance of the Roman Catholics was that higher education, suitable to them, and in accordance with their religious views, was not endowed in the same manner as that for Protestants in the University of Dublin, with its richly endowed Trinity College, or that of the Queen's University, with its unsectarian colleges at Belfast, Cork, and Galway, mainly supported by State grants.

Trinity College was at that time largely sectarian. It had been part of the machinery for maintaining Protestant ascendancy in Ireland. When, at the time of the Reformation in England, the Irish Roman Catholic Church was transformed by English law into a Protestant institution, with the intention of converting the population of Ireland from Popery, Trinity College was founded with the same object, largely out of funds derived from a suppressed Roman Catholic monastery. No Catholic could graduate or become a student there. In 1793 it was thrown open by the Irish Parliament, to the extent that Catholics were allowed to enter as students, and were admitted to degrees ; but the religious tests for scholarships and fellowships were maintained. In 1844, Sir Robert Peel admitted the grievances of Catholics, and endeavoured to deal with the question, but the authorities of Trinity College refused to throw open their endowments. He found himself unable to compel them to do so. He dealt with the question by establishing the unsectarian Queen's University, with affiliated colleges at Belfast, Cork, and Galway supported by State grants. But the Catholics did not want unsectarian colleges. The University and its colleges were condemned

and tabooed by the Catholic hierarchy.   Later a so-called
Catholic University was founded by the Bishops, scantily
supported by voluntary contributions ; but it had no charter
from the Crown.   Its degrees were unrecognized by law.
The Conservative Government of 1867 tried to deal with the
question.   They opened negotiations with the Catholic
Bishops.   But Protestant feeling in Ireland was aroused, and
nothing came of this attempt.   The problem before Mr.
Gladstone was how to give the Catholics the benefit of higher
education, largely at the expense of the State, without raising
the susceptibilities of Protestants, who had shown in the
past that they would oppose the endowment of Catholic
religion.

Mr. Gladstone set to work on the question with resolution
and self-confidence.   He devised his own scheme, quite independently of the Irish Government, and of the Chief Secretary
for Ireland, then Lord Hartington, and devoted immense
labour to it.   He did not consult the Irish Catholic Bishops,
or the Irish representatives in the House of Commons.   It
was to be expected that as the success of the measure would
depend upon the views which the Catholic Bishops would take
of it, he would have sounded them on the subject before
announcing it to the House of Commons.   In his opening
statement on the Bill he gave excuses for not doing so.   He
said that the authorities of Trinity College had already
introduced a Bill, propounding a scheme of their own for
dealing with the subject, in the direction of removing religious
tests. This, in his view, made it impossible for him to negotiate
with them, and as it was necessary to treat other religious
communities equally, he was precluded from negotiating with
the Roman Catholics.   The explanation does not carry conviction.   The measure was intended as a remedy for Catholic
grievances.   It would seem to be essentially necessary that the
Government should know whether it would be accepted by
those for whom it was intended.   On the other hand it was
scarcely conceivable that any plan could be devised which
would be acceptable to the authorities of Trinity College.
The Government would have to fight them in any case.   To
consult them in advance would give them an advantage
in the Parliamentary contest.   The sequel showed how far
wiser it would have been to negotiate with the Catholic Bishops.

It may have been that Mr. Gladstone's immense Parliamentary success in the two previous Irish measures, affecting the Church and the land, where he followed the same course, led him to believe that he could produce a scheme for the University question which, by its fairness and completeness, would meet with support from all sections of the Liberal Party, including the Irish Catholic Members. It will be seen that he over-estimated his powers in this case, and under-estimated the forces which were ultimately arrayed against him.

Mr. Gladstone's scheme was a most ingenious one. It was such as in ordinary times, and if the Irish Bishops had not been led by so ultramontane and masterful a prelate as Cardinal Cullen, might have been successful. He proposed to constitute a single great University for Ireland, for teaching as well as for examining purposes, on a purely unsectarian basis, to which colleges of either sectarian or unsectarian character were to be affiliated. The existing University of Dublin was to be detached from Trinity College, and was to form the nucleus of the new University. Trinity College was to be affiliated as a sectarian institution, closely connected with the Dis-established Church. The Queen's University was to be done away with. The Colleges of Belfast and Cork were to be affiliated to the new University, as was the Catholic College representing the so-called Catholic University. No endow-ment or grant was to be given to the Catholic College, but the University was to be endowed with £50,000 a year, provided in part by a contribution of £15,000 a year from Trinity College, and partly by a State grant. The affiliated Colleges would all benefit equally from the endowed University. Professorships were to be provided by the University, subject to a proviso, which came to be described as "a gagging proposal," that there were to be no Professors of Religion, Morals, or History. These subjects were to be left to the Colleges to deal with, in any manner they might think best. Professors and teachers were to be liable to removal if they wilfully gave offence to the religious opinions of any students. The Governing Body of the new University was to consist of twenty-eight members, to be nominated by the Act in the first instance, and later were to be appointed in part by the Crown, in part by co-option, and in part by election of the graduates.

Mr. Gladstone expounded this scheme with a persuasive earnestness, a fullness of knowledge, and an enthusiasm for the subject, at least equal to his efforts on introducing his two previous Irish Bills. He seemed fairly to mesmerize the House of Commons, with the result that in the debate which followed his scheme was generally applauded, and scarcely a dissentient voice was heard. It was admitted that if a vote could have been taken at once, the Bill would have been almost unanimously agreed to. But closer examination of its details soon dissipated this favourable impression. Cardinal Cullen assumed from the first a hostile attitude to it. His view prevailed with the Irish Bishops. It might possibly have been accepted in this quarter under other auspices than Cullen ; for Archbishop Manning, also an ultramontane, was in favour of it and did his best, but in vain, to induce Cullen and the Irish Bishops to accept it. Nor was it more favourably received in other quarters. The Presbyterians of the North of Ireland denounced it ; so also did the Governing Body of Trinity College. Professor Fawcett and other academic experts were vehemently opposed to the Government scheme, largely on account of the " gagging " clauses.

The Tory Party, as was to be expected, could not resist the opportunity of making a party question of it. An ingenious motion was devised for rejecting the second reading of the Bill, which, admitting that legislation was necessary, amounted to a declaration of want of confidence in the Government. In the four days' debate the Bill was attacked from every quarter of the House. It was condemned by the Irish Catholic Members, because it did not give an endowment to the Catholic College, and by the Irish Protestant Members, because it detached some of the funds of Trinity College, and might lead to the endowment of Catholics. It met with little support from any speakers but those connected with the Government. But most serious of all was the fact that it failed to enlist a majority of the Irish Members in its favour.

Towards the end of the debate Mr. Disraeli made a rattling party speech against the Bill, denouncing it from many opposite points of view, but carefully committing himself to none of them. He seemed, at one time, rather to favour concurrent endowment, which, he pointed out, had been the policy of Pitt, of Peel, of Russell and Palmerston, but this was only for the purpose of attributing to the Government the alternative policy of confiscation. This last was the main *refrain* of his discourse. " You have had," he said, " four years of this policy of confiscation. You have despoiled the Irish Church. You have threatened every corporation and every interest in the country. You have criticized every profession and vexed every trade. No one is certain of his property, and nobody even knows what duty he will have to perform. This is the policy of confiscation as compared with that of concurrent endowment. The Irish Roman Catholics were perfectly satisfied when you were despoiling the Irish Church. They looked on, not unwillingly, upon the plunder of Irish landlords ; and they thought the time had arrived when the great drama would be fulfilled, and the spirit of confiscation would descend upon the celebrated walls of Trinity College, and would level it to the ground, and endow the College of St. Stephen's Green [the Roman Catholic College]. I ventured to remark, at the time when the policy of the Government was introduced, that confiscation was contagious. I believe that the people of this country have had enough of this policy of confiscation. From what I have seen, the House of Commons, elected to carry out that policy, is beginning to experience some of the inconveniences of satiety, and if I am not mistaken, you will give some intimation to the Government to-night that these are your views." [1] The proposal of the Government to hand over a small part of the huge endowment of Trinity College to the unsectarian University, whose scholarships and prizes the College would share equally with other Colleges, was a very small peg on which to hang these charges of confiscation, but the speech was intended for the hustings, and should not be too closely scanned for consistency and accuracy. It presented the case on which he was to enlarge at the next General Election, and to which his party was largely indebted for victory.

When Mr. Gladstone rose to reply he had been informed by the Whips of the party that the Irish Members, who were generally supporters of his Government, would vote against the Bill. Cardinal Cullen had signed a pastoral letter a few days before to be read in all the Catholic churches of Ireland, denouncing the Bill for endowing non-Catholic and godless

[1] *Hansard*, March 11th, 1873.

colleges, without giving a shilling to Catholics. This determined the votes of the Irish Catholic Members. The fate, therefore, of the Bill was in the balance. Mr. Gladstone must have felt that, even if the Bill were carried by a narrow majority, its fate was sealed, for it would be impossible to proceed with it, when rejected by the great majority of those for whom it was proposed as a remedy for their grievances. In no way discouraged by the bad news, Mr. Gladstone made one of the ablest and most effective speeches he ever delivered in the House of Commons. It still remains in the memory of those who, like the writer, heard it, as on the highest level of his achievements. It was marked by the greatest dignity. There was no trace of resentment or anger. It was at times pathetic in reference to his past efforts to do justice to Ireland. He made it clear that the vote of the House would determine the fate of the Government. He was not, however, over-insistent or defiant. He spoke with pride of what he had accomplished for Ireland in the past. There was a serenity in his demeanour and language which I had not observed in previous speeches. It seemed to be inspired by the well-known lines :

> " Virtus repulsæ nescia sordidæ
> Intaminatis fulget honoribus."

He made it clear, not so much by words as by manner and expression, that if the verdict was against him he would retire from power without misgiving or regret.

It may be doubted whether this admirable speech changed any considerable number of votes—at all events not a sufficient number. When the division was called the Government was defeated on the hostile motion by a majority of 3—287 to 284—and the Bill was rejected. Thirty-five of the usual Irish supporters of the Government voted against it, twenty-five of whom were Catholics and ten were Protestants. Of eighty-three Irish Members who were present only fifteen voted with the Government. The measure, therefore, was rejected by an overwhelming majority of the Irish Members. It could not have been proceeded with even if the majority of Members for Great Britain had been sufficient to carry it.

The Bill passed into limbo. Thirty-five years elapsed before Parliament finally dealt with this question. Mr. Birrell, in

1908, with the general consent of all parties in the House of Commons, succeeded in passing a measure of University reform in Ireland.

After the adverse vote in the House of Commons, Mr. Gladstone brought the matter before the Cabinet. They acted on his advice and authorized him to tender their resignation as a body to the Queen. Mr. Disraeli was sent for, but he declined to take office and to form a Government. " He could not," he said, " carry on the government in face of a House of Commons, where the majority was so adverse to him, and he could not ask for the dissolution of Parliament upon a question where there was no direct issue which could be laid before the electors." In the end, after some further correspondence through the Queen, Mr. Gladstone and his colleagues resumed office—most unwillingly, so far as the Prime Minister was concerned, for he said that past experience had shown that Governments resuming office, after defeat and resignation, had never enjoyed a healthy existence. His anticipations, it will be seen, were realized. Little was done in the remainder of that Session. The most important measure carried was that of Mr. Fawcett for relieving Trinity College of Tests in respect of its scholarships and fellowships—a measure which converted it into an unsectarian institution, but which, in fact, made hardly any difference in its future personnel and influence. It should also here be stated that in 1872 the Ballot Act passed into law, after a year's delay, due to its rejection in the previous year by the House of Lords. It will be seen that while it did not much affect the result of the next General Election in Great Britain, it was fraught with enormous consequences in Ireland.

CHAPTER VI

IN 1870 a new movement arose in Ireland in favour of self-government, known as Home Rule, a phrase most happily devised by an eminent Professor of Trinity College, Dublin, Mr. Galbraith, a Conservative in politics, who had recently been converted to the national cause. It was not on party lines. It was supported by many well-known landowners, and others of the dominant class in Ireland, even in the Province of Ulster, and was due in part to their loss of confidence in the Imperial Parliament, and to disaffection arising from the Disestablishment of the Protestant Church, or from the Land legislation then under discussion. The chief exponent of the new policy was Mr. Isaac Butt, who was to play a most important part in the Parliament of 1874–9 as Leader of the Irish Party.

Born in 1815, Isaac Butt was the son of a Protestant clergyman in Donegal. He was educated at Trinity College, Dublin, where he had a most distinguished career. In 1838 he was called to the Bar and met with such rapid success, that two years later he was selected by the Corporation of Dublin, then under the control of the Protestant Ascendancy Party, to represent them in their petition against the Irish Municipal Reform Bill before Parliament. He appeared on their behalf at the Bar of the House of Lords, and made a speech conspicuous for its fire and ability. It led to his being elected an Alderman by the Corporation. When, three years later, after the reform of the Corporation, O'Connell was elected Lord Mayor of Dublin, and brought before its Council his celebrated motion for the repeal of the Act of Union, which inaugurated his great Repeal agitation, Butt undertook the leading part in opposition to him, in a speech worthy of the occasion, and of his great antagonist. O'Connell was much struck by the speech. He recognized that behind the powerful argument of the advocate there was a latent sympathy for the national cause, and he predicted that the time would not be distant, when Butt would be found ranged on the side of the cause which he then opposed. Butt was made a King's Counsel, after only six years of work at the Bar. His reputation was such that his political opponents were glad to avail themselves of his advocacy. He was retained as counsel by most of the Young Ireland Party, who were prosecuted, in 1848, for their abortive attempt at insurrection. He defended Smith O'Brien, Meagher, John Martin, and O'Doherty. The earnestness, patriotism, and devotion to the national cause of these men made a great impression on their advocate.

In the General Election of 1852 Butt was returned as a Conservative Member for Youghal, which he continued to represent until 1865. He did not, however, make any mark during these thirteen years of his first essay in Parliamentary life. It was indeed unfortunate for him that his attendance in the House of Commons withdrew him so much from his practice at the Irish Bar, at a critical period of his professional life. He was exposed in London to temptations which he could not resist. He was most reckless in expenditure. His purse was always most generously open to demands on it from needy or suffering friends, even when it was at a very low ebb. He contracted debts from which he was never able to free himself during the rest of his life. In 1864, he ceased to attend the House of Commons, and did not seek re-election in the General Election of 1865. He returned to work at the Bar in Dublin, where he soon regained a lucrative practice and was recognized as the leading man in the Irish Courts.

Butt was again employed, between 1865 and 1868, as counsel by many of the Fenians prosecuted by the Government for the abortive conspiracy, and was again deeply impressed by the patriotic fervour and honesty of their convictions. From this time Butt was gradually drawn to the national cause. He took the leading part in favour of an amnesty for the Fenian convicts. He devoted also much labour and time to the claims of the tenants in Ireland for greater security of tenure. His numerous and weighty writings on this subject did much to promote the legislation of 1870, and later to expose its defects.

In 1870 Butt declared himself in favour of Home Rule for

Ireland on the federal basis, and at once became the recognized leader of the movement. He was well equipped for the position. No speaker on the public platform, since O'Connell, had a greater command over an audience. His speeches were persuasive and sympathetic. They teemed with humour and wit, and with passages of genuine pathos. They were made attractive by a voice of singular musical tone. In appearance he was of the same type as O'Connell, of robust presence and open and attractive expression. His Parliamentary knowledge and experience were great ; his power of debate was recognized as inferior only to that of Mr. Gladstone. No one had a greater knowledge of the constitutional and legal questions which he dealt with.

The Home Rule Movement was started at a meeting of leading merchants and professional men at Dublin, sixty in number, of whom one half were Protestants and Conservatives, the other half men of opposite politics, from Whig Catholics to extreme Nationalists and even Fenians. It was unanimously agreed to form an association, for the purpose of obtaining for Ireland the right and privilege of managing its own affairs, by a Parliament assembled in Ireland, leaving to the Imperial Parliament the power of dealing with all questions affecting the Empire, its relations with foreign States, and the defences of the country. The new movement was not favoured, in the first instance, by the Catholic Church. *The Freeman's Journal* opposed it. The Association, however, made rapid progress, and was welcomed in every part of Ireland. It soon made its influence felt in the by-elections. In 1871 four such elections took place in the counties of Meath and Westmeath, and in the cities of Galway and Limerick. In all of them Members were returned pledged to the new policy of Home Rule. Butt himself was returned for Limerick. In 1872, two more by-elections of great importance took place for the counties of Kerry and Galway. Lord Kenmare, in Kerry, and Lord Clanricarde, in Galway, were members of Whig families, which had an almost recognized claim to nominate representatives in these counties. Candidates in their interest were put forward and received the support of the whole landed interest in their districts, both Liberal and Tory. Independent candidates were brought forward by the Home Rule Association—in the case of Galway, Captain Nolan, and in Kerry, Mr. Blennerhassett. Captain Nolan was elected by a majority of four to one in spite of the whole landlord interest. Mr. Blennerhassett was returned by a majority of over 700, after a fierce contest, in which all the landlords, the Catholic Bishop of the Diocese, Dr. Moriarty, and even the O'Connell family supported his opponent, a well-known and highly respected Catholic Whig. It was considered a victory equal in significance to that in the county of Clare, in O'Connell's time, which was the turning-point of Catholic Emancipation.

Inspired by these successes and by many other evidences of the trend of public opinion in Ireland, it was decided, in 1873, to summon a Home Rule Conference representative of the whole of Ireland. The requisition for it was signed by 24,000 persons from every part of the country. It was attended by 900 delegates, including a large contingent from Ulster. Men of all parties and religions gave it a national character, which had been wanting in the meetings held by O'Connell.

The Conference was presided over by Mr. William Shaw, a well-known Cork banker. Isaac Butt was the principal speaker at this great meeting at the Rotunda. A passage from his speech on the occasion explains the motives, which led him to head this movement, and is a good illustration of his eloquence : " Mr. Gladstone has said that Fenianism taught him the intensity of Irish disaffection. It taught me more and better things—the breadth, the sincerity of that love of Fatherland, that misgovernment had tortured into disaffection and had exaggerated into revolt. State trials were not new to me. Twenty years before I stood near Smith O'Brien, when he braved the sentence of death, which the law pronounced upon him. I saw Meagher meet the same sentence, and then asked myself this : ' Surely the State is out of joint, surely all our social system is unhinged, when O'Brien and Meagher are condemned by their country to a traitor's doom.'. . . Years passed away, and once more I stood by men who had dared this desperate enterprise of freeing their country by revolt. They were men who were run down by obloquy ; they had been branded as the enemies of religion and social order. I saw them manfully bear up against all. I saw the unflinching firmness by which they testified the sincerity of their faith in that cause—their deep conviction of its righteousness and truth.   I saw them meet their fate with a manly fatalism that made them martyrs. . . . I asked myself again : ' Is there no way to arrest this ?   Are our best and bravest spirits ever to be carried away, under this system of constantly resisted oppression and constantly defeated revolt ?   Can we find the means by which the national quarrel which has led to all these terrible results may be set aside ?   I believe in my conscience we have found it.   I believe that England has now the opportunity of adjusting the quarrel of centuries."

The essential feature, he said, of the Home Rule scheme was the maintenance of the connection between the two countries, and the full representation of Ireland in the Imperial Parliament, while securing to it the control of its own affairs in an Irish Assembly.   " I prefer our federal proposal, not only because it gives better security for the connection between the two countries, Ireland and Great Britain, better security against the arising of occasions to disturb their amity, but I prefer it even on grounds which are more particularly Irish." He insisted on the complete and undiminished participation of Irish representatives in the Empire.   Without federation Ireland would have no part in the vast colonial system.

A resolution in favour of Home Rule, in this sense, was carried unanimously with great enthusiasm.   It was decided that an Irish Party should be formed, independent of all other parties, and pledged not to take office till their objects were attained.   An attempt was made to carry unity of action yet further, and a motion was proposed that a Committee should be appointed by the Irish Members to control their action in the House of Commons ;   that the Irish Members should always vote in a body, or abstain from voting, as the majority of them should direct ;   and that no Bill should be introduced, or motion made, without the consent of the majority.   This was opposed by Butt.   He declared that he would betray his own principles, his dignity, his personal honour and personal honesty, if he gave a pledge that he would submit his future conduct to the absolute control of any tribunal on earth, except his own conscience.   He thought they would find that every high-minded man would shrink from pledging himself to act in accordance with the decision of a majority, no matter what the decision might be.   The motion obtained little support in the large assembly. Discussion arose as to the policy of obstruction in the House of Commons. On this Mr. Butt said: " Even if they were ready to act on the principle of universal obstruction, that policy ought not to be avowed. The power was one that was lost in the declaration that it would be used. Extreme cases might justify such a policy of obstruction. If ever they did, obstruction would probably be carried on in other and more decided ways." These passages from Mr. Butt's speeches at this great Conference have been quoted because they show how widely his policy differed from that of his successor in the leadership of the Irish Party, Mr. Parnell.

In January, 1874, shortly before the date when it was expected Parliament would meet, Mr. Gladstone suddenly made up his mind to dissolve it, and to appeal to the constituencies for a new lease of power for his Government. The debate on the Irish University Bill, in the previous Session, had weakened its position in the House of Commons. Several by-elections had gone against the Liberal Party. Mr. Gladstone felt that his Government had no longer a sufficient momentum to carry any considerable measure. He determined, therefore, to appeal to the country, and to claim renewal of confidence mainly on financial grounds. The state of the revenue, resulting from great prosperity in trade, assisted by economies in the great spending Departments, the Army and Navy, would enable the abolition of the Income Tax, a reduction in the taxes on articles of consumption, and a large subvention to local rates. He made this the main topic of his electoral address.

In Ireland, however, the sole issue before the electors in the General Election which then ensued was that of Home Rule. It was the first occasion on which an election took place under the recent Ballot Act; and though the franchise in Ireland was still very limited in the Counties, as compared with England, and though many very corrupt small Boroughs still returned Members, there was a better chance than ever before of the popular will making itself known. The General Election, however, came upon the Home Rule Association as a thief in the night. They were taken by surprise and they were almost destitute of funds. They had not completed their organization. Their leader, Mr. Butt, was himself at the lowest ebb of his finances. He was, in fact, arrested for debt on the very day that the Dissolution of Parliament was announced ; and though he was able to come to some arrangement, under which he was released from prison, he was obliged to avoid other Irish creditors by flight to England, and was therefore unable to take an active personal part in the electoral contests, such as was to be expected of a leader.

In spite of all these difficulties, so great was the strength of the popular movement that 60 out of the 103 Irish Members were returned to the new Parliament pledged to the policy of Home Rule. Of the remaining 43, 12 were Whigs not committed to this policy, and only 31 were Conservatives. The result was even more fatal to the old Whig Party in Ireland than to the Conservatives. Among the defeated candidates was Mr. Chichester Fortescue, who had represented for twenty-seven years the County of Louth. This made a profound impression. The Home Rule Party, thus returned, included not a few old Members, who swallowed the pledge, when they found that they could not be re-elected without it, but who were anything but ardent supporters of the cause. Later they were classed as " nominal Home Rulers." They were seldom to be found in the Lobby with their party. Mr. Butt was again returned for Limerick, and Sir John Gray, Mr. Mitchell Henry, Mr. William Shaw, and Mr. John Martin were elected. Amongst other new Members who distinguished themselves later in the national cause were Mr. A. M. Sullivan, Mr. Richard Power, Mr. Shiel, and Mr. Biggar. They formed the nucleus of the national party, which later under Mr. Parnell swept four-fifths of the Irish constituencies. It may be taken that of the sixty Members returned as Home Rulers, not more than one-half were to be relied upon by Mr. Butt as his followers. Most of the other thirty, however, were present at a Conference of Home Rule Members held at Dublin immediately after the elections, at which the Parliamentary Party was constituted. Whips were appointed, and a resolution was unanimously adopted, at the instance of Mr. Butt, affirming their independence of other political parties in the House of Commons.

The effect of the resolution, however, was much weakened by the refusal of the Conference of 1873, at the instance of Mr. Butt, to enforce combined action of the Home Rule Members, in the sense that a majority of them were to bind the minority and that no action was to be taken in the House of Commons by any independent Members, without the sanction of the majority. The subsequent policy of the Home Rule and the Nationalist Party showed that without such concerted action, and the submission of all to the will of the majority, the party would be little better than a rope of sand, would have no cohesive strength, and would be ineffective for any purpose as against the combined forces of the two main parties in the House of Commons. This was undoubtedly the experience of the six years of the Parliament of 1874–9, during which Butt was for a short time the real head, and later the nominal head of the Home Rule Party in it. The leader of such a party had great difficulty in keeping it together. He had nothing to offer in the way of immediate or prospective office or honours. The party tie was a very loose one. On rare occasions only were its members found voting together. Practically nothing was effected by Butt and his supporters. No legislation whatever, of any importance, was carried through Parliament to meet the wishes of the overwhelming majority of the Irish people, and no advance was made towards converting English and Scotch opinion to the principle of Home Rule for Ireland.

Mr. Butt was over sixty years of age. His health, already the worse for some years of self-indulgence, was further impaired by the great efforts he had to undergo in carrying on his heavy business in the Law Courts in Dublin, and at the same time in leading the Home Rule Party in the House of Commons, and taking part in frequent debates. This involved incessant and fatiguing travelling between the two capitals. It seemed also to the writer that Mr. Butt, during this time, though immeasurably superior to all others of his party, in Parliamentary qualification, was physically unable to cope with the powers arrayed against him as O'Connell had done. He was too deferential in his manner to the House. He did not stand up to his opponents. He was essentially of a conservative type of mind, a Parliamentarian, with great respect for the traditions of the House of Commons. He hoped to attain the objects of his party by persuasive argument, and by gaining, for himself and his followers, the confidence of their opponents. There was never any prospect of success for such a policy. The leadership of the forces by which alone an impression could be produced, fell, as the sequel showed, to younger, stronger, more daring, and less scrupulous hands.

The result of the elections in Great Britain had been very different from that in Ireland. While the Conservatives succeeded in retaining only 31 out of 103 Irish seats, they obtained in England and Scotland a majority of nearly 100, sufficient to outvote the majority of the Irish Members by 60. The great work of Mr. Gladstone's Government during the previous five years, now admitted by all historians to have been one of the most capable and best of all Governments in the century, seemed to count for little with the British electors. The two great Irish Acts did not interest them. An Education Act, which established a national system of education for England and Wales, beneficent as it was, alienated a large section of Nonconformists—the backbone of the Liberal Party. An abortive measure, for reducing the number of licensed houses, lashed the brewers and publicans into fury, and led to unlimited supplies of drink during the elections. The rigid economies enforced by Mr. Gladstone were locally unpopular. His foreign policy of peace and abstention from intervention, and particularly his agreement with the United States Government to refer their claims for the depredations of the Confederate cruisers to arbitration, caused resentment to large classes of swashbucklers. It was claimed by Lord Salisbury that the great increase in the liquor bill of the nation was caused by the desire to drown in drink the humiliation of the surrender to the American claims, and the *mot* had a wide circulation.

As a result of these combined influences, the Government was defeated by a large majority in Great Britain. Mr. Gladstone and his colleagues, without waiting for the meeting of Parliament, accepted the verdict and resigned office. Mr. Gladstone himself, a short time later, withdrew from the leadership of the Liberal Party, under the belief that he had reached an age when he could not look forward to another spell of office—so little did he anticipate the future. Mr. Disraeli was commissioned by the Queen to form a Government. He did so without any programme of future policy, other than that of antagonism to the Government which he had displaced. Lord Hartington was elected by the Liberals as their leader in the House of Commons.

As regards Ireland, its position was this. It had returned a majority in favour of Home Rule, and a still larger majority against the Conservative Party. A Government was installed at Dublin, with Sir Michael Hicks-Beach (now Lord St. Aldwyn) as Chief Secretary (not in the Cabinet), responsible in no way to the majority of the Irish people, but to a small minority in that country—a position which was certain to create discontent and disaffection.

At the opening of the new Parliament, Butt made haste to raise the question of Home Rule for Ireland in an amendment on the address. He was answered by Mr. Gladstone, who advised the Irish Members, before insisting on a great constitutional change, to bring forward in the House of Commons their measures to remedy the evils they complained of, and promised them an attentive consideration. The motion was defeated by 314 to 50.

Nothing daunted by this rebuff, Butt, later in the Session, raised the question again by a more formal motion. His speech on the occasion was the best he ever delivered in the House of Commons—persuasive, argumentative, and with full knowledge of the history of Ireland, and of the constitutional and administrative questions involved in his proposal. To the charge that Home Rulers were ungrateful to Mr. Gladstone for his great measures of the previous Parliament, he declared that it was only when Ireland could be made useful for party purposes, that Irish questions were taken up by English statesmen. The motion led to a two nights' debate in which Lord Hartington, who had been Chief Secretary for Ireland in the Gladstone Government, took a leading part against it. Mr. Disraeli in reply, at the end of the debate, made a most amusing speech. He did not affect to treat the subject seriously. He bantered the Irish Members for having complained of being a conquered country. " I deny," he said, " that the Irish people are conquered ; they are proud of it ; I deny that they have any ground for that pride." The Normans, he said, had conquered Ireland, but only after they had conquered England. Cromwell had conquered Ireland, but only after he had conquered England. It was only in the last few sentences that he became serious. " I oppose the motion," he said, " because I think involved in it are the highest and dearest interests of the country. I am opposed to it for the sake of the Irish themselves, as much as for the sake of the English and the Scotch. I am opposed to it because I wish to see, at this important crisis of the world, that is perhaps nearer arriving than some of us suppose, a united people, welded in one nationality ; and because I feel that if we sanction this policy, if we do not cleanse the Parliamentary besom of this perilous stuff, we shall bring about the disintegration of the Kingdom and the destruction of the Empire." The motion was rejected by a large majority, only sixty-one members voting for it, of whom only forty-two were from Ireland. The constitutional claim of Ireland, therefore, was not a strong one, for a majority of its members did not declare themselves by their votes in favour of the policy.

Mr. Disraeli, by his humorous banter, gave the cue to the House of Commons for the treatment of Home Rule and other Irish questions, during the remainder of that Parliament. They were to be met with ridicule rather than argument. Butt himself was not taken seriously thenceforward. In vain he renewed his motion for Home Rule, session after session. He made no advance, but rather lost ground. In vain also he and his followers raised the question of Land Reform, the defects of the Act of 1870, and the growing difficulties of the tenants in Ireland. In vain his followers introduced Bills on subjects of deep interest to their country. The motions or Bills without exception were rejected or put aside. Public opinion in Ireland was disheartened, and was withdrawn from the Home Rule policy. The party in the House of Commons was discouraged and disorganized. The less earnest among them fell off from the cause, and lapsed into Whiggery. The more ardent among them took more violent courses, under the leadership of stronger men. It was admitted, after three years of trial, that with all his great Parliamentary qualifications, his efforts and his sacrifices, Butt's leadership was a failure.

CHAPTER VII

ON the 23rd of April, 1875, when a Coercion Bill was under discussion in the House of Commons, the only legislative proposal for Ireland of the new Government, two incidents occurred which had important bearing on the future course of Irish politics. Charles Stewart Parnell took his seat in the House, for the first time, as Member for the County of Meath, and Joseph Gillis Biggar made his début there, in a speech—if indeed it could be designated as such—four hours in length, of pure obstruction to the Bill under discussion. It was difficult to imagine two men differing more in their physical appearance, their antecedents, temperament, and capabilities; yet they were destined to be closely associated, during the next few years, in a new and militant policy in Parliament, which soon superseded the constitutional methods of Butt. Parnell was then a young man of twenty-eight years, tall and lithe, exceptionally handsome, with a pallid, delicate, and intellectual countenance, of American rather than English type. He came of most distinguished stock. The Parnells were a Protestant family of pure English descent. Natives of Congleton, in Cheshire, they had settled in Ireland in the time of the later Stuarts. They were distinguished there as statesmen, lawyers, and poets. A Sir John Parnell was for seventeen years Chancellor of the Exchequer in the Irish Parliament before the Act of Union. He was compelled to resign this post because he could not give his support to that measure. His eldest son rose to high office in the British Parliament, in the Ministries of Lord Grey and Lord Melbourne, and was made a peer under the title of Congleton. The second son of Sir John inherited the small but very picturesque property of Avondale, in the County of Wicklow, together with other landed property, and was grandfather to Charles

Parnell. His mother was daughter of Admiral Stewart, of the American Navy, better known as Commodore Stewart, who, when in command of the *Constitution*, in the war against England of 1815, fought and captured the two British vessels of war, the *Cyane* and the *Levant*. His dauntless courage and determination in this and other naval combats earned him the nickname of " Old Ironsides."

Charles Parnell inherited the intellectual qualities of his father's race, and much of the dogged courage and inflexible will of the American Admiral. There had been little, however, up to the date of his entering Parliament, to indicate any promise of distinction. His career at the University of Cambridge had been cut short by the authorities, on account of his complicity in a petty street brawl. His biographer, Mr. Barry O'Brien, and Mr. F. H. O'Donnell, who was closely associated with him in his early career in the House of Commons, agree in saying that he was almost totally ignorant of Irish history. He had, however, a turn for mathematics, and interested himself greatly in mechanical and engineering questions.

After leaving Cambridge he paid a long visit to a brother in the United States, and on his return settled at Avondale, where he lived, for a few years, as an Irish landowner of small income, hunting and shooting, and taking part in cricket matches like his neighbours. His mother and sisters lived in Dublin, and were strong Nationalists, with close relations to some of the Fenian leaders. There is no reason to believe that Parnell himself was associated with the same cause. His sympathies, however, were strongly enlisted on behalf of the amnesty agitation. In 1874, he joined in the movement inaugurated by Butt for Home Rule, and became a member of the Home Rule League. He wanted to come forward as a candidate for his County of Wicklow in the General Election of 1874. But he was High Sheriff for the County in that year, and the Irish Government refused to allow him to resign the post. He was therefore disqualified. Later, at a by-election in 1875, he contested the County of Dublin against Colonel Taylor, the Chief Whip of the Tory Party, and was beaten by a great majority, after a severe and costly contest, in which he showed little capacity for public speaking. In April of the same year another vacancy occurred in the County of

Meath, and at the instance of Butt, as leader of the Irish Party, Parnell was invited to become a candidate. He was elected without opposition. Few men have ever embarked on a career of public politics with less equipment of political knowledge and experience, and with less expectation or promise of what proved to be his future.

Compared with Parnell, Biggar had little in his appearance to commend him to notice. He was very short in stature, partly owing to his being a hunchback. He had a harsh and grating brogue, such as is common with the labouring people in Belfast. He had difficulty in stringing words together. A native of Belfast, he had, by great industry, rigid economy, and financial capacity, realized a considerable fortune as a provision merchant, but he continued to live in penurious style. He had shown great pugnacity in the local affairs of Belfast. He was a kind of stormy petrel there, and roused violent animosities. He was a good hater, especially of his political opponents. He was at one time a member of the Supreme Court of the Irish Republican Party, the Fenian Organization, and had taken the oath of that Association ; but he had been expelled by that body shortly after entering the House of Commons. He was a convert to the Roman Catholic faith.

Biggar was first returned to the House of Commons, in 1874, as Member for the County of Cavan. He very early showed that he had no respect for its traditions and conventions. He was absolutely fearless, and was undaunted by the hostile demonstrations, which his rough language and rude manners roused against him. One of his first essays was to call attention to the presence of strangers in the Gallery of the House, on an occasion when the then Prince of Wales was present. This led, under the then rules of the House, to the Prince having to leave the Gallery with other strangers. A storm of indignation was aroused. It resulted in the immediate repeal of the absurd and obsolete rule of the House, under which strangers, including members of the Press reporting the debates, were present only on sufferance, and so long as no single Member of the House objected.

In my personal recollection Biggar was regarded by a great majority of Members, in the early days of his membership, as a kind of mischievous imp, who alternately shocked and amused by his insolent audacity.   Later his fighting qualities gained for him a more general respect, and it was recognized that beneath his rugged and uncouth exterior, there was a kind and even generous heart.   There never was a more loyal or more disinterested colleague to those who worked with him.   His first great opportunity of showing his aptitude for obstruction arose in the debate on the Irish Coercion Bill, in 1875.   His leader, Mr. Butt, wishing, for some reason, to protract the discussion, asked Biggar to fill up a gap in the debate.   He was fully equal to the occasion.   Rising from the Irish bench, he spoke continuously for four hours. There happened in this case what was quite unique in the record of debates in the House of Commons.   In Hansard's report, instead of Biggar's speech, more or less condensed, there is a humorous narrative of the general effect of his grotesque proceedings and incoherent utterance.

It appears that early in his career in the House of Commons, Biggar had formed the opinion that Butt's constitutional method of presenting the Irish case for Home Rule and of advocating Irish reforms was futile, and could lead to no results. " Butt's a fool," he is reported to have said, " too gentlemanly —we're all too gentlemanly.   The English stop our Bills. Why don't we stop theirs ?   That's the thing to do.   No Irish Bills !   Then stop English Bills.   That's the policy.   We'll never do any good until we take an intelligent interest in English affairs."   It was not, however, till the beginning of the Session of 1877 that he was able to influence Parnell, and some half a dozen of the more advanced section of the Irish Members, in favour of a concerted movement in this direction.

In the first two years after his election, in 1875, Parnell had rarely spoken in the House of Commons.   In 1877, however, he came rapidly to the front.   Mr. F. H. O'Donnell, the able journalist who has published his reminiscences of that time, claims that he was largely concerned in influencing Parnell in favour of a more active policy in the House of Commons.   His proposal was that the Irish Members should take a leading part in English and Imperial questions of all kinds, and should not as theretofore confine themselves to Irish questions.   They should, in his view, " endeavour to associate the Irish cause with as many other good causes and righteous demands as possible, in order to oppose a mighty confederation of the wronged against the iniquities which oppressed Ireland. They should show a restless activity and should concentrate on a retaliatory and constructive propaganda." [1]

Parnell, in the past two years, had been closely watching the proceedings of the House of Commons in respect of Irish affairs ; he had come to the conclusion that Butt's policy was a failure, and that it was hopeless to expect any results from it. He is reported to have said to an Irish Member about this time :

" It is not by smooth speeches that we can get anything done in the House of Commons. We must show that we mean business. They are a great deal too comfortable in this House, and the English are a great deal too comfortable everywhere." And again : " If we are to have Parliamentary action it must not be the action of conciliation, but of retaliation."

Three measures of the Government, in 1877, offered a wide scope for the intervention of Irish Members in debate and discussion of details, whether with the object of obstruction, or of constructive propaganda—namely, the Prisons Bill of that year, the Annual Mutiny Bill, and the Bill for the Confederation of the South African Colonies. Parnell threw himself into the work with the utmost energy and zeal. He speedily developed debating power of a very exceptional and unexpected kind. He showed great faculties of searching criticism and lucid statement, and great ability in rapidly cramming himself with facts, sufficient to enable him to take part in detailed criticism. Not more than six or seven other Irish Members joined with him in this new movement. His principal aids were O'Donnell, on the one hand, always fertile in suggestion, and ready with amendments, and full of knowledge on subjects of which Parnell was totally ignorant, and Biggar, bent on pure obstruction, incapable of any sustained and intelligible argument, but always ready to fill up a gap in debate with prolonged and incoherent speeches. Every measure under charge of a Minister was systematically obstructed in this way, and day after day motions for adjournment were made, or personal questions were raised, with the object of making the conduct of business as difficult and protracted as possible. It was said of Biggar that he propounded

[1] O'Donnell's *History of the Irish Parliamentary Party*, I, p. 180.

and acted upon a gospel of obstruction under the following heads : (1) To speak only in the time set apart for the Government. (2) To aid any independent Member in expending the time of the Government. (3) When he saw a Government Bill to block it. (4) When he saw a raw of any kind in the proceedings of the Government to rub it. (5) Always to give way to any English or Scotch Member who had anything to say which the Government wished unsaid.

Parnell assisted in this policy by his fertility of resource in raising subjects of debate, and moving amendments, which could not be dubbed irrelevant, but which gave rise to discussions more or less prolonged. Some of his amendments to the Prisons Bill were of real value, especially those relating to the treatment of political prisoners. One of them which he succeeded in carrying was that persons convicted of seditious libel should be treated as first-class misdemeanants, and not with the severity to which ordinary criminals are subjected. But in many of these, and indeed in all his discussions on these three measures, he gave the impression to the House that he cared little or nothing for the demerits of the Bills, or the merits of the amendments he proposed, and that he was mainly bent on thwarting the policy of the Government, and making it more difficult for them to carry on their business. It seemed as though the more reasonable an amendment, the more he valued it as a means only of occupying time, and of harassing the Government. It was part of his skilful tactics that his interventions were nearly always rational, that they were supported by language of a moderate character, and that he seldom laid himself open to charges of mere frivolous waste of time. He was cool, calm, and business-like, kept to the point, and was rarely aggressive in voice or manner.

The development of this policy of Parnell and Biggar soon brought them into conflict with the leader of the Irish Party. Butt had great respect for the traditions of the House of Commons, and had no sympathy for a policy of obstruction. In the Committee on the Prisons Bill, on March 26th, 1877, when, after repeated motions for adjournment by a small band of three Irish extremists, the Government was compelled to give way at 3 a.m., Butt, on the suggestion of Sir M. Hicks-Beach, the Chief Secretary for Ireland, rose in his place and rebuked these turbulent members of his party. " I must express," he said, " my disapproval of the course taken by the Hon. Member for Meath. I am not responsible for him and cannot control him. I have, however, a duty to discharge to the Irish nation, and I think I shall discharge it best when I say I disapprove entirely of the conduct of the Hon. Member." Parnell sat calmly, and with a cynical smile, while this reproof was being administered. He attempted no immediate reply. But a few days later a correspondence took place between him and Butt, which appeared in *The Freeman's Journal*. " I claim in future," wrote the former, " the liberty of action on Imperial and English matters which has hitherto been granted to every member of the party, while I shall continue to follow your lead in regard to Irish questions." In reply Butt dissented from this view of the obligations of a member of the Home Rule Party. He reminded Parnell that the pledge taken was clear and distinct. " I see no objection to your taking part in the debates on English and Imperial questions, provided only they are bonâ fide. But it is impossible not to see that your action in the House is conducted as an organized system of obstruction. It must tend to alienate our truest and best English friends. It wastes, in aimless and objectless obstruction, time which might be obtained for the discussion of Irish grievances."

Parnell returned to the charge. " I cannot sympathize with your conclusion as to my duty towards the House of Commons. If Englishmen insist on the artificial maintenance of an antiquated institution, which can only perform a portion of its functions, by the concurrence of those entrusted with its working, I cannot conceive it my duty to connive in the imperfect performance of them."

Later in the Session, on July 25th, when the House was in Committee on the South African Bill, after a long course of obstruction on the part of some seven or eight Irish Members, under the leadership of Parnell, a violent scene took place, in which Parnell denounced the Bill as mischievous to the Colonies and to the native races of South Africa, and drew a comparison between Ireland and these Colonies. " As an Irishman," he said, " coming from a country which had experienced to its fullest extent the result of British interference in its affairs, and the consequences of English cruelty and tyranny, I feel a special satisfaction in preventing and thwarting the intentions of the Government in respect of this Bill."

The Leader of the House, Sir Stafford Northcote, moved that the words be taken down, and that the Speaker should be sent for. After a violent speech in justification from Parnell, Sir Stafford Northcote moved that " Mr. Parnell, having wilfully and persistently obstructed the public business, is guilty of contempt of the House, and that he be suspended from the service of the House till Friday next." It was then, however, pointed out that the motion misdescribed Mr. Parnell's language. He had not declared his interest in thwarting the designs of the House, but of the Government. The one would have been obstruction which the House could take notice of ; the other, if reprehensible, was not illegitimate. Sir Stafford Northcote was compelled to withdraw his motion, and Parnell resumed his speech as though the incident had not occurred. Later again, on July 31st, a prolonged conflict occurred between the Government and this small band of Irish Members. It was determined by the former that the Committee stage of the South African Bill should be concluded that night. Parnell, O'Donnell, Biggar, and a few others, seven in all, accepted the challenge and determined to carry on the contest to the very extreme of their power. They succeeded in keeping the Committee at work for twenty-six consecutive hours. It was not till 2 p.m., on the following day, that the last amendment to the Bill was disposed of. The House by that time had filled again, and Sir William Harcourt, on behalf of the main body of Liberals, entered a strong protest against the action of the small band of Irish Members. He quoted from a recent speech of Parnell in Manchester to the effect that " if they are to have a Parliamentary policy it must not be one of conciliation but of retaliation." Mr. O'Donnell spoke at length, defending the policy of retaliation. " What was wrong about it ? They were only paying the Government back." He spoke for the advanced party in Ireland, and he said if they could not have conciliation, they would have retaliation. Butt thereupon intervened with great warmth. " I deny," he said, " that those who act contrary to the pledges given to the Irish Party are members of that party. I know that the Irish Party repudiate the Member for Dungarvan.

I would be false to myself, I would be false to my country, if I did not repudiate him. If I thought he represented the Irish Party, and the Irish Party represented my country, which it does not, I would retire from Irish politics, as a vulgar brawl, in which no man could take part with advantage or honour to himself." In the division which followed, the last in this scene, seven Members only, including the Tellers, supported the motion, and the great majority of Irish Members followed Mr. Butt into the Lobby with the Government.

While these events were occurring which were to disintegrate and ruin the then Irish Party, Butt had been quite as active as in previous Sessions in pursuit of his policy of endeavouring to persuade Parliament to concede the Irish demands for self-government, for reform of the Land Laws, and for other Irish measures. On April 24th, an important motion was brought forward, at his instance, by Mr. W. Shaw for a Committee to report on the demands of the Irish people for an Irish Parliament. Butt spoke at length in support of it. The debate was important, as it led to declarations by leaders of the Liberal Party against Home Rule in any shape, namely, Lord Hartington, Mr. W. E. Forster, and Mr. Fawcett. Mr. Forster, in his speech, declared that Home Rule was not an open question. Until the House of Commons had become convinced that separation was desirable the question could not be an open one which could be submitted to a Committee. His own opinion was that the House of Commons would never entertain that conviction, and he had a sanguine hope that, year by year, fewer Irish Members would support Home Rule. The motion was defeated by 417 to 67, twelve English Members voting in the minority.

Later, Butt himself moved the second reading of an Irish Land Tenure Bill. It proposed perpetuity of tenure to existing tenants, excluding all grazing farms with a rental of over £50 a year, and those on which the tenant did not reside. Where there was dispute as to rent, the landlord and tenant were to appoint an arbitrator to decide between them. The Bill was rejected by a majority of 323. On April 27th the subject was reopened on a motion of The O'Donoghue that in order to ensure to the Irish tenants the benefits intended by the Act of 1870, it was essential that steps should be taken to prevent the exaction of rents, which virtually confiscated their interest in

their improvements. It was absolutely necessary, he said,
to give further protection to the tenants.   Cases occurred
where landlords threatened tenants with eviction if they did
not assent to what might be in the first instance small increases
of rent.   He quoted the case of a Mr. Buckley, a Lancashire
manufacturer, who bought an estate in Tipperary under the
Encumbered Estates Act, at eight years' purchase of the
rental, and immediately after increased his rents by 100 or
150 per cent.   Lord Hartington opposed the motion, which
was defeated by 189 to 65.

On June 11th Butt made another motion for the appointment of responsible Ministers at the head of the Local Government Board and the Board of Works in Ireland.   He was
supported on this occasion by Parnell, who declared that
" by the past administration of Irish affairs the Government had
set the people of Ireland in direct antagonism to the upper
classes and landlords of Ireland."   The motion was rejected,
as was also another on June 5th on the subject of Irish taxation.   The Government majority on this was comparatively
narrow—152 to 118.   With the above exception Parnell and
his small band of followers took no part in the discussions on
the motions of Butt and the main body of the Irish Members.

It was clear, however, beyond all question that Butt could
get nothing from the Government and that his policy was a
failure.   Sir M. Hicks-Beach, one of the ablest and most con-
scientious of statesmen who had held the post of Irish Secretary, did nothing during his four years of tenure of office
to meet the demands of the great majority of the Irish
Members.   His own contribution to legislation was unim-
portant, beyond the extension of the Coercion Act for a term
of five years.

CHAPTER VIII

DURING the year 1877 I personally saw much of Mr. Butt in the House of Commons. Early in this year, after two visits to Ireland, in the course of which I had seen some of the properties of the Disestablished Church, whose tenants had been able to purchase their holdings under the Act of 1869, I moved for a Select Committee to inquire into the causes of failure of the Bright clauses of the Land Act of 1870. In this view, I consulted Mr. Butt on the subject. Though he was in favour of my motion, and approved generally of the scheme of purchase of their holdings by tenants, he made no secret of his own view that schemes of this kind were quite inadequate as remedies for the existing state of land tenure in Ireland, and for the grievances of tenants. He maintained that the chief object of Land Reformers in Ireland should be to secure fixity of tenure for the tenants and arbitration of their rents.

In moving for a Committee I showed that the clauses of the Church Disestablishment Act had been successfully carried out in respect of the large landed property of the Irish Church, consisting of parochial glebes and episcopal and capitular estates, and that over six thousand tenants had been converted into owners, on the terms that two-thirds of the purchase money was left on mortgage, repayable by equal annual instalments of interest and sinking fund, spread over a term of years. On the other hand, the purchase clauses of the Land Act had been almost a complete failure. Though great numbers of properties had been sold under the Encumbered Estates Act, yet their tenants had not been offered any opportunity of purchasing their farms. In the seven years since the passing of the Act only nine hundred tenants had been converted into owners.

The House after a full debate agreed to my motion, and an important Committee was appointed, including among its members Mr. Butt, and Mr. Bright who was the author of the clauses in the Land Act of 1870. Mr. Plunket, then Solicitor-General for Ireland, and now Lord Rathmore, represented the Government. The Committee elected me as its chairman. The inquiry extended over two Sessions. Mr. Butt took some part in its early proceedings, but later ceased to attend, and in 1878 was not reappointed a member of it. Mr. Bright took a most active part on the Committee.

The evidence taken by the Committee conclusively proved my contention that no serious effort had been made by the officials of the Court administering the Encumbered Estates Act, and of other Departments of the Government in Dublin, to give effect to the Act. Practically the policy of the Land Act in this respect had been burked by the legal and other officials in Dublin.

On the conclusion of the evidence I submitted a draft report to the Committee embodying a full statement of the working of the clauses of the Church Disestablishment Act, in respect of the conversion of the tenants of the Church property into owners, and of the beneficial results of this policy as already manifest. It pointed out the causes of failure of the Act of 1870. It proposed a number of recommendations for amendment of the Act. It advised an increase in the proportion of the purchase money to be loaned by the State, and a prolongation of the term of repayment. A counter report was propounded on behalf of the Government of a most futile character. It was carried by a bare majority of the Committee in substitution for mine. When, however, the report of the Government was considered in detail, most of my recommendations were grafted upon it by majorities of the Committee, and as finally amended and adopted, it represented in the main my conclusions. In the Session of 1879 I made a motion in the House of Commons affirming the conclusions of the Report, and directing the Government to give effect to them as soon as possible. I was supported by a most powerful speech of Mr. Bright, and also by one from Mr. Gladstone. An admirable speech was also made in favour of my motion by Mr. Justin McCarthy, who had been returned as Member for Longford only a few days previously.

The Government, in the first instance, was unfriendly to the motion, but the general feeling of the House was so strongly expressed in favour of it, in the course of the debate, that it was compelled to change front, and the motion was ultimately agreed to unanimously. Mr. Parnell and the group of Irish Members associated with him took no part in these discussions and proceedings.

Reverting to the year 1877, it remains to point out that the annual motion, in favour of an amnesty for the remaining Fenians in convict prisons, was made in the course of this Session by Mr. O'Connor Power. Mr. Butt supported it in an eloquent speech, in which he pointed out that only eight of these men were still in convict prisons, two of whom had been concerned in the release of the prisoners in the Manchester affair, and five were soldiers, who had been convicted of taking part in the conspiracy ; the remaining convict was Michael Davitt, who had been convicted of collecting and distributing fire-arms to Fenians in Ireland, and had been sentenced to fifteen years of penal servitude. The leaders of the movement, including O'Donovan Rossa, had been already released. " Was it wise," Mr. Butt said, " to prolong the exasperation and ill-feeling in Ireland, and to undo the good effected by the release of the leaders by keeping in prison these few miserable men ? " Of those implicated in the Manchester attack, he said that at most it was a case of " constructive murder " and not such as was popularly held to be murder. The motion was strongly resisted by the Government. The Irish Secretary, Sir M. Hicks-Beach, repudiated Mr. Butt's contention that the term of murder was not rightly to be attributed to those engaged in the attack. Lord Hartington, on behalf of the main Opposition, supported the Government and contended that there was no reason for reversing the decision arrived at by the previous Government. Mr. W. E. Forster voted against the motion. The occasion, however, was taken by Mr. Gladstone for a speech urging the exercise of the prerogative of mercy, though he did not follow it up by his vote. Mr. Butt, he said, has called the Manchester case one of constructive murder. Independently of that it was a most gross outrage against the law, and an act most dangerous to the peace of Society, but it was going beyond the limits of accuracy to say that it was a deliberate and atrocious assassination. He hoped that the time had arrived when these cases might be examined with a view to the exercise of the prerogative of mercy. [1]

It was probably due to this intervention of Mr. Gladstone that, later in the same year, these few remaining Fenian prisoners were released. Michael Davitt was set free on a ticket-of-leave, after eight years of imprisonment as a convict. He was one of the most interesting, able, and independent of the men engaged in the Nationalist movement. On his release he devoted himself, at once, to an agrarian agitation in Ireland for the suppression of landlordism, and was very active in organizing Irish opinion in the United States with this object. The tardy exercise of the prerogative of mercy in the case of these few remaining political prisoners deprived the measure of much of its grace. It might well have been conceded much earlier. Instead of this the question was allowed to embitter Irish opinion for many long years. This, and the total failure of Parliament to listen to the demands of the Irish Members, and to provide any remedy for the grievances which they laid before it in the constitutional way, were fatal to Butt's policy of conciliation.

The scene above described, which occurred on the South African Bill, was also fraught with disastrous results to Butt and his policy. His intervention on behalf of the Government, in opposition to Parnell, was resented by Irish opinion outside Parliament, and led to his downfall as leader of the Irish Party. For some time past the militant attitude of Parnell had attracted and fascinated Irish opinion, especially that of Irishmen in England and in the United States, who had long been far more violent in their views than their compatriots in Ireland. Parnell had already stimulated this by speeches outside Parliament. At Manchester, on July 13th, 1877, he said :

" For my part I do not believe in a policy of conciliation of English opinion or English prejudices. What did we ever get in the past by trying to conciliate ? Why was the English Church in Ireland disestablished and disendowed ? Because there was an explosion at Clerkenwell and because there was a policeman shot in a prison-van at Manchester."

A few days after the scene in the House of Commons, on

[1] *Hansard*, 1877.

September 1st, 1877, the annual meeting of the British Home Rule Confederation took place at Manchester. The Association had been founded, a few years before, by Butt, who had been elected as its President in each succeeding year. He was present as usual at this meeting, expecting re-election as a matter of course. Parnell was also there. Some member rose and proposed Parnell as President for the coming year. There was no counter proposal on Butt's behalf. Not a single voice was raised for him. Parnell was unanimously elected. The old chief was deeply mortified. Tears were seen to fall from his eyes. " I never thought," he said, " that the Irish in England could do this to me." He appealed to his supporters in Ireland against this revolt of the Irish in England from his leadership. In an open letter to his constituents, later in the year, he wrote :

" The difference between the majority of the Home Rule Members and certain Members is not merely of greater or less activity, or as to an improper use of a legitimate instrument of opposition, but is deep and vital, embracing the whole of their Parliamentary conduct."

In spite of his appeal, public opinion in Ireland veered against Butt. It was deeply offended by the neglect and refusal of the House of Commons to meet any of the demands of the great majority of the Irish Members. It had practical proof in this of the inutility of methods based on constitutional lines, and of the failure of Butt's policy. Resentment against him was stimulated by the action of Parnell and Biggar and their small group of adherents, who had bearded the House of Commons. This struck the imagination of the Irish people. The action, however, of the Irish in Ireland was more considerate and deferential to Butt than that of the Irish in England.

At a Home Rule Conference held at Dublin on January 14th and 15th, 1878, a vast majority of those present were still favourable to Butt's leadership, though evidently dissatisfied with his conduct of affairs in the House of Commons. A large majority, however, were in favour of the policy of obstruction. Butt made a passionate appeal for unity of the party.

" I have no objection," he said, " to Irish members taking part in the discussion of English and Imperial affairs. I have even held that they did not take a part often enough.

We should do something for the sufferers of wrong throughout the Empire. What I object to, what I hold to be fatal to the dignity and usefulness of the Irish Party, and to the good name of Ireland throughout the world, is obviously not the intervention in English and Imperial concerns, but the manifestation of a certain Irish party without regard to the matter in hand and the interests involved. I laid down, at Limerick what I believed was the policy to pursue, and that was to make an assault all along the whole line of English misgovernment, and to bring forward every grievance of Ireland and to press the House of Commons for its redress. I believed, and still believe, that if once we get liberal-minded Englishmen fairly to consider how they could redress the grievances of Irish misgovernment, they would come, in the end, to the conclusion that they had but one way of giving us good government, and that is by allowing us to govern ourselves."

To this Parnell replied in a moderate speech : " I gladly agree with Mr. Butt that it is very possible, and very probable, that he would be able to persuade a few fair-minded Englishmen in the direction he has indicated ; but still I do not think that the House of Commons is mainly composed of fair-minded Englishmen. If we had to deal with men who were capable of listening to fair arguments, there would be every hope of success, but we are dealing with political parties, who consider the interests of their political organization as paramount beyond every other consideration." He went on to defend his own action. As a result, Butt's friends found it inexpedient to press their original motion that no Irish Member ought to persevere in any course of action, which should be condemned by a resolution, adopted at a meeting of Home Rule Members, as calculated to be injurious to the National cause. On the other hand, a motion of Mr. O'Connor Power, in the interest of Parnell, urging determined and vigorous action of the Parliamentary Party, was also withdrawn, and a neutral resolution was agreed to.

Although the immediate result of this conflict was a drawn battle, Butt recognized that his leadership was practically brought to an end. In April, he addressed a manifesto to the electors of Limerick condemning obstruction, but announcing his intention to resign the leadership of the Irish Party, and alleging ill-health as his reason. He followed this up by tender-ing his resignation to the Irish Party in the House of Commons. It was not accepted. He was induced to continue as nominal leader, but with the understanding that the same regular attendance, in the House of Commons, was not to be expected of him in the future. This was the more necessary to Butt as his finances were in a desperate condition. Subscriptions to the party funds had fallen off, owing to the division of opinion in the ranks of the party, and the hostility of the extreme section. A national subscription was started in Ireland by Butt's friends to recompense him for the great professional losses he had incurred by devotion to the Irish cause. It was a complete failure. Butt was thrown upon his own resources, which consisted solely of his income from professional work at the Bar. He was harassed by creditors in respect of old and accumulated debts. It was necessary to make every effort to recover his practice at Dublin. His sacrifices to the national cause had been very great. He had declined overtures for appointment to a very high position on the judicial Bench, to which, as the most eminent man at the Irish Bar, he was fully entitled. Like O'Connell, he would not give up his leadership of the national cause for professional advancement. But it was necessary to find the means of living. During the year 1878 he relaxed his attendance in Parliament. He devoted himself mainly to the Law Courts at Dublin. He was seldom at Westminster in comparison with the three previous years. He made great efforts to pick up again his professional practice. But it was too late. His health was rapidly failing. It was obvious to his friends that his end was approaching. It was to be regretted that Parnell did not appreciate this, and by generous and sympathetic treatment, relieve the gloom of the few remaining months of the old chief. Instead of this he continued his opposition in the party. At his instance a vote of censure on Butt was passed by a majority of the Home Rule Association of England.

The last speech which Butt made in the House of Commons was on July 4th, 1878, on an annual motion for inquiry into the Land Laws of Ireland and the failure of the Land Act of 1870, made by Mr. Errington, one of the most moderate of the Irish Party. Butt's speech was short, but vigorous and persuasive. Mr. James Lowther, who had succeeded Sir M.

Hicks-Beach as Irish Secretary, and who was an uncompromising Tory of the old school, expressed a detestation of the principle of the Irish Land Act, and banged the door against any amendment of it, in the interest of the tenants. It was an incident of the debate that Lord Randolph Churchill, at that time an undistinguished Member of the House of Commons, but who had seen something of Ireland, where his father was Lord-Lieutenant, first showed sympathy for the Irish Party, by speaking in favour of the Bill. Parnell and his associates took no part in the discussion. The motion was defeated by 124 to 67.

Butt's last presence at a public meeting was at Dublin on February 9th, 1879. His appearance there was a shock to his friends. There was no mistaking the signs of his approaching end. In spite of this, the reception by the audience was unsympathetic, if not hostile. Old friends gave him the cold shoulder. Butt took the opportunity of defending himself against the recent vote of censure by the British Home Rule Association. His speech, in spite of his failing strength, was worthy of his old reputation. It was persuasive, and closely reasoned, with passages of pathos. He succeeded in defeating a hostile motion by a small majority. It was his last speech. He went home to die. The end came a few weeks later—on May 5th. Butt died of a broken heart, if ever man did so, with a bitter sense of failure, of ruined fortune, and of political defeat by insurgent members of his own party, unredeemed by any generous appreciation of his great services to the Irish people, and of the great personal sacrifices he had made to their cause.

Isaac Butt's was the last attempt to combine the moderate section of Irish Liberalism, and representatives of Tory landowners, in Ireland, in a national policy of Home Rule and Land Reform. He was the first to propose, in a definite and practical form, the alternative to Repeal of the Act of Union, of a federal scheme, which was to give to Ireland an executive responsible to its representatives, and a legislature empowered to deal with purely Irish questions, while reserving to an Imperial Parliament matters of common interest and of Imperial concern. His speeches on this main topic have stood the test of subsequent experience. They were the text-book for the next generation. He was the first also to formulate specific proposals in the House of Commons for fixity of tenure and judicial rents and to clothe them with legal forms.   It may safely be presumed that Mr. Gladstone owed much to Butt's writings and speeches, when he came to deal with the Irish land question in 1881, and when later he made his proposals for Home Rule in 1886.

CHAPTER IX

ON the death of Mr. Butt in 1879 the Irish Home Rule Party in the House of Commons chose as their leader Mr. William Shaw, Member for Cork, and Chairman of the Munster Bank, with a high repute as a financier, and at that time a man of substance. He was a Protestant, a shrewd and forcible speaker, with a certain quality of dry humour which attracted the House of Commons, but without the gift of eloquence. His election in preference to Parnell, who had already acquired a Parliamentary position, far in advance of any others of the party, showed that a majority of it were imbued with Butt's principles of moderation and conciliation, rather than the more advanced view of Parnell and his followers.

Though nominally leader of the Irish Party, Mr. Shaw appears to have had very little influence. The germs of dissension had already, in the previous year, developed in the party. There were very few subjects on which they agreed. Parnell went his own way, and paid little, if any, deference to Mr. Shaw's leadership. The main subject which occupied him, in 1879, was the Army Discipline Bill. This was a measure consolidating all the law on the subject. It was the result of the labours of a Committee of the previous Session, which had been due to Parnell's obstruction to the Annual Mutiny Bill. It offered endless opportunities for discussion, and raised the important question of flogging in the Army. Parnell, O'Donnell, and Biggar availed themselves freely of them. Their main object was to abolish flogging. They organized obstruction to the whole Bill for this purpose. They were aided in their opposition to flogging, in the first instance, by a small section of English Liberals, including Mr. Joseph Cowen and Mr. Hopwood. Later Mr. Chamberlain came to their aid. He bore testimony to the great public service performed by Parnell and Biggar in obstructing the Mutiny Bill of the previous year. " Nothing," he said, " can be done without obstruction. The friends of humanity and the friends of the British Army owe a debt of gratitude to the Member for Meath [Mr. Parnell] for standing up alone against this system of flogging, when I myself, and other Members, had not the courage of our convictions. I hope that his efforts will be crowned by success."[1]

These efforts to abolish flogging were opposed at first by Lord Hartington, as Leader of the Liberal Party and former Minister of War, and by Sir William Harcourt ; but later public opinion outside the House of Commons declared itself so unmistakably against flogging, that the whole of the Liberal Party in the House veered round in the same direction. Mr. Chamberlain taunted Lord Hartington on the subject, and referred to him contemptuously as " lately the Leader of the Liberal Party." Mr. Callan, an Irish Home Ruler, not one of Parnell's followers, succeeded in getting specimens of the different kinds of cat, used for flogging in the two Services, exhibited in the Library of the House. This added to the excitement on the subject, both in and outside the House. After seven weeks of discussion in Committee on the Bill, Colonel Stanley, the Minister in charge of it, who, in the first instance, had asserted that flogging was, in the opinion of the highest military authorities, indispensable for the maintenance of discipline in the Army, began to waver. He made a series of concessions, giving way from point to point, as the discussion progressed, and eventually took his stand on the maintenance of flogging only in time of war, and for cases where death was the only alternative. Lord Hartington also, who had originally supported the Government, ultimately yielded to the general feeling of the party behind him, and, on the report stage of the Bill, moved a resolution condemning in every case the punishment of flogging in the Army. This was resisted by the Government and was defeated on a party division.

The Bill, as ultimately passed, limited flogging to the rare cases above referred to. In other respects the severity of the measure was much mitigated. The discussion on it occupied the House for twenty-three nights, and according to *Hansard*,

[1] *Hansard*, June 10th, 1879.

Parnell and O'Donnell spoke, each of them, over 150 times. To them, and to others of their small band of Irish followers, the main credit of the practical abolition of flogging in the Army was due. It cannot therefore be said that their obstruction was without justification. It was, in fact, successful. If time was wasted, the fault lay with the Members in charge of the Bill, and with the Government, who, by early concessions, might have disarmed opposition and avoided obstruction.

The Session of 1879 was not unfruitful of Irish measures. It was claimed by Parnell and his followers that their general policy of obstruction and of hostility to the Government, as distinguished from Butt's policy of conciliation, compelled the Government to propose or agree to measures of appeasement. An Irish University Act was passed, which substituted for the Queen's University an examining University on the model of that of London. It passed without much difficulty or discussion. It failed, however, in its result to give satisfaction or to afford a remedy for the complaints of the Catholics in Ireland. Another measure, important in its political effect, due to a private Member, was the virtual repeal of Lord Clare's Convention Act of 1798. The Act, which was passed by the Irish Parliament of that year, was part of the panic legislation caused by the French Revolution. It prohibited the election of delegates to any central convention in Ireland. The repeal of the Act was supported by a most powerful speech of Mr. Joseph Cowen, which virtually carried the Bill. He showed that the Convention Act did not interfere with the common law right of holding meetings in Ireland. The Irish people could muster in immense numbers on the classic hill of Tara or at Trim or Mullaghmast. But if, instead of holding threatening assemblies 500,000 strong, such as gathered together, under O'Connell, a deliberative assembly of representative men met quietly in a room in Dublin and strove, not by force but by persuasion and agreement, to put their case for the repeal of a specified law, or the reform of a social usage, the law would step in and prevent them. The Act might be said to offer a premium to passion and violence, and to put a penalty on representation and reason.

The Bill was opposed by the Attorney-General for Ireland, Mr. Gibson, who claimed that the Act was enforced only with the greatest discretion, so as not to abridge the holding of representative meetings. In reply to him I pointed out that the Act extended far beyond what its framers apparently intended, for its preamble contemplated the prohibition of meetings of delegates claiming the attributes of a Parliament, while the enacting clauses prohibited delegations of all kinds. I suggested that the Bill should be amended so as to maintain the prohibition of meetings arrogating the functions of Parliament. This was supported by Parnell in a closely reasoned and conciliatory speech, which showed what advance he had made in Parliamentary debate. He pointed out that under the common law assemblies aping Parliament were illegal. The Irish Secretary, while saving the face of the Government, by saying that the Bill could not be amended as proposed, promised to support one, which would have the desired effect of repealing the Convention Act, but which would maintain the prohibition of assemblies arrogating the functions of a Parliament. This was agreed to, and an Act was passed which repealed the objectionable features of the Convention Act.

Another important Bill, introduced by an Irish Member, for permitting the enrolment of volunteers in Ireland, also passed the House of Commons. It was supported by Mr. Shaw and Colonel King-Harman. There was unanimity in the House of Commons in favour of it. The Attorney-General for Ireland, Mr. Gibson, said that as an Irishman he was always glad when it devolved on him to make any reasonable concession to Irish opinion. It will scarcely be credited that this most reasonable Bill, passed unanimously by the House of Commons, and supported by the Government, was rejected by the House of Lords by a majority of 36 to 16. The majority consisted mainly of Irish Peers, while the 16 included Lord Beaconsfield, the Duke of Richmond, Lord Cairns, and Lord Cranbrook, members of the Cabinet, and the leaders of the Liberal Opposition, such as Lord Spencer. Lord Bury, who represented the War Office, said that it would be a grave responsibility for the Government to express its opinion that the Irish nation was unfit to be trusted with arms. That, indeed, was not their opinion. It was felt by the Government that there could be no danger or difficulty in allowing the volunteer system to be extended to Ireland. In spite of this the reactionary Peers rejected the Bill.

Before the close of the Session (1879) the condition of agriculture both in England and Ireland occupied the serious attention of the House of Commons. The two previous years, 1877 and 1878, had been very unfavourable. Crops were very deficient, and prices did not rise in proportion to the deficiency as in past years. In July Mr. Chaplin called attention to the prevalent depression of agriculture, and moved for a Royal Commission to inquire into its causes and to suggest remedies. His speech was strongly flavoured by his well-known views in favour of Protection. Speaking of the distress in Ireland, he said that the profits of farmers were reduced by the amount of one half, and often of the whole of their rent. The O'Donoghue, on behalf of the Irish Party, moved an amendment pointing to the necessity of including an inquiry into the Land Laws of Ireland, and their failure to protect the interests of tenant farmers in years of bad harvests and low prices. Agricultural depression, he said, meant inability to pay high rents. The rent question had become a grave one in Ireland, where the overwhelming majority of tenants had agreed to their existing rents under compulsion. They had to choose between accepting the landlords' terms and eviction, which meant ruin, and they naturally preferred the alternative, which, at all events, gave them a chance of security till happier times. . . . The real, the only method, he contended, of dealing with the agricultural depression was to establish a fair system for the adjustment of rents.

Much discussion followed, and it was ultimately agreed that the subject of the adjustment of rents should be included in the reference to a Royal Commission. A Commission was accordingly appointed with the Duke of Richmond as its President. Mr. Chichester Fortescue and Mr. William Shaw represented Irish interests upon it.

The harvest which followed on this, in 1879, was the worst which had occurred in Ireland since 1846. Successive weeks of rain ruined the crops of corn and potatoes, and made it impossible in many cases to dry the turf. Agricultural distress was not confined to Ireland. It was almost equally severe in England. The corn crops were less than one-half of the average of past years. It resulted that there was little demand for the employment of the migratory labourers from the west of Ireland, who yearly crossed the Channel for work at harvest time in England, and who reckoned on paying rent for their small holdings and homes out of wages thus earned. The West of Ireland was consequently in a deplorable condition.

The year 1880 opened under most gloomy conditions in Ireland. The gravity of the state of things there, as regards the western half of it, was now fully recognized. Famine was stalking through the land. Evictions, pauperism, and crimes were largely increasing. Relief funds were opened by the Duchess of Marlborough, the wife of the Lord-Lieutenant, and by the Lord Mayor of Dublin (Mr. E. D. Gray). Large contributions were made through the Roman Catholic Bishops from the United States, and by emigrants there to their relatives at home. There was also a relief fund collected by Parnell and Dillon in their political tour in the States. But the aggregate of these funds was little compared to the total deficiency caused by the three bad harvests.

The distress was not confined to the west of Ireland. It was also, though in a less degree, prevalent in every part of Ireland, among the large as well as other farmers, and generally throughout Great Britain. Lord Beaconsfield, in a speech at Oxford, during the recess, impressed upon the landowners of England the necessity of meeting the emergency by large remissions of rent to their tenants. No similar exhortations to reduce their rents were made to the landlords of Ireland by any responsible member of the Government. Many land-owners did, in fact, make abatements, especially in Ulster, where the distress was least, and where the tenants' interest in their holdings was fully recognized. But in a great part of Ireland no reductions were made, and rents were either fully insisted on, or were allowed to accumulate in arrears, which kept the tenants in bondage till three years later, when relief was afforded by the Legislature. In some cases landlords took advantage of the occasion, and began to clear their estates of tenants, without paying any compensation for eviction, thus appropriating the tenants' interest in their holdings, which it was the object of the Land Act of 1870 to recognize and protect. Eviction processes alarmingly increased. In 1879 they were double the number in the previous year, and in the first half of 1880 they were again double the rate of 1879. The recollection of the clearances effected by landowners in many parts of the south and west in previous years of bad harvests were still fresh in the memories of the peasantry.

It was at this juncture that the ill effect of the mutilation by the House of Lords of the Land Act of 1870 became apparent. The Act as it left the House of Commons gave discretion to the judge to award compensation in cases of eviction for non-payment of rent if there were special circumstances to warrant his doing so. This would have provided for the case of a succession of bad seasons when the payment of full rent, or even any rent at all, became impossible. The action of the House of Lords, in striking out these words of discretion to the judge, was now to produce its malign effect, for the tenants were at the mercy of their landlords, and could be evicted wholesale, without any compensation as intended by the Act. The least that could be expected under these conditions was that the Government would make some proposal for the protection of the smaller tenants at least against the legal consequences of their failure to pay rent, owing to the succession of bad harvests.

When, however, Parliament met early in 1880 there was no suggestion in the Speech from the Throne of any amendment of the law for the purpose of saving the smaller tenants from eviction for non-payment of rents which had been made impossible by causes beyond their control. Mr. Shaw moved an amendment to the address raising the question of distress in Ireland. A debate prolonged over three nights took place on this motion. Sir Stafford Northcote's explanation on the part of the Government gave a most alarming account of the state of things in Ireland. His statistics showed that there had been a failure of the principal crops in Ireland, as compared with previous years, of 10 millions, or more than one-half, and that the value of the potato crop was 6 millions behind the average—or less than one-third of an average crop.

It appeared from Sir Stafford Northcote's explanation that the chief action taken by the Irish Government to meet this state of things was the issue of a circular to the Boards of Guardians, impressing upon them the importance of making due provision beforehand of ample stores of bedding and clothing, to meet any pressure on the workhouse which was likely to occur. Nothing had been done in the way of relaxing the order prohibiting outdoor relief, which could only be effected in Ireland by an Act of Parliament. Nor was anything done immediately, or proposed, with reference to the quarter-acre provision, under which no relief could be given by the workhouse authorities, if the applicant was tenant of more than a quarter of an acre of land, without surrendering his holding. A circular, however, had been issued to landowners and local authorities reminding them of their powers to borrow public money, under various Acts of Parliament, for works of drainage, planting, etc., involving the employment of labour, and offering somewhat more favourable terms by the postponement of the commencement of repayment for two years. The applications in response to this were trivial in amount. Lord Hartington, on behalf of the Liberal Party in opposition, refused to join in a vote of censure. He left the responsibility of meeting the distress on the Government. Mr. Plunket (later Lord Rathmore), then Solicitor-General for Ireland, speaking on behalf of the Government, attacked the Irish Home Rule Party. " To the Irish agitator," he said, " the present distress seemed a good occasion to call up the grievance of the past, to rake up buried sorrows, to exasperate the people, and to make them as little as possible ready or patient to bear their suffering." Mr. Shaw's motion, after a fierce debate, was rejected by a majority of 216 to 66. A few days later Mr. Shaw asked the Irish Secretary whether the Government intended to do anything for Land Reform, in the direction of extending to the rest of Ireland the security enjoyed in Ulster. Mr. Lowther replied that to extend the Ulster custom as proposed would be pure and undiluted confiscation. He added that the Land Laws had nothing to do with the state of distress in Ireland.

A Relief Bill was introduced early in the Session by the Government, authorizing the advance of a million out of the surplus funds of the Disestablished Church for loans to Irish landowners, on favourable terms, to be expended on works providing for the employment of labour. The Bill led to protracted debate. In the course of it a clause was inserted enabling Boards of Guardians to relax the rigid provision as to outdoor relief. Mr. Hugh Law, an eminent lawyer, later Solicitor-General for Ireland in Mr. Gladstone's Government, succeeded in inducing the Government to agree to a clause modifying the landowners' rights as regarded evictions in cases where they borrowed money under the Relief Act. But this clause, so eminently just and expedient under the existing conditions of Ireland, was rejected by the House of Lords.

The Irish Secretary, Mr. James Lowther, throughout these discussions showed a harsh and cynical attitude to Irish questions. In answer to a deputation suggesting a distribution of seed potatoes to the poorer tenants, he said that what Ireland needed was grass seed, hinting by this that more land should be devoted to grazing purposes—a measure which would obviously entail a further depopulation of the country. No more unsympathetic statesman ever filled the post of Irish Secretary. Before, however, he could do more mischief his official career was brought to an end by the sudden determination of the Government in April, 1880, to dissolve Parliament. The favourable result of two by-elections had led them to believe that public opinion was in their favour and that the opportunity was a favourable one for an appeal to the electors.

CHAPTER X

THE year 1879 was memorable in Ireland for the commencement of an agrarian agitation, and for the foundation of the Land League, which played so great a part in the next three years. The country was ripe for such a movement, owing to the grave distress of agriculture, and to the failure of the Government to hold out any hope of a remedial measure for the protection of the tenants.

Parnell took no part in the discussion on this subject in the House of Commons during this Session. After his great and successful fight on the Army Discipline Bill, he was mainly occupied in attending public meetings in Ireland on the Land question. He appears to have hesitated for some time whether to advocate legislation for fixity of tenure and judicial rents, or the creation of a peasant proprietary, by means of State loans, and the expropriation of landlords by purchase. In 1878 he had paid a visit to the west of Ireland, and for the first time, as later he told the Special Commission, became aware of the misery of its people. He drove for miles through rich grazing land, without meeting any one, though he saw the ruins of many houses, while in other parts he found a dense population living, from hand to mouth, on holdings quite insufficient to support life. He began, he said, to think that a measure for merely fixing rents would be insufficient.

Later in 1878 Michael Davitt returned from America and commenced an active agitation on the Land question in the west of Ireland. He advocated the extinction of landlords, and the adoption of a scheme of land nationalization. Taking advantage of a case of gross hardship on a property at Irishtown, in Mayo, which had recently come into possession of a Catholic priest, Canon Burke, and where the tenants were threatened with wholesale eviction, for non-payment of large arrears of excessive rents, he summoned a meeting there to protest against the evictions, to demand a reduction of rents, and to denounce the whole system of landlordism.

The meeting was an immense success. Upwards of 7000 persons were present ; 600 mounted farmers acted as a bodyguard to the speaker. Many advanced land reformers attended the meeting. Very strong speeches were made. "Down with landlordism," "The land for the people," were the watchwords of those present. Resolutions were passed demanding an immediate reduction of rents in Mayo, and the ultimate expropriation of landlords.

The immediate result of the meeting was the announcement by Canon Burke, within a few days, that his rents would be reduced by 25 per cent. These reduced rents were, later, still further reduced by the Land Commission, under the Act of 1881, by 40 per cent—showing that the tenants had very strong ground for their complaints.

The result of the meeting, the first of its kind, aiming at a reduction of rents, through the pressure of public opinion, was enormous. The Irishtown meeting has always been considered as the commencement of the new agitation, of a revolutionary character, for the extinction of landlordism. It was the more important, as the meeting was immediately directed against the action of a Catholic clergyman. Warnings were given from their altars by many priests in Mayo against the holding of such meetings, " called by irresponsible people and showing disrespect to priests." Undeterred by this, and influenced by the prospect of obtaining reductions of rent in this way, meetings of the same kind were soon multiplied in the County of Mayo. Parnell appears to have been greatly interested by the accounts of these meetings. He had many conversations on the subject with Davitt, who pressed him to take a leading part in this new movement. Eventually Parnell promised to attend a great meeting at Westport, in Mayo. The meeting was discouraged by the priests of that district, and was openly and fiercely denounced by Dr. McHale, the veteran Archbishop of Tuam, the bosom friend and colleague of O'Connell in the Repeal movement, and who exercised immense influence throughout Ireland.

"Against such combinations in the diocese," the Archbishop wrote, "organized by a few designing men, who instead of the well-being of the community, seek only to promote their personal interests, the faithful clergy will not fail to raise their warning voice, and to point out to the people that unhallowed combinations lead invariably to disaster, and to the further riveting of the chains, by which we are unhappily bound as a subordinate people to a dominant race."

In spite of this episcopal manifesto, Parnell addressed a great meeting at Westport on June 8th, 1879. Eight thousand people were present. This speech was a momentous one.

"I am one of those," he said, "who believe that the institution of landlords is not a national institution in the country. I believe that the maintenance of the class of landlords in a country is not for the greatest benefit of the greatest number. Ireland has suffered from them more than any other country. In Belgium, Prussia, France, and Russia the land has been given to the people—in some by the iron hand of revolution ; in others, as in Prussia, landlords have been purchased out. If such an arrangement could be made, without injuring the landlord, so as to enable the tenant to have the land as his own, and to cultivate it as it ought to be, it would be for the benefit and prosperity of the country. I look to this as the final settlement of the question. But meantime it is necessary to ensure that as long as the tenant pays a fair rent he shall be left to enjoy the fruits of his industry. A fair rent is a rent which the tenant can reasonably pay according to the times, but in bad times the tenant cannot be expected to pay as much as in good times, three or four years ago. Now what must we do in order to induce the landlord to see the position? You must show the landlords that you intend to hold a firm grip on your homesteads and lands. You must not allow yourselves to be dispossessed as you were in 1848. You must not allow your small holdings to be turned into larger ones. I am not supposing that the landlords will remain deaf to the voice of reason, but I hope that they may not, and that on those properties on which the rents are out of proportion to the time, a reduction may be made and that immediately. If not, you must help yourselves, and the public opinion of the world will stand by you and support you in your struggle to defend your homesteads. If we had the farmers of

Ireland the owners of the soil we should not be long in getting an Irish Parliament."

Parnell spoke later at Limerick and Tipperary in much the same sense. Indeed, at the former place on August 31st his language was stronger. The bad season had already made it certain that the harvest would be a complete failure, and that the pressure on the small farmers would be very great.

" It is the duty of the Irish tenant farmers," he said, " to combine among themselves and ask for a reduction of rent, and if they get no reduction of rent, then I say it is the duty of the tenants to pay no rent."

At Tipperary on September 21st he again enforced his advice to farmers to keep a firm grip on their homesteads and to show a determined attitude to the landlords.

These speeches, and especially the remarkable one at Westport, made an epoch in the Land question, and must be judged of by the light of subsequent events. At the time they appeared to most people in England to be revolutionary and dangerous, if not illegal, in a very high degree. But what Parnell then recommended has since been carried out almost in its entirety, after long years of agitation and suffering in Ireland. But for the agitation, which Parnell then initiated, it must be admitted that these great changes would never have been effected. It may be that these great and revolutionary results were not achieved without much of most reprehensible violence. But impartial historians must look broadly at results, and compare them with the original policy laid down. They must make allowances for much that occurred in the course of the movement which led to such results. Measured and judged in this way, Parnell must be held to have shown most remarkable prevision, when he made the speech at Westport which has been quoted.

In September Parnell was again urged by Davitt to join in expanding the Land League of Mayo into a National League for the whole of Ireland. He hesitated for some time to do so. In his evidence before the Special Commission in 1888 he thus described his motives in consenting to do so :

" Mr. Davitt was very anxious that the Land League should be formed, and that the tenants should be supported by an agrarian movement. I had in my mind advice given to me by Mr. Butt, two or three years previously, when I pressed upon him the extension of the Home Rule movement, by the formation of branches throughout the country. He said, looking at it from a lawyer's point of view, that we should be made responsible for every foolish thing done by the members of the branches. I was rather disinclined to entertain the idea of the formation of an extensive agrarian movement on account of the caution which I received from Mr. Butt. But ultimately I saw that it was necessary to take the risk. . . . Mr. Davitt spoke to me with regard to the desirability of a combined social and political movement, a movement which would interest the tenant farmers by directing attention to their condition, and proposing remedies for their relief, and a movement which, at the same time, would interest the Irish nation, at home and abroad, in the direction of the restitution of an Irish Parliament."

He finally consented to take the leading part in forming a National Land League for Ireland, upon the understanding that the platform put forward should be such as could be advocated as freely in the House of Commons, as on the platform in Ireland. Invitations were accordingly sent out, in his name, to the leading men interested in Land Reform, for a Conference at the Imperial Hotel, Dublin, on October 21st, for the purpose of forming a Land League Association for appealing to Irishmen abroad, and especially in America, for assistance, in forwarding land agitation in favour of the ownership of the soil by the occupier, and also for the purpose of upholding the tenants, during the present terrible season, by the promotion of organization.

Parnell moved the principal resolution : " That the objects of the League can best be attained by promoting organization among the tenant farmers, and defending those who may be threatened with eviction for refusing to pay exorbitant rents ; by facilitating the working of the Bright Clauses of the Land Act of 1870 during the winter ; and by obtaining such a reform in the laws relating to the land as will enable any tenant to become the owner of his holding by paying a fair rent for a limited number of years." He was appointed President of the League, and he was requested to visit the United States in company with Mr. Dillon, who had already gained distinction on the platform, as a Land Reformer, for the purpose of inviting assistance to the League, and contributions toward the relief of distress in Ireland due to the bad seasons.

The Land League thus formed was largely in the hands of extreme men in sympathy more or less with Fenians. Mr. Biggar and Mr. Patrick Egan were its honorary treasurers. Mr. Davitt, Mr. Kettle, and Mr. Brennan were honorary secretaries. Land League meetings were organized throughout Ireland, at which language at least as strong as, and not unfrequently stronger than that of Parnell was used. For speeches at Gurteen, in Sligo, closely resembling that of Parnell at Westport, Davitt, Daly, and Kettle were arrested by the Government, and were brought before a magistrate and charged with sedition and seditious language. The magistrate, after some days of inquiry, committed them for trial at the Assizes in Sligo. When the Assizes came on the Government, finding that there was no prospect whatever of obtaining a verdict against them, changed the venue to Dublin. Eventually the prosecutions were dropped, just before the General Election. The only effect, therefore, of these abortive proceedings was to give wide advertisement to speeches, which would otherwise not have been published in any but the local papers, and to show that, under the existing law, they could be delivered with impunity. They had the effect also of postponing the visit of Parnell to America. To go there, while these prosecutions were pending, would look like running away from the post of danger. Remaining in Ireland, he addressed numerous meetings in the same tenor as the speech delivered at Gurteen. At a meeting at Liverpool he repeated the very speech for which Davitt was prosecuted, and challenged the Government to bring him before an English jury. They refrained from doing so. It was not till November 21st, 1879, that Parnell found himself able to embark with Dillon on their American tour.

The mission was a very great success. It aroused the greatest interest in every part of the United States. On their arrival at New York, they were met by a deputation of 300 gentlemen, including senators, judges, merchants, and authors, and Parnell addressed a meeting of 8000 persons. He said that the object of the mission had been modified by the pressure of events, and the increasing distress in Ireland, caused by the failure of crops. It was their original intention to address the people in the States on behalf of the political organization, newly created, for the purpose of Land Reform, but the course of events had compelled them to abandon the original intention. They now proposed to open two funds, one for the relief of distress in Ireland, the other for the purely political purpose of forwarding their organization. They would be kept wholly distinct. In this view meetings were held in every part of the States, and were everywhere attended by thousands, including many leading men of the districts. At Brooklyn the eminent divine Mr. Ward Beecher spoke on their behalf. At Boston Mr. Wendell Phillips, the great anti-slavery leader, was present.

" I came here," he said, " as you have done, from a keen desire to see the man that has compelled John Bull to listen. Half the battle is won when the victim forces his tyrant to listen, gains his attention, and concentrates on his wrongs the thought of Christendom and the civilized world."

At Washington the very rare honour was conferred on Parnell of inviting him to address the House of Representatives. Lafayette and Kossuth had been among the few privileged in this way. Parnell, on being called before the Assembly, made a very judicious and moderate address.

" We do not seek," he said, " to embroil your Government with the Government of England, but we claim that the public opinion and sentiment of a free country like America is entitled to find expression whenever it is seen that the laws of freedom are not observed. . . . The most pressing question in Ireland is at the present moment the tenure of land. . . . Many of us, who are observing the course of events, believe that the time is fast approaching when the artificial and cruel system of land tenure prevailing in Ireland is bound to fall, and be replaced by a more natural and a more just one. . . . The remedy we propose for the state of affairs in Ireland is an alteration of the land tenure previously there. We propose to imitate the example of Prussia and other countries where the feudal tenure has been tried and found wanting and abandoned, and we propose to make or give an opportunity to every tenant occupying a farm in Ireland to become the owner of his own farm." After referring to Mr. Bright's proposals in this direction, he said : " The radical difference between our proposition and that of Mr. Bright is that we think that the

State should adopt the system of compulsory expropriation of the land, whereas Mr. Bright thinks that it might be left to self-interest and the force of public opinion to compel the landlord to sell."

Nothing was said in this speech of Home Rule, still less of the independence of Ireland. He was more expansive as to his ultimate views at other places.

At Cincinnati on February 23rd he was reported to have said : " When we have given Ireland to the people of Ireland we shall have laid the foundation upon which to build up our Irish nation. The feudal tenure and the rule of the minority have been the corner-stone of English misrule ; pull out that corner-stone, break it up, destroy it, and you undermine English misgovernment ; when we have undermined English misgovernment we have paved the way for Ireland to take her place amongst the nations of the earth, and let us not forget that is the ultimate goal at which all we Irishmen aim. None of us, whether we are in America or Ireland, or wherever we may be, will be satisfied until we have destroyed the last link which keeps Ireland bound to England."

Parnell, before the Special Commission of 1888, when questioned as to this passage, said that it was improbable that he had used the expression as to " severing the last link with England," and that if he did it must have been " qualified with other matters, as it was entirely opposed to anything he had ever thought or said." The Commission did not accept his disclaimer. They found that he had spoken these words.

It is to be observed that the Special Commission did not include Parnell's name among those against whom they found that the charge of conspiring to bring about a separation between England and Ireland was established. The sentence in the Cincinnati speech as to " the last link " is the only one of the kind which was detected out of many hundreds of speeches. It was distinctly opposed to the general tenor of Parnell's speeches and policy.

At the conclusion of his tour of meetings in the United States Parnell went to Canada, leaving Dillon behind him. He was joined in Canada by Mr. T. M. Healy, then a clerk in a London warehouse, but who had earned distinction as a writer in *The Freeman's Journal*. Parnell, who had come across him, was impressed by his ability, and now telegraphed to ask his assistance as secretary. Mr. Healy commenced in this way his political career which has been so distinguished, if at times somewhat erratic. He took part with Parnell in meetings in Canada, but within a short time they were recalled to England by the sudden announcement of the Dissolution of Parliament.

CHAPTER XI

ON March 8th the announcement was made that the six-years-old Parliament of 1874–80 was to be immediately dissolved. On the next day Lord Beaconsfield issued a manifesto, in a letter to the Lord-Lieutenant of Ireland, in which the attempt was made to draw off the attention of the electors from the Foreign policy of the Government and other issues, and to present disaffection in Ireland, and the demand for Home Rule, as the main, if not the sole, issue at the coming General Election.

" A danger," it said, " in its ultimate results scarcely less disastrous than pestilence and famine, and which now engages Your Excellency's anxious attention, distracts Ireland. A portion of its population is endeavouring to sever the constitutional tie which unites it to Great Britain in that bond which has favoured the power and prosperity of both. It is to be hoped that all men of light and leading will resist this disastrous doctrine. . . ."

This turgid manifesto missed fire. It met with no response from the country. In a counter address to his constituents Lord Hartington, who still led the Liberal Party in the moribund House of Commons, wrote : " I know of no party which challenges the expediency of the Imperial character of this realm. . . . No patriotic purpose is gained by the use of language of exaggeration in describing the Irish agitation for Home Rule. I believe the demand to be impracticable. . . . I have consistently opposed it in office and in opposition, and I shall continue to oppose it. The agitation has existed during the whole of the continuance of this Parliament. It has been treated by the Government, till now, if not with indulgence, with indifference. . . . The agitation must be met, not by passionate exaggeration, but by firm and consistent resistance, combined with the proof that the Imperial Parliament is able and willing to grant every reasonable and just demand of the Irish people for equal laws and institutions."

Mr. Gladstone, on his part, in an address to the electors of Midlothian, wrote : " Those who endangered the Union with Ireland were the party that maintained there an alien Church, an unjust Land Law, and franchises inferior to our own ; and the true supporters of the Union are those who uphold the supreme authority of Parliament, but exercise that authority to bind the three nations by the indissoluble ties of liberal and equal laws."

The only result of Lord Beaconsfield's move, which by the light of subsequent events must now be considered to have been premature, rather than wholly wanting in justification, was to draw from the Irish Home Rule Association of Great Britain a counter manifesto, drawn up by Mr. O'Donnell, calling upon all Irish electors, " in the presence of the atrocious and criminal manœuvres which had been attempted, to vote against Benjamin Disraeli, as the mortal enemy of their country." It urged that no pledges should be asked of Liberal candidates. In deference to this instruction from the Home Rule head-quarters, the large number of Irishmen, who were qualified as electors in Great Britain, voted for Liberal candidates. They formed a most important factor in the rout of the Tory Party.

Ireland, for all other purposes, dropped out of the political controversy in Great Britain. The elections in Great Britain turned wholly on the misdeeds of the Tory Government during their six years of office, and especially on their aggressive and militant policy in every part of the world. Mr. Gladstone, in his great Midlothian campaign, during which he made sixteen important speeches, devoted himself wholly to these topics, and hardly mentioned the subject of Ireland. No promise whatever was held out to the Irish people of Land Reform. As a result, the elections in Great Britain were largely determined by these efforts of the Leader of the Liberal Party, and nearly 100 seats were won from the Tory Party, making a difference of about 200 in the relative strength of the two parties.

It was very different in Ireland. There the elections turned wholly on the Land question. Home Rule itself became a subordinate issue for the time being. The electors took no interest whatever in Imperialism, and the aggressive Foreign and Colonial policy of Lord Beaconsfield's Ministry. The only question was the extent to which Land Reform should be carried.

There was an almost universal demand for a radical amendment of the Land Act of 1870. In Ulster, quite as much as in the west of Ireland, there was profound dissatisfaction with the results of that Act. While it had purported to recognize and give validity to the Ulster custom, it had failed to secure the tenants from the raising of rents, such as to expropriate the tenants' interest in their holdings. Still less did it provide for a reduction of rent, which a fall of prices made necessary, if the tenants' interest was not to be swallowed up by the landlord. The Ulster tenant farmers, therefore, with one voice, demanded a more complete protection, and the legalizing of their custom by the judicial determination of rent. So strong was this demand that the Tory landowners' candidates for County constituencies in Ulster were compelled to support it. Lord Castlereagh, now Lord Londonderry, who was candidate for County Down, obtained and published a written promise from Sir Stafford Northcote that, in the event of the Government being maintained in power after the General Election, it would legislate on the land question in accordance with the demands of the Ulster tenants. In the rest of Ireland there was also unanimity as to the necessity of a measure securing the three F's, that is, fixity of tenure, fair rents to be determined by a legal tribunal, and free sale of the tenants' interest. But in many constituencies the electors took up a more advanced demand for the extinction of landlordism, on the lines indicated by Parnell's speeches, namely, the purchase by the State of the landlord's interest, based on rents not higher than the Poor Law valuation.

Parnell, suddenly recalled from Canada by the Dissolution of Parliament, displayed enormous activity in the elections. He rushed about Ireland addressing meetings in favour of his candidates. He seemed to be equally concerned in opposing and defeating moderate Home Rulers who followed Mr. Shaw, especially if they were landowners. He was returned himself for three constituencies, the two Counties of Meath and Mayo, and the City of Cork. He elected to sit for Cork, where he was returned at the head of the poll by a majority of 200 above the Tory candidate, and 500 above the two Whigs, who were supported by the Catholic Bishops and clergy and by most of the business men of the city.

Parnell was largely, if not mainly, responsible for the selection of candidates in other constituencies. They were mostly young men, quite unknown to fame, or to the constituencies where they came forward; but they abundantly justified the selection. Among them were John Dillon, elected for Tipperary County in spite of his absence in the United States; Thomas Sexton, for Sligo (County); John Redmond, for New Ross; T. P. O'Connor, for Galway (City); James O'Kelly, for Roscommon; Arthur O'Connor and Lalor, for Queen's County; T. D. Sullivan, the poet of the National cause and journalist; Richard Power and Leamy, for Waterford; Barry, for Wexford. Of those in the previous Parliament O'Connor Power, A. M. Sullivan, O'Donnell, Biggar, and Dwyer Gray were again returned.

Not less remarkable than the return of these men was the fact that they defeated so many of the old and respected Liberal Members. Most of the Members representing landlord interest, whether Whig or Tory, outside of Ulster, were rejected. Many more seats would probably have been won by Parnell and the Land League, if there had been more time to organize, and more money at their disposal. Their only resource appears to have been the sum of £2000 borrowed from the funds of the League, which could not by their rules be devoted to such a purpose.

The success of the party was the more remarkable as the priests were generally opposed to them. Archbishops McHale, of Tuam, and McCabe, of Dublin, published violent manifestos against the Land League. As a result of Parnell's efforts his seven supporters in the defunct Parliament were increased nearly sixfold in the new one, mainly by newly elected men, but in part by the accession to his party of Members hitherto followers of Mr. Shaw. Of the 103 Members for Ireland in the new Parliament, the Tory Party returned only 26; 15 of the remainder were pure Whigs not committed to either section of the Home Rule Party, representing Ulster constituencies or small Boroughs elsewhere. The Home Rule followers of Mr. Shaw numbered no more than 22, and the residue (39) were to be relied on as members of the new party led by Parnell.

As soon as the results of the elections, as a whole, were made known, Lord Beaconsfield tendered the resignation of his Government to the Queen. The Queen then invited Lord Hartington to form a Government, but it was obvious that no Liberal Government could be formed without Mr. Gladstone, who had been the main agent in bringing about the fall of the previous Government. He could not be a member of a Government, except in the position of its Chief. After a brief consultation with some of his political friends, Lord Hartington found himself unable to comply with the Queen's invitation. Her Majesty thereupon, but very unwillingly, committed to Mr. Gladstone the charge of again forming a Government.

The new Cabinet was quickly constructed. It consisted of fourteen members, a small number compared with more recent Cabinets. Mr. Gladstone gathered round him most of his old colleagues, with the inclusion of Mr. Chamberlain, as a single representative of the new Radicalism. The Cabinet did not contain a single Irishman, or any one who was in sympathy with Home Rule, or with the new demands for Land Reform in Ireland.

Lord Hartington, generously oblivious to his claims to the Premiership, arising from the fact that he had led the Liberal Party with conspicuous ability for five years, after the retirement of Mr. Gladstone in 1875, was content to take the post of Secretary of State for India. Mr. W. E. Forster, who was almost his equal in status in the Liberal Party, and who might well have expected to be one of the principal Secretaries of State in the new Ministry, accepted the post of danger and difficulty, that of Chief Secretary for Ireland. Mr. Forster had served in Mr. Gladstone's previous Government of 1869–74 as Vice-President of the Council, the virtual head of the Education Department, and in that capacity had carried through the House of Commons three of the most important measures of that Ministry so famed for great legislative work : the Endowed Schools Act, the Education Act, and the Ballot Act. He had impressed himself greatly on the House of Commons, in the conduct of these measures, and by his administrative capacity. He was a powerful, if not a polished, speaker, fearing neither foes nor friends. He had shown in the Education Bill that he was ready to take his own line in the interest of the whole community, against the extreme men of his own party, and to risk his popularity with the Nonconformists. It was known that in early life, during the great famine of 1847–8, he had paid visits to Ireland, and had administered charitable funds raised by the Society of Friends, of which he was then a member, among the starving peasantry of the south and west of Ireland, and had formed a strong opinion as to the miserable condition of the tenantry there, and the necessity for land reform. It was doubtless thought by Mr. Gladstone that he had that mixture of strength and sympathy which specially fitted him for the Irish post. Public opinion in England unanimously ratified the appointment. He did not covet the position. He took it as a soldier would take orders from his chief to go under fire.

The post of Chief Secretary for Ireland, thus conferred on Mr. Forster, was the more conspicuous and important from the fact that the new Lord-Lieutenant, Lord Cowper, an orthodox Whig of the older type, was not to have a seat in the Cabinet, and consequently the Chief Secretary, with Cabinet rank, though officially subordinate, was practically in supreme command in the Irish Office. Mr. Bright became Chancellor of the Duchy of Lancaster, a position which involved but little real work, and left him free to advise in the Cabinet, and to take part in important debates. Mr. Chamberlain was President of the Board of Trade.[1]

Nothing was decided, on the formation of the Cabinet, as to Irish policy. The subject of land reform, however important in Ireland, and however unanimously demanded by members of all parties in that country, was never even mentioned at this early stage of the Government.

I may mention, as matter of personal reminiscence, that, since the conclusion of my Committee on the Purchase Clauses of the Land Act of 1870, I had kept in touch with many of the principal witnesses from Ireland, who had given evidence before it, and who had helped me in the inquiry. I had arrived at the conviction that my proposals as to land purchase, and the conversion of tenants into owners, however desirable and beneficial in the long run, were quite inadequate to meet the agrarian crisis in Ireland, and that nothing short of the adop-

[1] I was myself appointed Secretary to the Admiralty in the new Government, a post rather out of the stream of contentious politics.

tion of the three F's could suffice to meet the just claims of the tenants. I represented my views to Mr. Forster on his appointment as Irish Secretary. I urged the importance, and indeed the necessity, of dealing with the Irish land question immediately on the meeting of Parliament. I pointed out that Irish opinion had expressed itself at the General Election unanimously in favour of the three F's, and that there could be no stronger or safer basis for legislation than the declared opinion of the electors. I said that, looking at the state of Ireland, it was almost certain that if legislation was delayed, the agitation there would be aggravated, and that exceptional measures for restoring order would be forced upon the Government, and that coercion would again, as so often in the past, have to take precedence of remedial legislation. I maintained that the clear and certain lesson to be drawn from Irish history was that by applying coercion before a great remedial measure the effect of the latter was seriously impaired, and that at least half its value was lost ; and that, on the other hand, a remedial measure, if applied at once, in answer to the constitutional demands of the electors, might make it possible to dispense altogether with coercion.

Without committing himself to any specific proposal, Mr. Forster appeared to be impressed with the expediency of pressing at once whatever legislation could be conceded. He said that he would speak to Mr. Gladstone on the subject, and he asked me to represent my views in that quarter. I took an early opportunity of doing so. I found that Mr. Gladstone was quite unprepared for so radical an amendment of his Land Act of 1870, but he admitted that whatever could be done in the way of Land Reform would best be done at once. A few days later he told me that he had consulted Mr. Hugh Law, the newly appointed Solicitor - General for Ireland, as to immediate legislation on the Land question, but had been met by the assurance that it would be quite impossible to frame a measure, whatever direction it might take, within a reasonable time, so as to present it to Parliament and carry it in the Session of 1880. Mr. Forster told me that he had arrived reluctantly at the same conclusion. In any case the Government decided not immediately to deal with the subject. It met the new Parliament without any such measure, and without any definite promise of one in the future.

I have always thought that this was an initial error of the new Government, of a most serious character, the cause of many and grave difficulties. In an Irish Parliament, there cannot be a doubt, in view of the practical unanimity of the electors, that a measure of land reform would have been decided on, and that some lawyer would have been found equal to the task of framing it.

But even if a full measure of reform could not have been devised in time for legislation in the coming Session, it would have been wise policy to have provided a temporary measure, with the object of putting a stop to evictions, and of allaying the agitation. As it was, the Government met the Irish Party in the new Parliament without any land policy, and was soon compelled, at the instance of the extreme section of the Irish Party, to frame a temporary measure. They had the appearance, therefore, of conceding to pressure of the extremists, what should have been freely recognized as necessary to meet the emergency in Ireland.

Another early error of Forster, as it seemed to me, at least, as serious as the above, was that from the very first he assumed a position of antagonism to Parnell and his party in the House of Commons. He appeared to consider them as beyond the pale of responsible politicians. He refrained from having any communication with them. It was still thought in official circles that Shaw and his supporters were the true representatives of Irish opinion. But, in fact, Parnell had already ousted Shaw from this position. On the meeting of Parliament the former was elected Leader of the Irish Party in preference to Shaw, and after accepting the position he was faithfully followed by 38 members, while the other 22 members of the old party held aloof with Shaw, and soon ceased altogether to be counted as members of a Home Rule Party. This cleavage of the Irish Party in the House of Commons was accentuated by the fact that Parnell and his 38 followers took their seats in the House of Commons on the benches opposite to those of the Government, while Shaw and his smaller band of followers sat on benches on the Ministerial side of the House. There could be no stronger evidence of the break of unity of the Irish Party. Thenceforward Shaw's influence waned. His party was disintegrated, and at the next General Election it completely disappeared.

CHAPTER XII

THE COMPENSATION FOR DISTURBANCE BILL

THOUGH the Speech from the Throne at the opening of the Session of 1881 was silent as to Land Reform, it promised to Ireland a measure for assimilating its Borough franchise to that in England, and it announced the intention of the Government not to renew the Coercion Act of their predecessors, which was to expire on June 1st. This could not be expected to content the Irish Members. Mr. O'Connor Power, on behalf of the party led by Parnell, moved an amendment to the Address to the effec. that the condition of Ireland required the immediate attention of the Government, in order to secure to the tenants of land the fruits of their industry. He was supported by Parnell in a vigorous speech which described the terrible condition of the tenants in the west of Ireland. Mr. Shaw followed on behalf of his section of the Irish Party, presenting himself as the moderate politician, compared with his more extreme rival, though substantially his story and his claim were much the same.

Mr. Forster pleaded as an excuse for the Government, in not dealing at once with the subject, that it had been quite impossible, in the short time since the accession of the new Government, to come to a decision, or to frame a measure, on so difficult a subject. He announced, however, the immediate appointment of another Royal Commission, to report on the grievances of the tenant farmers of Ireland, and their claim for fixity of tenure, and he expressed the confident hope that its report would be ready for legislation in the following Session. His plea for delay was generally admitted by the Irish Members ; but they insisted that some immediate and temporary measure was needed to save the tenants from the peril of evictions, which were already being cruelly carried out, or were threatened. "If," said Parnell, "in consequence of the delay caused by the Chief Secretary requiring time to consider the subject, thousands of tenants run the risk of being driven from their holdings, the Irish Members may fairly ask the Government to give them the benefit of some temporary measure."

There was no response from the Government to this very reasonable appeal. A Bill was therefore introduced by the Irish Party to amend the grave defect in the compensation clause of the Land Act of 1870, by undoing the work of the House of Lords, and by providing that compensation should be paid in all cases of eviction, even in the case of non-payment of rent.[1] The Bill, by some chance, escaped the notice of opponents, and came on for discussion at a very late hour of the night. Mr. Forster, after some hesitation, promised, on behalf of the Government, to deal with the subject by a clause in a Bill for the further public relief of distress which he had already introduced. Strong objection was raised by the Opposition to this course, and ultimately the Government consented to introduce it in a separate Bill. The measure, entitled Compensation for Disturbance Bill, dealt with the subject in a much more halting manner than the Bill of the Irish Party. It was limited to the half of Ireland where the main distress existed. It excluded Ulster. It was to be in force only till the end of the current year. It was to apply only to tenancies rented at £30 a year. Subject to these limitations, tenants, who were unable to pay full rent, by reason of the two last bad harvests, and who were willing to continue their tenancies, on just and reasonable terms, as to rent or otherwise, in the event of such terms being unreasonably refused by their landlords, were to be entitled, on eviction, to the compensation payable under the Act of 1870. Judged by subsequent legislation, the Land Act of 1881, the Arrears Act of 1882, and subsequent amending Acts, this proposal of the Government was moderate in the extreme. It met, however, with the most determined and prolonged opposition in the House of Commons, and was rejected with contumely by an

---

[1] I was at this time on friendly terms with Parnell. He consulted me as to a Bill which he contemplated for suspending evictions altogether for two years. I suggested to him the much more moderate course which he adopted in Mr. O'Connor Power's Bill,

overwhelming majority of the House of Lords. It caused a serious defection in the Liberal Party. Lord Lansdowne, the owner of large estates in Ireland, who had joined the Government as Under-Secretary of the Home Department, resigned his post on account of this Bill, and commenced a new career, which led him ultimately to the Leadership of the Tory Party in the House of Lords. The measure was assailed as one of pure confiscation, and as interfering with contracts between landlords and tenants. Many of the Whig Members joined in the attack.

Mr. Forster made a powerful defence of the Bill. He showed the great increase of evictions in Ireland. Defending himself for not having brought in the Bill at the commencement of the Session, he said: " We did not do so because we hoped that we might put off legislation until we had all the facts before us, and knew how the Land Act of 1870 was working. It may be said, Why, then, have you brought it in now ? Well, for this reason, that we could wait no longer. Facts are accumulating upon us. Evictions have increased and are increasing. I have here the figures as to the evictions which the constabulary have had to conduct. They are not all that have been effected, only those in which the aid of the constabulary has been required, and I deduct from them all the cases where the evicted tenant has been readmitted as caretaker. This last, moreover, has nothing to do with process-serving. The average of evictions for the five years ending 1877 was 503 for each year. In 1878 the number was 743. In 1879 it was 1908, and up to June 20th of the present year it was 1073. During these few months also upwards of 15,000 notices of eviction had been served. . . ."

The evictions, he said, had to be supported by large bodies of police. In the West Riding of Galway alone, upwards of 3000 police were engaged in protecting process-servers, and 600 in carrying out evictions. In many cases 100 police were insufficient to protect a single process-server ; upwards of 200 were required to protect a single eviction. He desired the passing of the Bill in the interests of law and order and for the preservation of peace in Ireland. In any case, he said, the law would be enforced.

One of the ablest speeches on behalf of the Bill was that of Lord Hartington, who, as an Irish landowner, might have been expected to be frightened by the tendency of the legislation, and who, in the Cabinet, had strongly opposed the measure.

" The Bill," he said, " was but the logical sequel of the Land Act of 1870. In some parts of Ireland the impoverished circumstances of the tenants have placed in the hands of the landlords a weapon which the Government never contemplated, and which enables the landlords to clear the estate of hundreds of tenants whom, in ordinary circumstances, they would not have been able to remove except by a heavy pecuniary fine. I ask whether that is not a weapon calculated to enable landlords absolutely to defeat the main purposes of the Act. Supposing a landlord wishes to clear the estate of a number of small tenants ; he knows that this is the time to do it, and if he should lose the opportunity he can never have it again without great pecuniary sacrifice."[1]

Mr. Gladstone threw himself into the struggle for the Bill with his accustomed ardour. In one of his speeches he made use of the historic expression that eviction was to the small tenant in Ireland equivalent to a sentence of death.

" In the failure of the crops," he said, " caused by the year 1879, the act of God has replaced the Irish occupier in the condition in which he stood before the Land Act of 1870. Because what has he to contemplate ? He has to contemplate eviction for his non-payment of rent and, as a consequence of eviction, starvation. It is no exaggeration to say that in a country where the agricultural pursuit is the only pursuit, and where the means of the payment of rent are entirely destroyed for a time by the visitation of Providence, the poor occupier may, under these circumstances, regard a sentence of eviction, coming for him, very near to a sentence of death."[2]

I took part myself in the debate and showed that under the Roman Law the most just and complete code which had ever, in the world's history, been framed, when some unexpected calamity occurred, which made the payment of full rent for the year impossible, the tenant was relieved of the payment

---

[1] I was sitting next to Lord Hartington while he spoke. When he sat down I said to him that his speech for the Bill could not have been better. "I hope," he grimly replied, "it persuaded others. It did not persuade me."

[2] *Hansard*, 253, p. 1003.

of one-half of it. This had been followed by the codes of almost every country in Europe, except that of our own. In England it had been held by the Judges, in the time of Charles I, that where land had been devastated of its crops by a force under command of Prince Rupert, and there was no produce out of which to pay rent, yet the full rent, under the terms of the tenancy, was payable.

The main opposition of the Tory Party to the Bill was based on a total misconception of the relations of landlord and tenant in Ireland. It was assumed that the relation was that of free contract, as in the case of landlord and tenant in England. It was left out of sight that the tenants in Ireland had an interest in their holdings, universally claimed by Irish opinion, and practically admitted by the Act of 1870. " The measure," said Mr. Plunket, " is not a relief Bill, but a political one. As between landlord and tenant it will do the greatest injustice. It is a direct confiscation of the income of one class for the benefit of the other. It will strengthen and confirm the disastrous agitation in Ireland." " It is the commencement of a war between landlords and tenants," said Lord Randolph Churchill. " If the Bill passed," said Mr. W. H. Smith, " no tenant will pay any rent till 1881. It will shake all confidence."

The Bill was read a second time by a majority of 295 to 217. About 20 Liberals voted against it, and not less than 50 abstained from voting. They included many representatives of the old historic Whig families. It occupied the House in Committee for many weeks. Parnell and his followers had supported the second reading. But they soon got into conflict with Forster, and there began that personal antagonism between him and Parnell which was so conspicuous and unfortunate a feature of the following two years. The Bill, as framed, was on the most moderate lines. Less could not be expected to be of the smallest benefit, or to content the Irish Members. Yet Forster, in the hope of warding off opposition from the Tory Party, offered two concessions of a most serious kind. He proposed to make a further exception to payment of compensation for eviction in cases where the landlords were willing to allow the tenants to sell their interest in the holdings ; and he proposed to reduce the class of tenants to benefit from the Bill from those paying rent of £30 a year to £15. Both of these concessions were vehemently opposed by Parnell. He showed, as regards the first of these, that in the then state of Ireland, there were no possible purchasers of small holdings, and that the amendment would reduce the Bill to a nullity. He attacked Forster, and applied to him the text, " Unstable as water, thou shalt not excel." He had intended to support the Bill, he said, but could not now take the responsibility of voting for it, or wasting the time of the House. The measure would be useless.

After vehement debate, in which Parnell had all the best of the argument, Mr. Gladstone, on behalf of the Government, withdrew in part the amendment, substituting the words " without the offer of any reasonable alternative " for the proposed words " offer to the tenant to sell his interest "— words which, in the view of the Irish leader, were still open to grave objection. The Government were also compelled by the strong opposition of Parnell to withdraw their proposed limitations as to the class of tenant to be dealt with. It was finally read a third time by a majority of 57, considerably less than one-half the normal majority of the Government. The Parnellites abstained from voting, angered by the weakness shown by Forster, and unwilling to admit that the Bill would suffice as a remedy for the existing perils to tenants in Ireland.

In the House of Lords the opposition of the Whigs was fatal to the Bill. Lord Lansdowne made the ablest and fiercest attack upon it. "The Bill," he said, "singles out a particular section of the community, and a special contract into which that section has entered, and it announces with all the solemnity of an Act of Parliament that the Legislature is going to revise the terms of one of the parties to it, so that if that party fails to fulfil its obligations, the Legislature will shield it from the consequences, which in every civilized society result from a breach of contract. . . . It will debauch the conscience of the tenants, and hopelessly extinguish in their minds all self-reliance and honesty. . . . Ireland will be brought within measurable distance of civil war."

The Duke of Argyll, who was soon to part company with Mr. Gladstone and the Liberal Party on another Irish Land Bill, on this occasion gave effective support. He showed that whole-ale evictions were taking place in Ireland, under conditions of great hardship. " I have been asked," he said, " whether we know of any cases where the landlords have taken advantage of the state of things in Ireland to make wholesale evictions. The Government must speak with reserve, but I must say frankly that there have been cases in which undoubtedly landlords have shown a disposition to make wholesale evictions, for non-payment of rent, when the non-payment was clearly due to the failure of crops." He gave as an illustration the case of a property in Galway where 89 tenants paid an aggregate rent of £1370. Notices of eviction were served, and when it was endeavoured to enforce them, they met with great resistance. " You have in this case," he said, " a population of five hundred at the mercy of the landowner, who, under the existing law, can be evicted without one shilling to carry them to America." After a discussion of two days only the Bill was rejected by the Lords on August 3rd by 282 to 51, more than half of the usual supporters of the Government voting against it.

Of the many misdeeds of the House of Lords in rejecting Irish Bills passed by great majorities of the other House, and supported by overwhelming majorities of the Irish Members, this was probably the worst, for it was asked for by the Irish Government as a temporary measure, to enable them better to maintain order in Ireland during the coming winter, and with a clear conscience that no injustice was being done, to support the landlords in the collection of their rents. The Irish Government were practically directed by the House of Lords to enforce evictions for non-payment of rent which they knew to be excessive and unjust, having regard to the two bad seasons, and to use all the force at their disposal for the purpose.

How was the Government to meet this rebuff by the House of Lords ? Was it to dissolve Parliament at the bidding of the Peers, and to take the opinion of the electors on the Bill ? To do so would be to admit that the House of Lords had the right to compel a dissolution of Parliament, a claim never admitted by any Liberal Government. Would it also be reasonable to submit to the electors of Great Britain a question of land tenure affecting only Ireland, of which they understood nothing and cared less ? An overwhelming majority of the Irish Members had declared in favour of the Bill. Was their opinion to be set aside by a majority of Members for Great Britain ? The majority of the House of Commons had been returned with the special mandate to overrule and reverse the Foreign and Colonial policy of Lord Beaconsfield's Government. The new Government had as yet been able to do little in this direction. Was their new policy to be risked by another appeal to the electors on a totally different issue ?

The Government rightly decided neither to resign nor to appeal to the electors, but to rub on in Ireland, as best they could, till the next Session, and then to deal with Irish Land Reform on a larger scale. Mr. Forster at first threw out hints that he might be compelled to resign his post, if Irish landlords should insist on demanding full rents, rather than enforce the law on evictions which he knew to be unjust ; but he ultimately decided to struggle on in office through the winter. Resignation would mean desertion of his colleagues. It would compel the Government itself to resign, for no one of his colleagues could be expected to take his place and carry on the government of Ireland. The position not the less was a most cruel one for him. For the rest of his life he spoke with the greatest indignation and impatience of this action of the House of Lords.

The sequel showed that the House of Lords were not only in the wrong, but that they had done the very worst possible thing for the cause they had at heart. During the next six months evictions and consequent outrages increased enormously in Ireland. They compelled legislation in the Session of 1881 far more serious to Irish landlords than that of 1880. If they had passed the Compensation for Disturbance Bill, and it had produced the expected effect of quieting agitation, it may be doubted whether a Land Act, so extreme and revolutionary as that of 1881, would have been adopted by the Government, or would have been passed by Parliament.

Later in the Session the House of Lords added to their list of wrongs to Ireland, by rejecting a measure passed by the Commons for assimilating the law for the registration of Irish electors to that of England. Parnell indignantly pressed the Government to tack this Bill to the Appropriation Bill. The Government refused, but Mr. Forster gave a crumb of comfort to the Irish Members for the rejection of this Registration Bill, by the assertion that if such a course were taken often, it would be very difficult for the two Houses to go on, and the House of Commons might think that some change in the constitution of the House of Lords was desirable and might be necessary. The House of Commons must not forget, he said, that they were representatives of the people, and that the power which the House of Lords had was simply owing to an accident of birth. This seems to have been regarded as a very radical pronouncement in those days. By the light of recent events it would seem to be a very mild one.

It remains only to state of this short Session of 1880, that a new party bent on obstruction came into existence in it—the Fourth Party, as it was called, consisting of Mr. Gorst, Sir H. Drummond Wolff, Lord Randolph Churchill, and Mr. Arthur Balfour. In a discussion on obstruction, Lord Hartington pointed out that three members of this small party had made 247 speeches and asked 140 questions, as compared with 152 speeches and 34 questions of the three most active members of the Irish Party.

Parliament was not prorogued till September 6th. Nearly the whole of the Session had been expended on Irish questions. The only result, so far as Ireland was concerned, was a Relief Act providing an additional million, by way of loan to land-lords under the Act of the late Government, for the employ-ment of labour in the distressed districts.

CHAPTER XIII

THE WINTER OF 1880–1

THE rejection by the House of Lords of the Compensation Bill speedily produced a most malign effect in Ireland. Discontent was everywhere intensified. Agitation became fiercer. Evictions were multiplied. They were resisted with greater determination and violence. Agrarian crimes followed in their wake. Those who took the farms from which tenants had been evicted were assaulted ; their property was damaged, their cattle were maimed. Outrages of all kinds increased in number, and became more brutal in quality. From the foundation of the Land League, at the Irishtown meeting, in April of the previous year, till the rejection of the Compensation Bill, there had been very few, if any, agrarian murders in Ireland. They now became frequent, not, indeed, by any means so numerous as in past times of agrarian and political agitation, but still such as greatly to alarm the landowning classes in Ireland, and to impress unfavourably public opinion in England. Speeches at Land League meetings became more violent. Large funds in aid of the cause were remitted from America. They were spent in relief of evicted tenants, in building huts for them, and in defending persons prosecuted for resisting process-servers and evictions. The Land League branches assumed the function of courts for the determination of what reductions of rent ought to be made in their districts, what evictions were unjust, and in what cases it was permissible to take farms from which the tenants had been evicted.

Parnell crossed over to Ireland, as soon as the Session was at an end, and addressed a series of great meetings. The most important was at Ennis, on September 19th. His speech there was marked by distinct hostility to Mr. Gladstone and

Mr. Forster. He pointed out that the Government had failed
to carry the measure which it had proclaimed to be necessary
for the protection of vast numbers of Irish tenants from
eviction for non-payment of rent, which the bad seasons
had made impossible ; that there was no certain promise of
adequate legislation on the Land question in the coming year ;
that a Royal Commission had been appointed, with the
personnel of which the Irish Members were dissatisfied ; and
that the Chief Secretary had proclaimed that the law would be
maintained—in other words, that the landlords would be
supported by all the force of the police in their evictions under
the existing state of the law. He advised the tenants to place
no confidence in the Government Commission. Though he did
not advise them to refrain from giving evidence before it, he
warned them against the danger of accepting responsibility
for its proceedings and conclusions—most sensible advice to
them under the circumstances. He then proceeded in these
strong words :

"Depend upon it, the measure of the Land Bill of next
Session will be the measure of your activity and energy this
winter ; it will be the measure of your determination not to
pay unjust rents ; it will be the measure of your determination
to keep a firm grip of your homestead ; it will be the measure
of your determination not to bid for farms, from which others
have been evicted, and to use the strong force of public opinion
to deter any unjust men amongst yourselves—and there are
many such—from bidding for such farms. If you refuse to
pay unjust rents, if you refuse to take farms from which others
have been evicted, the Land question must be settled, and
settled in a way that will be satisfactory to you. It depends
therefore upon yourselves, and not upon any Commission or
any Government. When you have made this question ripe
for settlement, then and not till then will it be settled." He
then proceeded to suggest to them a method to give effect to
their determination.

"What are you to do," he said, " to a tenant who bids for
a farm from which another tenant has been evicted ? "

Several voices: " Shoot him."

Mr. Parnell: " I think I heard somebody say ' Shoot him.'
I wish to point out to you a very much better way—a more
Christian and charitable way, which will give the lost man an

opportunity of repenting. When a man takes a farm, from which another has been unjustly evicted, you must shun him in the roadside, when you meet him ; you must shun him in the streets of the town ; you must shun him in the shop ; you must shun him in the fair-green and in the market-place, and even in the place of worship, by leaving him alone ; by putting him into a moral Coventry ; by isolating him from the rest of the country, as if he were a leper of old—you must show him your detestation of the crime he has committed."

In a later speech, at New Ross, he developed his own views as to what should be the goal of land reformers in Ireland :

" We seek as Irish Nationalists for a settlement of the Land question which shall be permanent—which shall for ever put an end to the war of classes which has unhappily existed in this country . . . a war which supplies the strongest inducement to the Irish landlords to uphold the system of English misrule, which has placed these landlords in Ireland. Looking forward to the future of our country, we wish to avoid all elements of antagonism between classes. I am willing to have a struggle between classes in Ireland—a struggle that should be short, sharp, and decisive—once for all ; but I am not willing that this struggle should be perpetuated at intervals, when these periodic revaluations of the holdings of the tenants would come under the system of what is called fixity of tenure at valued rents."

" Now, then, is the time for the Irish tenantry to show their determination ; to show the Government of England that they will be satisfied with nothing less than the ownership of the land of Ireland. . . . I see no difficulty in arriving at such a solution, and in arriving at it in this way ; by the payment of a fair rent, and a fair and fixed rent not liable to recurrent and perhaps near periods of revision, but by the payment of a fair rent for the space, say, of thirty-five years, after which time there would be nothing further to pay, and in the meantime the tenant would have fixity of tenure."

At Galway he explained the ultimate object he had in view.

" I wish," he said, " to see the tenant farmers prosperous ; but large and important as is the class of tenant farmers, constituting as they do, with their wives and families, the majority of the people of their country, I would not have taken off my coat and gone to this work if I had not known that we were laying the foundation in this movement for the regeneration of our legislative independence." By "legislative independence " he clearly meant Home Rule and not separation. At Kilkenny, October 3rd, he expressed disbelief in the possibility of any partnership between landowners and tenants. One of them must go.

Parnell's speeches must be studied and compared with subsequent results of the agitations, or rather the succession of agitations in the next twenty years, and with the final settlement propounded in 1903 by Mr. Balfour's Government, at the instance of Mr. Wyndham, of universal ownership of their holdings by tenant farmers, in order to estimate at their true worth his statesmanship and prevision. The settlement he aimed at has, in fact, been approved by the Imperial Legislature, and is in course of being carried out upon terms much more favourable to the tenants than Parnell could have conceived to be possible.

A few days after the Ennis speech, Parnell's advice as to social ostracism was given practical effect to in an historic case. Captain Boycott, the agent for Lord Erne's property at Lough Mask, in Mayo, who farmed himself a considerable extent of land, had a dispute with his farm labourers as to their wages, and failing to come to terms, dismissed the whole of them. No other labourers in the district could be induced to take their place. Captain Boycott then, by way of reprisal to the district, proceeded to take action against the numerous tenants of Lord Erne. He insisted upon payment of full rent and arrears, and threatened them with eviction. The tenants refused to pay anything unless a fair reduction was made. The local Land League then took up the case. The system of ostracism was brought into play. In furtherance of this, no one could be found willing to serve the writs of eviction. The local tradesmen refused to sell food to Captain Boycott, or to shoe his horses, or otherwise to supply his wants. No one was willing to help him in gathering his crops. His domestic servants left him. Captain Boycott appealed in the Press for sympathy and aid. In response to this, fifty Orangemen from Ulster volunteered their services to gather his crops, and dig his potatoes. It was thought necessary by the Government to give special protection to them. Two thousand soldiers formed an escort for them. Large bodies of the constabulary were collected in the district. These invaders were left severely alone. No one would supply cars for them. They could obtain no food in the district. By the aid of these intruders from Ulster, guarded in this way, crops to the value of £350 were harvested at a total cost to the Government of £3500.

In the end Captain Boycott was compelled to admit defeat. He resigned his agency and left the country. The case attracted universal attention and comment. A new word, "boycotting," was coined and added to the English language, to take its place beside those of " lynching " and " burking," also of Irish origin. It has been adopted in most languages in Europe. The process of boycotting spread widely in Ireland, and was applied freely to other cases of dispute between landlords and tenants, and to disputes in other trades of all kinds. It proved to be most efficacious in deterring landlords from eviction.

While these speeches were being made, and while evictions on the one hand and outrages on the other were being multiplied, Mr. Forster faced the position with courage and determination. He was in a very solitary position, at the headquarters of the Irish Government at Dublin. He was between two antagonistic forces, the landlords and the Tory Party on the one hand, and the Land League, the tenants, and the great majority of the Irish people on the other. He had nothing to offer in appeasement of public opinion. He had no authority, at that time, to promise a wide and popular measure of Land Reform. The only expectation held out was that of a possible report from a Royal Commission, the constitution of which did not inspire any confidence in the National Party. All that Mr. Forster could actually undertake to do was to maintain the law in Ireland, and that meant to the tenant farmers the support of evictions for the non-payment of rents which under the conditions of the past two years could not be paid.

Mr. Forster was deeply pained and horrified by the outrages which were committed. They appeared to lessen, if they did not extinguish, his sympathy for the tenants in the numerous evictions which were being carried out, and which he had to support with police and soldiers. He did not connect these two classes of events as cause and effect. He was obsessed with the belief that the outrages were the result only of the agitation of the Land League, and of the violent speeches made at its meetings.

In Mr. Forster's letters to Mr. Gladstone, and in those of Lord Cowper, the Lord-Lieutenant, to the Cabinet, we can trace the inception and progress of the policy to put down outrages, and the agitation, which they believed to be the cause of them, by a strong coercive measure.

Early in October, within one month of the prorogation of Parliament, we find Mr. Forster writing to Mr. Gladstone from Dublin that he was contemplating the prosecution of Parnell and other leaders of the Land League. The Law Officers had been asked for their opinion. There were, he said, the strongest moral grounds, but doubtful legal grounds, for such a prosecution. In any case he could not expect a conviction. He did not feel sure that it would stop or materially check the outrages. Parnell, he said, had incited these crimes, but they might now be beyond his control. If the prosecution should fail the Government might be driven to call a special Session of Parliament for a coercive measure, in the direction of a suspension of the Habeas Corpus Act.

A few days later Mr. Forster wrote again to Mr. Gladstone : " We may find that nothing will check outrages but the arrest and detention of men under suspicion of committing them. . . . When the whole population sympathizes with men who commit outrages, juries will not convict. The suspension of the Habeas Corpus Act is a most violent and brutal remedy. We must be sure that it is the only remedy." A fortnight later, on October 25th, he wrote again, " The last two or three days there has been some diminution of outrages. It is owing to the Land League getting their way and not needing outrages." " Unless real improvement takes place I cannot face the winter, in January and February, without special legislation. I do not believe that any Bill will be of use, short of suspension of the Habeas Corpus Act." " The state of the country is undoubtedly most serious. Nor do the number of outrages by any means represent the gravity of the situation, and for this reason—that, in many places, those who profit by outrages are completely masters of the position, and thus the temptation is removed. Nobody dares to evict. Tenants of evicted farms, even those who have been in possession for more than a year, are daily giving them up.

. . . The sudden imprisonment of some of those who are known to instigate, or to commit crime, would strike home in a way that nothing else could do, for no man would know whether his turn would not come next."

On November 8th Mr. Forster again wrote : " October is very bad. There have been very few evictions. Parnell is quite right in saying that the Land League has stopped evictions, though he ought to have said—the Land League and its attendant outrages. . . . The present outrages, or rather the condition of the country which produces the outrages, is owing to the action of the League, but I believe that now these outrages are very much beyond their control. . . . The actual perpetrators and planners are old Fenians, and old Ribbonmen and *mauvais sujets*. They would shrink into their holes if a few were arrested." [1]

The question of summoning Parliament for the special purpose of passing a coercive measure for Ireland was then brought before the Cabinet. It led to a great and prolonged struggle. It was vehemently opposed by two of its leading members, Mr. Bright and Mr. Chamberlain. Mr. Gladstone also seems to have been much opposed to the form of coercion asked for, namely, the suspension of the Habeas Corpus Act. In a letter to Mr. Forster he pointed out the grave objection to the imprisonment of men under suspicion and without any trial.

While this conflict was proceeding Mr. Forster wrote on November 18th : " Evictions 82 in the last six weeks against 671 for the previous three months." That is a reduction from 50 a week to 12. " Outrages," he added, " are not caused at present by evictions. Parnell can claim the credit of stopping evictions. Outrages and fear of outrages have done their work."

Both Mr. Forster and Lord Cowper threatened resignation, if their demand for a speedy suspension of the Habeas Corpus Act was not agreed to. It was not till November 27th that this conflict in the Cabinet was brought to an end by a compromise. Mr. Forster's demand for a suspension of the Habeas Corpus was conceded ; but Parliament was to be summoned for the purpose, early in January, and not earlier as pressed for by the Irish Government. Rather than break up the

[1] *Life of W. E. Forster*, II, 265.

Cabinet, Mr. Forster determined to carry on his work in a way he disapproved of for another month, throwing the responsibility upon his colleagues.

Lord Cowper also, writing to Mr. Gladstone, said that he was in great doubt whether he was justified in retaining the position of Lord-Lieutenant, unless the remedy he asked for was provided, but as he was unwilling to leave the ship in the middle of the storm, and as he felt that Mr. Forster's position would become untenable, if he left, he had come to the conclusion not to do anything until January, when if the legislation he asked for was not conceded, he would place his resignation in the hands of the Government.

Mr. Gladstone's answer was interesting and important. While expressing satisfaction that Lord Cowper had deferred until January any intention to resign his office, he wrote : " What I personally think a very doubtful remedy is a suspension of the Habeas Corpus Act, proposed alone, carried after much delay in the teeth of two-thirds of the representatives of Ireland (without taking English allies into account). You may rely upon it, when the time you name comes, the Cabinet will look at the duty of defending proprietary rights, without any mawkish susceptibilities. . . . It is with regret, perhaps with mortification, that I see the question of Land Reform again assuming, or having assumed, its large proportion. My desire certainly would have been to remain on the lines of the Act of 1870, such as it left the House of Commons." [1]

It appears, then, that so late as November, 1880, Mr. Gladstone had not arrived at the conclusion that it would be necessary to embark on another great measure of Land Reform for Ireland. The patching up of the Act of 1870 was the outside of what he then contemplated. Another point brought out clearly by the correspondence is that in the opinion of the Irish Government the Land League had been successful in putting a stop to evictions. It had done what the rejected Bill of the Government (the Compensation for Disturbance Bill) had been intended to do.

No one who looks dispassionately at the facts of the time can doubt that, but for the action of the Land League, evictions, instead of coming nearly to an end, would have been greatly multiplied, and that they would have led to a great increase of

[1] *Life of Parnell*, II, 260.

outrages and crime, as in many past agitations in Ireland. This view is strongly confirmed by the fact that when Mr. Forster succeeded in inducing Parliament to give him power to suspend the Habeas Corpus Act, and when he had arrested and imprisoned every man under suspicion of committing outrage or inciting to outrage, and when finally he had gone the length of arresting and imprisoning the leaders of the Land League, including Parnell, crimes and outrages, instead of being put an end to, or even greatly reduced, were seriously increased in number and violence.

To Parnell must be mainly credited the advice to substitute the scheme of boycotting for the more violent and criminal acts, which had always been the feature of agrarian agitation. Of the ethics of the system of boycotting, not for the first time devised, but then recommended in public speech by a responsible leader, as a substitute for more violent acts, there is much to be said. From a legal point of view it seems that the mere refraining, by one or more persons, without combination directed against a particular person, from intercourse or trading with a neighbour, by way of protest against some action of his, held to be unjust, or against the public interest of the district, is certainly not unlawful or criminal. Nor can a speech indicating that such a course is open to the hearers, and is justifiable and expedient in certain cases, not directed against a particular person, be held to be an illegal act, as inciting to violence or crime. But, on the other hand, a combination of persons, aimed at a particular person, to refrain from dealing with him, and with the deliberate intention of injuring him in his trade or occupation, on account of his action in some matter obnoxious to them, may undoubtedly be held to be a criminal conspiracy ; and a speech advising such a course and pointing specially to the obnoxious person may equally be held to be an incitement to a criminal act. But in each of these cases it is a question for the Jury to determine, and not for the Judge who tries the case. The question of motives then arises, and it is competent for the Jury to take into account the motives of those engaged in the combination, and the conduct of the person against whom it is directed.

However this may be, boycotting, at the time we are

dealing with, was a method by which Irish opinion, deprived of the power of effecting its object, through the legitimate and constitutional method of a legislative measure, sought to effect it, indirectly by combination, and by the use of a method, open to grave abuse, and resulting in not a few cases in great hardship, but not the less a rough-and-ready way of enforcing public opinion against injustice and wrong.   It is quite certain that by the use of it evictions were practically stayed, and we have the high authority of Mr. Gladstone for the admission that, but for the Land League and its agitation and its boycottings, the Land Act of 1881 would not have been passed by Parliament.

Meanwhile, on November 3rd, Mr. Forster decided to prosecute fourteen of the leaders of the Land League, including Parnell, Dillon, Biggar, Sexton, and T. D. Sullivan.   The charge against them was that of conspiracy to prevent the payment of rent, to resist the process of eviction, to prevent the taking of farms from which the tenants had been evicted, and to create ill-will amongst Her Majesty's subjects.   Parnell and Biggar met this move with characteristic contempt and defiance.   " I regret," said the former, in a speech at Dublin two days later, " that Mr. Forster has chosen to waste his time, the money of the Government and our money on these prosecutions.   He has begun in a bad way, and I fear the result of his attempt to govern Ireland will be to shatter his reputation for statesmanship, which he formerly acquired in another branch.   He is surrounded by a landlord atmosphere at the Castle of Dublin, and although he may be able to resist the effect of that atmosphere longer than most men, yet sooner or later it is bound to tell upon him."   Biggar, on his part, is reported to have exclaimed when he heard the news of the intended prosecutions, " D—d lawyers, sir, d—d lawyers. Wasting the public money.   Wasting the public money.   Whigs d—d rogues.   Forster d—d fool." [1]

The prosecutions appear to have been entered upon without much hope of conviction.   The usual course of packing the Jury, so familiar to the Irish legal authorities, was not adopted on this occasion, and without that, it must have been known to the Government that conviction was impossible.   The trial took place before Mr. Justice Fitzgerald and Mr. Justice Barry.

[1] *Life of Parnell*, I, 253.

It lasted for twenty-two days, and was not concluded till after the meeting of Parliament in 1881. The Jury could not agree in their verdict. In the quaint language of the foreman, " They were unanimous that they could not agree." Ten of them were for acquittal and two only for conviction. The result led to rejoicings all over Ireland. It may be doubted whether anywhere in the United Kingdom a conviction could have been obtained. While it may have been necessary to show that the law was powerless to convict, before asking for coercive powers from Parliament, there is no doubt that the abortive prosecution brought the Irish Government and Mr. Forster into contempt, and did much to strengthen the Land League.

CHAPTER XIV

THE COERCION ACT, 1881

IN 1881, Parliament was summoned to meet on an exceptionally early day, January 7th, for the double purpose of carrying a drastic Coercion Act for Ireland, and of effecting some change in the Land Law, the extent of which had not as yet been decided by the Government.

On the second day of the debate on the Address, Parnell made one of the two best speeches of his Parliamentary career. He defended the Land League, and repeated in the House of Commons the advice to the tenants, which he had given at numerous meetings in Ireland, and for which he was, at the very moment, being prosecuted at Dublin. The tone of his speech was moderate and conciliatory. Coercion, he said, would contribute to crime and outrage by encouraging landlords to evict their tenants. The question was whether there should be an open organization or secret societies. What the Land League had effected was to organize the Irish people to resist unjust laws by constitutional means. This course had been forced upon them by the rejection of the Compensation for Disturbance Bill in the last Session. The Irish people had unfortunately an evil and unhappy history. They had been tempted and driven too much in the past to rely on murder and outrage for redress of their grievances. The politician, who attempted to originate a movement, would do so with the knowledge that there would be crime and outrage, when there was distress, and when there were evictions, and that he would be made personally responsible for the unhappy results. Resistance to unjust laws sometimes became a high duty, and he could conceive of no higher duty on the part of the Irish people than a willingness to go to jail to endure hard labour, and to encounter other sufferings, rather than surrender this right. Those for whom he spoke had undoubtedly called upon the Irish people to resist constitutionally—without violence, but by organization, by refusing to take farms from which tenants had been evicted, and by refusing to deal with the persons who took the farms, and to supply them with provisions—the unjust laws which were the result of the legislation of England. But the emergency was such that there was no other course open to them. He entreated the House of Commons not to be again the cat's-paw of the landlords. He warned the Government that if they attempted to take away from the people the right of meeting publicly and discussing their grievances—if they prevented them from organizing, if they prevented them from bringing to bear the strong force of public opinion on individuals, who defy the public opinion of their neighbours, they would see murder and outrage walking abroad through the land, notwithstanding all their Coercion Acts. He moved as an amendment that " the peace and tranquillity of Ireland cannot be promoted by suspending any of the constitutional rights of the people."

Mr. Forster retorted in angry terms, and while acknowledging the moderation of Parnell's speech, expressed regret that he had not spoken with the same reserve in Ireland. Experience, he said, had shown that the Land League meetings were usually followed by attacks on persons or property. Quoting from Parnell's Ennis speech, he found in it a clear recommendation not only not to take farms from which tenants had been evicted, but a threat that those who took them would be cut off from all social intercourse and treated as lepers. It was clear from this and other similar advice that it was the object of the Member for Cork to replace the law of the land by the unwritten law of the League. He did not charge Mr. Parnell with having himself incited to the outrages which had occurred, but he held that he must have known what would be the result of his speeches and of his action. This remark drew an angry protest from the Irish Members, and an appeal to the Speaker. Mr. Forster, in deference to the protest, slightly modified his language. " Mr. Parnell," he said, " with his knowledge of the Irish character, and with his ability, ought to have known, and it is a wonderful thing if he did not know, what the natural effect of his speeches would be. At any rate, the outrages undoubtedly followed upon the meetings of the Land League." He dwelt on the long list of outrages committed during the closing months of the past year, and on the wide spread of cases of intimidation. He then proceeded to defend himself against the Tory attack for not doing enough to protect law and order. " We have thought it our duty," he said, " to try and exhaust the constitutional powers we possessed, and we have exhausted them. We are driven to the distressing conclusion that further powers must be asked for. We believe that our first duty is to protect liberty and person and property. We cannot quietly sit by and allow the law of the land to be replaced by another law. We cannot allow men to be interfered with in the daily walks of life by a system of terrorism. But we do not for a moment suppose that the fulfilment of this painful duty constitutes our whole duty to Ireland. We still intend, and we still do believe that we shall be able to look into the grievances of Ireland connected with her principal industry, grievances which we fully admit are at the foundation of the state of things which now exists."

Mr. Shaw, the late leader of the Irish Party, and still the leader of the section which refused to support Parnell,[1] followed Mr. Forster in a speech, in which he defended the Land League from the charge of having been the cause of outrage. He expressed his belief that none of the agrarian outrages of the preceding months could be traced to the meetings of the Land League. Mr. Davitt, he knew, ever since his return from America, had earnestly set himself the task of discouraging anything like crime, arguing that crime must be detrimental to the people's cause. Nevertheless, there was an immense deal going in connection with local Land Leagues that was not at all creditable, and was most injurious to the real interests of the people. The country was absurdly and cruelly over-rented, and the outcome of the policy was the permanent pauperization of the people. It would be better not to touch the Irish Land question at all, than not to deal with it firmly and effectively. Measures of coercion might be pressed forward, and might, after a few weeks or months of struggle in that House, become the law of the land, but the seeds of sus-

---

[1] On January 12th, a few days after this speech, Mr. Shaw retired from the Home Rule Party, and was followed in this by about twenty Irish Members who sat with him on the Government Bench side of the House.

picion and distrust would be sown, and would not fail to produce results which would be most prejudicial to the success of any legislation of a remedial character. As to coercion, what, he would ask, was the use of it in dealing with 500,000 or 600,000 farms, and with the whole people of the country banded together ?

Mr. Parnell's motion was rejected by 435 to 57. Of the Irish Members 51 voted with Parnell, 30 abstained from voting, and only 22 supported the Government. The debate on the Address was prolonged for eleven days, most of them occupied with the Irish question. When at last it was concluded, Mr. Forster moved for leave to introduce his Coercion Bill for Ireland. He proposed to give power to the Lord-Lieutenant to issue a warrant for the arrest of any person, whom he might reasonably suspect of treasonable or agrarian offences. Persons so arrested were to be treated as unconvicted prisoners, but might be detained until September 30th, in the following year. He supported this proposal by statistics showing the great increase of agrarian crime. He attributed this to the Land League. Personal insecurity had, in consequence of the Land League, increased so rapidly that no less than 153 persons were attended, day and night, by two constables each, and 1149 were watched by the police. The serving of writs was as impossible as the collection of rents, and the shopkeepers were as unable to obtain justice as the landlords. " In Ireland," he said, " the Land League is supreme, and there is a real reign of terror over the whole country. No man dares take a farm from which another person has been ejected, nor work for a man who pays his rent and who refuses to join the Land League. Those who defy the law are safe, while those who keep it, the honest men, in short, are in danger. The ordinary law is powerless. The unwritten law is powerful, because punishment is sure to follow its edicts."

The particular form of coercion applied for by Mr. Forster was strongly disapproved by Mr. Gladstone. " I considered," he wrote, late in his life, in a memorandum, " that coercion should be applied by giving stringency to the existing law, and not by abolishing the right to be tried before being imprisoned." To his distress, however, he found that Chamberlain and Bright, who had for weeks strongly opposed coercion in any form, when at last they acquiesced in its necessity, had arrived at the conclusion that if there was to be coercion at all, there was something simple and effective in the suspension of the Habeas Corpus Act, which made such a method preferable to others.   He therefore gave his consent, for otherwise his resistance would have broken up the Government, and have compelled his own retirement, before a commencement had been made of the work which had been specially commissioned by the constituents, in relation to the Foreign policy of the country.

" Forster," he added, " was a very impracticable man, placed in a position of great responsibility.   He was set upon a method of legislation, adapted to the erroneous belief that the mischief lay only with a limited number of well-known individuals—that is to say, the suspension of the Habeas Corpus Act. . . . I must say that I never fell into this extraordinary illusion of Forster about his village ruffians."[1]

The sequel will show that Mr. Gladstone was right in his diagnosis, and that Mr. Forster was completely misled by the police and the Dublin officials as to their power of laying their hands on the perpetrators of crime.

Meanwhile the debate on the introduction of the Bill was protracted over several nights.   It was vehemently opposed by the Irish Members.   Mr. Gladstone, whatever his opinion on the scheme of coercion in the Bill, gave his most loyal support to Mr. Forster.   His speech, however, showed most clearly that the measure was directed against crime and outrages only, in the ordinary sense of the term, and not against political combinations, or meetings, or speeches, even when they recommended breaches of contract.

" We aim by this Bill," he said, " and aim solely at the perpetrators and abettors of outrage.   I stand upon the words of the legislation we propose, and I say that they do not in the slightest degree justify the suspicion that we are interfering with the liberty of discussion.   I will go farther.   We are not attempting to interfere with the licence of discussion.   There is no interference here with the liberty to propose the most subversive and revolutionary changes.   There is no interference here with the right of association, in the furtherance of these changes, provided the furtherance be by peaceful

---

[1] Morley's *Life of Gladstone*, III, 49.

methods. There is no interference with whatever right Members may think they possess, to recommend and to bring about, not only changes of the law, but in certain cases breaches of positive contracts. I am not stating these things as a matter of boast, I am stating them as a matter of fact. I must say it appears to me that it is a very liberal state of law which permits honourable gentlemen to meet together to break contracts into which they have entered."[1]

On the fifth night of the discussion it was decided by the Government that it must be brought to a close, if possible, and Mr. Gladstone, at the commencement of the sitting, intimated that it would be prolonged till the motion for the introduction of the Bill was carried. This was taken as a challenge by the Irish Members. They carried on the discussion, at first, by repeated motions for adjournment, and later by long speeches on the main motion, all through the night and the following day and the second night. During one of their nights Mr. Sexton spoke for nearly three hours, between two and five o'clock in the early morning. I was one of the six or seven English Members who were present, and heard the whole of it. I had rarely listened to a more closely reasoned, eloquent, and cogent speech. There was no reiteration, and scarcely a word was redundant. It was a presage of many speeches of the same quality from Mr. Sexton, which gained him so great an influence in his party, and so high a reputation in the House. It was a surprise to me that he had been told off by his party to waste such an exhibition of power and close reasoning, at a time when practically he had no audience.

The closing scene of this long sitting was dramatic. When the hour of nine of the second morning arrived, after forty-one hours of continuous debate, the House had filled again, under the impression that a crisis was imminent. Mr. Gladstone and Sir Stafford Northcote, the two leaders, were in their places. Mr. Biggar, by an apt coincidence, was on his legs, the very personification of obstruction, delivering one of his lengthy and incoherent speeches. The Speaker, on resuming the Chair, in place of Mr. Playfair (later Lord Playfair), who had filled it as deputy during the small hours of the morning, caused a break in Biggar's oration. Without calling on him to resume, the Speaker delivered the well-known historic pro-

[1] *Hansard*, 257, p. 168.

nouncement from the Chair, pointing out that a necessity had
arisen demanding the interposition of the Chair. " The credit
and authority of the House," he said, " are seriously threatened,
and it is necessary they should be vindicated. . . . A new and
exceptional course is imperatively demanded, and I am satisfied that I shall best carry out the wish of the House if I decline
to call upon any more Members to speak, and at once proceed
to put the question to the House."

The Speaker thereupon put the question, and the amendment to Mr. Forster's motion was negatived by 164 to 19.
On the main question that the Bill be introduced, Mr. Justin
McCarthy rose to speak on it, but the Speaker declined to hear
him. The Home Rulers thereupon stood up *en masse*, and for
some time with raised hands shouted " Privilege," and then
bowing to the Chair left the House. Leave was then given to
introduce the Bill. There can be no doubt that the Speaker's
action was in the nature of a *coup d'état*. It was effected with
the approval of Mr. Gladstone, and upon the promise that the
rules of the House would be strengthened against obstruction,
and with the knowledge, and without the disapproval, of the
Leader of the Opposition, Sir Stafford Northcote. It led to
an immediate change in the rules of procedure of the House,
not at once going the length of adopting the closure, but
expediting the progress of business which by formal resolution
should be declared to be " urgent."

Before the discussion on this another violent scene occurred.
It was announced that Michael Davitt had been sent back
to a convict prison, his ticket-of-leave being cancelled. On
February 3rd a question was put to the Home Secretary,
whether this statement was true. Sir William Harcourt
replied that the Law Officers had given their opinion that
Michael Davitt's conduct, as one of the most energetic apostles
of the Land League, was not compatible with the ticket-of-
leave of which he was the holder ; but he declined to explain
what conditions of the ticket had been violated. On Mr.
Gladstone rising to move his resolution for expediting the
business of the House, he was interrupted by Mr. Dillon, who
desired to raise the question of Davitt's arrest. The Speaker
refused to allow Mr. Dillon to speak. He insisted on doing so,
and stood with his arms folded, exclaiming, " I demand my
privilege of speech." There followed a scene of unprecedented

THE COERCION ACT, 1881 141

excitement, which ended by Mr. Dillon being named by the Speaker as wilfully disregarding the authority of the Chair. Mr. Gladstone then moved that Mr. Dillon should be suspended. The motion was carried by 395 to 33. Mr. Dillon refused to leave the House, and the Serjeant-at-Arms was directed to remove him. Mr. Dillon avoided the employment of force by rising and walking out of the House amid cries of "shame" from the Irish Party. Mr. Gladstone thereupon resumed his speech, but he was again interrupted by Parnell, who moved that "he be no longer heard." Parnell was then named by the Speaker. He left the House, after a demonstration of force by the Serjeant-at-Arms. The Irish Members had refused to vote on the motion for the suspension of Parnell. They were named in a body by the Speaker, and were suspended from attending the House by a majority of 410 to 6. They successively declined to leave the House till a demonstration of force was made by the Serjeant-at-Arms. Finally, Mr. O'Donnell and Mr. O'Kelly were dealt with in the same way, with the result that 36 Irish Members in all, practically the whole of the Parnellite Party, were suspended. Among them was Mr. John Redmond, the future and present leader of the party. He took his seat for New Ross for the first time that very day, and had the experience of being suspended before he had completed a day's work in the House.

Looking back at the arrest of Davitt, and his consignment to a convict prison, it is quite impossible to justify it. He had certainly not committed any act in breach of the condition on his ticket-of-leave. He had been most active in founding the Land League, but the prosecution of the leaders of that body had failed. If he was engaged in committing acts aimed at by the Coercion Bill it would have been reasonable to wait till the Act was passed, and then to arrest him under its provisions ; but to consign him again to a convict prison was a hardship and unjustifiable insult to the man, and a needless provocation to public opinion in Ireland. It is right to say that Sir William Harcourt gave orders that Davitt was to be treated with exceptional lenity. In doing so, he assumed the right of the Home Secretary to interfere with the treatment of persons convicted of political offences, which it will be seen was denied by the Tory Government at a later stage of the Irish question. There can be no doubt that among the many mistakes made in dealing with the Irish question, there were few graver than this treatment of Davitt. It did much to aggravate public discontent in Ireland.

This incident being disposed of, Mr. Gladstone was able to move his resolution. He did so in a speech of great dignity and pathos, which produced a profound effect on the House. He implored Members not to allow the House which had been the mainstay and power and glory of the country to degenerate. His proposal was that in cases where the House of Commons voted by a majority of three to one that the business before them was urgent, the whole conduct of it was to be under the control of the Speaker. The motion was carried with general assent. The Speaker then framed rules of urgency. The most drastic of them was the power secured to him of closing discussion by fixing a time when all the remaining amendments to a Bill should be passed without further discussion. With the aid of these very drastic powers the Coercion Bill passed through its various stages, not, however, without heated and protracted discussion. Four days were devoted to the second reading of the Bill. Mr. Bradlaugh moved its rejection. He was followed in his opposition by several other Radical Members for British constituencies, among them Mr. Joseph Cowen, who predicted that the Act would have the exact opposite effect to that intended, and would lead to a further outbreak of crime and to a general state of lawlessness in Ireland. He denounced the imprisonment of Davitt in no measured terms. Lord Randolph Churchill also spoke of it with disapproval, and attributed the state of things in Ireland to the action of the Government rather than of the Land League. The Bill was read a second time by a majority of 389 to 56. Some few Radical Members voted against it, and many more abstained from voting.

In the Committee stage, the Bill was contested by the Irish Members, line by line, and word by word, with the greatest pertinacity. Parnell was occupied most of the time in Ireland, and was seldom at the House. The brunt of the battle fell on Dillon, T. P. O'Connor, Sexton, Healy, the two Sullivans, Biggar, O'Donnell, and others who showed great skill in attack and debate. Mr. Forster made some slight concessions. He made it more clear that persons imprisoned were to be treated as political prisoners. He gave a personal undertaking that no persons should be imprisoned without his personal investigation of the case. On the other hand, the demand that no arrests should be made, except on the sworn information of two credible witnesses, was refused. So also was the effort to get a precise definition of the crimes to which the Act was to apply, and that the warrant should specify the crime with which the arrested man was charged, and that he should be furnished with a copy of the warrant. These amendments met with some support from Radical Members of the House, and especially from Cowen, Labouchere, and Bradlaugh. They brought into strong relief the arbitrary nature of the measure, and how completely the liberties of the Irish people were placed in the hands of the Chief Secretary.

After five days of debate in Committee, only one section of the first clause was disposed of. It was thought necessary for the Speaker to frame a new rule applying a more severe method of closure. By the aid of this, after eight more days of discussion in Committee, the Bill was passed. Two more days were occupied on the Report stage, and a further application of the closure took place, and finally two days on the third reading—in all, twenty-five days were expended on the Bill. On February 24th, the last day of debate on it, Mr. Forster, in his reply to a motion of Mr. Justin McCarthy for the rejection of the measure, claimed that he was conferring a great benefit on Ireland. Pointing to the Irish Members, he said: "We have been delivering Ireland, or doing our best to deliver Ireland, from a great grievance, and have been saving her, or believing we are saving her, from a still greater peril." Mr. McCarthy's motion was rejected by a majority of 321 to 51. The Bill passed without opposition, and with scant discussion, in the House of Lords. The sequel will show the futility of the measure, and that the Irish Members were justified in their predictions that it would aggravate the agitation in Ireland, and would lead to an increase, rather than a diminution, of crime.

The Parliamentary battle for coercion, however, was not concluded. There remained the Arms Bill, which was to enable the Government to search for and seize arms in proclaimed districts, and to forbid the sale of them. The Home Secretary, Sir William Harcourt, took charge of it, in the absence of Mr. Forster, who had crossed the Irish Channel in order to set going the machinery for giving effect to his Coercion Act. It led to further heated discussion and protracted obstruction. Sir William Harcourt did not mince his words in dealing with the Irish Members. Mr. Dillon took the lead in opposing the Bill, and a battle royal occurred between him and Sir William Harcourt.

Dillon said that the Irish had no means of waging civil war. He wished they had. He was called to order for this language, and withdrew it, but he attacked Harcourt for his cynical tone. " If," he said, " the peaceful, the loyal, and the constitutional agitation of the Land League failed, the people of Ireland would be driven back to the dark and desperate methods, which the League had almost successfully induced them to give up. The whole blame of the murders which would be committed would be at the door of the men who struck from the hands of the League the weapon of open and legal agitation."

Harcourt, in reply, suggested that the debate should close at once. The House, he said, had heard an authorized agent of the Land League explain its doctrines to be those of treason and assassination. He insisted that Dillon had advised the Irish farmers to shoot those who resisted the Land League. Healy warmly defended his colleague, and charged Harcourt with want of truth. He was at once suspended by a vote of 253 to 15. In Committee, the Irish Members, by their pertinacity, obtained some concessions. Not a few violent scenes took place, and the Bill was only carried by the application of the closure. Parnell moved its rejection on the third reading, and took the opportunity of again defending the Land League. The debate which then occurred was a most interesting one. The opposing parties came to close quarters, and concentrated their bitterness in short speeches. Parnell taunted Mr. Bright for his support of Coercion, and quoted from a speech made a few years ago in which he said :

" I entirely disagree with those who, when any crisis or disturbance arises in Ireland, say you must first of all restore order and then later you may remedy the grievance. After having asserted the supremacy of the law the grievances are forgotten and there is no consideration for them. This has been done in Ireland for 200 years, and nothing has been done except under the influence of terror."

Sir William Harcourt denied that Irish opinion was against the Bill. In no single division, he said, had a moiety of the Representatives of Ireland voted against it. If Ireland were against it, would not all its representatives have been found voting in opposition to it ?

It was worthy of note that Sir William Harcourt, with his plain, and almost brutal, language, was more acceptable to the Irish Members than Mr. Forster, with his professions of sympathy for Ireland. Mr. Justin McCarthy gave voice to this in his speech on this occasion. He complimented Sir William Harcourt on the skill, moderation, and good feeling with which upon the whole he had discharged a very difficult task. The Irish Members expected nothing from him ; he had made no profession of sympathy or protestation of sturdy, rugged honesty. They were not disappointed in him.

Mr. Forster, in a general reply, speaking for the first time on this Bill, defended it on the ground that repeated advice had been given to the people of Ireland to arm themselves. Many had followed the advice thus given. Foolish young men had begun to arm themselves all over the country in Ireland. He doubted whether the Irish Members represented the real opinion of the Irish people. He would not object, if that was the time to do it—even in their present excitement—to appeal from the Members opposite to the people of Ireland. His own belief was that if a real reform of the Land Laws was introduced and carried, the attacks which had been made on the Government would very speedily be forgotten. He was sure that he could venture to appeal with confidence from the Irish Members opposite to their constituents.

The third reading was carried by 255 to 36—the minority was the largest of the many divisions in the course of the Bill. It was clear that there was by no means the same hostility to it as to the other and main Coercion Bill.

CHAPTER XV

THE LAND ACT OF 1881

THE Coercion Act carried, the Government devoted the whole of its energies to the Land question of Ireland. It did so under great disadvantages, for the majority of the Irish people had been completely alienated by the unfortunate coercive measures of Mr. Forster. Nor had they ground for supposing that any effective measure would be proposed, which would result in a reduction of rents, and would give security against rack-renting for the future. The indications were that nothing more was intended by the Government than an amendment and moderate extension of the Land Act of 1870. I can personally confirm this, for in January, 1881, after the meeting of Parliament, Mr. Gladstone asked me to put in writing, for the Cabinet, my views as to what should be the main lines of a measure of Irish land reform. In my memorandum, I urged that the mandate given by the Irish electors was clear and unmistakable, namely for fair rents, fixity of tenure, and free sale of the tenant's interest. Mr. Gladstone remarked to me a few days later that he was greatly surprised at my having recommended so extreme a measure, an indication that he was far from having himself arrived at such a conclusion.

Several occurrences, however, contributed to a rapid development of policy, and to the production of a measure of a much more advanced character than originally contemplated. Early in 1881, the two Royal Commissions above referred to produced their reports, or rather a litter of reports, as Mr. Gladstone called them. That appointed by the late Government, presided over by the Duke of Richmond, issued a report signed by a majority of its members, in which the necessity for giving greater protection to tenants of land in

Ireland was fully admitted. It pointed to a scheme of arbitration of rents, though in guarded and halting language. A minority of six members of the Commission, led by Lord Carlingford and Mr. Joseph Cowen, strongly asserted the expediency of adopting the full policy of the three F's. The smaller Commission, more recently appointed by Mr. Gladstone's Government to report on the Irish Land question only, with Lord Bessborough as its Chairman, while issuing three separate reports, was unanimous in favour of the three F's. This last Commission examined no less than 800 witnesses. They included a large number of land agents, landowners, and County Court Judges, who agreed as to the necessity for this policy. They showed conclusively the causes of failure of the Act of 1870, namely, that many landlords, with the object of evading that Act, had raised their rents by successive degrees, each time such that the tenants could not be expected to refuse, and give up their farms claiming compensation under the Act, but in the aggregate such as to amount to excessive rack rents, infringing on, if not wholly appropriating, the tenant's interest. In view of these reports, it became clear that the intended Land Bill must be a radical one. There were members, also, of the Cabinet who had only agreed to the Coercion Act, upon the express understanding that a wide measure of Land Reform should follow. Mr. Forster's correspondence with Mr. Gladstone shows that he was fully in accord with this view, and that he had made up his mind that no measure short of the three F's would be of any use.

These converging influences had their effect on Mr. Gladstone. But there can be no doubt that it was with reluctance that he came to the conclusion that his Land Act of 1870 was a failure, and that a measure drawn on very different lines was necessary. He never quite admitted that he had adopted the scheme of the three F's in its entirety. He had, moreover, much difficulty with some members of his Cabinet. One of them, the Duke of Argyll, could not be persuaded to adopt the scheme. He resigned the office of Privy Seal, and brought to an end his political association with Mr. Gladstone of twenty-nine years' standing.

The Bill, as ultimately agreed upon, was, in fact, a most revolutionary measure. In this view it was much to be regretted that no attempt was made to obtain the consent and support for it of the representatives of those mainly interested in it, the great mass of the Irish tenants. Parnell's course in the discussions did not indicate that he was impracticable. On the contrary, the effect of his speeches and amendments was, in my opinion, such as to show that it would have been possible to come to terms with him. If this had been effected, how different would have been the reception of the Bill in Ireland. But the whole attitude of Mr. Forster to Parnell and the Irish leaders precluded the possibility of negotiation with them. The ultimate success of the measure would necessarily depend on its reception by the Irish people, yet it was not thought necessary to consult their representatives, or to come to terms with them on the details of the scheme.

Mr. Gladstone introduced his Land Bill in the House of Commons on April 7th, in a speech of two hours in length, not a word of which was superfluous. It was cogent, lucid, persuasive, and tactful, but not adorned with passages of eloquence as some of his other great speeches. He appealed to the reasoning powers, and in no sense to the passions, or even the enthusiasm of his audience. He described the task before him as far the most difficult he had ever been called upon to perform. He admitted that his Land Act of 1870 had to a large extent failed. He attributed this in part to the action of the House of Lords in forcing concessions from him, and in part to the inherent defects of the Act. He discussed the litter of reports. He showed that there was almost unanimity in them in favour of a wide measure of Land Reform, involving the independent determination of rents. He vindicated the Irish landlords from the imputation of the Land League. " They had," he said, " been tried and acquitted." He quoted from the Bessborough Commission to the effect that the greatest credit was due to the landlords for not exacting from their tenants all that they might have done, under the law as it then stood—a somewhat doubtful compliment. But a few, he admitted, had taken advantage of their position, and had done great injustice, by arbitrary raising of rents and harsh evictions. He described the scheme of the Land League as aiming at public plunder. He based his proposals mainly on the inability of the tenants, on account of their weakness and poverty, to contract freely with their landlords, and attributed the raising of rents largely to the land hunger which existed in Ireland, owing to the scarcity of land in proportion to the number of those desirous of making a living out of it. This made inevitable, he said, the institution of a Court to arbitrate between landlords and tenants as to rent.

He proposed, therefore, to constitute a Commission or Court of three members to which tenants might apply to determine the rents of their farms. The term for which the rent was to be fixed was fifteen years, at the end of which the tenant was to be permitted to apply to the Court for another term, and a fresh declaration of rent, and so on, *toties quoties*. The tenant was to have the right of assigning his interest in his farm to a solvent incomer, subject, however, to a right of pre-emption to the landlord on terms to be fixed by the Court. The scheme therefore provided for the adoption of the three F's with little or no restriction. There were also clauses giving greater facilities for the purchase of holdings by their tenants, embodying all the recommendations of the Committee of 1878–9. This brief description, however, gives but a faint idea of the complexity of the Bill.

Looking back at Mr. Gladstone's explanations on introducing this great measure, it seems now, as indeed it seemed to me at the time, that he did not base it on the best ground that was open to him. His main argument was that the weakness and poverty of the Irish tenants, and the intense land hunger that existed, made it impossible for them to enter into free bargains with their landlords as to rent. The better justification for the great change appeared to me to be that the tenants, having effected, themselves and their predecessors, all the improvements on the land, everything which added to its prairie value, in the shape of houses, farm buildings, etc., they were *de facto* part owners with their landlords in the holdings, and that such interest, though recognized as their property by the Act of 1870, being inadequately protected, they were not in a position to bargain on equal terms with their landlords as to the rent which should be payable for the landlord's interest ; and that it was essentially necessary, in point of justice, that some independent authority should be called in, in the event of dispute, to determine what the rent should be. This view of the case was more fully developed by Lord Carlingford in his speech on introducing the Bill in

the House of Lords. He was, to my mind, more imbued with
the true Irish view of the tenant's position in Ireland than
Mr. Gladstone. But such was the force of lucid persuasion
by a supreme master of all the arts of an orator, that
while the speech of the latter produced the most powerful
effect, and, when supported in Committee by all his immense
dialectical powers, carried the measure to success, Lord
Carlingford's speech produced little or no effect, either on the
House of Lords or on the country. Yet of the two speeches
it is now, when read in after years, the more cogent and
convincing. Another observation to be made on Mr. Gladstone's great speech, is that it minimized the case on behalf
of the tenants as against the landlords. He uniformly spoke
in most generous terms of the latter. He gave the impression
that the cases of rack-renting were comparatively rare, that
the reduction of rents by the Commission would be small, and
that the landlords, as a body, would not be losers by the Act.
Yet no one could read the evidence of the Bessborough Commission without coming to a very different conclusion, namely,
that in a very large number of cases rents had been raised to
a point, when they appropriated the tenant's interest. The
result also of the proceedings of the Land Court, after the
passing of the Act, showed that rack-renting was the rule and
not the exception. The effect of the speech was to give a
handle to those who were interested in depreciating the
effect of the measure, to point out to the tenants in Ireland
that they had little to expect from it in the way of reduction
of rent. It will be seen that Parnell played upon this theme
in criticizing the Bill, both in the House of Commons and
at meetings in Ireland. With these reservations, it must be
admitted that Mr. Gladstone's speech on introducing the Bill
was one of his greatest performances in persuasive exposition and argument.

The Bill, as introduced, even with the limitations which
were inherent from Mr. Gladstone's description of it, evidently
took the Irish Nationalists by surprise. They had not expected
a measure so wide in its scope, and so favourable to the
tenants. There was great difference among them as to what
should be their attitude to it. The majority were in favour of
accepting it in principle, and endeavouring to amend and
extend it in Committee. A more militant minority were in

favour of rejecting the Bill as worthless, and of continuing their battle with the landlords on the lines of the existing agitation, and by the methods of the Land League. A convention of the League was held at Dublin between the introduction of the Bill and its second reading. After two days' discussion it was decided, in view of their differences, to leave the Irish Members unfettered in their action in the House of Commons, as regards the Bill, and to oppose, or not, as they should individually think best. But just before the second reading of the Bill, at a meeting in London of the Irish Parliamentary Party, Parnell personally informed them that he had come to the conclusion that the best course would be to abstain from voting on the Bill, and, without waiting for any discussion by his colleagues, declared that if his advice was not taken he would resign his position of their leader. He imposed his will upon them much against the opinion of many. His motion for abstention was carried by 19 to 12.

Parnell has been much blamed in some quarters for this. It was said that he showed want of gratitude to the Liberal Party for the great measure of Land Reform. But impartial consideration of the position will, I think, lead to the conclusion that he was justified in his action. The Irish Members had not been consulted by the Government, and they were in no way responsible for the measure. Though it greatly altered the status of Irish tenants, giving them fixity of tenure, and preventing the unjust raising of rents, it was by no means clear that it would result in a reduction of rents, which, in their opinion, was absolutely necessary, in consequence of bad seasons and falling prices, and of arbitrary increases of rent of late years, such as to encroach upon and to confiscate the tenant's interest. There were grave defects in the Bill, and everything would depend on the extent to which these might be made good, and on the administration of the Act when it became law. Why should the Irish Party make itself responsible for it ? The alternative was to hold aloof, to express dissatisfaction with its details, and to press for amendments. This policy must now, by the course of the Bill, and by the experience of its working, when passed into law, be held to have been wise and prudent. It was pursued throughout the proceedings in the House of Commons with ability and persistence.

If the position of the Irish Party was difficult, so also was that of the Tory Party. The measure realized the best hopes and wishes of the Ulster tenants, and was therefore supported by the Tory Members for County constituencies in Ireland *bon gré, mal gré*. The Irish landlords, who dreaded the Bill, found little support from their Members. On the other hand, the Tory Members for England and Scotland hated the Bill. They looked at it from the point of view of English law. The very phraseology of Irish Land Law was unknown to them. They looked on the relation of landlord and tenant in Ireland as one of free contract. In this view the landlords were entitled to all that the existing law gave to them, and to any rent they could get for the land by competition. They believed the Bill to be a scheme of pure confiscation. They dreaded its extension to England and Scotland.

On the second reading a debate took place extending over eight days. The speech of the greatest interest in this long palaver was that of Parnell. He adopted a neutral attitude to the Bill in language of great moderation. He pointed out many defects in it. He contended that it would have very little effect on rents, and would therefore not satisfy the tenants, under the existing condition of things. He favoured, himself, a scheme of Peasant Proprietors in Ireland. " We do not," he said, " desire to confiscate anything. The Land League doctrine is that any attempt to reconcile the respective interests of landlords and tenants is impossible. . . . The League does not believe that landlords have yet touched bottom. It has recommended compulsory expropriation, but not of all landlords. It proposes that power should be given to a Commission to expropriate compulsorily those landlords who may be acting as centres of disturbance, the price to be fixed at twenty years' purchase of the Poor Law valuation. The mere threat of expropriation will do more to reduce rack rents than all the legal proceedings of the Bill. The Land League also proposed that those who have bought under the Encumbered Estates Act should be called upon to give up their purchases on repayment of the money given for them. Parliament will thus undo the mischief it has done by passing the Act."

With respect to the proposed judicial rents, he contended that every point would be contested in a court of law, and that the costs would eat up any profit which the smaller tenants might expect from a reduction of rent. He complained that the arrears of excessive and unjust rent were not dealt with, and that leaseholders were not included in the benefit of the Bill. He advised the migration of small tenants from the congested districts in the west of Ireland to the thinly populated districts elsewhere, rather than their emigration. He suggested that the Commission should be empowered to buy land and erect labourers' cottages on it. He concluded with these words, which pointed to conciliation and agreement rather than to active opposition to the Bill:

" I think I have said enough to show why I ought not to compromise myself and those whom I represent by accepting a measure which I fear cannot be either a final or satisfactory solution of this question. I regret very much that the Government appear determined to miss the great chance which is open to them. . . . I hope the result will prove that I am wrong in my forecast as to the chief effect of the Bill. No one hopes more sincerely than I do that the measure will turn out better for the Irish tenants than I fear it can. I and my friends have no desire to keep things in a perpetual state of Irish confusion. We desire to see the Land question and every other question settled. We desire to see this division among classes done away with. We do not want the Irish landlords and the Irish tenants continually to live in opposing camps. As individuals, the landlords are well fitted to take their place as the leaders of the Irish nation. They have been placed up to the present time by legislation in a false position, and they would have been more than human if they could have filled it without shame and disgrace. I implore the Government to reconsider the question, and to endeavour in Committee to make the measure more healthy to the poor people and less hurtful, and to bring about such an improvement in it that we, the Irish Members, may vote for it without feeling that we are compromising the position we have hitherto occupied and maintained."[1]

The only other speech eminently worthy of notice was that of Lord Hartington, as representing the Whig element of the Government. He denied that the agitation in Ireland, or the obstruction of Irish Members in the House of Commons, was the

[1] *Hansard*, May 18th, 1881.

cause for the introduction of the Bill. But one of the causes which rendered legislation necessary was the then condition of Ireland. In some parts of the country there actually existed civil war between landlords and tenants. Rent could not be collected except by the threat of wholesale evictions, and numbers of landlords were deprived of their just rights. He defended the methods of the Bill.

" In my opinion," he said, " the law of Ireland has too long neglected to recognize the customary and equitable rights of the tenants. We have gone all this time on the assumption that the tenants in Ireland were able to protect their equitable rights, and that there ought to be freedom of contract. But we cannot do so now. We have to acknowledge that freedom of contract does not exist in Ireland, and that the tenants never have been, and are not now in a position to protect themselves in the possession of their equitable rights. . . . The law has given everything to the landlord, and nothing to the tenant. . . . The Act of 1870 has been found practically inadequate, and what the Bill proposes to do is to supplement that Act by other and more direct provisions, intended to secure to the tenants their equitable and customary rights."

Mr. Forster made an admirable speech, but without presenting any new view, as also did Mr. Bright. The latter was, I believe, the originator of the expression, " the prairie value of land in Ireland." In illustration of the position of tenants there, he said :

" If all that the tenants have done were swept off the soil, and all that the landlords have done were left upon it, the land would be as bare of houses and farms, fences and cultivation, as it was in prehistoric times. It would be as bare as an American prairie, where the Indian now roams and where the white man has never trod." After this description it is difficult to understand how he arrived at the conviction which he affirmed to the House that rents would be reduced under the Bill in not more than one case out of ten. The views of the Ulster farmers were ably expounded by Mr. Macnaghten, K.C., then Member for Antrim, now Lord Macnaghten. While supporting the second reading of the Bill, but objecting to some of its details, he said that " it would be nothing less than a national calamity if the House did not put aside all party feeling and do its best to settle the question as speedily as possible."

If I refer to my own speech on the occasion, it is only for the purpose of pointing out that what I have said above as to the best ethical defence of the Bill, and as to the necessity which existed for large reductions of rack rents, were equally the views which I then expressed.

The general drift of the debate was greatly in favour of the Bill. A hostile amendment moved by Lord Elcho was rejected by a majority of 352 to 176, a proportion of 2 to 1, in spite of the abstention of the Parnellites. Twenty-four Home Rulers, thirteen Tory and fifteen Whig Members for Irish constituencies voted for the Bill, and only eight Irish Members voted with the minority against it. There was therefore an overwhelming weight of Irish opinion in favour of its main principles.

The real difficulties of the measure were encountered in the Committee stage. It was there that Mr. Gladstone's incomparable skill and versatility, knowledge of details of the subject, patience, tact, and dialectical powers were chiefly manifest. He had to face enormous difficulties, for though there was general admission that a reform of the Land Law was necessary, so as to give more or less protection to the tenants, there was great difference of opinion as to how this was to be effected. The English landowners and the great majority of the Tory Members hated the Bill, looked at it from the point of view of English law and English land tenure, and held it to be pure confiscation of the landlords' rights. The Irish Nationalists, on the other hand, thought it was inadequate to meet the grievances of the tenant farmers, and made every effort to extend it.

It was a stupendously difficult task to steer the Bill between these two opposing forces, especially for a leader in his seventy-third year. I was better able to judge of this, for I was one of a Committee consisting of Sir Farrer Herschell (the Solicitor-General), Mr. Hugh Law, the Irish Attorney-General, and Sir Henry Thring, the draftsman of the Bill, who were asked by Mr. Gladstone to advise as to the amendments proposed to the Bill. We met every morning, during the passage of the Bill through Committee, examined the amendments which were likely to be discussed during the sitting, and reported on them to Mr. Gladstone. But I am bound to say we were of very little use to him. We found that he knew more of the subject than all of us together. He was never for a moment at a loss how to meet his many opponents. He did the work almost alone through thirty-three sittings of the Committee, five days of the Report stage, and four more devoted to consideration of the Lords' Amendments.

The record in *Hansard* gives a very inadequate impression of the difficulties encountered, and of the way in which Mr. Gladstone handled them. It was currently said that there were only two Members of the House besides himself who understood the details of this complicated Bill, namely, Mr. Hugh Law and Mr. T. M. Healy, who won a great reputation by the ability, legal knowledge, and dexterity of debate he showed in the discussions.

It was generally thought at the time that the Irish Party were too critical, too hostile to the Bill, and too pertinacious in their amendments. But when comparison is made between the amendments which they pressed on the Government, with what has since been conceded by Parliament, after years of further demands from Ireland, and long agrarian agitation, it must now be admitted that they were justified in pressing them, and that they knew better what were the just needs of the Irish tenants than did their irresponsible critics. It would have been better for all parties, even for the landlords, as it turned out, if all the demands of the Irish Party had been conceded. Their amendments were directed mainly to the following points. They contended that the direction in the Bill as to the principle on which " fair rents " were to be awarded by the Land Commission was unsatisfactory, and that it was not clear that the rents would be fixed at a rate which would secure to the tenants the full value of the improvements effected by themselves and their predecessors.

Mr. Healy did, in fact, succeed in obtaining a most important amendment on this point. He moved a new clause to the effect that rent should not be charged on improvements. Mr. Law, the Irish Attorney-General, accepted the clause, without much discussion or demur, and it was adopted in the Bill, without discovery by the Opposition of its supremely important effect. But the clause embodying this principle is now recognized at its true value, and goes by the name of

" Healy's clause." Apart from this direction, there was no definition of a fair rent. It was left wholly to the discretion of the Commission, and to the Judges on appeal. The Irish Judges, in construing the clause, gave it a meaning favourable to the landlords, which was not intended; and later in 1897 Parliament was compelled to interfere, and to set aside the decision of the Judges. Parnell, therefore, was justified in his criticism of the Bill in this respect.

Another main point insisted upon by the Irish Party was the necessity for dealing with accumulated arrears of excessive and unjust rents. They contended that the Commission should be empowered to reduce these arrears, in the same proportion as they reduced future rents. After much discussion, the Government agreed to deal with the question. Mr. Forster moved and carried a new clause providing, on the joint application of the landlord and his tenants, for the advance, by way of loan out of the surplus funds of the Disestablished Church, of one-half of the arrears due by tenants paying rent of less than £30 a year, the interest and principal to be repaid by an addition to the rent spread over a term of years. The Irish Members objected that it was insufficient and would not work, and so it proved in practice, for nothing came of the clause, mainly because the assent of the landlords was necessary. In 1882, the Government was compelled to deal with the subject in a far more drastic manner. The Irish Party, therefore, were fully justified in their demands.

Another demand of Parnell and his followers had reference to leaseholders, who, they claimed, should be admitted to the benefit of the Bill. Here, again, a concession was made by the Government. A clause was inserted, providing that on the termination of a lease, the tenant was to be entitled to rank as a tenant under the Act, and to have the benefit of a judicial rent, and perpetuity of tenure. The clause was rejected by the House of Lords, and was not insisted on by the Government. In 1887 the Government of Lord Salisbury gave way on this point, and admitted leaseholders at once, and not at the end of their leases, to the full benefit of judicial rents. It is clear, therefore, that the demands of the Irish Members should have been conceded in 1881.

With respect to the Land Purchase clauses, the Irish Party urged the advance by the Government of the whole of the purchase money to the tenant purchasers, contending that this measure, if restricted to the advance of three-fourths, would be ineffective. The Government resisted this demand. In 1885, under Lord Ashbourne's Act, provision was made for the advance of the whole of the purchase money, and the terms were successively improved by Mr. Balfour's Acts of 1891 and 1896 ; and Mr. George Wyndham's Act of 1903 goes beyond the demands of the Parnellites in 1881. Mr. Parnell and his followers also strongly objected to the Emigration Clauses, and suggested as an alternative the migration of small occupiers of land from the congested districts in the west of Ireland to the thinly peopled districts elsewhere, a measure which, rejected in 1880, was adopted later in the Acts passed by Mr. Balfour and Mr. Wyndham.

It will be seen then that every one of the important amendments supported by Parnell, in the course of the discussion on the Land Bill, has since been adopted by Parliament. It may well be asked why they were not conceded in 1881 in defiance to the demand of the great majority of Irish Members. It is not to be gainsaid that the Bill was already heavily laden. There were many occasions when it was in great danger from attack by the Tory Party, backed up by a large section of Whigs in the House of Commons.

The general effect of the proceedings in Committee was that some few amendments were conceded at the instance of the Irish Members favourable to the tenants, and that practically no concessions of importance were made to the landlords. The case for the Bill, however, was greatly strengthened by the long discussion. The third reading was carried by a very great majority, only fourteen Members voting against it. The Tory leaders and most of their followers abstained from voting : so also did Parnell and six of his followers ; but the bulk of the Irish Members voted for it.

This acceptance of the Bill by so great a majority of the House of Commons had its effect on the House of Lords. It was vehemently attacked by the Duke of Argyll, who took the opportunity of comparing his recent colleagues, in an amusing sally, to a row of jelly fishes—"most beautiful creatures in the world, endowed with elaborate and delicate nervous systems, but hitherto found destitute of a skeleton or backbone." "They make," he said, "the most convulsive movements in the water, and, you see, the poor creatures think they are swimming, but when you take the bearings of the land, you find that they are floating with the current and with the tide." He then proceeded to tear the measure in pieces. Lord Lansdowne followed in the same strain. "This is not an attempt to remove imperfections from the existing law. It is an attempt to quell a grave rebellion by the wholesale concession of proprietary rights to the peasantry of Ireland—a concession which has been extorted by violence and agitation. These rights we are asked to create." Lord Carnarvon, Lord Lytton, and a bevy of Irish Peers joined in denouncing the Bill. It was severely criticized by Lord Cairns, who admitted, however, that its main provisions must be accepted. It was ably defended by Lord Carlingford and Lord Selborne, and by the Irish Chancellor, Lord O'Hagan. One Irish landowner, Lord Dunraven, alone defended it in point of principle, but claimed that the landlords were entitled to compensation, while other Irish Peers, like Lord Waterford and Lord Monteagle, denounced its methods, but could not take the responsibility of voting for its rejection.

Lord Salisbury, who since the death of Lord Beaconsfield had led the Tory Peers, inveighed against the Bill in the most trenchant terms. "It gave to the tenant the right to sell that which he had never bought, and to tear up contracts by which he was bound." He denied that it would be accepted in Ireland as a message of peace. Landowners would, in future, look upon Parliament as their worst enemy, and in view of recurring General Elections would be living in perpetual apprehension of earthquakes. These vehement denunciations were, however, only a presage to a complete surrender. He could not advise the House to reject the Bill. He gave the following reasons for this course.

"The state of Ireland, the condition into which her population has been allowed to drift by the culpable leaders of the Executive Government, is a consideration which must greatly govern us in deciding on the course we shall take. If this Bill is rejected on the second reading, we must, of course, remember that we have not in our hands the Executive Government. I confess, though with some reluctance, I have been led to the belief that it may be wise for us not to vote against the second reading of the Bill, but to see whether in

Committee we cannot remove from it some of its most glaring acts of impolicy, some of its greatest injustices." [1]

Once again, therefore, the Tory Leader in the House of Lords, as his predecessors had done in the notable cases of Catholic Emancipation, Irish Tithe Reform, the Disestablishment of the Irish Church, and the Land Act of 1870, advised his followers to concede to agitation in Ireland and to violence and outrage what they denied to arguments founded on justice and reason.

After debate extending over two days, the Bill was read a second time without a division. In the Committee stage the Government was powerless to prevent havoc being made of the clauses. Shoals of amendments were carried by majorities of about three to one, in the interest of landlords in Ireland, completely altering the structure and effect of the Bill. Two sittings were occupied in this wrecking work. On the return of the Bill to the House of Commons, Mr. Gladstone, instead of moving the rejection *en bloc* of these amendments, asked the House to consider them *seriatim* and in detail. Four nights were occupied on this. Some concessions of no great importance were made, but substantially the Lords' Amendments were rejected. The House of Lords again dealt with the Bill in the spirit of " no surrender," and insisted upon their amendments. But in the end wiser and more prudent counsels prevailed, and after some negotiations between the leaders of the two parties some few concessions were made by the Government. It was unfortunate that the two main amendments of the Lords which were conceded by the Government were on points which, after long discussion in the House of Commons, the Government had accepted on the proposal of the Irish Party. The one was the clause admitting leaseholders to the benefit of the Act at the end of their leases. The other was a provision which gave some protection to tenants against being evicted for non-payment of rent in the interval between the application to the Law Courts and the fixing of the judicial rent. Apart from these, this great and revolutionary measure passed almost in the shape in which it was originally introduced by Mr. Gladstone—a monument to his skill, versatility, dialectics, and tactics. It is safe to say that no other statesman of the century could have achieved

[1] *Hansard*, August 2nd, 1881.

such a success. The measure, indeed, as passed, had grave defects, which, from time to time, were remedied in later years, but its main principles—the independent valuation of rents as between landlords and tenants, the recognition of the tenants' permanent interests in their holdings, and of their right to assign them—have stood the test of experience, and have been recognized in Ireland as charters of the Irish tenantry.

It has been the fashion, of late, in some quarters, to speak of this great measure as founded on error ; that it created a position of unstable equilibrium between two opposing parties, the landlords and the tenants, which necessitated its being superseded by a scheme for buying out the landlords, and turning the tenants into peasant proprietors. It is to be observed, however, that no scheme of purchase could have been adopted, without a preliminary valuation, determining the relative interests of landlords and tenants in the holdings, and this must have necessitated an arbitration by a Commission or a Court, and must have been based on the rent. A scheme of purchase also could not have been carried out all at once. It must have been spread over a long term of years. It would be impossible for the State to raise and advance 200 millions for this purpose within a short period, without greatly disturbing the money market, and raising the rate of interest, on which the whole scheme would be based. It has been found lately that not more than 5 millions a year can conveniently be raised by the State for this purpose, and at this rate forty years or more would be occupied by the transaction. Meanwhile, the tenants waiting to be turned into owners would require protection from their existing rack rents. It was therefore absolutely necessary that there should be a process for determining fair rents, both as a basis for purchase, and as an interim protection pending the completion of the scheme.

It has undoubtedly been a defect of the Act of 1881 that it involved so much of legal expense in determining the rents payable in 300,000 small tenancies. The process has brought a harvest to lawyers, and has been a burden to the smaller tenants. Much of this might have been avoided. When, in 1886, the Scotch Crofter Act was passed, applying the principles of the Irish Act to the crofters in the west and north of

Scotland, instead of leaving it to each tenant to make his application to the Commission for a determination of rent, the Commission was directed to make personal investigation of districts, and to determine what rents should be payable in future by classes of tenants, and this arrangement avoided the process of individual litigation involved in the Irish case. It would have been far better to have adopted some such scheme in the case of the small tenants in Ireland. But the framers of the Act of 1881 proceeded under the belief that the applicants for judicial rent would be the exception and not the rule. These and other defects in the Act might have been avoided if there had been consultation with the Irish leaders before it was framed and introduced, or if more attention had been paid to their demands, when the Bill was in Committee.

It cannot, in fact, now be denied that the main criticisms by Parnell and his followers of the Land Bill of 1881, and their demands for its amendment and extension, which seemed at the time to be unreasonable and excessive, have been justified and confirmed by experience and later legislation. The moral to be drawn is that the best, and in fact the only safe guide for legislation for a community like Ireland, with separate interests and wants, is to be found in the demands of its representatives. This principle was adopted in the main by the Act of 1881, but it was not carried out sufficiently in detail. As a result, it failed to give satisfaction in most important respects, and, after further long agitation, had to be supplemented by other and more complete measures.

It should be understood, however, that the Bill, as introduced by Mr. Gladstone, was already heavily freighted with a valuable cargo. If more had been put on board the vessel might have foundered. I recollect Mr. Gladstone pointing out to me, about this time, the great difficulty a Minister had in carrying successfully any great remedial measure involving much detail. The Minister in charge of it had first to meet objections raised in the Cabinet. Concessions had often to be made in order to get the consent of his colleagues. Later, the measure had to run the gauntlet in the Committee stage of the House of Commons, where it was often advisable to ease the position, and to ward off opposition, by making further concessions. Lastly, there was the House of Lords always hostile to Liberal measures and ready to mangle the Bill. Concessions had to be made, in considering their amendments, to avoid the loss of the Bill.   The Minister was fortunate if his measure escaped all these difficulties ; but in any case it was seldom that serious changes affecting its remedial effects were not imposed on him.   In spite of its grave omissions, the Land Act was a very great and beneficial measure.   It effected a revolution in the Irish land system, and prepared the way for a still greater one.

The carrying of such a measure through a Cabinet in which there was no Irish representative, through a House of Commons in which the Irish Party was in so small a minority, and where the bulk of Members understood nothing of the Irish land question, and through a House of Lords, where the only Irish interest was that of the landlords, was a very great feat, perhaps the greatest, though not the most complete, in Mr. Gladstone's career.   If it had not been handicapped by coercion it would have been received with enthusiasm by the Irish people ; and with some amendments it might have been a settlement of the question.

" I must make one admission," said Mr. Gladstone in 1893, " and that is that without the Land League the Act of 1881 would not now be upon the Statute Book." [1]

[1] *Hansard*, April 21st, 1893.

CHAPTER XVI

THE ARREST OF PARNELL

IT was perhaps to be expected of Mr. Forster that, having obtained from Parliament the great and arbitrary powers of the Coercion Act, he would hold them in reserve for a time, while the remedial measure, the Land Bill, was being discussed in the House of Commons. It would probably have been wise policy to see what effect so great a measure of Land Reform would have on public opinion in Ireland. But this was not Mr. Forster's view of the position. He began as soon as possible to put his coercive law in force. He had obtained the consent of the House of Commons to the Act upon the assurance that it was aimed at "*mauvais sujets*" and "*village ruffians,*" who were the actual perpetrators of outrages. The police, he had said, were fully cognizant who these persons were, and could lay their hands on them. Mr. Gladstone also had given his personal assurance that the Act would be put in force only as against the perpetrators and abettors of outrages, and not against those who by speeches, or combinations, advised and promoted breaches of contract as to rent.

It was, however, soon discovered that the police were at fault in the assurances they had given, and that they were unable to lay their hands upon the actual perpetrators of crime. Mr. Forster divided the disturbed parts of Ireland into six districts, and put at the head of them men with the duties of magistrates and inspectors of police combined. They were invested with the power of putting persons in prison, who were under suspicion of being implicated in outrages. Some of them were men of singular indiscretion, and did much to aggravate local opinion by their arbitrary proceedings. Mr. Forster himself took infinite pains to prevent injustice being done, but he soon found that it was necessary to support his agents in their summary proceedings, and to defend their action in the House of Commons.

By the end of April, forty persons were under arrest, and this number was doubled in another month. The numbers continually increased, till, in a few months, the total in jail exceeded eight hundred, in spite of numerous releases. It was obviously impossible that Mr. Forster could be personally responsible for the arrest and imprisonment of all these under his *lettres de cachet*. He was obliged to leave the responsibility with subordinates. As a result large numbers of persons were imprisoned, merely because they were connected with local Land Leagues, and without other evidence of their implication in outrages in their districts. This produced a very bad effect. Disturbances and outrages increased, as had been foretold by objectors to the Coercion Act.

From a letter of Lord Cowper to the Cabinet, in September,[1] it appears that the question of the arrest of the leaders of the Land League was then under consideration. The letter is of great importance, for it shows that up to that date, in the opinion of the legal advisers of the Irish Government, the Land League was not an illegal association ; and also that the Government was not justified in arresting the leaders of the League for openly preaching and advising breaches of contract. Lord Cowper wrote : " There is no doubt that, in the opinion of many lawyers, the Land League is an illegal association, and if our law officers had shared this opinion, it might have been a grave question in the early autumn whether it should not have been put an end to. . . . To strike at the leaders is undoubtedly the right thing, and this is just what we have been accused of not doing. But openly teaching the doctrine of breach of contract, which is their real crime, does not, unfortunately, enable us to take them up. We are hampered in our action by an express agreement that we will not arrest any man, unless we can say, on our honour, that we believe him to have actually committed or incited to outrage. This has at first prevented us from attacking the leaders as vigorously as we might have done, but latterly some of them have been less cautious, and we have also prevailed

---

[1] *Life of Parnell*, I, 287. The date of this letter is not given, but it is evident from the context that it was written in September.

upon ourselves to give a wider interpretation of our powers. For my part, I should be inclined to say that, in the present state of the country, everybody, who takes a leading part in the Land League, does, by the very act of doing so, incite to outrage. And there is now hardly anybody, whose detention policy would demand, that I would not personally arrest."

In another part of the letter there is an important admission as to the Land League. " If," he writes, " the restraining influence of the central Land League were withdrawn and the local branches were driven to become secret societies, crime, and especially assassination, might increase ; for though the central body gives unity and strength to the movement, it does to a certain extent restrain crime."

Any scruples, however, which Mr. Forster may have had on the subject of arresting the leaders of the Land League under the Coercion Act were soon dissipated. He had begun early by arresting Mr. Boyton, the Secretary of the League, and Mr. Brennan. A little later, and during the discussion on the second reading of the Land Bill in the House of Commons, he arrested Mr. Dillon, who had taken the place of Davitt as general manager of the Land League. Later he authorized the arrest of the leading men of local Land League Committees in every part of the country. It soon became a distinction to be arrested and imprisoned as suspects. The suspects on release from prison were met with ovations. They became local heroes. Twenty-one ex-suspects were elected as Members of Parliament at the next General Election in 1885.

Their treatment while in prison had nothing of severity. They were not ranked with ordinary prisoners and subjected to prison fare and prison clothing. They were allowed to see their friends and to communicate freely with them.

The Land Act received the Royal Assent on August 22nd. From Mr. Gladstone's letters it appears that very soon after he began to urge on Mr. Forster a policy of conciliation in Ireland, and a mitigation of the arbitrary imprisonments under the Coercion Act. He had not, indeed, much hope of the effect of this on the leaders of the Land League, but he looked to the more general effect, in combination with the working of the Land Act. Mr. Forster does not appear to have responded to these suggestions.

On September 14th a Land League Convention was held in Dublin, at the Rotunda, for the purpose of determining the action to be taken as regards the Land Act. It was a remarkable assembly. It was attended by delegates from more than a thousand local Land League associations in every part of Ireland. It was a truly representative body of the tenants. Orangemen from Ulster, descendants of the Cromwellian settlers, sat beside the more fiery men from the south and west. One feature of the meeting was the large number of priests who spoke in favour of the Land League. There was much difference among the delegates as to what should be done under the Land Act, and what should be the attitude of the Land League, and the tenants generally, to the Land Commission, which was about to open its proceedings. Many of the delegates were of opinion that the tenants should be advised to shun and boycott the Commission, and treat the Land Act as a farce. They held that the League should continue to apply its methods, which they believed would be more efficacious in compelling a reduction of rents than the Land Commission. Others, and the larger number, were of opinion that a fair trial should be made of the Land Courts. Parnell, who was in the chair, advised a course between these two extremes. The duty of the League, in his opinion, was to watch the proceedings of the Land Courts, to study their actions by test cases, and to see, as far as lay in their power, that justice was done to the tenants.

At his instance, a resolution was adopted that the Act should be tested by selected cases of application for reduction of rents, and, pending decision on them, that the tenants should be advised not to apply to the Land Court. " Nothing," said Parnell, " could be more disastrous to our case, or our organization, and to your hopes of getting your rents reduced, than any indiscriminate rush of the tenantry into the Land Courts, and it is with a view to prevent this that we desire to take the tenantry in hand, and to guide them in this matter, because, depend upon it, if we don't guide them for their advantage, there will be others who will guide them for their destruction."

A few days after this Convention a popular demonstration took place at Dublin, in honour of Parnell, of a most enthusiastic character. Never, indeed, had Parnell received a greater ovation. It was the apogee of his fame. He was drawn in triumph, through the Dublin streets, from the station to the offices of the Land League, accompanied by an enormous crowd carrying torches. On the day of this great popular ovation to Parnell at Dublin, Mr. Forster, incited by the previous proceedings at the Dublin Convention of the Land League, wrote to Mr. Gladstone, suggesting that Mr. Parnell should be arrested under the Coercion Act. Mr. Gladstone was, in a few days' time, to be present at a great political demonstration at Leeds, where he was expected to make an important speech, defending the past policy, and explaining the future intentions of the Government. Mr. Forster suggested that he should take the opportunity of denouncing Parnell's action and policy. Mr. Gladstone, acting with the greatest loyalty to Mr. Forster, made a very strong speech at Leeds on October 7th. He attacked Parnell, compared him unfavourably with O'Connell, and accused him of proclaiming a gospel of plunder. Parnell, he said, after doing everything he could to destroy the Land Act, was now urging the people of Ireland to test the Act and not to use it. " The people of Ireland, we believe, desire, in conformity with the advice of patriots and of their Bishops and best friends, to make a full trial of the Act, and if they do make a full trial of the Act, you may rely upon it, it is as certain as human contingencies can be, to give peace to the country. . . . If it should appear that there is still to be fought a final conflict in Ireland between law, on the one side, and lawlessness, on the other—if the law freed from defects is to be rejected and refused, the first condition of political security remains unfulfilled, and then I say, without hesitation, the resources of civilization are not yet exhausted." He proceeded to complain of the want of support to the efforts of the Government from the landlords and other classes threatened, and made the admission that the Government were expected to keep the peace with no moral support behind them.

Parnell made a passionate reply to Mr. Gladstone, in which he made a full use of the admission that the Government had no moral force behind them in Ireland. Speaking two days later, on Sunday, October 9th, at Wexford, where he met with a most enthusiastic and even frenzied reception, he said :

" You have gained something by your exertions during the last twelve months; but I am here to-day to tell you that you have gained but a fraction of that which you are entitled to. And the Irishman who thinks that he can now throw away his arms, just as Grattan disbanded the volunteers in 1789, will find, to his sorrow and destruction, when too late, that he has placed himself in the power of the perfidious and cruel and relentless British enemy. . . .

" It is a good sign that this masquerading knight-errant, this perfidious champion of the rights of every other nation, except those of the Irish nation, should be obliged to throw off the mask to-day, and stand revealed as the man who, by his own utterances, is prepared to carry fire and sword into your homesteads, unless you humbly abase yourself before him and before the landlords of the country. . . .

" In one last despairing wail Mr. Gladstone says that the Government is expected to preserve peace with no moral force behind them ! The Government have no moral force behind them in Ireland ; the whole Irish people are against them. . . . He admits that England's mission in Ireland has been a failure, and that Irishmen have established their right to govern Ireland by laws made by themselves."

On the same day Mr. Forster, before reading the report of this speech, wrote to Mr. Gladstone :

" Parnell's reply to you may be a treasonable outburst. If the lawyers clearly advise me to that effect, I do not think that I can postpone immediate arrest on suspicion of treasonable practices."

The letter is the more important as it shows that, up to that date, there was not sufficient justification for arresting Parnell under the Coercion Act. The Law Officers in Ireland must have given their opinion on the above speech on the succeeding Monday. On Tuesday Forster crossed the Channel to attend a meeting of the Cabinet on the Wednesday, when, after five hours of deliberation, it was decided to give orders to arrest Parnell. On the following morning the Irish Leader was arrested at Morrison's Hotel, Dublin, and was conveyed to Kilmainham. Later, on the same day, Mr. Gladstone received the Freedom of the City of London, at the Guildhall. In the course of his speech he made the dramatic announcement that Parnell had been arrested. " Within these few minutes," he said, " I have been informed that towards the vindication of the law, of order, of the rights of property, and the freedom of the land, of the first elements of political life and civilization, the first step has been taken in the arrest of the man, who has made himself pre-eminent in the attempt to destroy the authority of the law, and substitute what would end in being nothing more than anarchical oppression exercised upon the people of Ireland."

The announcement was received with immense enthusiasm, and with salvos of applause, almost, it was said, "as if it had been the news of a signal victory gained by England over a hated and formidable enemy."

It is clear, from Mr. Gladstone's speeches at Leeds and the Guildhall, that the cause of the arrest of Parnell was not his alleged treasonable language at Wexford; but that he had endeavoured to set himself above the law, and had advised the Irish tenants not to rush promiscuously to the Land Commission, for the determination of their rents, but to submit, through the Land League, test cases. "We arrested Parnell," said Lord Cowper to Mr. Barry O'Brien, "because we thought it absurd to put lesser men into jail and to leave him at large. Furthermore, we thought that his test cases would interfere with the working of the Land Act."[1]   Dillon, Sexton, and O'Kelly were arrested at the same time as Parnell, and warrants were issued for the arrest of Healy, Arthur O'Connor, and Biggar. By the express instruction of Parnell these last three avoided arrest, by remaining in England and not returning to Ireland.

Looking back at these proceedings, it is difficult for us now to justify the arrest of Parnell, and his imprisonment under the Coercion Act, for advising the tenants of Ireland not to rush headlong into the Land Courts, but rather to submit test cases to the Courts through the medium and advice of the Land League. It may well be asked whether the advice given to the tenants was reasonable or not, under the circumstances. It has been already pointed out that many leading members of the Government, including Mr. Gladstone, had expressed the confident opinion that landlords generally would not suffer in the reduction of their rents by the Commission, In the view of Parnell and the Land League, so far from

[1] *Life of Parnell*, I, 342.

rack-renting being the exception, it was almost universal, and no settlement could be satisfactory which did not result in a large and general reduction of rents. The process of ascertainment of values, and the determination of rents would necessarily be a slow one and a costly one. Under these circumstances it would seem that the course suggested by Parnell was not only not unreasonable, but was a wise one. The Commission could have been tested by a few leading cases. If satisfactory reductions were made agreements might have been arrived at between landlords and tenants, subject to confirmation by the Land Court. In this way much delay, and a great expenditure on legal costs, might have been avoided. We must conclude that the imprisonment of Parnell was not justified by the terms of the Coercion Act, and still less by the Parliamentary assurances, and that it was unwise and unnecessary, even from the point of view of the Government, in the interest of the Commission, which they hoped would lead to a pacification of Ireland.

Whatever the justification in law and policy, this high-handed and arbitrary act of imprisoning the leader of the Irish Party produced the very worst effect in Ireland. In Dublin there were riots, and serious conflicts between the people and the police. Everywhere the greatest indignation was expressed. In many parts of Ireland shops were closed, as in the case of general mourning. Parnell took the treatment with philosophic composure. On being asked in Kilmainham by other suspects there what led to his arrest, he replied : " Forster thought that I meant to prevent the working of the Land Act, so he sent me here to keep me out of the way. I don't know what he will gain by this move."[1] And to a pressman who interviewed him he said : " I shall take it as evidence that the people of the country did not do their duty if I am speedily released."

Five days after the arrest of Parnell a meeting was held at the Central Branch of the Land League on October 18th. A manifesto to the Irish people was agreed upon.

" The executive of the National Land League," it ran, " forced to abandon the policy of testing the Land Act, feels bound to advise the tenant farmers of Ireland from henceforth to pay *no rents* under any circumstances to their land-

[1] *Life of Parnell*, I, 315.

lords until the Government relinquishes the existing system of terrorism and restores the constitutional rights of the people. . . . The funds of the National Land League will be paid out unstintingly for the support of all who may endure eviction in the course of the struggle. . . . Our exiled brothers in America may be relied upon to contribute, if necessary, as many millions of money as they have already contributed thousands to starve our landlords and bring English tyranny to its end.

" Landlordism is already staggering under the blows which you have already dealt it with the applause of the world. Pay no rents under any pretext. . . . No power of legalized violence can extort one penny from your purses against your will. If you are evicted you shall not suffer. The landlord who evicts will be a ruined pauper, and the Government, which supports him with its bayonets, will learn in a single winter how powerless is armed force against the will of a united, determined, and self-reliant nation."

This manifesto was written by William O'Brien at the instance of Ford and Egan. It was signed by Parnell, Dillon, Sexton, Kettle, and Brennan, who were in Kilmainham Jail, and by Egan, the Treasurer of the League, at Paris. Dillon is said to have been strongly opposed to it. Parnell also was against its issue in the first instance. It was submitted to a vote of the leaders in Kilmainham and was agreed to by a majority. The minority then signed it. Davitt's name was appended to the document without his knowledge. He was in Portland Jail, and could not be communicated with. Later he expressed his strong disapproval. He had been in favour of such a course at a certain stage of the land struggle, but now " with the leaders of the movement the Chief Secretary's prisoners, and the new land system coming into operation, the no-rent shell fired from Kilmainham could only demoralize and could not explode. Its fuse had fallen out." " A strike against rent," Dillon is reported to have said, " cannot be carried out without the consent of the Bishops and priests. And the priests cannot support so barefaced a repudiation of debt as this. Rome would not let them."

The issue of the " No Rent " manifesto was followed immediately by a proclamation of the Irish Government, signed by Mr. Forster, declaring the Land League to be an illegal association, on the ground that it assumed to interfere with the Queen's subjects in the free exercise of their lawful rights, and especially to control the relations between landlords and tenants in Ireland.

It may be doubted whether this was a legal proceeding authorized by law. Two State prosecutions had failed to convict the Land League of a violation of the law, and there was no clause in the Coercion Act authorizing its suppression. But whether strictly legal or not, it was not matter for surprise that the Government should reply to Parnell in this way.

The " No Rent " manifesto was one of the gravest errors of Parnell's political career. There was something almost burlesque in the action of men, who had just been imprisoned, calling on the tenants in Ireland to abstain from payment of rent till they were released from jail. Nothing could justify such a course but its complete success. If the tenants as a body had acted upon it, this would have been a most striking demonstration of the strength of the movement and the power of its leaders, and would have placed the Government in grave difficulties and embarrassments. But it was not so. What Dillon had anticipated came about. The Catholic Bishops and priests rejected the policy and denounced it from their altars. The tenants as a body ignored it and paid their rents. There were some districts where it had effect. There were large bodies of the poorer tenants in the west of Ireland who, by the previous advice of the Land League, were already refusing to pay full rent and arrears without deductions, and who were now confirmed in their action by the new manifesto. The position in these districts was greatly aggravated. Landlords felt themselves justified in proceeding against these tenants for full rents and arrears, on the ground that the " No Rent " policy was being carried out. The agrarian war, therefore, was intensified and social disorder was increased, without any political advantage to the Nationalist cause. English opinion also was greatly incensed by the " No Rent " circular.

The arrest of Parnell and the leaders of the Land League was followed by the arrest of the local leaders of the League in the disturbed parts of Ireland, and the Coercion Act was used without scruple in aid of the landlords for collection of rents, however excessive they might be. The assurances given by the Government when the Act was under discussion were flung aside, and jails were filled with men, arrested not for suspicion of crime, but because they were prominent in agrarian disputes as to rent.   Evictions were multiplied.   Outrages increased in number.   Secret societies were stimulated, and took the place of the open agitation of the League.

CHAPTER XVII

COERCION IN MAYO AND GALWAY

IN January, 1882, at the suggestion of Mr. Forster, I paid a visit to Ireland. He wished me to form an opinion as to the then condition of the country, and the administration of the Coercion Act, with a view to discussion in the House of Commons. He thought it possible I might succeed him in the post of Chief Secretary, of which, as we now know, he was then contemplating resignation. I spent a few days at his house in the Phœnix Park. During this time I occupied myself in seeing as many persons as was possible of different parties and opinions in Dublin. My official position, as member of a Government, which was then enforcing coercion in Ireland, made it impossible for me to have any communication with representatives of the Nationalist Party; but I met men of all other grades of opinion.

The period was one of the greatest gloom in Ireland. Most of the prominent leaders of the Nationalist Party were in prison as suspects, under the Act of 1881. The manifesto issued by the Land League, advising tenants of Ireland to refrain from paying rent until their leaders were released, was still in circulation. In most parts of the country it had produced no effect. Where landlords made reasonable reductions of rent to meet the bad seasons they were obtaining their rents. Where arrears had accumulated, and landlords were pressing for their full rents, there was a firm determination, on the part of the tenants, to refuse payment. Many landlords, who would perhaps have been willing to deal generously with their tenants, were induced by the " No Rent " circular to press their claims to the utmost. Agrarian crimes and outrages were alarmingly frequent throughout the west and south of Ireland, and since the Coercion Act they had increased in number and gravity.   The Land Commission had recently begun its work of reducing rents.   The Irish leaders had advised the tenants not to apply for judicial rents in great numbers, but to wait till certain test cases should be decided. This advice, however, was not generally followed.   Immense numbers of tenants had made applications to the Court, and a small proportion of them had been dealt with.   The decisions of the Commission had already given more or less satisfaction to those who had applied.   On the other hand, many landlords were alarmed at these reductions, and were the less inclined to make any abatement of arrears of rent owing to them.   By threatening to insist on the payment of arrears they were able to prevent their tenants going into Court for a reduction of rent.

I found a growing feeling among moderate men, that the imprisonment, under the Coercion Act, of the leaders of the Irish Party, and of the local leaders in rural districts, was a grave mistake.   They held also that the shutting up without trial of so many hundreds of the local leaders under the plea that they were " village ruffians " was of little avail in quieting the country.   There was reason to believe, in spite of every care and precaution taken by Mr. Forster, that many persons were thus dealt with only to gratify the caprice of local authorities, or because they were obnoxious to the local landlords. After a few days spent in informing myself of opinions in Dublin, I went, at the suggestion of Mr. Forster, to the west of Ireland, with the object of personally seeing what was then considered the most disturbed part of the country.   I first visited Lord Dillon's property in Mayo and Roscommon.   It was one of the largest in the west of Ireland, consisting of 85,000 acres, with about 4500 tenants.   The holdings of the vast majority of these people did not average more than ten acres.   They were, in fact, labourers rather than farmers, migrating to England and Scotland during the summer months, either for harvest work, or for work in the brickfields, or other work which required additional hands during a part of the year.   They returned home in the autumn in time to dig their potatoes, and did not leave again till after the planting in the spring of the next year.   Their rent was wholly paid out of the earnings which they thus made.   They were an industrious and thrifty set of men, and though their standard of living was low, their children were healthy, and grew up into strong and vigorous men. The depression of agriculture and of trade in England had told very heavily on these men. Great numbers of them had been unable to find their usual employment in England, or had returned with very much less than the average of savings. These two causes had brought them into great difficulties, and they were in heavy arrears of rent. Lord Dillon's agent, Mr. Strickland, resided in a part of the family mansion, in the middle of one of the largest and most beautiful parks in the west of Ireland. The house, with the exception of that part of it occupied by the agent, was unfurnished and dilapidated, and no member of the Dillon family had resided there since the beginning of the nineteenth century. During these eighty years they had drawn their large rental from the district, and had spent it in England. No capital had ever been expended by them in improving their Irish property, unless it were money lent by the State for drainage, for which the tenants had paid interest. Every improvement which had gradually brought the land into cultivation from its original condition of waste bog had been effected by the tenants. All the houses and buildings had been erected by them.

When Arthur Young visited this district near the end of the eighteenth century the rental of this estate was £5000 a year. This had been gradually increased to £24,000, the nominal rental when I was there. This, it was stated, was far beyond the real value of the land, and could only be paid out of the earnings saved by the tenants, during their yearly visits to England. None of the functions of landowners, as generally understood and acted upon in England, had ever been performed by the Dillon family. They had not, however, followed the example of many other landowners, of this part of Ireland, in clearing their property of the smaller tenants, and turning the land into large holdings and grazing farms. Mr. Strickland told me that in average years, when the tenants could get employment in England, the rents were well paid without deduction, but that in bad years when the potatoes failed, or when employment fell short in England, rents could not be paid, and it was necessary either to make large abatements or to allow arrears to accumulate.

At the time of my visit to this district Lord Dillon had

offered no abatements of the rent and arrears then due. The agent justified this on the ground that the Land Commission would certainly make large reductions of rent in the future which he considered would be unjust, and, in fact, confiscation, and that the only way of meeting the " No Rent " manifesto was to insist upon the full payment of what was due. He said that the tenants were refusing to pay any rent, and he attributed this to the advice of the Land League. He admitted, however, that there had been a great failure of employment in England for these migratory labourers, owing to the great depression of agriculture, and the bad season of 1878–9, and, generally, to the depression of trade. He also allowed that the tenants had suffered much from the wet years of 1878, 1879, and 1880, when their potatoes had failed, and it had been impossible to dry the turf, and that, consequently, the pressure upon them was very great. He represented the district to be in a most lawless state. Notices were at the very time posted up calling a Land League meeting in the park itself, and a large body of police was expected for the purpose of suppressing this gathering. The contrast between this beautiful park and its deserted mansion and the small holdings and cabins, by which it was surrounded, was very striking.

From Lord Dillon's property I drove to Tuam. I had intended to stop at two or three of the small towns on the way for the purpose of making inquiries, but there was not a single person in them to whom Mr. Strickland or the police could give me a recommendation. It was alleged that the people of these small towns were even more disaffected than those of the country round them, and that I could not obtain from them any information of value.

At Tuam I made the acquaintance of the Catholic Archbishop, Dr. MacEvilly, and had an interesting conversation with him on the state of the country. He was very much opposed to the " No Rent " circular. He considered it most unjustifiable and immoral, and the cause of untold mischief ; but he held that a grave error had been committed by the Government in arresting the leaders of the Irish Party. He thought that Mr. Gladstone and Mr. Forster should have had greater faith in their own remedial measure, the Land Act. If this were supplemented by one dealing with arrears of rent, he had the utmost confidence the country would be quieted, but it would be necessary also to release all the suspects. From Tuam I drove to Athenry, where I met Mr. Blake (now Sir Henry Blake), then one of the chief inspectors of the Irish Constabulary, recently appointed by Mr. Forster, and later Governor of several colonies. I drove with him from Athenry to Loughrea.

At Loughrea I found myself in the centre of the Clanricarde property, which extends from Athenry to Portumna, a distance of nearly thirty miles, intermixed, however, with other properties such as those of Lord Dunsandle, Sir Henry Burke, and Mr. Lewis. The whole town of Loughrea belonged to Lord Clanricarde. My position, as the friend of Mr. Blake, made it most difficult for me to get any information from independent sources. It was not, however, impossible to pick up some facts, even in quarters friendly to the Government, and to the landlord interest, which threw much light on the condition of the district.

Lord Clanricarde's property consisted of about 52,000 acres, with 1900 tenants, and a rent roll of £25,000 a year. He had never visited the estate since he came into possession of it, in 1873, except once, when he came over from England to the funeral of his father. He had drawn this great income from it, without ever expending anything in the way of improvement. He had left uncompleted the great mansion commenced by his father in Portumna Park, a most beautiful and romantic demesne of great extent. He lived in London, but his tenants did not know his address. He never answered any letters forwarded to him through his agent.

Very grave complaints were made on the part of the people of Loughrea, even those favourable to the landlord party, of Lord Clanricarde's treatment of them. It was said that he refused to do anything which would lead to the improvement of the district, or to the prosperity of his tenants. In spite of bad times, and of the severe depression of agriculture, he had refused to make any general abatement of rent. He had, however, in response to a petition from the tenant farmers, promised not to press them unduly, but to allow what rent they were unable to pay to go to a suspense account, and to be treated as arrears. It was alleged that he had not kept even this meagre promise, and that the tenants were unduly pressed for rent. It is fair to add that the rents were not considered to be high, as compared with those of other land-lords in the district. This was claimed as a justification for not making general abatements in bad seasons. The passing of the Land Act of 1881, and the action of the Nationalist leaders in the issue of the " No Rent " circular, were also alleged as reasons for refusing any concessions.

Most of the other landlords of the district were also absentees. Of the few who resided there, some were represented to be very deficient in those personal qualities and habits which create respect and confidence among the people. In this respect, it was said, there was a very great contrast with what in past times had been the condition of the gentry in this part of Ireland. There could be no doubt, from what I heard in the district, that the landlords—whether through ignorance, as absentees, of the true condition of things, or other reasons—had not met their tenants during recent bad times in a reason-able spirit of concession. The tenants were pressed for rent which they could not possibly pay ; abatements were refused ; arrears of rent accumulated ; evictions were carried out, or were threatened, on a large scale ; resistance followed ; combinations, for the most part secret, took place ; outrages and crime became frequent—the work of individuals driven to despair, or inspired and incited by secret societies and Ribbonmen.

Nearly a hundred persons in this district alone had been arrested and sent to prison, under the Coercion Act of 1881, without trial—not, as I was assured, for complicity in actual crime, but for connection with combinations which insisted on abatements of rent. Among them were many of the leading tradesmen of Loughrea. Their arrest and detention had not quieted the district, but rather the reverse. The worst out-rages and murders took place after the arrest of these people. Meanwhile the great remedial Act of 1881 was not receiving a fair chance, as great numbers of the tenants were unable to go into Court for a reduction of rent, on account of the arrears which hung round their necks. I came to the conclusion that the question of arrears was a most pressing one, and that it was hopeless to expect the district to be quiet, until a measure were passed dealing with them.

My visit to the district of Loughrea was cut short by pro-ceedings of a very strange and exceptional character, which opened my eyes as to what was possible under the Coercion Act. Mr. Blake informed me that he had received instructions from the Government in Dublin to search the two towns of Athenry and Loughrea for arms and treasonable correspondence, which there was reason to believe would be found there. For this purpose a large body of military and police were collected in the neighbourhood, and he proposed to surround the two towns, at daybreak, and to carry out his task. Telegrams on this subject were continually passing between Mr. Blake and the authorities at Dublin Castle, and the morning was already fixed, when the proceedings were to take place. I felt that it was undesirable that a Member of the Government should be present on the occasion, the more so as Mr. Blake thought it not impossible that the proceedings would result in a serious disturbance. I therefore left Loughrea on the day previous to that on which this manœuvre was to be carried out.

The operation was carried out on the morning after my departure, in the manner intended. The two towns were surrounded by a large force of police, and a great number of houses were entered and searched by them. Nothing, however, was found of the smallest importance. This was only what was expected by Mr. Blake, for the cipher telegrams which he had received from the Dublin Castle authorities were so ill constructed—only a few of the most important words being in cipher—that nothing was more easy to an intelligent person than to make out the purport of the messages. The head of the post office at Loughrea was said to be in the interest of the Land League, and Mr. Blake thought it probable that the intentions of the Government would be discovered, and made known to the local Land League, and that consequently arrangements would be made to make the search fruitless. Whatever the cause, the operation was a failure, and no discoveries were made of arms or treasonable correspondence. That such proceedings could take place in any part of the United Kingdom, that they were submitted to without disturbance, and that no notice was taken of them by the English Press, impressed me not a little.

My observations in this district, added to the information and opinions I had obtained at Dublin, led me to the conclusion that the policy of coercion, as carried out under the Act of 1881, was a grave error, and that more especially mistaken had been the arrest and imprisonment, without trial, of the leaders of the Nationalist Party. These measures had greatly aggravated the position, and had prevented the great remedial measure, the Land Act, of the same year, from having effect in quieting the country. This Act also, however beneficial as regards the future, was defective as regards the past, in not having dealt with the question of accumulated arrears of rent. So long as these arrears hung round the necks of so large a proportion of the smaller tenants, placing them completely at the mercy of their landlords, and preventing them from going into the Land Court for a reduction of future rents, it was impossible to expect that the tenants would be satisfied, or that order would be restored. On the other hand, I was equally impressed by the mischief effected by the " No Rent " circular. It had greatly aggravated the ill-feeling between landlord and tenant. It was used as a justification by many landlords for refusing to make abatements, and for pressing for arrears.

On my return to Dublin I submitted these views to Mr. Forster. I suggested to him that the wise course would be at once to release from prison the suspects, and to apply to Parliament for a measure to relieve the tenants from a great part of the arrears of rent, which had accumulated during the bad seasons of 1878–80 ; and that subject to these measures it would be possible to support the landlords to the utmost power of the ordinary law against the " No Rent " movement. The agrarian outrages, I contended, had their origin in the agrarian difficulty, and this arose chiefly from the action of many of the landlords in pressing for arrears of excessive rent. I held that when this difficulty was removed, and when it was made clear and certain that the Government would, subject to this and to the Land Act of 1881, support the landlords in the collection only of just rents and reduced arrears, the " No Rent " circular would be completely defeated, and agrarian outrages would cease. As a first condition, however, to a better state of things, it was necessary that the suspects should be let out of prison, with the exception of those against whom there was certain evidence that they had been guilty of actual crime. I was unable to convince Mr. Forster of this view of the position. He said that the Government were quite unable to devote any considerable part of the time of the coming

Session to another Irish measure, such as one dealing with arrears of rent, and he disagreed with me absolutely as regards the policy of releasing the suspects. Indeed, he declined to discuss the question further with me. On my return to London I did not feel free to communicate my views to Mr. Gladstone.

My visit to Ireland, on this occasion, suggested to me for the first time grave doubts whether the system of administration of that country, known as the Castle Government, and its relations to the Imperial Parliament, were beneficial or defensible. The logical sequence of events seemed to me to be very distinct. The neglect of remedial measures for Ireland by the Imperial Parliament was due to want of knowledge, and want of time, and to failure to consult the majority of Irish Members. This neglect resulted in disturbances and outrages of an agrarian character. These outbreaks were seized on by the Irish officials as an excuse for resorting to their well-worn policy of coercion. Coercion was used locally, in the interest of landlords, to support their extreme rights, and, consequently, only aggravated the evil, and led to an increase of outrages. Parliament was then compelled to apply remedial measures; but the remedial measures lost a great part of their efficacy in appeasing public opinion in Ireland by the long delay, and by being connected with coercion. I came to the strongest conclusion adverse to coercion, and I determined that I would never myself be responsible, in the future, in any position connected with the government of Ireland, for renewing or administering a Coercion Act.

A few weeks after my visit to Loughrea, Lord Clanricarde's agent, Mr. Blake, was brutally murdered. He was driving on a Sunday morning into Loughrea with his wife and servant, on an Irish car. About half a mile from the town two shots were fired from behind a stone fence, and Mr. Blake and the driver were killed on the spot. Mr. Blake was seventy years of age, and had filled the post of agent of the Clanricarde estate for many years, and, until within a recent period, had not been unpopular in the district. Great complaints, however, were prevalent as to his conduct to the tenantry, during the two years previous to the murder. It was said that he was personally responsible for the refusal of Lord Clanricarde to make any abatements of rent, during the period of depres-

sion. His widow proposed to vindicate his memory by pub-
lishing his correspondence with his employer, with the
object of showing that he had received express instructions
to insist upon the payment of full rent, in spite of his own
advice that abatements should be made.   His employer,
on being informed of Mrs. Blake's intention, obtained an
injunction, in the Law Courts in Dublin, prohibiting her from
making any use of her late husband's correspondence with
him.[1]

[1] A part of this chapter was included in *Incidents of Coercion,* a journal
of visits to Ireland, published in 1888.

CHAPTER XVIII

THE KILMAINHAM NEGOTIATIONS

THE imprisonment of Parnell and other leaders of the Land League, and the suppression of the League itself, was followed by the creation of a new agency for carrying on the same work with far greater activity, and more bitter hostility to the Government, under the name of the Ladies' Land League. It was presided over by Miss Anna Parnell, who, with her sister, Miss Fanny Parnell, were much more extreme in their views and objects than their brother, the Irish leader. This Ladies' League had been founded by Davitt some time before, with a view to the possibility of the suppression of the main Land League, and was now ready to take its place. Though Davitt was in Portland Prison during the period of its activity, he made himself fully acquainted with its proceedings, when he was released, and must be accounted as a good authority on the subject. The following is his description of the work of the Ladies' Land League, between the arrest of Parnell and his release six months later.

" Boycotting, more systematic and relentless than had ever yet been practised, was the weapon with which the Ladies' Land League were to fight Forster, and to beat him. The responsible League leaders, now in prison, had, to some extent, checked, where that was possible, extreme boy-cotting. The line was drawn at violent intimidation. Out-rages were never encouraged except by eccentric characters, or wild men, who held no responsible position, and exercised no influence, while the meetings of the local branches gave some stability to the movement in rural districts, and offered opportunities for venting angry feeling by the channel of speeches and resolutions. Mr. Forster put these restraining powers and influences down, by imprisoning those who wielded them, with the result that for the one thousand or more local leaders whom he had arrested as suspects, double that number of less careful and less scrupulous men volunteered, in one form or another, to carry on the fight of the League, on more extreme lines, under the encouragement lent to their efforts by a body of patriotic ladies in Dublin, led by the sister of the imprisoned national leader.[1] . . .

" It was neither the business nor the desire of the Ladies' League to inquire too closely into the motives or methods of those who, driven from open combination and public meetings, resorted to such expedients as were available in carrying on the fighting policy of the movement. That was Mr. Forster's doing, and not that of Miss Parnell. Her purpose and policy were to render Ireland ungovernable by coercion, and this she and her lieutenants succeeded completely in doing. . . . The system of operations of the Ladies' League was perfect in its way. Thanks to the continued generous help from America, and also from Australia, they were supplied with abundance of money by Mr. Egan from Paris. Agents passed to and fro between the Treasurer of the League and the new League government. Organizers of both sexes were employed to distribute copies of the ' no-rent ' manifesto throughout Ireland, to visit the new local leaders, to organize opposition at process-serving and evictions, and to encourage and stimulate resistance and intimidation. The evicted families were looked after as usual, and the relatives of suspects were supported by grants from the central office. In fact, under the nose of Mr. Forster, and in utter defiance of his most strenuous application of the arbitrary powers at his disposal, everything recommended, attempted, or done, in the way of defeating the ordinary law and asserting the unwritten law of the League, except the holding of meetings, was more systematically carried out, under the direction of the Ladies' executive, than by its predecessors in existence and authority. The result was more anarchy, more illegality, more outrages, until it began to dawn on some of the official minds that the imprisonment of the male leaders had only made confusion worse confounded for Dublin Castle, and made the country infinitely more ungovernable under the

[1] Miss Anna Parnell.

sway of their lady successors. . . . Tenants going into the land courts were denounced. Secret League meetings were encouraged." [1]

It was stated that between October, 1881, when Parnell was arrested, and April, 1882, when he was liberated, no less a sum than £70,000 was expended by the Ladies' Land League in the manner above described.

In spite of all these efforts, it is certain that the "No Rent" movement was a failure. The Bishops and priests used their influence to defeat it. They were confirmed in this by a letter addressed to the Irish Bishops by the Pope (Leo X), in which the League and its policy were censured, and the people were admonished " not to cast aside the obedience due to their lawful rulers." " We have confidence," the rescript said, " in the justice of the men who are at the head of the State, and who certainly have great practical experience combined with prudence in civil affairs."

The Irish Bishops issued a manifesto in accordance with these injunctions from the Pope. Forster, in his speeches, in defence of his policy, claimed credit for having defeated the " No Rent " manifesto by the use of the Coercion Act. The better explanation seems to be that where the rents were low, or where reasonable reductions were made to meet the bad seasons, the tenants, whether under the influence of their spiritual advisers, or of their own instincts, paid no attention to the "No Rent" circular, but paid the rents which they admitted were justly due. There were some districts where this was not the case; but, as a general rule, the "No Rent" manifesto was a failure. This was admitted by Parnell and other leaders of the League. It is equally certain that the advice of the League to tenants to avoid the Land Courts was not adopted. The tenants resorted to the new Courts by thousands. Twelve Sub-Commissions were appointed by Mr. Forster, each consisting of two members, and they were hard at work hearing applications. They made reductions of rent which averaged about 23 per cent.

When Parliament met early in February, 1882, Mr. P. J. Smyth raised the question of Home Rule in a most eloquent speech, on an amendment to the Address. It led to a short discussion. It was important because Mr. Gladstone, for the

[1] *The Fall of Feudalism*, by Michael Davitt, p. 340-1.

first time, in the House of Commons, indicated a leaning in that direction : " With regard to local government in Ireland," he said, " and local government in general, and its immeasurable benefits, and to the manner in which Parliament is at present overcharged by a too great centralization of duties, I, for one, will hail with satisfaction and delight any measure of local government for Ireland, or for any portion of the country, provided only that it conforms to this one condition, that it does not break down or impair the supremacy of the Imperial Parliament." He discussed some of the proposals for Home Rule, and pointed out that neither Mr. Butt nor his followers had ever produced a definite and practical scheme. Mr. David Plunket, on behalf of the Conservative Party, at once seized upon Mr. Gladstone's statement, and declared that it was most dangerous to hold up a signal for the renewal of the agitation for Home Rule, which had been steadily resisted by both parties. The motion was quickly rejected by 97 to 37 votes. The House, in fact, was not disposed to debate the question. Members were eager to enter upon a discussion raised by Mr. Justin McCarthy, on behalf of the Irish Party. His motion arraigned the policy of Mr. Forster along the whole line of his action as Irish Secretary. It led to a debate of four nights, in which the case against Forster was ably put forward by McCarthy, Sexton, Dwyer Gray, and Redmond, on the part of the Irish Members, and by Gibson and Plunket, on the part of the Tory Party, from a very different point of view, but almost equally hostile to Forster's administration.

They were replied to by Forster in a speech of two and a half hours in length. Mr. Forster said that without the Protection Act (as he always called it, in preference to Coercion) law in Ireland would have been powerless ; industry would have been impossible ; liberty would not have existed. He accused Parnell of aiming at the abolition of all rent, with the object of making the tenants the owners of their farms ; and of promising tenants whose interests in their farms were sold, that the Land League would keep the farms vacant by means of boycotting. This meant personal violence, destruction of their means of living, and deprivation of the necessaries of life. The Government was obliged to arrest Parnell, unless they were prepared to allow the Land League to govern Ireland, and to determine what rents should be paid, what shops should be left open, what men should be allowed to buy, what tenants were to be permitted to take advantage of the Land Courts, what decisions of the Law Courts should be respected and what laws obeyed. The Government had to arrest the local leaders, and could not therefore, leave the central leaders at large. . . .

As regards the suppression of the Land League the Government had to be convinced that it was an intimidating organization, and that active membership of it was a crime punishable by law, being an act of intimidation, and an incitement thereto. He quoted cases of outrages. He considered that some of the Irish Members were morally responsible for them. They had happened in consequence of the incitement and advice to the effect that those who paid rent would be visited with penalties. There had been no attempt of the leaders to prevent these outrages—no stepping forward to disown them. He claimed that there had been some improvement as a result of putting the Act in force. The figures of outrages lately had been better, and there had been less boycotting. Tenants, he said, were discovering that they had been misled by Parnell. The Coercion Act was beginning to tell. He could hardly have hoped a few weeks ago to be able to meet Parliament without asking at once for further powers ; but matters had improved, and if there was less intimidation it might be possible to revert to the ordinary law.

Turning, then, to the complaints of landlords against the Land Act, he said that the worst cases of over-renting had gone first into the Land Courts ; but he admitted that it would turn out that rents in Ireland were higher than the House had expected, not higher than he himself had expected from information in his possession. The pull of the market had been in favour of the landowners for the last hundred years, and there was consequently greater justification for the Land Act than some of them had expected. There was no foundation for the statement that the Government had made concessions to agitation. Those who conducted the agitation were the greatest foes of those who proposed remedial legislation. He thought that agitation would soon be starved out by the Land Act. He concluded by saying that he was "not altogether without hope and faith in the Irish people."

Mr. Sexton, in reply, explained at length the objects of the Land League. He denied that it aimed at the abolition of all rents without compensation. Its object was to put an end to rack-renting, and landlord oppression, and ultimately to buy out the landlords at twenty years' purchase of the Poor Law valuation. He defended boycotting. The tenants, if dealt with one by one, were isolated and powerless. To obviate this, it was necessary that they should band together, and offer such rents only as enabled them to live in ordinary times. The pivot of the whole system on which landlord power in Ireland rested was the hungry competition for land. Whenever a farm fell vacant, no matter through what injustice, some miserable creature driven to his wits' end for means of living, was willing to come forward and offer whatever rent the landlord asked. The Land League established the rule, based on voluntary action, that the tenants should act together in the matter of rent. When any man acted against the interest of others, and preferred his own selfish ends to those of the community, they were justified in discountenancing such a man by refusing to work for him, or to take a farm from him. Were they to suffer sneaks and traitors to perpetuate a bad and tyrannical system ?

Boycotting, he maintained, when confined to social discountenance and to negative action, was a method not only necessary to the success of the movement, but largely justified on grounds of expediency and even morals. The Land League had as little to do with boycotting, which included outrage, as with the transit of Venus. The speeches at Land League meetings had, on numerous occasions, denounced outrages and violence. Parnell himself had, on many occasions, done the same. In his speech at Wexford he concluded by saying : " We are warned by history that we must fight within the lines of the Constitution." He had himself made one hundred speeches between May and October. He was arrested because of one line in a single speech made at the torchlight demonstration in Dublin. He was proud to admit that he had signed the " No Rent " circular when in prison at Kilmainham. As a punishment for this he was condemned to seven days' solitary confinement and to indignities and pains which he would hesitate to describe. The " No Rent " circular was due not to the arrest of Parnell, but to the suppression of the Land League. At the very moment when the League was preparing hundreds of test cases for the Land Court the Government arrested all its staff. He defended the policy of test cases. Their conviction was that when test cases to the number of 1000 or 1200 were decided on, there would be a sufficiency of record decisions, to enable landlords and tenants to dispense with this costly litigation. The motion was rejected. The minority of 30 included no English Members. In the enforced absence of some members in jail, and of others on a mission to America, it represented the strength of the Parnellite section.

While the main attack in the House of Commons was from the Irish Members in the interest of the tenants, in the House of Lords the landlords were the aggrieved party seeking redress. Lord Donoughmore, an Irish landowner, moved for a Committee to inquire into the working of the Land Act of 1881. He complained that the Act had been passed by Parliament, on representations by the Government that it would have very little effect in reducing the rents of average landowners. In its actual working, he showed that large reductions of rent had been made by the Sub-Commissions, and had been approved by the head Commission in almost every case. The reductions had averaged 23 per cent. He complained that the Sub-Commissioners, twenty-four in number, were mere partisans appointed for party purposes, and were unfair in their awards as against the landowners. The motion was opposed by Lord Carlingford, Lord Spencer, and the Lord Chancellor (Selborne), on the ground that it was wholly unprecedented to inquire into the working of an Act so recently passed. Lord Carlingford predicted that the Act would ultimately be found to have increased the security of property in Ireland. On the other hand, Lord Lansdowne, in a lengthy and powerful speech, insisted that the Act was not being administered in accordance with the intentions of Parliament, and Lord Cairns contended that, if the motion was unprecedented, so also was the Act itself. It had proved to be a measure for strangling landlords, and alienating the fee simple of their property. The motion was carried by 96 to 53.

The Government met the rebuff of the Peers by declining to take any part in the proceedings of the Committee, or to give it any assistance. They also contended that the motion amounted to a vote of censure on the Act of the previous year.

In this view, Mr. Gladstone gave notice of a counter resolution in the House of Commons, to the effect that a Parliamentary inquiry into the working of the Land Act would tend to defeat its object, and would be injurious to the interest of good government in Ireland. Four days were spent in discussing this motion. Mr. Gladstone, on moving it, maintained that the confidence of the Irish people in the Act would be vitally impaired if there was any tampering with it. It was to the Act that the Government looked mainly for the restoration of law and order in Ireland.

Mr. Sexton, on behalf of the Irish Party, demanded inquiry into the working of the Land Act. He believed it could not be made effective except through inquiry leading up to further remedial legislation. A Committee of the House of Lords would be better than none at all. He went at length into the defects of the Act, the arrears question, the non-inclusion of leaseholders, the imperfect definition of the tenants' interest, and other matters, and ended by saying that the Irish Party would vote with the Tories against the motion of the Government. In spite of this, the motion was carried by 303 against 255 votes—39 of the Irish Members voted with the minority. It was the first occasion in that Parliament, on which the Irish Party were found, in a party division, voting in the same Lobby with the Tories. Thenceforward through the remainder of the Parliament this was their general course, by way of protest against the Coercion Act of 1881, and of its successor of 1882.

A little later Mr. Forster himself began to admit in his correspondence with Mr. Gladstone that his statements in the debate on the Address, and in the more recent discussion, were over-sanguine. On April 7th he wrote to Mr. Gladstone to the effect that while there were some good signs, such as that the November rents had been generally paid, that there was no longer open resistance to the law, that the Land League had been defeated in preventing any rent being paid, and that there was less boycotting, yet there were exceptions, important and frequent, mainly in Connaught, and in poor districts elsewhere, where the arrears were hopeless. He showed also that there had been an increase of agrarian crime of the more serious kinds. He attributed this to two causes—(1) the fierce passions evoked by the "No Rent" struggle for which the Land League leaders were mainly responsible; and (2) the immunity of crime from punishment.

The course he proposed was (1) new and increased powers to try agrarian offences by special commissions without juries; (2) making districts contribute for special police protection; (3) giving compensation for injury to persons as in the case of injury to property; (4) giving power to the police to arrest persons at night under suspicious circumstances. He also proposed a renewal of the Coercion Act of 1881.

"Can we let the Act expire? I dare not face the coming autumn and winter without it. The Act does not deter murders through fear of punishment, but it enables us to lock up persons suspected of them."

Nothing was said in this letter as to an Arrears Bill, or other measures of a remedial character. His policy was, in fact, a continuance of the existing Coercion Act, strengthened by the abolition of juries in agrarian cases and by greatly increased powers to the police and magistrates.

The reply to this of Mr. Gladstone has not been made public, but a few days later he wrote to Mr. Forster the important letter of April 12th, printed in Lord Morley's work, which shows how far he had already travelled in the direction of a policy of Home Rule for Ireland.

" About local government for Ireland, the ideas which more and more establish themselves in my mind are such as these. Until we have serious responsible bodies to deal with as in Ireland every plan we frame comes to Irishmen, say what we may, as an English plan. As such it is probably condemned. At best it is a one-sided bargain, which binds us and not them. . . .

" If we say we must postpone the question till the state of the country is more fit for it, I should answer that the least danger is going forward at once. It is liberty alone which fits men for liberty. This proposition, like many others in politics, has its bounds; but it is far safer than the counter doctrine—wait till they are fit."

He went on to urge the importance of " relieving Great Britain from the enormous weight of the government of Ireland, unaided by the people, and from the hopeless contradiction in which we stand; while we give a Parliamentary representation, hardly effective for anything but mischief, we refuse the local institutions of self-government which it pre-supposes, and on which alone it can have a sound and healthy basis."[1]

Here we have the main principle of Home Rule asserted. On the same day, April 12th, Mr. Forster wrote a yet more gloomy account of the state of things in Ireland :

" My six special magistrates all bring me very bad reports. They are confirmed by constabulary reports. The immunity from punishment is spreading like a plague. I fear it will be impossible to avoid very strong and immediate legislation."

There were many indications about this time that public opinion in England was dissatisfied with the administration of the Coercion Act, and was convinced as to its failure.

The Pall Mall Gazette, under the inspiration of its then editor, Mr. John Morley, had for some time past written strongly against the continuance of coercion, and had recommended the removal of Mr. Forster. Mr. Morley's views were believed to be those of Mr. Chamberlain and Sir Charles Dilke, who were strongly opposed to Mr. Forster's policy. Even the Tory organ, *The Quarterly Review,* spoke in a sneering way of the arrest of cart-loads of suspects.

Everything, therefore, tended to a change of policy, and it must have been obvious that it would necessitate a change in the personnel of the Irish Government. Lord Cowper had already tendered his resignation of the post of Lord-Lieutenant—for private reasons, it was said—and only held on till new arrangements were complete. Mr. Gladstone induced Lord Spencer, who had previously held the post, and who was then a member of his Cabinet, as President of the Council, to succeed Lord Cowper, retaining his position in the Cabinet. This, we are told, was suggested by Mr. Forster, though it is quite certain that his position would be very different if the Lord-Lieutenant was in the Cabinet. The administration of Ireland would practically be taken out of his hands and placed in those of the Lord-Lieutenant.

While these arrangements were being made important events were being hatched in Kilmainham Jail. Parnell had been interned there for six months. The treatment he was subjected to was most lenient, consistently with his being confined within the prison walls. He had his separate apartments, which were large and cheerful. Food was provided from outside. He was amply supplied with literature. He could associate with other suspects there. Permission was readily granted to him to see his friends, and to communicate with them by letter. But, in spite of all these relaxations of prison rules, the deprivation of liberty to a man of Parnell's age and temperament must have been increasingly irksome and even intolerable. It is probable that it had a permanent bad effect on his health, and contributed to his premature end. I was myself greatly struck by the change in the appearance of Parnell on his release from prison. He looked haggard and in bad health, and he was never again the same strong and healthy man he had been before his imprisonment.

Parnell was also profoundly dissatisfied with the action of the Ladies' Land League during his absence from head-quarters. He recognized that the state of the country had become deplorable, and was going from bad to worse. Mr. Barry O'Brien says: "The country was drifting out of his hands and drifting into the hands of reckless and irresponsible men and women, whose wild operations would, he felt sure, sap his authority and bring disaster to the national move-ment. It was quite time for him to grasp the reins of power once more, and to divert the course of events. His release from prison became, in fact, a matter of paramount im-portance."[1]

Everything therefore pointed to the necessity for making an effort to get out of jail. Parnell had come to the con-clusion that the existence of large arrears of rent on the part of the vast body of the poorer tenants was the main cause of disturbance leading to murder and outrage. He recognized that the "No Rent" manifesto had completely failed, and that tenants by thousands were rushing into the Land Court. The poorer tenants, however, were prevented doing so by their indebtedness for arrears which the land-lords insisted on. He had, while in jail, drafted a Bill dealing with this, and other defects of the Land Act of 1881, namely, the exclusion of leaseholders, the imperfect protection of the tenants' interest, and the insufficiency of the purchase clauses. The Bill thus drafted was introduced, at his instance by one of his followers, at the beginning of

---

[1] *Life of Parnell*, I, 235.

the Session, and stood for second reading on April 26th. The Bill offered the opportunity for a negotiation with the Government. Chamberlain and some other members of the Cabinet were known to be hostile to the Coercion Act. Davitt says that " this was a vital turning-point in Parnell's career. Hitherto he had been in everything but name a revolutionary reformer. He now entered, as an opportunist statesman, upon a phase of a purely political movement." Without any consultation with his colleagues in Kilmainham, or beyond its walls, and without even informing any of them of his intentions, he entered into negotiation with the Government, using as his intermediary Captain O'Shea, a Home Rule Member of the Shaw section, and a personal friend, but not one of his followers.

Captain O'Shea had several interviews with Forster, and by his leave, with Parnell in Kilmainham, and also with Mr. Chamberlain, and later with Mr. Gladstone.

On April 10th Parnell asked the permission of the Irish Government to leave Kilmainham for a few days on *parole*, in order that he might visit at Paris his sister, Mrs. Thomson, whose son was dying there. Permission was granted to him, as it had been to other suspects for similar reasons. On his way to Paris he stopped for a day in London, and met there Mr. Justin McCarthy, and had a long conversation with him on the state of Ireland.

It does not appear that he told McCarthy that he intended to enter into negotiation with the Government. But the next morning he saw Captain O'Shea. It seems to be certain that he authorized O'Shea to communicate with members of the Government. At all events O'Shea wrote to Mr. Gladstone and Mr. Chamberlain, suggesting the feasibility of some arrangement by which the suspects might be released, and an Arrears Bill passed. Mr. Gladstone replied that he would communicate with Forster on the important and varied matter in O'Shea's letter. " I am very sensible of the spirit in which you write. . . . The end in view is of vast moment, and assuredly no resentment, personal prejudice, or false shame, or other impediment extraneous to the matter itself will prevent the Government from treading in the paths which may most safely lead to the pacification of Ireland."

Mr. Chamberlain also replied in a most judicious letter.

Mr. Gladstone forwarded O'Shea's letter to Forster, who, in his reply, was sympathetic as to the Arrears question, but did not see his way to the release of Parnell and the other suspects. " The difficulties and the dangers," he said, " of dealing with the Arrears question are very great . . . but we must interfere. The evictions in Mayo and elsewhere are becoming very serious, and many of the poorer tenants and many of those who are most rack-rented feel it useless to resort to the Land Court. The helpless, miserable position of these poor men is the foundation of the agitation." [1] He suggested a scheme for dealing with arrears. It was to be based on the voluntary and combined application of both landlords and tenants ; and the advance from the Government was to be by loan and not by gift. The scheme would no more have been a settlement of the question than that of the Act of 1881.

As regards the release of the leading suspects, Forster said : " I expect no slight pressure for their immediate and unconditional release. . . . My own view is clear. I adhere to our statements that we detain these suspects solely for prevention, and not for punishment. We will release them as soon as we think it safe to do so."

There were three events, he said, in which it might be effected : (1) The country being quieted ; (2) the passing of a fresh Act (i.e. a new Coercion Act), which might warrant the attempt to govern Ireland when the suspects were released ; (3) an assurance that Parnell and his friends, if released, would not attempt in any manner to intimidate men into obedience to their unwritten law. " Without the fulfilment of one or other of these conditions I believe their release would make matters worse than they are. At any rate, I could not, without this fulfilment, administer affairs as Irish Secretary with advantage." [1]

It will be seen that this was an ultimatum from Forster, to which he strictly adhered in the negotiations which followed, and which resulted in his resignation.

[1] *Life of W. E. Forster*, II, 425.

CHAPTER XIX

ON April 22nd there was a meeting of the Cabinet, specially called to consider the Irish question. Forster crossed the Irish Channel the previous night to attend it. It was his last journey as Irish Secretary. Later, on the trial of the murderers of Lord Frederick Cavendish and Mr. Burke, it transpired that the band of assassins had lain in wait, at the railway station at Dublin, with the determination to murder Forster on that evening. They must have obtained information as to his movements, and fully expected to find him at the station. By a most fortunate accident, on the suggestion of his private secretary that they should dine at the Yacht Club, at Kingstown, before going on board the steamer, instead of at Dublin, they took an earlier train, and escaped the fate which a few days later befell his successor as Irish Secretary.

At the Cabinet the case of the release of Parnell was presented by Chamberlain, who had been in personal communication with O'Shea. In spite of Forster's objections, the Cabinet agreed to Chamberlain negotiating further with O'Shea. On the same day, April 22nd, Parnell arrived in London on his return from Paris, and met O'Shea, who expressed to him the hope that, as the result of negotiations then going on, he and the other suspects might be permanently released. " Never mind the suspects," said Parnell ; " get the question of the arrears satisfactorily adjusted, and the contribution made not a loan, but a gift on compulsion. The Tories have now adopted my creed as to a peasant proprietary. The great object to be attained is to stay evictions by an Arrears Bill." [1]

[1] Captain O'Shea's speech, *Hansard*, May 15th, 1882.

After the return of Parnell to Kilmainham, O'Shea had further interviews with Chamberlain and Forster, and then went over to Ireland, by leave of the latter, and visited Parnell in Kilmainham. A letter was then written by Parnell to O'Shea, for the purpose of being shown to Forster and Chamberlain.

"I desire," he wrote, "to impress upon you the absolute necessity of a settlement of the Arrears question, which will leave no remaining sore connected with it behind, and which will enable us to show the smaller tenantry that they have been treated with justice and some generosity.

"If the Arrears question be settled upon the lines indicated by us, I have every confidence—a confidence shared by my colleagues—that the exertions which we would be able to make, strenuously and unremittingly, would be effective in stopping outrages and intimidation of all kinds.

"As regards permanent legislation of an ameliorative character, I may say that the views which you always shared with me as to the admission of lease-holders to the fair-rent clauses of the Act, are more confirmed than ever. So long as the flower of the Irish peasantry are kept outside the Act, there cannot be a permanent settlement of the Land Laws, which we all so much desire. I should also strongly hope that some compromise might be arrived at this Session with regard to the amendment of the tenure clause. It is unnecessary for me to dwell upon the enormous advantages to be derived from the full extension of the purchase clauses which now seem practically to have been adopted by all parties.

"The accomplishment of the programme I have sketched would, in my judgment, be regarded by the country as a practical settlement of the Land question, and would, I feel sure, enable us to co-operate cordially for the future of the Liberal Party in forwarding Liberal principles ; so that the Government, at the end of the Session, would, seeing the state of the country, feel themselves thoroughly justified in dispensing with future coercive measures."

It will be seen that the last part of this letter was practically a new proposal for a wider agreement with the Government, which was not adopted. Mr. Forster has given an account of his interview with O'Shea when Parnell's letter was shown to him :

"After carefully reading the letter, I said to O'Shea, ' Is that all that Parnell would be inclined to say ? ' He said, ' What more do you want ? Doubtless I could supplement it.' I said, ' It comes to this, that upon our doing certain things he will help us to prevent outrages,' or words to that effect. He again said, ' How can I supplement it ? '—referring, I imagine, to different measures. I did not feel justified in giving him my own opinion, which might be interpreted to be that of the Cabinet. So I said, ' I had better show the letter to Mr. Gladstone, and to one or two others.' He said, ' Well, there may be faults of expression, but the thing is done. If these words will not do, I must get others, but what is obtained is '—and here he used most remarkable words—' that the conspiracy which has been used to get up boycotting and outrages will now be used to put them down, so that there will be a union with the Liberal Party.' And, as an illustration of how the first of these results was to be obtained, he said that Parnell hoped to make use of Sheridan, and to get him back from abroad, as he would be able to help him to put down the conspiracy (or agitation, I am not sure which word was used), as he knew all its details in the trial." [1]

It is to be observed on this conversation, as repeated by Forster, that it is quite impossible to believe that anything which Parnell had said to O'Shea justified the quotation from the former, that the "conspiracy which had been used to get up boycotting and outrages will now be used to put them down." The words may have been correctly quoted by Forster, though O'Shea denied that he had spoken them ; but if he had, they could not have been the words used by Parnell, who was far too careful and precise in his use of language to have made such a compromising admission. Parnell, in his cross-examination before the Special Commission, denied that he had ever made such a statement. The Commission did not impute it to him in their report, as they would undoubtedly have done if they believed he had made it. So far as one can reasonably conclude from the whole circumstances the words, as quoted, were never uttered by Parnell.

Parnell's letter was forwarded by Forster to Mr. Gladstone, together with the account of the conversation with O'Shea. "I expected little from these negotiations," was Forster's

[1] *Life of Forster*, II, 436.

comment on the whole transaction. But Mr. Gladstone was highly gratified. " This," he wrote to Forster, " is a *hors d'œuvre*, which we had no right to expect, and I rather think have no right at present to accept." He was doubtless referring in this to the new proposals of Parnell for a wider settlement of the whole Land question.

Meanwhile, on the 26th, Mr. Redmond's Bill had come on for discussion in the House of Commons, and led to an important debate. The Bill proposed to deal with four principal subjects, by way of amendment of the Land Act of 1881, namely, " Arrears of excessive rent," " The admission of leaseholders to the benefit of the Land Court," " The amendment of the tenure clauses," so as to make it certain that the improvements effected by tenants and their predecessors in title would not be excluded in assessing the rents, and " The extension of the purchase clauses by the advance from the State of the whole of the purchase money."

It must be repeated that all these four main points had been urged by the Irish Party in amendments to the Land Act of 1881. Agreement might then have been arrived at. They have all later been conceded by Parliament. There was now another opportunity of agreement. So far from finding fault with the Government for coming to an arrangement with Parnell, it seems to me that they erred in not going far enough, and not taking the opportunity of settling the whole question.

In the debate on Redmond's Bill, Mr. Gladstone, having in view the communications already opened with Parnell, spoke in most conciliatory terms. He welcomed the Bill as an authentic expression of the desire of the Irish Party to make the working of the Land Act an effectual security for the peace of the country. The Government could not, however, support the second reading, because they still thought, as they did, when they opposed the Lords' Committee, that the tenure clauses of the Land Act ought not to be reopened and disturbed. He admitted that the recent decision of the Irish Judges did not carry out the intentions of Parliament; but the scope of the discrepancy was not so great as to justify an immediate reopening of the question.

As regards the purchase clauses, he pointed out that a notice of motion had been given by Mr. W. H. Smith, when a proposal of importance would doubtless be made, which it was not expedient to anticipate. With respect to land under lease, the Government was not prepared to interfere with covenants, or to place leaseholders in the same position as yearly tenants. With regard to arrears, the Government was willing to recognize the duty of legislating at an early date, on a basis which should be impartial and in accordance with public opinion in Ireland.

The Irish Members, through Sexton, Healy, Shaw, and others, expressed themselves as satisfied with the latter part of the statement. Mr. Forster agreed with Mr. Gladstone as to the necessity for dealing with arrears of rent, and admitted that it was most urgent. Mr. Gibson, on behalf of the Tory Party, expressed no hostility to this part of the speech. The debate was adjourned without a division.

On May 1st the subject was again brought before the Cabinet. The letter of Parnell of the 28th was laid before them. Chamberlain appears to have again taken a leading part in insisting on the release of Parnell, and the principal Land League leaders. The Cabinet was in favour of this course. Forster alone stood firm against it, and was irreconcilable. The Cabinet was adjourned till the next day, in the hope that some *modus vivendi* might be found, which would avoid the resignation of Forster.

The Cabinet met again the next day at twelve. Mr. Gladstone then read a memorandum, on which, with one exception, they agreed :

" The Cabinet are of opinion that the time has now arrived when, with a view to the interests of law and order in Ireland, the three Members of Parliament who have been imprisoned on suspicion, since October last, should be immediately released ; and that the list of suspects should be examined, with a view to the release of all persons not believed to be associated with crimes. They decided at once to announce to Parliament their intention to prepare, as soon as necessary business will permit, a Bill to strengthen the ordinary laws of Ireland for the security of life and property, while reserving their discretion with regard to the Life and Property Protection Act of 1881, which, however, they do not at present think it will be possible to renew, if a favourable state of affairs shall prevail in Ireland."

The one exception was Mr. Forster, who resigned his office. Mr. Gladstone, in reply to his letter of resignation, wrote :

" I have received your letter with much grief, but on this it would be selfish to expatiate. I have no choice ; followed, or not followed, I must go on."

On Tuesday, May 2nd, after the crucial Cabinet, Mr. Gladstone announced in the House of Commons the resignation of Lord Cowper and Mr. Forster. He stated that directions had been sent to Ireland for the release forthwith of the three Members of the House who had been imprisoned since October last. The list of persons similarly imprisoned would be carefully examined, with a view to the release, in accordance with like principles of consideration, of all persons who were not believed to be associated with the commission of crime. This measure, he said, had been taken by the Government, after gathering all the information which it was in their power to extract, either through the medium of debate in the House, or by availing themselves of such communications as were tendered to them by Irish representatives, and this, without the slightest reference to their previous relations to those Irish Members, but simply with relation to what they believed to be the public interest.

He disclaimed that the release was in any way the result of a negotiation. " It is an act done without any negotiation, promise, or engagement whatever." " It has entailed upon us a lamentable consequence—the resignation of Mr. Forster, who would make his personal explanation on Thursday, after obtaining the sanction of the Queen to his resignation." [1] He then proceeded to state the intentions of the Government as regards legislation. It was not at present in contemplation to renew the Coercion Act of 1881. They proposed, as soon as possible, to introduce a Bill for strengthening the ordinary laws in defence of private rights, and for the enforcement of law, and the maintenance of peace and tranquillity in Ireland. It would be proceeded with as soon as the new rules of procedure of the House had been concluded. An Arrears Bill would also be proceeded with.

The Government was taunted by the Opposition with a change of policy, but generally there was a disposition to adjourn discussion until Mr. Forster should make his personal

[1] *Hansard*, May 2nd, 1882.

explanation.   In answer to a challenge as to the release
generally of the suspects, Mr. Gladstone said that, in the belief
of the Government, it was conducive to the interests of law
and order and security in Ireland.

Mr. Sexton, on behalf of the Irish Party, said: " It might
be true that the present policy of the Government was in
condemnation of that they had pursued in October last.   He
was not concerned to drive the comparison home.   It was
enough for him if the policy they now foreshadowed was a
better policy for his country than that which they had adopted
before, and he most certainly believed it was so. . . . Mr.
Gladstone, in his long and varied life, had never spoken truer
words than when he said that the release of the suspects
would lead to the advancement of law and order in Ireland.
Every day that they maintained these men in prison was
a day added to the inflamed passions and deepening hatred
towards the British Government which existed in the minds
of the Irish people."

Two days later, on May 4th, Mr. Forster made his promised
personal explanation of his resignation.   Mr. Gladstone,
he said, had rightly stated that the reason for his resignation
was that he did not think it right to share the responsibility
for the release of the three Members.   He would gladly have
done so, if he thought it right.   " According to the repeated
promises I have made to the House, we have only detained
persons in prison without trial, for the purpose of prevention
of crime, and not for the purpose of punishment.   That is
why I am opposed to their unconditional release at this moment.
. . . I believe it will tend to the encouragement of crime. . . ."

He then proceeded to justify the arrest of the three Members.
At this moment a most dramatic scene occurred.   Parnell
entered the House and took his seat there, confronting Forster,
his accuser and judge.   He was greeted by a long burst of
cheering from the Irish Members.   After this interruption,
Mr. Forster continued his explanation.   The three Members,
he said, were not arrested simply for illegal agitation.   " It
was our duty to arrest them upon what we considered reasonable suspicion of the commission of a crime punishable by
law, being either an act of intimidation or an incitement
thereto.   Now, it is a common notion that Mr. Parnell was
arrested merely for obstructing the action of the Land Act. . . .

The real reason why these gentlemen were arrested, and why many others were arrested, was because they were trying to carry out their will—their unwritten law, as they often called it—and to carry it out by working the ruin and the injury of the Queen's subjects by intimidation of one kind or another. If Mr. Parnell had not been placed in Kilmainham, he would very quickly have become in reality what he was called by many of his friends—the King of Ireland. I do not for a moment say that he, or the other two Members, incited to outrage and the intimidation of special individuals ; but what they did was, to my mind, far more dangerous than that. They organized and instituted a system of intimidation of individuals generally, punishing them for obeying the law of the land, and doing what they had a right to do, and very often what it was their duty to do. . . . Under what circumstances could I have approved their release ? I will at once admit that it was impossible to detain them for ever. . . . I would have released them as soon as I obtained security that the law of the land would no longer be set at naught and trampled under foot by them. There are three conditions on either of which I could have considered their release safe ; but, to my mind, not one of the three conditions has been fulfilled. There should have been a public promise on their part, or Ireland quiet, or the acquisition of fresh powers by the Government. . . . What do I mean by a public promise ? I mean a public undertaking or promise to make no further attempt to set up their will, or rather their law, against the law of the land, and, under no circumstances, to aid or abet or instigate intimidation to prevent men from doing what they had a right to do. Mr. Parnell has in no way disowned his famous Ennis speech, the system of intimidation, of tabooing people, and ruining people, because they did not do what he was trying to make them do. What I want is the avowal of a change. . . . A surrender is bad, but a compromise or arrangement is worse. I think we may remember what the Tudor King said to a great Irishman in former times : ' If all Ireland cannot govern the Earl of Kildare, then let the Earl of Kildare govern Ireland.' . . . If all England cannot govern the Member for Cork, then let us acknowledge that he is the greatest power in Ireland to-day. But I believe that with all England, helped by a large portion of Ireland, no concessions are necessary, and that the Government should not be weakened by concessions. My first condition has not been fulfilled. There has been no public undertaking to cease from intimidation under any circumstances ; there has been merely a hope held out publicly yesterday week that if Parliament passed a certain Bill, and that if it settled this difficult question of arrears, then the party below the gangway [the Irish Party] would cease to obstruct the law. . . . I would have taken their word. Mr. Parnell knows how I differ from him, he knows what a wonder and surprise it is to me that he can bring himself to do what he has done ; but he is not only a gentleman in station, he is also a man of honour, and I would have taken his word. But his word we have not got."

Mr. Gladstone, in reply, accepted responsibility for the original arrest of Parnell and the other Members. With respect to the words used by Mr. Forster more than once, which were equivalent to saying that he desired to obtain from Mr. Parnell, and those with whom he acted, an avowal of change, it was, in effect, much like asking for a penitential confession of guilt. He disclaimed for himself and his colleagues the desire and the right to ask of Mr. Parnell, or any of those who sat with him, anything of the sort.

" In considering whether we should be justified in closing the prison doors on these Members, I had no title to ask any question but the one whether I believed that the effect of their release would be prejudicial to the public tranquillity. I do not believe Mr. Parnell would ever come with a declaration of that kind, and certainly I am not the man to go to any Member of the House and ask him for any statement involving his humiliation."

Referring to Forster's protests against buying obedience to the law, or entering into any arrangements, or paying blackmail, he held them to be without application to the case. He disclaimed that the release of Parnell and the other suspects was part of any bargain or arrangement.

Mr. Parnell, speaking after Mr. Gladstone, asserted that he had never referred to his release in any of the verbal or oral communications with his friends ; but he had said and had written that a settlement of the Arrears question would have an enormous effect in the restoration of law and order, and would take away the last excuse for outrage ; and that, if such a settlement were made, the Irish leaders, in common with all persons who desire to see the prosperity of Ireland, would be able to take such steps as would have a material effect in diminishing those exceptional, those lamentable outrages.

Mr. Dillon, who followed, asserted that he had never, directly or indirectly, had any communication with the Ministers or with the Government of Ireland. He was aware of the drafting of an Arrears Bill by Mr. Parnell, and he never took any trouble to conceal his conviction that, if the proposals of the Bill were passed into law, and the Coercion Act were withdrawn, it would be easier to maintain law and order in Ireland. He did not care in the least degree whether it reached the ears of the Government or not. He felt himself just as free to take any course which might seem right and judicious to him, as he did when he went into Kilmainham Jail. If the Government believed that he felt himself in any way bound to shape his actions otherwise than might seem right to him, they were greatly mistaken.

Mr. O'Kelly also affirmed that there was no shadow of foundation for the suggestion that he entered into agreement with the Government, and said that he would have died sooner than give the assurances which Mr. Forster required, as a condition of his release from jail.

It was not till some days later that the letters of Gladstone, Chamberlain, Parnell, and O'Shea, and the records of conversation between Forster and O'Shea, above referred to, were made public. Their publication was mainly due to O'Shea. On May 12th and 13th debate took place upon them, and the Government was attacked with the greatest virulence. It was contended that the correspondence showed that a treaty had been virtually concluded between the Government and Parnell, of which the terms, on the one side, were the release of the suspects and the passing of an Arrears Bill, and, on the other, that Parnell would use his influence in the future to put down outrages, and that the Irish Party would give its support in Parliament to the Government. The transaction was dubbed the Kilmainham Treaty.

On May 13th Mr. Arthur Balfour moved the adjournment of the House in a most violent speech, accusing the Government of infamous conduct. They had, he said, degraded themselves, by treating on equal terms with men whose guilt they had so fervently believed that they felt themselves justified in imprisoning them for months, without trial, and by negotiating with men whom they had asserted to be steeped in treason, with men who had used their organization for purposes adequately to describe which the vocabulary of the Government had scarcely proved equal. The agitators in Ireland would thenceforward have the conviction that, by holding out to the Government alternately the threat that they would promote outrages, and the promise that they would stop outrages, they would be able to exact whatever legislative measures they might wish. He charged the Government with infamous conduct, in negotiating with treason in order to get Parliamentary support.

The speech is interesting from an historical point of view, as it was the first incursion of Mr. Balfour into Irish affairs, a prelude, and perhaps a key, to much that he said and did when Irish Secretary five years later. His speech stung Mr. Gladstone into an instant reply, hot with indignation and passion. It led to a fierce debate, such as gives intense interest in the House of Commons, when the leaders take off the gloves, and hit out in short, impromptu speeches, without measuring their words, or concealing their scorn for their opponents. The substance, Mr. Gladstone said, of the charge was that a compact had been made, under which Parnell was to get his release, and to get legislation for arrears, and the Government was to obtain through him peace in Ireland and Parliamentary support. There was not a word of truth in that. Parnell never knew that he was to be released until he was actually released.

Mr. Gibson, Sir William Harcourt, and Mr. Chamberlain joined in the fray. The latter insisted that there was no condition in Parnell's assurances as to his release ; that never in these transactions had anything been said indicating, on the part of Parnell, any allusion as to his own personal position. It was impossible for the Government to conclude that the continued imprisonment of Parnell was any longer necessary for the peace of Ireland. On the contrary, they believed that his release would contribute to peace.

It remains to give the explanation afforded by Parnell to his followers of what had led to his release, and to the downfall of Forster. It was made, apparently, on May 7th, a few days before the debate last referred to. The substance, as vouched for by Davitt, was as follows :[1]

" The ' No Rent ' manifesto had failed. The tenants, instead of working out the plan of testing the Land Act, had entered the Land Courts, and had contracted obligations for fifteen years. The ruined tenants, mostly those of small holdings, would be sacrificed, unless an Arrears Act could be obtained, which would wipe out most of their indebtedness, and give them a clear road into the Land Court. To accomplish this, a parley with the Government was necessary. But the reasons by which he was chiefly influenced were the growing power of the secret societies, and the alarming growth of outrages. . . . He believed the obnoxious societies to be more or less local. . . . He saw in the development and in the growth of the revolutionary feeling inside the movement a menace to the constitutional agitation, and a peril to the country, which could only be successfully resisted and arrested by the release of those who would wield a counter influence, and who would calm down the popular feeling. Then it was evident that Mr. Chamberlain and his friends in the Ministry were equally anxious for other—that was Cabinet—reasons to abandon coercion, and to face the larger question of self-government, which could not be done while Ireland continued in a condition of semi-anarchy. Nothing was said of his letters from Kilmainham, which had not then been disclosed, or of his undertaking to slow down the agitation."

" Mr. Gladstone," says Lord Morley, " was always impatient of any reference to ' reciprocal assurances,' or ' tacit understanding,' in respect of the prisoner at Kilmainham. Still, the nature of the proceedings was plain enough. The object of the communication, to which the Government were invited by Mr. Parnell, through his emissary, was, supposing him to be anxious to do what he could for law and order, to find out what action on the part of the Government would enable him to adopt this line."[2]

The agreement or understanding was that the Government, on its part, would pass an Arrears Act, and, on the part of Parnell, that he would do his best to slow down agitation.

[1] Davitt's *Fall of Feudalism*, 361.
[2] *Life of Gladstone*, III, 64.

Whether it can be rightly said that the release of Parnell and
the suspects was part of the agreement is another matter.
There was no mention of this in Parnell's letter. It was
obvious, however, that the suspects could not be detained in
prison, in view of what was otherwise settled on.

We must look at the whole transaction by the light of subsequent experience. Tested in this way, it was, beyond all
question, a wise and successful proceeding. In spite of the
overwhelming misfortune, which occurred a few days later, in
the murders of Lord Frederick Cavendish and Mr. Burke, which,
it will be seen, altered the whole current of events, and prevented the full realization of the new policy, it is certain that
the release of the suspects did produce a most excellent effect
on public opinion in Ireland, and that the passing of the Arrears
Act did put a stop to evictions, and did ultimately lead to a
great reduction of outrages. It will be seen also that Parnell
did, with absolute good faith, use his influence, and successfully, to slow down the agitation.

As regards Mr. Forster, it has been shown that he was
not averse to coming to an agreement with Parnell and the
other leaders ; but he insisted on conditions which would
have been humiliating to them. It was impossible to expect
they would agree to a penitential admission of their past
conduct, and a promise of good behaviour in the future. If
his advice, therefore, had been followed, the Irish leaders,
and all the hundreds of suspects, would have remained in
jail, without trial, while another Coercion Act was being
discussed. As a result, it may be safely concluded that
the state of things in Ireland would have worsened, rather
than improved.

The difference between the two policies was marked by
a well-defined line. That carried out by Mr. Gladstone,
against the advice of Forster, led to conciliation, the other
would have widened the breach between the Government
and the Irish leaders and people. We must conclude that
a wiser and bolder new departure was seldom made by Mr.
Gladstone, or by any other statesman. He had supported
Forster, up to a certain point, with the utmost loyalty and
without any reserve. There came a time, however, when
he was convinced that Forster's policy was a mistaken one,
that the imprisonment of the Irish leaders and of hundreds

of other local leaders, on suspicion and without trial, only aggravated the position of the Government in Ireland, and was the cause of outrages, and not a means of putting them down. He then took the matter into his own hands. He performed what is the highest and most important duty of a Prime Minister—he overruled a colleague in his departmental work, and insisted on a change of policy. The Coercion Act of 1881 was set aside. The bulk of the suspects were set free. Another method was devised of strengthening the criminal law against crime, and a remedial measure of the highest importance was passed. It was impossible that this new policy could have been carried out by the Minister who was responsible for the policy which was reversed and discarded. The resignation of Forster, therefore, was necessary and inevitable. In forming judgment of Forster's two years of administration, as Irish Secretary, every allowance must be made for the enormous difficulties under which he worked. The first of his misfortunes was that his legal advisers in Ireland were not prepared, on his assumption of office, with a measure of Land Reform, to meet the universal demand of the Irish electors at the General Election. The second was the rejection, by the House of Lords, of his temporary measure, the Compensation for Disturbance Bill, which, if it had been passed, might have bridged over the interval before the passing of the Land Act in the following year. In default of such a temporary remedy, evictions, and their necessary consequence, disturbance and outrages, multiplied to an extent which induced the Government to apply for increased power to deal with them by the Coercion Act of 1881, and to give precedence to it over their remedial measure, the Land Bill. For the unfortunate method of coercion adopted in the Act, Forster must be held to be largely responsible. It was framed against the advice of Mr. Gladstone. It was also put in force in a manner distinctly contrary to the promises made to the House of Commons during its passing.

No statesman ever went to Ireland with higher ideals, or with greater determination to do justice, and, above all, to ameliorate the condition of the smaller class of tenants there. No man ever administered an odious Coercion Act with greater leniency to those who were imprisoned under it. But there was in him a dogmatic self-confidence, which, added to a brusque manner, made it difficult for those, with whom he did not agree, to present their views, and prevented him from learning, by free communication with all classes of persons, the effect of his measures, and the necessity for a change of policy.

Complaints are made by his biographer that Mr. Forster met with unfair treatment in the Cabinet, and not obscure hints are given that Mr. Chamberlain was the centre of an intrigue against him. On review, however, of what is known to the public, it appears that Mr. Chamberlain did no more than his duty in opposing a policy which he saw was leading to bad results. It is an essential object of a Cabinet to afford the opportunity to Ministers to criticize, and, if necessary, overrule, the policy of a colleague. The sequel showed that Mr. Chamberlain was perfectly justified in his opposition in the Cabinet to the coercive measures of his colleague Mr. Forster.

CHAPTER XX

THE PHŒNIX PARK MURDERS

ON the resignation of Mr. Forster, it was the general belief that Mr. Chamberlain would succeed as Irish Secretary. He appears to have expected this himself. The offer, however, was not made to him. It is difficult to understand the reason for this, unless it were that Lord Spencer, who must have been consulted as to the appointment, was unwilling to have as Chief Secretary one who was so masterful. There could not well be two Kings of Brentford in the Irish Office. It was, however, to be regretted that, on a change of policy so important, the statesman, to whom it was so largely due, was not employed to give executive effect to it. The post was offered, in the first instance, to Sir Charles Dilke, who was known to be in complete harmony with Mr. Chamberlain. In spite of the fact that he was to be admitted to the Cabinet, he declined the post, on the ground that, although in the Cabinet, he would be subordinate to Lord Spencer, and would have to defend acts of administration for which he was not responsible.

The offer of the post was then made to Lord Frederick Cavendish, brother to Lord Hartington, whose wife was niece, and almost in the relation of a daughter, to Mrs. Gladstone. Lord Frederick had been, for a short time, Secretary to the Treasury—the most important post in the Government outside the Cabinet. He was a man of the highest character and public spirit, modest and diffident of his own powers, with no reputation as a speaker in the House, but recognized by his friends as of great ability, and as a sound Liberal. He was in complete agreement with Mr. Gladstone's views about Ireland. It was thought that Mr. Gladstone, by this appointment, hoped to strengthen his political relations with Lord

Hartington, who had already shown signs of divergence on many questions.

The appointment was made on May 4th, and was announced in the House of Commons that night. On that morning, when crossing the Horse Guards Parade on the way to my office in Whitehall, I met Lord Frederick Cavendish, and had some conversation with him. He told me that he was going to Downing Street, where he expected Mr. Gladstone to offer him the Irish Secretaryship. He was very unwilling, he said, to accept it, as he preferred his then post of Secretary to the Treasury ; but he thought that he should have to take the post, as a matter of duty, if pressed upon him. Turning to me, he said, " Would you like to go to Ireland in place of Forster ? If so, I will refuse the post, and I think it will probably be offered to you." I replied that I could not answer the question, without knowing what was to be the new policy, as I was strongly opposed to renewing coercion. With that our conversation ended, and I never saw Lord Frederick Cavendish again. Two days later he met his end gallantly defending Mr. Burke, the Permanent Secretary for Ireland, from the band of assassins, who murdered both of them.

Meanwhile, Parnell, who was released from Kilmainham immediately after the Cabinet of May 2nd, crossed the Channel on the next day, and on May 4th made his dramatic reappearance in the House of Commons, as above described. On Saturday, the 6th, Parnell, Dillon, and O'Kelly, the three released suspects, went to Portland to meet Davitt, at the gates of the convict prison, on his release, which had been directed by Sir William Harcourt, in pursuance of the new policy. Davitt had been in prison there for fifteen months as a convict, whose ticket-of-leave had been revoked ; though by special orders of Harcourt he had not been subjected to all the rigours and indignities of the convict prison rules, he had been entirely cut off from the outside world, and knew absolutely nothing of what was taking place. His surprise, at his release and at meeting Parnell and his colleagues, was very great. They travelled together to London. " All the way," says Davitt, " Parnell talked of the state of Ireland ; said it was dreadful ; denounced the Ladies' Land League ; swore at everybody, and spoke of anarchy, as if he were a British Minister bringing in a Coercion Bill. I never saw him so wild and angry. The

Ladies' Land League, he declared, had taken the country out of his hands, and should be suppressed. I defended the ladies, saying that, after all, they had kept the ball rolling while he was in gaol. ' I am out now,' he said, ' and I don't mean to keep the ball rolling any more. The League must be suppressed, or I will leave public life.' "[1]

There seems to have been amusing conversation between the four Irish leaders, thus released from prison, about a future Home Rule Government in Dublin. Parnell laughingly assigned posts in it to the other three. Dillon was to be Home Secretary, Davitt to be Inspector of Irish Prisons, and O'Kelly, the future head of the Constabulary.

" We are on the eve of something like Home Rule," Parnell said. " Mr. Gladstone has thrown over coercion and Mr. Forster, and the Government will legislate further on the Land question. The Tory Party are going to advocate land purchase, almost on the lines of the League programme, and I see no reason why we should not soon obtain all we are looking for in the League movement." On their arrival in London, they were welcomed by a crowd of friends.

Their rosy expectations for the future were destined to be cruelly dispelled by the grave events, of which Dublin was the scene, on the same day. Lord Spencer and Lord Frederick Cavendish had crossed the Channel the previous night ; they took the oaths of their respective offices on the Saturday. The new Lord-Lieutenant made his state entry into Dublin, and was cordially, if not enthusiastically, received by the people. The change of policy, which his appointment seemed to indicate, gave general satisfaction. It raised hopes of yet further development. Late in the afternoon, Lord Frederick, after transacting business with Lord Spencer at the Castle, drove on a car to the Phœnix Park. At the entrance he dismounted, and being overtaken by Mr. Burke, the permanent Under-Secretary, walked with him towards the Viceregal Lodge. There was gross negligence, on the part of the police, in not affording to him the same vigilant protection which they had always provided for Mr. Forster. When a short distance from the Lord-Lieutenant's residence, and within sight from its windows, the two officials were suddenly attacked by a band of assassins, armed with long knives. Their object of

[1] *Life of Parnell*, I, 364.

attack was Mr. Burke. Lord Frederick tried to defend his colleague with his only weapon—an umbrella. Both were stabbed to death. Their dead bodies were found by passers-by within a few minutes. The assassins escaped without recognition, though it was still light, at seven o'clock in the evening, and there were many people in the Park. Those who saw the affray from a short distance, and from the windows of the Viceregal Lodge, thought that it was a mere scuffle of men at play.

It transpired some months later, when the murderers were on their trial, that they were members of a secret society called " The Invincibles," formed expressly for the purpose of political assassinations, and with the deliberate intention of taking the lives of Mr. Forster and Lord Cowper. They had, on several occasions, devised elaborate schemes for waylaying Mr. Forster, but had been foiled by some mischances. Finding that he had escaped from them by his final departure from Ireland, they had decided to wreak their vengeance on Mr. Burke. They did not know Lord Frederick by sight. It was the accident of his being in company with Burke which led them, through fear of recognition, to slay him. They were much surprised to learn that he was the newly appointed Chief Secretary. Months passed before any clue was obtained as to the murderers.

The details of this terrible deed reached the members of the Government in London the same night, when many of them were at an official reception at the Admiralty. Mrs. Gladstone, who was there, returned at once to Downing Street, and thence, with Mr. Gladstone, went to Carlton Terrace on the mournful errand of breaking the dreadful news to Lady Frederick Cavendish. That brave and heroic lady bore her bereavement with fortitude. It afforded some consolation to her to know that her husband died in the performance of his duty, and in the attempt to save the life of his colleague in the Irish Government. She tried to assuage the grief of Mr. Gladstone by saying that he had done right in sending her husband to Ireland. She wrote to Lord Spencer that she would have given up her husband, if she had known that his death would work good to his fellow-men, for that, indeed, was the whole object of his life.

It was not till the next morning (Sunday) that Parnell

heard of what had occurred. He was distressed beyond measure. In an interview with Dillon, Cowen, Davitt, and others, he is described by the latter as being completely unnerved by the terrible event. He said he would retire from the leadership of the Irish Party, and give up politics. " How can I carry on a public agitation if I am stabbed in the back in this way ? " He spoke of the crime as the work of extreme men, who were hostile to his leadership, and were incensed by his compact with the Government. His friends endeavoured to persuade him from resignation. By their advice, a manifesto to the Irish people was drawn up and signed by Parnell, Dillon, and Davitt, condemning the crime, and expressing the hope that the assassins would be brought to justice. It concluded with the following sentence, suggested by Mr. A. M. Sullivan :

" We feel that no act has ever been perpetrated in our country, during the existing struggle for social and political rights of the past fifty years, that has so stained the name of hospitable Ireland, as this cowardly and unprovoked assassination of a friendly stranger, and that until the murderers of Lord Frederick Cavendish and Mr. Burke are brought to justice the stain will sully our country's name."

Later, Parnell called on Mr. Chamberlain and met Sir Charles Dilke. They strongly dissuaded him from resignation. Strange to say, also, he wrote to Mr. Gladstone, not, as has been alleged, offering to resign his leadership, but asking for advice. Mr. Barry O'Brien gives Mr. Gladstone's version. " On the Sunday after the Phœnix Park murders, while I was at lunch, a letter was brought to me from Parnell. I was much touched by it. He wrote evidently under strong emotion. He did not ask me if I would advise him to retire from public life or not. That was not how he put it. He asked me what effect I thought the murders would have on English public opinion in relation to his leadership of the Irish Party. Well, I wrote expressing my own opinion, and what I thought would be the opinion of others, that his retirement from public life would do no good, but, on the contrary, would do harm. I thought his conduct on the whole matter very praiseworthy." [1]

This advice appears to have determined Parnell, and no more was heard of his resignation. There is no doubt, how-

[1] *Life of Parnell*, I, 357.

ever, that he was profoundly affected, and regarded the crime as aimed, in a great measure, at the constitutional agitation of which he was the leader. His communications on the subject with Mr. Gladstone, Mr. Chamberlain, and Sir Charles Dilke were significant as to the *entente* which had been arrived at.

On Monday, the 8th, Mr. Gladstone moved the adjournment of the House of Commons, at its meeting, as a mark of respect and grief for the murdered men, and of horror of the crime. He said of Mr. Burke that he was one of the ablest, the most upright, the most experienced, the most eminent men in the Civil Service ; and, of Lord Frederick, that one of the very noblest hearts had ceased to beat, when it was just devoted to the service of Ireland, full of love for that country, full of hope for her future, full of capacity to render her service. Most appropriate references and eulogies were made by Sir Stafford Northcote, Mr. Forster, and Mr. Lowther. Mr. Parnell, in a few well-chosen words, expressed, on behalf of all Ireland, unqualified detestation of the crime, and his conviction that it had been committed by men who absolutely detested the cause with which he had been associated, and who had devised the crime and carried it out as the deadliest blow which they had in their power to deal against their hopes, in connection with the new course on which the Government had just entered. Mr. Gladstone also gave notice, that all previous arrangements and intentions of the Government must be reconsidered, and that, on the following Thursday, a measure would be introduced for the repression of crime in Ireland, and that another measure, dealing with arrears of rent, would also be introduced as soon as possible. On this, Mr. Parnell said that he did not deny that it might be impossible for the Government to resist the situation, and that they might feel themselves compelled to take some step in the direction indicated by the Prime Minister.

The House then adjourned. Three days later upwards of three hundred of its Members were present at the funeral of Lord Frederick Cavendish, at Edensor, a remote village in Derbyshire, the burial-place of his family—a most striking testimony of the respect in which he was held, and of horror of the crime which had deprived the country of his services. With respect to the Irish Government, Mr. Forster at once offered to go back to Ireland, to help temporarily in its administration, until new arrangements could be made. It was not thought well to accept this generous offer. A successor to Lord Frederick was quickly found in Mr. Trevelyan (now Sir George), then Secretary to the Admiralty, than whom there could not have been a stronger or abler man for the post. He was not to be in the Cabinet. Lord Spencer, therefore, was to be mainly responsible for the executive work in Ireland ; but the new Secretary was to have the heavy burden of defending, in the House of Commons, the action and policy of his chief against the powerful attacks of the Irish Party.

CHAPTER XXI

THE CRIMES ACT OF 1882

THE effect of the Phœnix Park murders on public opinion in England was very great. It was thought by many that Mr. Forster had been justified in all that he had charged against Parnell and the Land League. No Government could have survived for a day which did not take instant steps to strengthen the law in Ireland against crime. All schemes, whatever they may have been, of giving to Ireland some rudiments of self-government, as regards its own affairs, went by the board. The measure for dealing with crime was greatly strengthened, and became a coercive one of harshness to Ireland. Public opinion there was again greatly embittered.

Looking back impartially at the new policy, one must now conclude that, although it was most difficult, if not impossible, in the then state of public opinion in Great Britain, to adopt any other course, it would have been more politic and statesmanlike to have taken Parnell into consultation, and to have come to terms with him, and the Irish Party, as to what measure should be proposed to Parliament for strengthening the law against outrages and murder. It is almost certain that Parnell, in view of the Phœnix Park horrors, would have agreed to a moderate measure for amending the Criminal Law. Public opinion in Ireland might have been conciliated and brought into harmony with that of England. No attempt was made in this direction. Parnell was never approached on the subject. He might well have considered himself as absolved, by the introduction of a new Coercion Bill, from whatever agreement or understanding had been arrived at with the Government. It will be seen that he did his best to carry out his undertaking, and to slow down the agitation.

It was decided by the Government to give precedence to the new Coercion Bill—the Prevention of Crimes Bill—as it was called, and to proceed with an Arrears Bill *pari passu*, thus reverting to the old Whig policy of giving precedence to a measure for restoring order, before applying a remedy to the evil which was the cause of disorder—a policy which deprived the remedy of most of its healing quality.

The Crimes Bill was introduced by Sir William Harcourt, the Home Secretary, on May 11th, and the Arrears Bill by Mr. Gladstone on May 15th. The former was read a second time on May 25th, after three nights of debate. The Crimes Bill was based on very different principles from that of the previous year. It proposed to put down crime, not by arbitrary imprisonment, for unlimited periods, of persons suspected only of crime, but by strengthening the law against persons who were guilty of actual crime, or of offences of a serious character. It had been an understanding with Lord Spencer, when he accepted the post of Lord-Lieutenant, that a measure of this kind would be proposed by the Government ; but the discussion on it was to be postponed until an Arrears Act was passed, and the House was agreed upon the new rules for procedure. As these measures would necessarily occupy the time of the House of Commons for many weeks, it was hoped in many quarters that the improved state of Ireland, due to the Arrears Act, and to the new attitude of Parnell, would dispense with the necessity for a Coercion Act. The Crimes Bill was to be of a moderate character. The Bill, as introduced, however, was tuned up to meet the altered state of public opinion, infuriated by the political murders. New clauses were added to the original Bill, and the measure, as finally adopted and presented to Parliament, was of a very drastic character. It corresponded closely with the demands which had been made by Lord Cowper and Mr. Forster.

The most serious change proposed, from a constitutional point of view, was the abrogation of the right of trial by jury. In grave cases of agrarian crime, the Government was empowered to dispense with juries, and to try them before a Court of three judges, who were to decide questions of fact, as well as of law, without juries. The Attorney-General was to have large powers of changing the venue in criminal cases. Power was conferred on the Lord-Lieutenant of forbidding public meetings, and of suppressing newspapers. Powers of search, and of arresting persons wandering about at night, were conferred on the police. Stringent provision was made against boycotting. The most serious, from the point of view of the Irish Party, were the increased powers given to magistrates of convicting persons of incitement to crime and of boycotting, and of membership of secret societies, offences which previously could only be tried before juries. These clauses enormously increased the powers of the special magistrates appointed by Mr. Forster, who had already shown that they were not to be trusted with the more limited powers already conferred on them. They were also empowered to hold secret local inquiries, and to compel the attendance of witnesses, and to interrogate them privately. Compensation was to be levied, in cases of injury to persons, on the ratepayers of the district—to be fixed by the Grand Juries, not responsible to them. Additional police might also be quartered in districts at the cost of the ratepayers.

This accumulation of strong provisions, which practically got rid of constitutional securities against injustice and wrong, caused in Ireland a revulsion of public opinion, which had been veering towards the Government, under the belief that a policy of conciliation was adopted, and which had been roused against crime by the political murders. It led to the bitter opposition of the Irish representatives in the House of Commons. Parnell made a comparatively moderate speech against the Bill, but his lieutenants, Dillon, Sexton, Healy, O'Donnell, and others, went far beyond him in violent opposition. Dillon's speech especially was impassioned and vehement to the highest degree. He would willingly, he said, have risked his own life to save that of Lord Frederick Cavendish. Let the Government, however, beware, if they send another man to carry out another Coercion Act, that a cursed stain may not again sully the page of Irish history. " Do we not read in the Bill before the House the condemnation of English rule in Ireland? What profit can you ever expect from governing a nation which nothing conciliates, and which nothing will subdue? In eighty-eight years since the Union there have been fifty Coercion Acts, and that before the House is the worst." If the Government had framed a measure against such crimes as that recently committed, he, for one, would have given no opposition to it, but the Bill, as drawn, aimed at every expression of opinion in Ireland. The Irish Party had offered assistance to the Government for the discovery of the criminals. If they abandoned the policy of conciliation, if they enacted a measure of the kind before the House, they would be carrying out the object of the assassins.

This speech has been referred to as an illustration of the temper which had been aroused by the strong coercive measure. The most reasoned speech against it was that of Mr. Sexton—full of contemptuous irony directed against Forster, whose failure he exposed, and full of predictions of failure of this new attempt against the liberties of the Irish people. The measure was ably defended by Mr. Trevelyan, in a first speech as Irish Secretary, and by Mr. Bright, who explained that his well-known, and oft-quoted, phrase, that " force is no remedy," was not inconsistent with support to the Bill. Force, he said, was occasionally necessary as against force, even if a remedy must be found in some other direction. Mr. Plunket, and Mr. Gibson, on behalf of the Opposition, made strong speeches in favour of the Bill. The second reading was carried, after a three nights' debate, by 383 votes against 45 ; seven English Liberals only voted in the minority—which included also Mr. William Shaw and Mr. Charles Russell. A majority of the Irish Members voting in the division were in favour of the Bill. The Committee stage led to most violent opposition. It was protracted over twenty-four sittings of the House. Some minor concessions were made by the Government, but substantially the measure passed in its original form, strengthened in one important respect against the will of the Government. No fewer than five days were devoted to the question of " boycotting," which the Government declared they were determined to put down.

The Irish Members, while admitting that boycotting had been carried, in some cases, to a dangerous point, and willing to put some limitations upon it, so as to prevent excesses, defended its use, under the conditions which existed in Ireland before the Land Act was passed. They claimed that it had been successfully applied in preventing unjust evictions. They maintained that the clause, as it stood, practically amounted to making all exclusive dealing criminal, and would be a most dangerous power to commit to magistrates. The

Government insisted that the clause was necessary to prevent the cruel excesses which had taken place. The debates which occurred on this subject were conducted by some of the ablest men, with the most subtle intellects, who ever sat in the House of Commons—Harcourt, Trevelyan, Forster, Gibson, Plunket and Gladstone on behalf of the clause; Parnell, Healy, Sexton, T. P. O'Connor, Charles Russell, and Cowen against it ; while Horace Davey (later Lord Davey) and Bryce took part in the debates, and contended that the clause went too far.

Mr. Gladstone, in the course of a keen debating speech, said :

" The evil, which there is in boycotting, dwells more or less in the breasts of most men—the question is, what is the amount of the evil ? In Ireland it is a great and serious evil, limiting most unduly the liberty of action of men, and seriously endangering the peace and order of the country. . . . The clause has been introduced because the system has become, in Ireland, a monstrous public evil, threatening liberty and interfering with law and order."

The whole of the speech, and indeed the whole of the discussion, on June 1st, when the principal debate on the clause took place, would be worth quotation. It was admitted by the Government that mere exclusive dealing—the refusal, for instance, to supply goods to a would-be purchaser, or to work for a particular person—was not criminal, or intended to be made so by the clause. On the other side, it was argued that there was no distinction in the clause, as drawn, between exclusive dealing, in the above sense, and the more serious cases which the Government hoped and intended to prevent and punish, and that it was dangerous to give to magistrates in Ireland the power to determine in what cases exclusive dealing became criminal.

Dillon, not for the first time, defended the action of the Land League in this respect. He had over and over again, he said, explained to the Irish people what he meant by the system of boycotting. He had told them that boycotting consisted in having no dealings with a man who had done certain things—such as taking a farm from which a tenant had been unjustly evicted ; assisting in any way in an unjust eviction ; breaking his engagement with his fellow-tenants, to hold out for certain terms as a reduction of rent, and then

making separate terms for himself. He had said : " Have no-
dealings with such a man, and have no association with him.
But do no injury to him, or to any one associating with him.
If you do, you destroy the system of boycotting, because you
break the law." So long as he (Dillon) and Davitt were at the
head of the Land League they never sanctioned, but strenuously set their faces against, any further interference with
individual liberty. But he was prepared to admit that after
the Land League leaders were arrested, the system of boycotting had been very grossly abused. He agreed frankly
that the system, defend it as best they could, was a rough
system ; but if it had not been adopted the most fearful
evils would have happened, which, by the course taken, the
Land League had been able in some measure to stave off.
In the end the clause passed with but slight amendment ; but
the discussion on it doubtless did good in preventing its being
put in force generally, and in other than most serious cases.

As the discussion proceeded the Irish Members disputed the
clauses, word by word, and their tactics became more purely
obstructive. On the clause enabling the levy of compensation
on the ratepayers of the district in cases of murder and maiming, an acrimonious debate took place with numerous attacks
on the late, and the new, Irish Secretary. The Committee
sat continuously for thirty hours, from 3 p.m. on the first day
till 8 p.m. on the second, with relays of Chairmen. I occupied
the Chair myself on this occasion, from half-past five in the
morning till nine, when the Chairman of Committees took his
place again. A little later the Chairman expressed the opinion
that it was necessary to stop the obstruction, and named sixteen of the Irish Members, including Parnell, Dillon, Justin
McCarthy, Redmond, Sexton, and Biggar. On the motion of a
member of the Government, they were suspended for the
remainder of the sitting by a vote of 126 to 27. Later, nine
more Irish Members were reported by the Chairman for wilful
and persistent obstruction, and were suspended, and the clause
was finally carried against a minority of only six.

On the next meeting of the House Mr. Gladstone moved
the resolution of the previous Session by which the business was declared urgent. This was carried by 259 to 31.
With the aid of new rules supplied by the Speaker, the
remaining clauses of the Bill were then carried with prac-

tically little discussion. The Irish Party, ejected from the House, as above described, passed a resolution protesting against the action of the House, and announcing their intention to take no further part in discussions on the Bill, which they affirmed would be devoid of moral force. In their absence the Government was defeated on a most important point. In deference to a promise given to Mr. Parnell in the Committee on the Bill, Mr. Trevelyan proposed to amend the clause, giving greater power of search to the police, by excluding night searches, except when there was reasonable cause to believe that a secret society was holding a meeting. This concession was violently opposed by the Tory Party, and by not a few Whig Members, on the ground that it would weaken the Bill. Mr. Gladstone, in vehement language, threatened resignation if the amendment was not carried. In spite of this the House, by a majority of 207 to 194, rejected it. Mr. Gladstone, however, did not carry out his threat. He explained that, under ordinary circumstances, after such a rebuff, he would have gone no further with the Bill, but in the condition of Ireland he could not do so. Nor could he resign on such a question. It would, indeed, have been absurdly quixotic to take such a course. It was within the power of the Executive Government of Ireland to refrain from using the power thus thrust upon them. But the fact that the House forced upon the Government larger powers of coercion than was thought necessary, or asked for, was very significant of its temper. Twenty-four Liberal Members voted against the Government on this occasion, and many more abstained from voting. This was the last difficulty in the Bill. It was read a third time, and sent to the House of Lords. It there passed all its stages in two nights. The only complaint was that the Bill was not strong enough.

CHAPTER XXII

THE ARREARS ACT

IT was greatly to the credit of the Government that, in spite of the very strong anti-Irish feeling of Great Britain, aroused by the political murders, it decided to press on its remedial measure for Ireland. The Arrears Bill was read a second time before the Committee stage on the Crimes Bill. It was substantially the scheme devised by Parnell, when in Kilmainham Jail, and which was incorporated in Mr. Redmond's Bill, already referred to. It differed from the scheme in the Land Act of the previous year, which had proved in practice to be a complete failure, on two vital points. The advance of one year's rent to the landlord, conditional on the payment of another year's rent by the tenant, and the wiping out of all other outstanding arrears, was to be a gift from the State, and not a loan, and the scheme was to be compulsory on both landlord and tenant, on the application of either of them, and not permissive only, and subject to the approval of the landlord. The money required for the purpose was to be provided out of the surplus fund of the Disestablished Church, which was expected to realize 1½ millions, and beyond this by the State. The scheme was limited to holdings of which the Poor Law valuation was £30 and under. Advances were only to be made in cases where the Land Commission, who were to administer the Act, were of opinion that the tenant was unable to pay the arrears for which he was indebted.

Mr. Gladstone, on moving the second reading of the Bill, admitted that it could not be supported on logical grounds, and that the interference of the State in the settlement of debts, legally due, by means of gift and compulsion, could not be defended on either economic or constitutional grounds. He justified it on the ground that the permissive clauses of the

Act of 1881 had failed, and that a vast body of tenants, encumbered by arrears of rent which they could not pay, were prevented from going into the Land Court, and obtaining a reduction of rent for the future, and that they were in danger of eviction on a large scale for these irrecoverable arrears ; that this was the cause of disturbance and outrages in Ireland ; and that it was necessary that this difficulty should be removed in the interest of peace in Ireland, and in order that the Land Act of 1881 should have its full effect.[1] In the course of the discussion on the Bill he spoke the following remarkable words :

" Eviction in the exercise of a legal right may be to the prejudice of your neighbours, may involve the highest reprehension, may even imply deep moral guilt. There may be outrages which—all things considered—the persons and the facts—may be less guilty in the sight of God than evictions."

The Bill was assailed by the Tory Party in full force, on the ground that it would have a demoralizing effect upon those for whose benefit it was designed, and would be a disastrous precedent in after years, and would be fatal to the future careers of Irish farmers. Mr. Chaplin declared that unless the Government made full compensation to those landlords, who had the right to claim arrears which were their due, they would be found guilty of wholesale confiscation. Sir M. Hicks-Beach (Lord St. Aldwyn) complained that all lawabiding in Ireland would be discouraged, and lawless people would be encouraged to further outrages. He did not believe it could be possible to restore peace and confidence by concessions to those who were responsible for criminal measures. Irreparable mischief, he said, had already been done by the mere introduction of the Bill. Mr. Arthur Balfour pointed out that three remedial land measures had been introduced by the Government in three years, all of which violated not only every principle of political economy, but every principle which had ever been recognized in English legislation ; all were introduced as the result of agitation, and all were recommended as a means of avoiding further agitation. The Bill would pauperize the tenants of Ireland by remitting debts which ought to be paid in full. Sir Stafford Northcote attacked the Government for taking measures from the Irish Party after opposing them. He did not object to

[1] *Hansard*, May 22nd, 1882.

the Bill because it was exceptional, but because it was bad and unjust, as regards the present, and mischievous, as regards the future. It would encourage a vicious system, of which they would feel the effect in after years.

The Bill was defended by Mr. Trevelyan in two admirable speeches, largely devoted to a description of what was going on in the parts of Ireland where the scheme would operate. At that moment, he said, in many parts of Ireland men were being turned out of their homes, actually by platoons, who were no more able to pay the arrears of three bad years than they were able to pay the National Debt. In Connemara, he said, in three days, since he had been in office, 150 families consisting of 750 persons were turned out of their homes for non-payment of arrears of rent. In that district thousands of persons, who had been beggared for years, were utterly unable to hold up their heads since the bad years of 1878–9. On many estates, he said, arrears were outstanding since 1847. The essence of the Bill was the clearance of accounts all through Ireland, once and for all. Never, since 1847, had there been years of distress which so utterly impoverished the people, that it was impossible for them to pay any rent at all. He pointed out that in recent famines in India the ryots had their land taxes remitted by a process as near as possible to that of the Bill.

An excellent debating speech was made by Mr. Bright, who rarely, on other occasions, spoke without elaborate preparations. Mr. Forster also spoke on behalf of the Bill. He had come to the conclusion that the House must make an effort to settle the Arrears question. If not, the Land Act would fail, as regards a vast number of tenants, and would be of little use in restoring peace and order. Compulsion could not be avoided. It was the interest of some landlords to clear their estates of tenants. It was the interest of the State that such clearances should not be made. If the Government had proposed to deal with the question by loan, the only effect would have been that the loan would be irrecoverable.

Looking at the debate as a whole it seemed to me at the time, and I have since been confirmed in the view, that the general line of defence for the Bill was rather timid and weak. Mr. Gladstone, as in the case of the Land Acts of 1870 and 1881, refrained from defending the measure on the grounds of justice. He based his defence on the grounds of expediency and policy, and the necessity of restoring peace to Ireland. But there was much to be said from the point of view of justice. The smaller tenants in the west and south of Ireland had made whatever improvements had added to the prairie value of their holdings, including the cabins in which they lived. The two Land Acts had already decided that these improvements were the property of the tenants, and ought to be protected, and that rent ought not to be levied on them. For years past they had been over-rented. These excessive rents could only be paid in good years. In bad years, when the crops were deficient, when the turf could not be dried, or when there was no employment in England for the migrating labourers, the full rent, or even part of it, could not be paid. Rent, in such cases, was not abated, but was allowed to accumulate as arrears, rolling up debt, so that the landlords had greater powers over their tenants, and could evict them at their pleasure. Since the Act of 1881 many of them had made use of these arrears to prevent their tenants going into the Land Court, and obtaining reductions of rent, which, in such cases, often amounted to 30 or 40 per cent.

In some cases the landlords would be better off if they cleared such estates of the tenants, and some of them were prepared to effect this by wholesale evictions. Evictions led to disturbance and outrages. When the principle of reduction of rent by independent authority was admitted, what could be more just, reasonable, and politic than to apply the same principle to the accumulated arrears of excessive rents? The same authority, which reduced the rents, should have been empowered to reduce, in the same proportion, the arrears of rents which were due, and which the tenants were unable to pay. This, it will be recollected, was the demand which Parnell made in Committee on the Act of 1881. If his demand had been acceded to, the difficulty would not have arisen.

A few years later, in 1886, the same question arose in dealing with the Scotch crofters, whose condition, legal and economical, was almost identical with that of the Irish cottier tenants. Under the Scotch Act a Commission was appointed to hold inquiries into the condition of the crofter communities, with power to reduce rents, to give security of tenure for the future, and with authority also to decide what arrears of rent should be payable, and to sweep away all excess beyond this. There was no gift or loan from the estate to make up a part of the loss to the landowners, in respect of the arrears thus annulled. The measure passed without any opposition, and this part of it was not even subjected to criticism.

As a result of that measure arrears of rent, owing by the crofters to very large amounts, were compulsorily reduced to very small proportions. If it was right and just to do this in the case of Scotch crofters, why not in the case of Irish crofter tenants ? The scheme of the Irish measure must be regarded as in the nature of a bribe to the Irish landlords from the State, an inducement to them to wipe off all arrears of rent, on payment of one year's arrears from the tenant, and another from the State—a most excellent bargain to the landlords.

In the House of Lords the Bill was read a second time, after a violent speech against it by Lord Salisbury. He had wished to reject the Bill, but had been overruled at a party meeting of the Opposition Peers, at the instance of the Irish Peers. He promised to eliminate some of its dangerous proposals in Committee. He moved an amendment to the first clause, making the consent of the landlord necessary for any application to the Land Court. He declared that " if there could be such a thing on the part of the State as stealing, and if it be possible for the State unjustly to take one man's property and give it to another, I cannot understand any offence more distinctly proved than confiscation is proved against the Bill." To bring the Bill into correspondence with the principles of common honesty, it was necessary to make it conditional on the consent of the landlord. Lord Derby and Lord Carlingford, on the part of the Government, said that the amendment was fatal to the Bill, and that it would be equivalent to its rejection on the second reading.

Lord Lansdowne, for once in his political career, supported a Liberal Government on an Irish Land Bill. The whole point of the arrangement, he said, was a compulsory composition of the tenants' liabilities. The optional system had been tried and failed. . . . The Government had prepared a twofold solution of the difficulties in Ireland. They had carried an effectual measure for dealing with disorders, and they were now proposing to do something to relieve the pressure which had no doubt tended to increase crime. He would greatly regret if, on the one hand, the House accepted legislation directed against crime, and, on the other hand, left unmitigated, the pressure would add to an increase of crime. In spite of his support, Lord Salisbury's amendment was carried by 169 to 98. Other small amendments were also carried, defeating the objects of the Bill.

On the return of the Bill to the House of Commons, on August 8th, Mr. Gladstone made some slight concessions, not substantially altering the character of the Bill, and, subject to this, proposed and carried the rejection of the Lords' amendments. In the interval, before the Bill came again before the House of Lords, a party meeting of the Opposition Peers took place, at which the Irish Peers rebelled against the hostile attitude to the Bill of the Tory leader, Lord Salisbury. The bait held out to so many of them of two years' rent, for arrears, which they knew were irrecoverable, was too tempting. In view of this Lord Salisbury found it necessary to drop his opposition to the Bill ; and when it came up for discussion on the amendments of the House of Commons he made the following remarkable statement on giving way, and agreeing to the passing of the Bill without his amendments.

" I believe that the Bill would be only defensible with the alteration in it which makes the consent of the landlord necessary before the measure can be put into operation. Without that alteration I believe it to be a most pernicious Bill ; that it will be an act of simple robbery ; and that it is a Bill which will bear the gravest fruits in the legislation of the future. These are my opinions. I have had the opportunity this morning of conferring with the noble Lords who formed the majority by whom the amendment was carried, and which was sent down to the other House ; and I found that the overwhelming majority of their Lordships were of opinion that in the present state of affairs, especially those which have recently arisen in Ireland, and in Egypt, it is not expedient that the Arrears Bill should be thrown out. I do not share in this opinion. If I had the power I would have thrown out the Bill. I find myself, however, in a small minority, and therefore I will not divide the House."[1]

He gave way on all the points at issue, and the Bill passed into law substantially in the form desired by the Government.

[1] *Hansard*, August 10th, 1882.

Lord Monck was appointed a Land Commissioner for the purpose of administering the Act. It worked with absolute success. Many thousands of tenants were able to relieve themselves of the burden of arrears, paying one year's rent. Great numbers of landlords obtained two years' rent, which they had considered to be hopelessly lost. It had a most undoubted effect in quieting the country, far more so, it may confidently be asserted, than the rigorous enforcement of the Crimes Act. It is only right that credit should be given to Mr. Parnell for devising the scheme of the Bill, and to the Government for coming to agreement with him about it. In the result a very much smaller sum than was expected sufficed to settle the question. The charge on the surplus fund of the Disestablished Church of Ireland did not amount to more than £700,000. None of the evil consequences predicted of the Act resulted from it.

It was unfortunate, however, that again, on the admission of Lord Salisbury, the Tory Party and the Irish Peers conceded a measure of this importance, not to arguments of justice, nor even to those of expediency and sound policy, but to the disturbed state of Ireland. It would seem to have been wiser statesmanship, on the part of Lord Salisbury, when he found that he was beaten by his own followers, to have avoided the admission that he gave way to agitation and violence.

CHAPTER XXIII

COERCION, 1882-4

THERE were two very opposite opinions among the followers of Parnell as to the merits of his action in effecting an arrangement with the Government and his consequent release from jail. Many, and probably a large majority of them, regarded it as a brilliant stroke of policy, by which he defeated the Irish Executive, compelled the resignation of Forster, and induced the Government to concede legislation for clearing away arrears of rent. During the first few days after his release he received ovations in Ireland, and congratulations from his colleagues in Parliament. Others, however, of the more extreme members of his party, took a different view of the transaction. It was, in their opinion, a deal with the Government, the last thing in the world which an Irish leader should have attempted. The militant members of the League were strongly opposed to the arrangement ; and many attributed it to an influence, concerning which scandal was already afloat. This difference might have caused a serious breach in the party, and have endangered Parnell's position. But the prolonged fight against the Coercion Act by the Irish Members, under his leadership, drew off opinion in Ireland from the Kilmainham arrangement.

Whatever adverse views there were of the arrangement, on the part of an influential section of his supporters, Parnell strictly adhered to it. He undoubtedly did his best to slow down the agitation. His first important act in this direction was to suppress the Ladies' Land League. This he effected by refusing further supplies of money to it. The Ladies' League had spent upwards of £70,000 while he was in prison. It was with difficulty that he was persuaded to advance

£500 more to enable them to meet their actual engagements. This was to be the very last advance. " The Ladies' Land League," he said, "has expended an enormous amount of money. They told me, after my release, that I ought to have remained in Kilmainham. I fear they have done much harm along with some good." The refusal of money meant their suppression. There was no formal dissolution, but the League died of inanition. This appears to have caused a quarrel with his sister, Miss Anna Parnell, the President of the Ladies' League, which was never completely healed.

Parnell was urged by Davitt and others, soon after his release from Kilmainham, to reorganize the Land League. He peremptorily refused to do so. He was unwilling to plunge the country again into the turmoil of violent agitation. Later, however, in September, under the pressure of some of the advanced members of his party, he agreed to the constitution of a new organization to be called the National League. At a conference held at Dublin on October 17th, at which a number of Members of Parliament were present, the programme of the new body was decided on. It was insisted upon by Parnell, as a condition of his consent, that the new League was to be on a strictly Parliamentary basis as regards the Land question. Home Rule, and not Land Reform, was put in the foreground.

The first article was the restitution to the Irish people of the right to manage their own affairs in their own Parliament. The second article aimed at the creation of an occupying ownership, a peasant proprietary, by an amendment of the purchase clauses of the Land Act of 1881 ; the protection from the imposition of rent on improvements made by the tenants, by an amendment of the Healy Clause ; the admission of leaseholders and other excluded classes to all the benefits of the Land Act. Other articles dealt with the creation of County Boards, the extension of Parliamentary and Municipal franchise, and legislation for the benefit of labourers. This programme, it will be seen, was strictly Parliamentary. There was nothing revolutionary about it. With the exception of Home Rule, every article in it has since been carried out by Parliament. " The outcome of the Conference," says Davitt, " was the complete eclipse by a purely Parliamentary substitute of what had been a semi-revolutionary organization.

It was, in a sense, the overthrow of a movement and the enthronement of a man ; the replacement of Nationalism by Parnellism." [1]

The proceedings of the Conference of October, and the programme of the National League, were proofs that Parnell, apart from any arrangement with the Government, had resolved to break with the extreme members of the Irish Party, and never again to engage in a land agitation such as that of the Land League. Egan and Brennan, the chief agents of the old League, were not connected with the new association. They were no more heard of in the movement led by Parnell. This change in the general direction of his policy by Parnell was not recognized, and apparently was not even perceived in England. It was still commonly believed there that the National League was only the old Land League under a new name. Parnell received no credit for this change, or for slowing down the agitation. He was still held responsible for whatever breaches of the law took place.

It must be admitted that when Parnell came out of jail the condition of Ireland was very bad. Many murders had recently taken place, without any of their perpetrators being discovered, and brought to justice. Forster's Coercion Act had been a complete failure. It had led to an increase of serious crime and murder, instead of a reduction. The task of Lord Spencer and Mr. Trevelyan of administering the Crimes Act, of endeavouring to restore order in Ireland, and of bringing to justice the perpetrators of the Phœnix Park murders, and other terrible crimes, was undoubtedly most arduous, difficult, and perilous. It required strong nerves, and a disregard of violent personal attacks in the Press and in Parliament. Lord Spencer had these qualities in a high degree, and no man with higher courage and greater public spirit ever filled the post of Lord-Lieutenant. " He was seconded," says Lord Morley, with absolute truth, " with high ability and courage by Mr. Trevelyan, whose fortitude was subjected to a severer trial than has fallen to the lot of any Irish Secretary before or since." [2]

A short time before his arrest, in the autumn of 1881, Parnell had bought, out of funds of the Land League, two newspapers, *The Irishman* and *The Flag of Ireland*, belonging

[1] *Fall of Feudalism*, 377.   [2] *Life of Gladstone*, III, 71.

to Richard Pigott, later so notorious in connection with the forgeries of Parnell's letters, but then believed to be a member of the extreme party, who were strongly opposed to the Land League. Parnell started, in place of them, a new paper, *United Ireland*, as the organ of the League. He selected as editor of this paper Mr. William O'Brien, who had already won distinction as an uncompromising supporter of the National cause, and as a brilliant writer in *The Freeman's Journal*. By his vigorous writing and literary ability he more than justified the selection.

Mr. O'Brien was arrested as a suspect the day after Parnell was lodged in Kilmainham Jail, and the paper itself, after a time, was suppressed by Forster. It continued a precarious existence, published sometimes in England and sometimes in Paris, and was circulated surreptitiously in Ireland. When O'Brien came out of prison, some months later, *United Ireland* was revived, and for three years was a thorn in the side of the Irish Government. Davitt says of the paper and its editor during this period :

" Week after week the paper poured broadsides of scathing criticism into the Castle camp, reviewing with remorseless severity the doings of the Coercionist Courts, the blundering of incompetent magistrates, the packing of juries, and the occasional brutality of the Castle police. Every resource of an aggressive journalism, and a widely informed political knowledge, was drawn upon in relentless war to the knife against the successors to the Forster policy." [1]

In this task Mr. O'Brien was powerfully aided by Mr. T. M. Healy, who contributed, it was said, most of the onslaughts on Mr. Trevelyan. These attacks in the Press were seconded by a ceaseless flow of hostile criticism in Parliament. It must be admitted that these passionate attacks were not without provocation from the Irish Government. It is of the essence of coercion that when arbitrary power is given to officials, to magistrates and police officers, the Government is powerless to control them. " Put power into a pot," it has been well said, " and it is certain to boil over." To a Government in the position of that in Ireland, especially when the Liberal Party is in power and is in conflict with the National Party, almost the only support it has is from

[1] *Fall of Feudalism*, 380.

these quarters. The Tory Party give it no support—and the National Party are estranged. It necessarily follows that the Government must support the officials and police in Parliament, whether they are right or wrong, for, if these classes are disaffected, the position of the Government becomes almost impossible.

This is probably the explanation of cases which occurred under the Crimes Act, which greatly envenomed public opinion in Ireland. Among others, there was the case of Mr. T. Harrington, who was Secretary to the new National League. A short time after his appointment, Harrington was prosecuted for a speech which he made in Westmeath. The charge against him was "for intimidating divers farmers in order to compel them to pay a certain rate of wages which they are not bound to do." In his speech, which was mainly devoted to the condition of labourers, he complained of the apathy of the farmers of Westmeath to the national movement. He would, he said, "be the last person in the world to set class against class, but he was now determined to organize against the men who would not give a fair day's wages for a fair day's work. The full force of the agitation would be directed against them."

It is scarcely credible that Harrington was prosecuted for intimidating the tenant farmers of Westmeath, by the use of these words, and was convicted by two resident magistrates, and sentenced to two months' imprisonment. The conviction was confirmed on appeal by the County Court Judge of the district. Harrington was subjected to the plank bed, and to all the other severities of a common prisoner. When he refused to perform some duty of peculiar indignity he was confined to his cell for a week, without any exercise in fresh air. While in jail a vacancy occurred in the representation of Westmeath, where he was resident as a prisoner. Harrington was put up as a candidate, and was elected without opposition by the farmers, who, in the days before the extension of the County franchise, constituted the bulk of the electors—the very men he was supposed to have intimidated. His election was reported to him in the jail. There could not be a stronger case of popular repudiation of injustice perpetrated under the guise of law.

In the course of the autumn of 1882 Mr. W. O'Brien was

prosecuted for a seditious libel. The case could not be withdrawn from a jury. In spite of every effort to pack the jury, and to obtain a conviction, the prosecution failed. A few days later a vacancy occurred in the representation of Mallow, by the elevation to the Bench of the Attorney-General, Mr. Johnson. The constituency was reckoned as an absolutely safe seat for a Government candidate, being small and corrupt. The new Law Officer, Mr. Naish, was sent by the Government to contest it. Mr. W. O'Brien was put up in opposition, and was returned by a good majority.

Two other cases of somewhat similar character, where Irish leaders were sent to jail, occurred in 1883. Mr. Davitt and Mr. Healy were prosecuted for speeches. In order to secure their imprisonment, articles were exhibited against them under an old Act of Edward III, long ago treated as obsolete in England, but which still existed, unrepealed, in Ireland. They were called upon to give bail for good conduct, or to go to jail. It was obviously impossible for these two men, in the face of public opinion in Ireland, to admit that they were in the wrong, and to give bail for good behaviour. They were, consequently, sent to jail for three months. Shortly after their release a vacancy occurred in the county of Monaghan by the death of its Member, Mr. Gavin. At that time there was not a single Parnellite Member for the Province of Ulster. It was thought desirable to make an effort to secure a footing in the province. Mr. Healy, who was already Member for Wexford, gave up his seat there, and came forward as a candidate for Monaghan. He was returned by a good majority, and his seat at Wexford was filled by Mr. William Redmond. Everything, therefore, tended to show that the electors revolted against the system of coercion, and that there was no passport so certain to secure election as imprisonment under it.

On the other hand, the Crimes Act undoubtedly did good work in bringing to justice the perpetrators of serious crimes, and especially of the Phœnix Park murders. This was mainly effected through the operation of the clause which gave power to magistrates to summon witnesses, and interrogate them in private. Early in 1883, before the meeting of Parliament, the Government, by means of this clause, was able to obtain full information of the conspiracy which had resulted in the murders of Lord Frederick Cavendish and Mr. Burke. More than one conspirator turned informer, to save their own lives from the halter. A man called Carey—a member of the Dublin Town Council—was the principal informer, and, on his evidence, the whole gang were put on trial and were found guilty. Five of them were hanged, and six were sentenced to penal servitude. Verdicts were obtained by a free use of the clause in the Coercion Act, which enabled the Government in serious cases virtually to form the panel from which jurymen were selected. The Irish Judges had protested most strongly against the clause, which enabled the Government to appoint special Commissions of the Judges to try cases without juries—and, in fact, this most objectionable course was never put in force by the Government. The clauses as to changes of venue, and as to framing panels of jurymen, were found to be sufficient, without resort to that so much objected to by the Judges. The evidence given before the magistrates in the Phœnix Park case greatly excited public opinion, and in some quarters it was firmly believed that the Land League, and Parnell himself, were implicated in the conspiracy.

At the opening of Parliament, in the beginning of 1883, the Speech from the Throne referred in terms of satisfaction to the improved condition of Ireland. Agrarian crime, it claimed, had sensibly diminished, and the law had everywhere been upheld. It went on to say that the continued existence of secret societies called for unrelenting energy and vigilance on the part of the Executive. On this Mr. Gorst, from the Opposition Benches, moved an amendment to the Address, which expressed the hope "that the recent change in Irish policy would be maintained, that no further concessions would be made to lawless agitators, and that secret societies would continue to receive the energetic vigilance of the Government." The debate raised on this was most important. It raised again the whole policy of the Kilmainham transaction.

Mr. Forster took the opportunity of paying off old scores, by making a most elaborate, long-prepared, bitter, and deadly personal attack on Parnell. He took advantage of the Phœnix Park murders, and of the excited state of public opinion on them, to prejudice Mr. Parnell and the Land League by raising suspicion of their implication in that terrible crime, and by charging them with responsibility directly for all the outrages and crimes of the past years. The recent disclosures, he said, at the trials before the magistrate in the murder cases, had increased the suspicions against the Land League, and made it incumbent on Mr. Parnell to give an explanation of their transactions.

" No mere disclaimer," he said, " of connection with outrages will suffice. We have had disclaimers before. Do not let the Hon. Member, Mr. Parnell, suppose that I charge him with complicity with murderers, but this I do charge against him and his friends, that he has allowed himself to continue as the leader, and the avowed chief of an organization, which not merely advocated, and ostensibly and openly urged, the ruin of those who offended by boycotting them, and making life almost more miserable than death, but which prompted or organized outrage and incited to murder. The outcome of this agitation was murder, and the Hon. Member ought to have known that this would be its natural result ; and it is hard to understand how he did not know it, and why he did not separate himself from it altogether, and disavow and denounce it. The Hon. Member was the man who, more than any other, derived advantage and power by the help of this terrorism, and he is bound to show how it was that he did not find out that this terrorism was used, and he ought to tell us the steps he took to find it out. We know that he took none, and we know that he has been content to reap the advantages."

He then quoted from speeches by Brennan, Boyton, Sheridan, and Redpath, all connected with the Land League, which, he said, were incitements to murder, also extracts from Mr. Patrick Ford's writings in *The Irish World*, and from *United Ireland*, of which Parnell and McCarthy were owners, in which murder, arson, and attacks on women were described as " incidents of the campaign," and " indications of the spirit of the country."

Mr. Forster went on to say : " This is the first time in the history of either England or Ireland, in which an agitation has been conducted by appeals to personal injury to individuals, and not by appeals to the voter or to public opinion. No wonder that from such an agitation as this has followed the first political assassination that has disgraced our annals for hundreds of years. There is abhorrence of it in England and Scotland. Until the Hon. Member expresses regret and repentance for having set on foot such an agitation as this, I can have no communication with him. Still, the abhorrence in Ireland is not so great as it ought to be, because of the efforts of the Hon. Member and his friends to demoralize the Irish people by intimidation and terror. . . .

" But there are grounds for hope ; one is that the Irish Government has now the power to uphold the law, and will use it, and the other is that the Member for Cork and his fellow-chiefs, in this so-called agitation, have been found out."[1]

Forster never, in his Parliamentary life, made a more powerful and effective speech. It was delivered amid frequent cheering of the Tory Party on the opposite benches, and of not a small section of the Liberals—a condition which is always most inspiring to a speaker. The speech was the outpouring of wrath pent up for nearly three years—a determination to destroy the character and influence of the opponent who had defeated him and caused his resignation. It is well to remember that only a few months before he had spoken of Parnell as a man of honour, whose word he would accept—yet if his present indictment was justified, such an appellation most certainly could not be given to him.

It was the general expectation that Parnell would at once reply to this scathing indictment. O'Connell and Butt would certainly have done so, and in passionate language would have done their best to dispel the impression produced. But Parnell's temperament was very different. He was cold and impassive. He had no command of passionate language. In spite of cries from all parts of the House, he sat silent, scornful, disdainful. The debate nearly collapsed for want of a reply to Forster. Parnell was pressed by his own colleagues to answer at once. He did not wish to make any reply. His friends had to force him to do so, if not at once, at least when the House should meet again. Later in the evening it was generally understood that he would reply the next day, and he moved the adjournment that night for the purpose.

Mr. O'Donnell, who by this time had ceased to be a follower

[1] *Hansard*, February 23rd, 1883.

of Parnell, says that he thought he knew how best Parnell should deal with Forster.

" I sought out Parnell," he says, " in order to render him the last service which his old comrade was ever to pay within that Parliament or elsewhere. I found Parnell in the Library of the House with a pile of papers like notes of speeches before him. ' O'Donnell,' he cried out, ' I want you. Sexton and Healy have given me a lot of splendid points for my reply to Forster, but I do not feel quite that they fit. My speech will be rather heavy, I fear. What a tremendous lot of ground Forster went over ! He must have had that speech on the stocks ever since he went out of office.' I pulled over a chair and sat down by him. ' Do you know, Parnell, my idea ? ' ' I am blest if I would answer Forster at all.' ' But I open the debate to-morrow.' ' Open it by all means.' ' But how ? ' ' You are the head of the Irish nation, and this Englishman has the impudence to stand you up for the decision of English opinion. If I were you, I should tell them all to go to the devil. You are responsible to Ireland alone. Give them contempt, nothing but contempt, and Ireland will go wild with pride for you.' Parnell leaned back on his chair for two seconds, and then with a sort of shout cried, ' O'Donnell the audacious. By God ! you are right,' and pushed the whole pile of notes off the table on to the floor. ' Let us come down on the Terrace. I shan't think of my speech till to-morrow.' As we went out of the door he half turned to look at the heap on the carpet, and with a chuckle that had something grim in it said, ' Those are great notes of Sexton's.' "[1]

Parnell acted on O'Donnell's advice. The next day the House of Commons was fuller than I had ever known it. The galleries were crowded. The Heir-Apparent to the Throne was there. The Peers were there in force. All had come to hear the reply of the Irish Leader, who had been distinctly arraigned for having connived at outrages and murders. Parnell was in his place, impassive as usual, but ready, as every one supposed, to meet his enemy at the gate and to dispel his facts.

To the surprise of all he made no attempt to do so. His speech was a scornful repudiation of any responsibility to the people of England for his past action, a denial that Forster

[1] *History of the Irish Parliamentary Party*, II, 147.

had any right or claim to call upon him for an explanation. His responsibility was only to the Irish people at home and abroad, and to them alone would he address the few words he proposed to say. He looked upon Mr. Forster, he said, as little better than an informer. After dealing with a few minor facts of the indictment, he turned on Mr. Forster and made a bitter onslaught on him. " Why," he said, " was Mr. Forster deposed—he, the Right Hon. Gentleman who has acquired experience in the administration of Ireland? . . . Why was he deposed, and Mr. Trevelyan, a prentice, although a very willing hand, put in his position ?   I feel that the Chief Secretary must say with the Scriptures : ' I am not worthy to unloose his shoe latchet.'   It would be far better to have the Act administered by the seasoned politician now in disgrace and retirement.   Call him back to his post ; send him to help Lord Spencer in the congenial work of the gallows in Ireland. Send him back to look after the secret inquisitions in Dublin Castle. Send him to distribute the taxes which an unfortunate and starving peasantry has to pay for crimes not .committed by themselves. All this would be congenial work to the Right Hon. Gentleman. We invite you to man your ranks and to send your ablest and best men to push forward the task of misgoverning and oppressing Ireland. For my part, I am confident as to the future of Ireland. Although the horizon may be clouded, I believe our people will survive the present oppression. . . . The time will come when this House and the people of this country will admit once again that they have been mistaken, and that they have been deceived by those who ought to be ashamed of themselves. . . . I believe that they will reject their guides and leaders with as much deter- mination and just as much relief as they rejected the services of the Right Hon. Gentleman the Member for Bradford."

The speech was an appeal to Irish opinion against that of England—a disclaimer that he owed responsibility to the latter. In this view it was received with acclamation by the Irish Party in the House of Commons, and by the great majority of the people of Ireland. It struck a note of defiance to England and its Government which appealed to Irishmen all over the world. It strengthened enormously the position of Parnell as Leader of the Party. It effaced the effect and recollection of his negotiations with the English Government.

Few people now believe that Parnell incited outrages and crimes or connived at them, or that the Land League organized them, though some of its members in their individual capacity may have been concerned in them. It may be doubted also whether, even at the time of Forster's attack, many persons were persuaded by him, and really believed in the complicity of Parnell. No one appears to have followed Forster's example in refusing to have any communication with Parnell, or with other leaders of the Land League in the House of Commons, because they did not express regret and repentance for having set on foot the agitation. Other Members of the House, so far as my observation went, continued to treat them as honourable political opponents.

It must be admitted, however, that the refusal of Parnell to answer Forster's charges, though approved by Irish opinion, produced a bad effect on English Members, and on English opinion outside Parliament. He was blamed chiefly for not having denounced outrages and murders, and for not warning his supporters, and the Irish people generally, against them. Comparison was made with O'Connell, who in his successive agitations for Catholic Emancipation, the abolition of Tithes, and the Repeal of the Union, very frequently warned his supporters against violence and outrages of all kinds, and protested that they only did harm to the causes he advocated. It should be recollected, however, that few people in O'Connell's time gave him any credit for so doing. He was frequently charged with responsibility for outrages and crime in language almost as strong as that used against Parnell. Nor did O'Connell's efforts in this direction have much effect in preventing outrages, which exceeded in number and virulence those committed during the Land Agitation. They were generally attributed to O'Connell's agitation, in spite of his efforts to prevent them. There was no reason to believe that condemnations of crime by Parnell would have produced any greater effect than did those of O'Connell. The outrages during the Land movement were the direct result of evictions. If evictions in the opinion of Mr. Gladstone were equivalent to sentences of death to the evicted families, in what light must they have been regarded by the evicted men themselves, and by the threatened peasantry of the district? Can we feel surprised that the *lex talionis* was enforced, when protection of the law was denied?

Though Parnell was personally silent on the subject, except on rare occasions, his principal followers were not so. Davitt, who founded the Land League, and who spoke at countless numbers of meetings, never did so without denouncing outrages and crime. He never received any credit for this. Nor did his action prevent his being sent back to a convict prison in the manner above described. In a circular issued by the Executive of the Land League, early in its proceedings, in the autumn of 1880, to the local organizers of the League, throughout the country, which must have been agreed to by Parnell, crime of all kinds, outrages, the maiming of cattle, and the use of threatening letters were denounced in the strongest language. The local meetings were largely attended by priests ; large numbers of them were presided over by the parish priests of the districts. These clerical speakers never failed to advise against violence of all kinds. They did not succeed in preventing such deeds, though doubtless they had some effect in reducing their numbers.

Reverting to the rigorous administration of the Crimes Act, it is to be observed that, in the last half of 1882, agrarian outrages were, month by month, greatly and progressively reduced. The average of such offences, including threatening letters, for the first five months was 462. For the next two months it was 257. For the next three months there was a further drop to an average of 139, and for the last two months of the year, generally the worst for such cases, the average was only 89, and this low rate was maintained during the next two years.

Was this great reduction to one-fifth only of the number at the beginning of the year due to the rigorous enforcement of the Crimes Act ? or was it due to the Arrears Act and the slowing down of the agitation by Parnell, of which the suppression of the Ladies' League was an important feature, in accordance with his promises ? The Government expected and intended, by its land legislation and by its arrangement with Parnell, to bring about a reduction of outrages and to restore peace and order in Ireland. They were advised that this would be the result of passing an Arrears Act, of releasing the suspects, and of the promise of Parnell to slow down the agitation. What could be more reasonable than to conclude that these measures had the desired result, and that the improved condition of the country was more due to them than to the Crimes Act, the administration of which incensed public opinion in Ireland ?   In any case credit ought to have been given to Parnell for slowing down the agitation, and for his advice and assistance in passing the Arrears Act.   It was ungenerous of Forster not to allude to this.

CHAPTER XXIV

THE IRISH FRANCHISE

THE Government was now entering upon its fourth year of office. During the first three years the time of the House of Commons had been almost wholly devoted to Irish questions. British legislation had been much neglected. It was impossible that this could continue. The autumn Session of 1882 was devoted to the discussion of the procedure of the House. New rules were prepared and carried by the Government, of a drastic character, for economizing the time of the House, and preventing the waste of it by merely obstructive discussion. The principle of the closure was then first proposed. It led to prolonged discussion. The main issue was raised on a motion of Mr. Gibson, on behalf of the Opposition, proposing that the closure of debates should only be adopted when supported by a majority of two-thirds of the Members present. It was obvious, if this were adopted, that it would only be used against small minorities, and not against the main Opposition. The amendment was strongly opposed by Mr. Gladstone, because it would be unjust to the majority, as it would hand over their rights to a minority. Parnell also opposed the amendment in the interest of the Irish Party. The closure, thus limited, would be used against them alone. He could not admit that the closure in any form would greatly facilitate legislation. The only remedy for the existing block was to restore to Ireland its right to deal with its own affairs in its own Parliament. The amendment was rejected by a majority of 322 to 288, the whole of the Irish Party voting with the Government—one of the very few occasions, when they did so, in this Parliament. Many Radicals abstained from voting. The main clause was carried by 306 to 262, the Irish Members on this occasion voting against it.

Thus fortified against obstruction, the Government entered on its fourth year. The Session was mainly devoted to Imperial and English legislation, and no Irish measures of importance blocked the way, though three or four useful Irish Bills of secondary importance, on tramways, fisheries, and the like, were carried with the support of the Irish Members. Parnell was seldom at the House during this and the next Session, partly owing to bad health; but he turned up when questions of importance affecting Ireland came before the House. He moved, on March 14th, the second reading of a Bill to amend the Land Act of 1881, in the direction already often explained, proposing to give effect to the Healy Clause, which had been all but defeated by the interpretation given to it by the Irish judges; to date the judicial rent from the time of application to the Land Court; to include leaseholders and other classes within the operation of the Act; and to amend the purchase clauses by the advance of the whole of the purchase money, and by the extension of the term for repayment. The Bill was strongly opposed by Mr. Gladstone. The Government, he said, differed organically from it. It amounted to a virtual reconstruction of the Land Act. The Government would give no encouragement to any plan for disturbing its main provisions. The Bill was rejected by 250 to 53. Nearly all the proposals of this Bill were conceded by Parliament, before many years were passed, most of them by the Tory Party when in office. It cannot therefore now be said that it was wise policy thus to bang the door in Parliament against all interference with the Land Act of 1881. It had the effect of confirming the position of Parnell in the leadership of the Irish people, and of destroying the Liberal Party in Ireland, as distinguished from the Parnellites on the one hand, and the Tories on the other.

The moderate and constitutional action of Parnell, so different from his earlier methods, though meeting with the general approval of the great majority of his party in Ireland, was indignantly resented by the more extreme men on the other side of the Atlantic. By way of protest against this moderation and inaction, *The Irish World*, the organ of extremists, at the instance of its editor, Patrick Ford, preached an active crusade against England, and proposed that its cities should be blown up with dynamite. Some dangerous

fanatics, in connection with the Clan-na-Gael, proceeded to put
these doctrines into practice, and, in the early part of this year,
made attempts to blow up public buildings in London, notably
that of the Local Government Board in Whitehall. A
manufactory of nitro-glycerine was discovered at Birmingham
fitted for such purposes ; and evidence was obtained of a
dynamite conspiracy, with definite intentions in this direction.
There was great public alarm on the subject. The Government
met the case with promptness and severity. Sir William
Harcourt introduced a Bill to strengthen the law against
such infamies. It was of a most stringent character. He
succeeded in persuading the House of Commons to pass the
Bill through all its stages in a single sitting of an hour and a
half. It passed the Lords with equal celerity. The Irish
Members raised no objection to it. Though no one suggested
that they had any connection with the dynamiters, yet the
Irish cause suffered in public estimation in England, and the
breach between the two countries became wider.

No one in England gave credit to Parnell for his changed
attitude and his strict adherence to his Kilmainham promises.
In Ireland itself Parnell's influence and prestige were never
higher. It has already been shown that the effect of Forster's
fierce attack on Parnell in the House of Commons, and the
defiant reply to it, appealing to Irish opinion against that of
England, was to add greatly to the popularity of Parnell in
his own country, and to confirm him in the leadership of his
party. His friends thought it afforded a good opportunity to
raise a fund by way of testimonial to him, in order to relieve
him from financial embarrassment due, in great part, to his
efforts for the national cause. He had suffered like other
landowners from a reduction of rent. Some one had asked him,
when he was in Kilmainham, how the " No Rent " manifesto
was being acted on. He replied, with a laugh, that he did not
know ; all that he could say was that his own tenants had
availed themselves freely of the excuse to abstain from paying
their rents. His property at Avondale was heavily mortgaged.
The mortgagees threatened to foreclose. It was proposed to
raise a fund to free the property from debt. The proposal was
backed by Archbishop Croke, and was cordially taken up.
It was hoped to raise £20,000. When, after some weeks, the
fund had reached the amount of £12,000, a most unexpected

impetus was given to it by the ill-advised action of the Government, in persuading the papal authorities at Rome to use their influence with the Irish Bishops, to discourage it.

It appears that early in the agrarian movement, in November, 1880, when many Catholic priests in Ireland were attending Land League meetings, and making violent speeches, Mr. Gladstone, through Cardinal Newman, made representations to the Pope, in the hope of inducing him to use his influence to restrain the clergy in Ireland from aiding the Land League movement. Lord Morley has quoted in full Mr. Gladstone's letter. It is well worth perusal. In the course of it he wrote : " You will hardly be surprised that I regard the supreme Pontiff, if apprised of the facts, as responsible for the action of these priests, for I perfectly well know that he has the means of silencing them. . . . If the persons complained of had been laymen, the Government would have settled their cases by putting them in jail. Mr. Errington [a Home Rule Member for an Irish constituency, not a follower of Parnell] is at Rome, and will, I hope, bring the facts, as far as he is able, to the knowledge of His Holiness. But I do not know how far he is able ; nor how he may use his discretion. He is not an official servant, but an independent Catholic gentleman." [1] Cardinal Newman replied that he would gladly find himself able to be of service, however small it might be, in a political crisis which he felt to be of grave anxiety to all ; but he thought that Mr. Gladstone overrated the Pope's powers in political and social matters. Mr. Errington, however, succeeded in inducing the Pope to bring his influence to bear on the Irish Bishops. He remained at Rome in a semi-official character, and it was doubtless due to his influence with the Pope that a rescript was addressed by the Prefect and Secretary of the Propaganda *de fide* to the Irish Bishops commencing, " *Quale cumque de Parnellio*," bidding them warn their clergy against taking part in collections for the testimonial to Parnell.

" Apostolic mandates," it said, " absolutely condemn such collections as are raised in order to influence popular passions, and to be used as a means for leading men into rebellion against the laws. The clergy must hold themselves aloof from such subscriptions, when it is plain that hatred and dissension are aroused by them, and that never in any way are censures

[1] *Life of Gladstone.*

pronounced against the crimes and murders with which wicked men stain themselves. . . . *Quibus positis*, it must be evident to your Lordships that the collection called the Parnell Testimonial Fund cannot be approved by this sacred congregation, and consequently it cannot be tolerated that any ecclesiastic, much less a Bishop, should take any part in recommending or promoting it."

The publication of this document caused universal indignation throughout Ireland. It was aggravated by the exultation in the English Press at the intervention of the Pope to suppress the turbulent priests. The result of this interference by papal rescript was an immense stimulus to the fund. There was a rush of new subscribers. It rapidly rose from £12,000 to £39,000. It was said the Peter's Pence from Ireland remitted to Rome that year was reduced in corresponding proportion. The day came, later in the year (1883), when a presentation of this handsome amount was to be made to Parnell on behalf of the subscribers, by the Lord Mayor of Dublin, to be followed by a banquet at the Rotunda. Mr. Barry O'Brien gives the following account of what took place :

" The Lord Mayor of Dublin with other leading citizens waited on Parnell, at Morrison's Hotel, to hand him a cheque for the £39,000. His Lordship naturally prepared a few suitable observations for the occasion. The deputation was ushered into a private sitting-room, and there stood the chief. The Lord Mayor, having been announced, bowed and began : ' Mr. Parnell——' ' I believe,' said Parnell, ' you have got a cheque for me.' The Lord Mayor, somewhat surprised at this interruption, said, ' Yes,' and was about to resume his speech when Parnell broke in: ' Is it made payable to order or crossed ? ' The Lord Mayor again answered in the affirmative, and was resuming the thread of his discourse, when Parnell took the cheque, folded it neatly, and put it in his waistcoat pocket. This ended the interview. The whole business was disposed of in five minutes, and there was no speech-making." [1]

On December 11th the banquet in Parnell's honour took place. Parnell made a long speech, but never said a word about the cheque, or of thanks for the public subscription. His speech was a vehement arraignment of Lord Spencer and Mr. Trevelyan. It was, however, important, for it was the first in

[1] *Life of Parnell*, II, 28.

which Parnell attempted to forecast the future, after the coming General Election. " Coercion," he said, " could not last for ever, but if it were to be renewed it should be by a Tory Government, and not a Liberal Government. Beyond a shadow of a doubt, it will be for the Irish people in England— separated, isolated, as they are—and for your independent Irish Members to determine at the next General Election whether a Tory or a Liberal English Ministry shall rule England. This is a great force and a great power. If we cannot rule ourselves, we can at least cause them to be ruled as we choose. This force has already gained for Ireland inclusion in the coming Franchise Bill. We have reason to be proud, hopeful, energetic, and determined that this generation shall not pass away until it has bequeathed to those who come after us the great birthright of national independence and prosperity."

This speech aroused great attention in England. It was regarded as an uncompromising defiance. It was a presage of what was to take place at the next General Election. That event was deferred in order to carry out the long-promised extension of the franchise in the Counties, and the necessary redistribution of seats. This occupied the attention of Parliament during the whole of the Session of 1884. Two questions deeply affected Ireland in relation to it, the one, whether that country was to be included in this extension of the franchise, the other, whether it was to retain its existing excess of Members in the House of Commons, in proportion to its population, and still more in proportion to its wealth, as compared with England and Scotland. These two questions were answered in the affirmative by the Government in their Franchise Bill and Redistribution of Seats Bill. The franchise in Ireland was to be assimilated to that of England, and the existing proportion of its Members was to be maintained, though there was to be a wide rearrangement of seats within its boundaries, and most of the small boroughs were to disappear. The extension of the County franchise in Ireland meant a much greater change in the addition of its electors, and in its disturbance of the balance of electoral power than in England. The existing franchise in the Counties of Ireland was a very limited one. It practically gave votes only to one class—the farmers. It excluded altogether labourers and cottier tenants. Household Suffrage meant the inclusion of these two classes, outnumbering greatly the existing electors. For the whole of Ireland the existing number of voters was only 200,000. The proposed lowering of the franchise meant the addition of 400,000.

It was to be expected that many Irishmen, of the landowning class, would be much alarmed at the great addition of new voters which would swamp the existing voters. They foresaw that it would completely change the complexion of County representation throughout a great part of Ireland, and would extinguish the Whig interest. On the other hand, Ireland, which at the time of the Union was very much under-represented in proportion to Great Britain, had, by the great reduction of its population, and by the great increase of that in England, come to be very much over-represented in the House of Commons. It returned 103 Members. If the number was reduced to the true proportion of its population there would be no more than 80, and if wealth were to be taken into account the number would be much less.

The first of these questions was discussed on two nights in Committee on a motion of Mr. Brodrick to exclude Ireland from the Franchise Bill. It led to a brilliant encounter between Mr. David Plunket (now Lord Rathmore), then representing the Dublin University, and Mr. Gladstone. Few of those now alive, who recollect the scene, can have forgotten the solemn warning by the former of the danger of the proposed extension. In beautifully chosen language, and with a mixture of passion and pathos, he contended that the measure was certain to result in the establishment of an Irish Parliament. The speaker had at times a slight stammer, which writers on oratory have held to be rather helpful in a great and passionate speech, by providing a short interval of expectation, on the part of the audience. His peroration of fervid eloquence, in which he dwelt on the benefits of the Union of the Parliaments of the two countries, and the danger of effecting a breach in it, was worthy of his reputation, and was emulous of his famous grandsire, the Plunket of the Irish Parliament in its last days, who, when translated to the English Parliament, held his own in the front rank of orators there.

The speech made a profound impression on the House. The question was a critical one. The division was uncertain. Many of the Whig supporters of the Government were doubtful as to their votes. It was necessary to supply an antidote at once. Only fifteen minutes remained before the rising of the House in which to apply it. Mr. Gladstone was equal to the occasion. He flung himself into the debate, striking at once the highest note of eloquence. He met passion and pathos by passion of a different character, impetuous and forcible in the highest degree. He dealt with the political and social alarms, and forebodings of evil, by appeals to the principle of justice as between two countries and two races. I know no better illustration of Mr. Gladstone's oratory at its best, concentrated in comparatively few sentences, and not diffused as in many of his speeches. It was also spontaneous and impromptu. It completely effaced the impression produced by Mr. Plunket's powerful appeal.

On the resumption of the debate the next day, Lord Randolph Churchill separated himself, not for the first time, from the majority of his party. He congratulated the Government on their decision to include Ireland in the Bill, and announced his intention to vote with them. He declared there was no difference between the mud cabin of the Irish, and the cottage of the English labourer, and that of the Member for Westminster (Mr. W. H. Smith). Strange to say, he contended that the enfranchisement of the Irish agricultural labourer would be favourable to the cause of the landlord, and to the British connection. He held strongly to the idea, that it was impossible to maintain the Union, if Ireland was not treated on a footing of perfect justice and equity. He preferred that the Separatists should be met in debates in Parliament, rather than by force and violence outside. Mr. Chamberlain also appeared to hold that the extension of the suffrage to labourers in Ireland would be favourable to its landlords. More rightly did Parnell divine the future, and estimate the effect on his party of the proposed extension. In a speech at an early stage of the Bill, while showing no enthusiasm for it, he claimed that, without extension of the suffrage, the strength of the Nationalist Party, in the next Parliament, would be seventy-five, and with household suffrage it would be ninety. But whether Ireland were included or not, the Irish Members would be able to carry out their policy. Lord Hartington, who only a few months before had pronounced the extension of the franchise in Ireland to be dangerous ,now gave it his full support. Mr. Trevelyan, in a forcible speech, said that he would not remain for five minutes a member of a Government which denied equality to Ireland. Mr. Brodrick's amendment in Committee was defeated by 332 to 157 votes, a conclusive determination by the House in favour of equality of treatment to Ireland, no matter what the consequences. Many Tory members voted with the Government, and others abstained from voting.

With respect to the other main question affecting Ireland—the redistribution of seats—many Members, in the course of the debates, declared in favour of the reduction of the Irish representation. Among them was Mr. Forster. The Government, however, stood firm. The question was ultimately determined in the negotiations between the Leaders of the two Houses in favour of maintaining the then number of Irish Members, and no specific amendment was discussed in the House of Commons raising the question of reduction.

I may here mention that in October of the year 1884 Mr. Trevelyan, after more than two years of excessive work, and of strained responsibility, under an unceasing stream of hostile criticism and invective in the Nationalist Press, and in Parliament, which visibly aged him and blanched his hair, was promoted to Cabinet rank with the office of Chancellor of the Duchy of Lancaster. Mr. Gladstone then offered the vacant post of Irish Secretary to me. Before giving him an answer, I asked Lord Spencer as to his intended policy. The question of the renewal of the Coercion Act, which was to expire in September of 1885, was already looming in the near future. I had a great aversion to Coercion, and was determined that I would never undertake the defence of such a measure as a Minister. If I had been offered the post immediately after the Phœnix Park murders, I could not have refused it ; for it was then a post of great danger. The danger had now passed. I learned from Lord Spencer that he was then determined to renew the Coercion Act. As eleven months remained before the expiration of the existing Act, I suggested that he should at once announce that he would cease to make any use of the powers of the existing Coercion Act, and would revert to the ordinary law. This would afford an experience of some months. If the effect of such a course should prove to be bad, and if there should be a renewal of disturbance, it would always be possible to revert to coercion, and the renewal of the Act would then become defensible. Lord Spencer was not disposed to adopt this suggestion. On this I declined to accept the post.[1]

---

[1] A few weeks later I was appointed Postmaster-General, on the death of Mr. Fawcett, and a little later I was admitted to the Cabinet.

CHAPTER XXV

IN the early days of 1885, when the Government was entering on its sixth year of office, there were many signs of its approaching dissolution. It was labouring in the trough of the political sea. The Cabinet was at sixes and sevens. It was held together only with the greatest difficulty and tact on the part of Mr. Gladstone. Frequent resignations took place of its members, and were recalled only after negotiations. Seldom was a Cabinet meeting held without some member threatening to resign. More than once a member left the Cabinet in dudgeon. Two discreet colleagues were then sent after him, and persuaded him to return. I recollect on one occasion that Mr. Gladstone, on coming out of the Cabinet, remarked to me that all his colleagues seemed to be " going off at half-cock." The condition of things reminded me of the saying of a cynical old Whig, who had been a member of several Cabinets, that after some years of continuous office the members of a Government, as a rule, began to hate one another more than they hated their opponents, and that this was the frequent cause of the end of Governments. It is not to be inferred that Mr. Gladstone's colleagues had begun to hate one another. But, politically, certain members of it were at daggers drawn. There was no longer a common purpose, or a determination, to carry on, and to compromise on points of difference. Some of its members were weary of office. Some had departmental difficulties, from which they desired to escape. Mr. Gladstone himself felt the advance of age, and the strain of work, and frequently discussed his approaching resignation with Lord Granville and Lord Hartington.

Mr. Chamberlain had already begun to strike out a new line of his own. He made speeches at Birmingham, Ipswich, and elsewhere, propounding a new departure of policy, intended to supply a programme for the party at the General Election, which could not long be postponed. He denounced the existing system of taxation as unjust to the poor. He advocated the graduation of the Income Tax, Free Education, and the purchase of land by local authorities for allotments and small holdings. He discussed many social changes which at that time seemed very radical, but which have since been adopted. His speeches were very obnoxious to some of his Whig colleagues, and added to the wish to part company. Mr. Gladstone met the difficulties and differences in his Cabinet, as Lord Morley has most justly said, " with unalterable patience, unruffled self-command, inexhaustible in resource, catching at every straw from the resource of others, indefatigable in bringing men of divergent opinion within friendly reach of one another, of tireless ingenuity in minimizing differences." It seemed to me that he treated the threatened resignations of his colleagues as part of the everyday business of his official life. He was ready to replace any or all of them, so long as he thought that the public interest would suffer by the resignation of his Government.

Whatever his personal views as to his own retirement, he played the great game of politics to the very end. He was determined that the Liberal Government should not be broken up on some by-question, not involving a point of principle which the country could understand. If the Government were to go out of office, it should be on some question not destructive of the integrity of the Liberal Party. He spared no efforts in this view. It has sometimes been charged against Mr. Gladstone that he dominated his Cabinet, and could not brook differences on the part of his colleagues. Nothing could be further from the truth, so far as I observed, in this the fag end of his Government. On the contrary, it seemed to me that he might at times, with advantage, have exercised his authority as Premier with greater force. He was sometimes treated in discussion in the Cabinet by two members of it in a manner which, I thought, should have been resented.

I was admitted to the Cabinet early in February of that year. Within a few days a division took place, in the House of Commons, on a vote of censure for the failure of the Government to relieve General Gordon at Khartoum. The Government escaped defeat only by fourteen votes. The question was mooted the next day, in the Cabinet, whether the Government should resign in view of the alarming reduction of its majority. There was great diversity of opinion on the subject. Mr. Gladstone asked for the opinion of all his colleagues. They were evenly divided, and Mr. Gladstone decided in favour of remaining in office. One member said that he had so recently become a member of the Cabinet that he would not express an opinion. If I had followed his example the majority would have been in favour of resignation.

The Parliamentary position of the Government was not much better than that in the Cabinet. There were some seventy or eighty Liberals who were restive under the Party Whip. Candid friends, such as Mr. Forster and Mr. Goschen, were firing broadsides at the Government from the back benches. The Irish Party of thirty-nine, under Parnell's lead, were now always on the side of the enemy. Ireland was, in fact, the main difficulty ahead. The question of Egypt and the Soudan, and that of Russia and the Afghan frontier, had been surmounted by the Government, not without great peril. In Ireland it was different. Two grave questions came up for determination—the one, whether the Coercion Act of 1881, which was to expire in a few months, was to be renewed wholly or in part, in which case early legislation would be necessary ; the other, whether some attempt should not be made to give Ireland some measure of self-government and greater control over its own affairs.

As regards the first of these, the condition of Ireland in respect of agrarian crime, was at the time satisfactory, whether that was due to the enforcement of the Coercion Act of 1882, or to the working of the Land Act of 1881, and the Arrears Act, 1882. Lord Spencer, however, would not dispense with coercion. He was supported by Lord Hartington, Lord Selborne, Lord Northbrook, and a majority of the Cabinet. He was strongly opposed by Mr. Chamberlain, Sir Charles Dilke, and myself. On the question of Local Government for Ireland there was also great divergence of opinion. Mr. Chamberlain laid a scheme before the Cabinet for a National Council in Dublin, of an elective character, in whom the work of all the numerous administrative Boards and Depart-

ments in Ireland was to be vested; but without power over
the police, or the administration of the law. No direct
communication had been attempted with the Irish leaders,
but it had been ascertained from the correspondence of one
of them, through Cardinal Manning, that Parnell approved
of the scheme, and if it were agreed to, would not oppose a
very limited Coercion Bill.

The scheme was very strongly supported by Mr. Gladstone.
He was prepared to go even further, and to invest the
National Council with control over the police as a beginning.
After long discussion in the Cabinet, a vote was taken upon
it—a very unusual course. The Cabinet was evenly divided.
All the Peers, plus Lord Hartington, were against the scheme;
all the Commoners in favour of it. On coming out of the
Cabinet I asked Mr. Gladstone whether he had observed the
remarkable cleavage between Peers and Commoners. " Indeed I did," he said; " the day will come when the Peers
will bitterly rue their decision." " The scheme," he wrote to
Lord Spencer, " will quickly rise again, as I think, in larger
dimensions."[1] For the present, however, he abandoned the
hope of solving the Irish question in this direction.

There still remained the question whether the Coercion Act
should be renewed. Lord Spencer, after much discussion, was
prepared to whittle down his Bill, but Chamberlain, Dilke, and
the writer still objected. For my part, I thought that some
of the most objectionable clauses of the Act of 1882 were
those giving power to resident magistrates to deal with
agrarian offences, which previously could only be determined
by juries. Irish opinion would be flouted almost as much
by the smaller Bill as by the larger one. If a small Bill, in
Lord Spencer's opinion, would suffice, all the more reason
for postponing it till the need for it was proved, and for
reverting in the meanwhile to the ordinary law. A Coercive
Bill of any dimensions would be bitterly opposed by the Irish
Party, and by a considerable section of Radical Members,
unless an agreement were come to with the Irish Party as
to a remedial measure in connection with it. It was a case
for negotiation, but Lord Hartington and the Whigs were
strongly opposed to any kind of negotiation or agreement
with Parnell.

[1] *Life of Gladstone*, III, 127.

It was hoped to make coercion more palatable by accompanying it with a Bill for extension of Land Purchase, but Chamberlain and Dilke objected to this unless connected with some kind of local government. A temporary agreement was patched up, and on May 15th Mr. Gladstone announced in the House of Commons that the Government proposed to introduce, what he described as certain clauses of a valuable and equitable description in the existing Coercion Act, and on May 20th he gave notice of a Land Purchase Bill. Mr. Morley, about this time, gave notice, in the House, that he would oppose the renewal of the Coercion Act in any form. Further negotiations took place between Mr. Gladstone and Mr. Chamberlain, and it seemed that some agreement was arrived at as to a measure of coercion, but whether it was to take effect only after proclamation by the Lord-Lieutenant, or immediately on the passing of the Act, was not settled. On June 5th, after the Whitsun recess, it was decided at a Cabinet that notice should be given in the House of Commons of a Bill to take the place of the Coercion Act. Some points, however, were still open, and it is very doubtful whether agreement was really arrived at. The end of the Government was at hand on another question—that of the Budget.

While, however, the Liberal Ministers in Mr. Gladstone's Cabinet were still haggling as to the details of a Coercion Bill, and could not see their way wholly to dispense with it, and were unwilling even to discuss with Parnell, or the Irish Party, a future policy for Ireland, which might have secured their acquiescence in a moderate measure of coercion, their opponents were secretly committing themselves to the very opposite policy. Lord Randolph Churchill is to be credited with having induced the other leaders of the Tory Party to adopt this course. He had recently been admitted to the inner council of the party leaders, and he was certainly, at this time, by far the most active and virile force in the party, almost the only one who had made any impression on the more democratic of its followers. He had very early perceived the advantage, and indeed the necessity, of an alliance with the Irish Party, as the only possibility, at that time, of a Tory Government coming into power. He was prepared to take every advantage of the announcement of the Government to introduce a Coercion Bill. In a speech at the Con-

DEFEAT OF MR. GLADSTONE 263

stitutional Club immediately after the notice given by Mr.
Gladstone, on May 15th, Lord Randolph declared himself
to be profoundly shocked by it. Ireland must be in an awful
state, or else the Radical members of the Cabinet would never
have assented to such unanswerable evidence that the Liberal
Party could not govern Ireland, without resort to that arbitrary
force, which their greatest orator had declared to be no remedy.
It was thought at the time that these were merely the
vagaries of a free-lance. No one, least of all the Tory rank
and file, dreamed that they indicated a policy, which Lord
Randolph had already persuaded their leaders to adopt.
Members of the party in the House of Commons were daily
hounding on the Government to renewed coercion in Ireland,
without dissent from leaders on the front bench. But three
months later, after the defeat and resignation of the Government, Lord Randolph, speaking as a Minister at Sheffield, let
the cat out of the bag. He told a surprised public that, early
in the year, when Mr. Gladstone was still in office, at the
very time when Lord Spencer, the head of the Irish Executive,
was assuring his colleagues that he could not safely govern
Ireland, without some coercive powers, the leaders of the
Tory Party had met in secret conclave, and had come to an
opposite conclusion.

After " immense deliberation," he said, they had determined that, in the absence of official information, they
could see nothing to warrant a Government in applying for
renewal of exceptional powers in Ireland, and that if they
were returned to power they would act on this conclusion.
This notable decision was kept secret from all the world. There
was good reason for this, as it would most certainly have
been repudiated by the rank and file of their party. If made
public, it is impossible to suppose that the Liberal Government would have proceeded farther with their intention to
renew a part of the Act of 1882. What, then, was the motive
for such an unprecedented course as that of the leaders of an
Opposition coming to a decision as to what they would do on
an administrative question, long in advance of any responsibility, and when they were without official information?
Can any one doubt that it was for the express purpose of
being made use of in negotiation with the Irish leaders?
It was obvious that the Irish Party would not assist in turn-

ing out the Liberal Government, if the only effect of it would be to replace them by a Government pledged to coercion.

Mr. Justin McCarthy, then acting as Leader of the Irish Party, in place of Parnell, who was temporarily indisposed, has put it on record that an assurance was given to him by emissaries from Lord Salisbury that the Tories, if returned to power, would not renew the Coercion Act. It has since been denied that there was any agreement between the two parties or their leaders. It was not necessary that there should be a written or sealed agreement. All that was necessary was a distinct intimation, on the part of the Tory leaders, of the decision arrived at by them not to renew coercion. This assurance would have its effect on the Irish leaders in determining their course.

That information to this effect was actually given by one of the Opposition leaders to the Irish Party is as certain as anything can be. It had the result of inducing the Irish Party to join in the vote on the division on the Budget against the Government. The assurance thus given was faithfully acted upon. On the earliest possible day, after the formation of the Government of Lord Salisbury, the newly appointed Lord - Lieutenant informed the House of Lords that his Government had come to a decision not to renew the Coercion Act. The policy thus announced, was later, not only carried out, but proved to be eminently successful. The expiring Coercion Act was no longer put in force. Its powers were allowed to drop. The Act was not renewed on its expiration in August. For nearly two years Ireland was administered under the ordinary law without any coercive powers. There were no bad results such as Lord Spencer feared. Public opinion in Ireland was appeased. What a commentary on Lord Spencer's policy and on the decision of the Liberal Cabinet to renew Coercion !

Whether the action of Lord Randolph Churchill, and the other Tory leaders, was in accord with a high standard of political ethics may be questioned. There was, indeed, nothing wrong, or open to objection, in negotiating with the Irish leaders, and coming to an agreement with them. That course was only what I have suggested would have been wise and sound policy on the part of the Liberal Government. But was it right to keep the transaction secret ? The Liberals had, perhaps, no right to complain of this. The aggrieved persons, if any, were the rank and file of the Tory Party, who, if they had known what was being done by their leaders, behind their backs, would certainly have objected. Secrecy, therefore, was the essence of the transaction. In this view the transaction was in the nature of a manœuvre not very creditable to those engaged in it.

The Liberal Government, meanwhile, wholly unconscious of this decision of the Tory leaders, pursued its policy in the direction of a modified and minimized Coercion Bill. Whether all its Members were fully and finally agreed upon a scheme is somewhat uncertain. The hostile motion on the second reading of the Budget Bill was moved by Sir M. Hicks-Beach. It was directed against the proposal to add to the duty on beer, and spirits, in the absence of any increase of the wine duties, and to increase the duty on real property, without remission of local taxation. The case made out was a very weak one, and the alternative suggested was the increase of the duties on tea and sugar, a very objectionable proposal. The House evidently voted irrespective of the immediate issue. The Government was defeated on a division, before the dinner-hour, by 264 votes against 252 ; a majority of 12. Six Liberals voted with the Opposition, as did also 39 of the Irish Party— their full strength. No fewer than 76 Liberals were absent unpaired. There was a remarkable absence of effort on the part of the Liberal Whips to bring up their full forces. Many absent Members complained that they had received no intimation that the division would be a critical one. It was impossible to ignore the fact that the defeat gave pleasure to the extreme men of both wings of the party—the Whigs and the Radicals. It relieved them from a position which had become unbearable. There was nothing in the motion itself, and in the Budget, which might not have been repaired if there had been the will to do so. But there was no such effort. I have myself always been of opinion that the real cause of defeat was the Coercion question looming in the background, and that many Liberal Members dreaded committing themselves to such a policy, immediately before a General Election. But it is a conclusion which is incapable of actual proof. The scene which occurred in the House of Commons, on the defeat of the Government, was one of indescribable excitement.   Lord Randolph Churchill stood on one of the benches, and, waving his hat, led the rounds of cheering. The Irish joined in the jubilation.   An Irish Member conveyed the news to a great meeting of Licensed Victuallers at the Crystal Palace, where he announced it as glad tidings of great joy to an enraptured audience.

Whatever the causes or motives which led to the defeat, Mr. Gladstone and the Government accepted it as final and conclusive, and tendered their resignations to the Queen. Thus came to an end, at the hands of the Irish Members, and virtually, though indirectly, on an Irish question, a Government which had spent three, out of its five years of office, on Irish questions, and which had carried out a revolution on Irish land laws more far-reaching in its effect, and more beneficial to the tenants, than could have been thought possible at the commencement of its career.   Looking back at its proceedings, by the light of subsequent experience, we are able to see that grave errors were committed, the chief of which was the failure to appreciate that Parnell had at his back the Irish people, and that it was advisable to take him into confidence before presenting a measure of Irish reform to Parliament.   It would seem that Mr. Gladstone, following the example of his great master, Sir Robert Peel, never thought it necessary to consult the leaders of those for whom he proposed remedial measures.   In a letter to Lord Hartington of May 30th, 1885, on the subject of Local Government in Ireland, quoted by Lord Morley, he explains this as a matter of policy :

" I do not reckon with any confidence upon Manning or Parnell ; I have never looked much in Irish matters at negotiation or the conciliation of leaders.   I look at the question in itself, and I am deeply convinced that the measure in itself will be good for the country and the empire."[1]

It may be permitted to differ from so great a master, and to suggest as a principle of practical politics that, in framing a great remedial measure, it is expedient to consult the leaders of those for whom it is intended.

Another error seems to have been that of coupling a great measure of land reform for Ireland with one of coercion, and of giving precedence to the latter.   This was a method insisted

[1] *Life of Gladstone*, III, 197.

upon by the earlier Whig statesmen, after the Reform Act of 1832. Experience showed that in doing so they predisposed the Irish people against their remedial measures, and deprived them of a great part of their efficacy. I cannot doubt, for my part, that Mr. Gladstone was aware of this danger, and that he was forced, against his will, into giving precedence to coercion. His difficulties were greatly enhanced by the un-homogeneous constitution of his Cabinet. The two extremes of the Whigs led by Lord Hartington, and the Radicals led by Mr. Chamberlain, went badly together in the harness of office. The jibbing of the one and the free-going of the other made them a most difficult team to manage. Never was Mr. Gladstone's tact more conspicuous than in his endeavour to make them step together. But the result was unfortunate, and the Government might have done better if it had relied on one or the other only of these incongruous sections.

CHAPTER XXVI

LORD SALISBURY'S FIRST MINISTRY

ON the resignation of Mr. Gladstone, Lord Salisbury was commissioned by the Queen to form a Government—passing over Sir Stafford Northcote, who, since the death of Lord Beaconsfield, had been the titular Leader of the Tory Party. Some delay occurred in Lord Salisbury's acceptance, owing to the fact that there could not be an immediate dissolution of Parliament. The Redistribution of Seats Bill had not passed through all its stages. It was necessary to allow time for the registration of new electors in the altered constituencies, and extended franchise. Meanwhile the House of Commons must be kept going to vote supplies, and to carry through other routine business. Mr. Gladstone refused to enter into a compact, on behalf of his party, to support the new Government. But, after some delay, he intimated that he, and his friends, would oppose no difficulties to such financial arrangements as were necessary. Upon this assurance Lord Salisbury undertook to form a Government—reserving for himself the post of Foreign Secretary as well as that of Premier—an arrangement open to much objection.

For the appointment of Ministers, in the House of Commons, Lord Randolph Churchill was chief adviser, if not dictator. At his instance, Sir Stafford Northcote was deposed from his position as leader, was shunted to the House of Lords, under the title of Earl of Iddesleigh, and was given the post of First Lord of the Treasury, reduced to a rich sinecure, when no longer associated with the Premiership.[1]

[1] In a memorandum written in 1899 Lord Randolph expressed regret at having treated Sir Stafford Northcote in this manner. "Lord Salisbury's intention," he wrote, "on being commissioned in 1885 to form a Government, was that Sir Stafford Northcote should become Leader in the House

Lord Randolph was content, himself, to take the second position in the House of Commons, as Secretary of State for India, putting Sir M. Hicks-Beach in the first position, as Leader of the Party, and Chancellor of the Exchequer. He provided posts for Lord Cross and Mr. W. H. Smith, whom he had irreverently, when a free-lance, nicknamed as Marshall and Snelgrove. Sir Hardinge Giffard became Lord Chancellor, as Lord Halsbury. Mr. Gibson, who for years had done yeoman's service for his party on Irish questions, became Lord Chancellor of Ireland, as Lord Ashbourne. The most significant appointment, however, was that of Lord Carnarvon, as Viceroy in Ireland—also in the Cabinet. Lord Carnarvon had been Secretary of State for the Colonies in the previous Tory Government—a post usually reckoned much higher than that now assigned to him. He had been mainly concerned in two great schemes of Colonial Federation—that of the Canadian Dominion, in 1867, when he was Under-Secretary of State, and the measure for the Confederation of the South African Colonies in 1877, which, however, was rejected by the Cape Parliament in 1880.

On the first day of the meeting of the House of Lords, after the constitution of the new Government, Lord Carnarvon announced that there was to be no more coercion in Ireland. He gave statistics which showed that the Act was no longer necessary. When the Act was passed, he said, Parliament had determined that it should come to an end in three years. It had produced the desired effect. There was no longer any exceptional crime in Ireland, and the Government was justified in the attempt to govern Ireland under the ordinary law, firmly and effectively. While there was much to be said for the renewal of some of the clauses of the Coercion Act, and they might with advantage be adopted as permanent changes of law for the whole country, yet, if adopted, as regards Ireland alone, they would be considered as exceptional legislation, making an invidious distinction between it and the rest of the country. He would therefore, for the present, trust the

of Commons. To this proposition I declined to agree, adhering to my former opinion as to the indisposition of Sir Stafford Northcote for acute party warfare. Whether I was right or wrong I do not argue. Public opinion in the party and outside was certainly not with me, and soon after, and since I have been strongly drawn to the conclusion that I was in error."
(*Life of Lord Randolph Churchill*, I, 407.)

people of Ireland, and though this would be an experiment, it was one which might diminish the ill-feeling between the two nations. On the more general question and the future, he said that he had been looking through the Coercion Acts, and had been astonished to find that, ever since 1847, with some very short intervals hardly worth mentioning, Ireland had lived under exceptional and coercive legislation. What sane man would admit this to be a satisfactory, or a wholesome, state of things ? Why should they not try to extricate themselves from the miserable habit, and aim at some better scheme? Just as he had seen in British Colonies across the sea a combination of English, Irish, and Scotch settlers, bound together in loyal obedience to the law and the Crown, and contributing to the general prosperity of the country, so he could not conceive that there was any irreconcilable bar, here in their native home and in England, to the unity and amity of the two nations. He went to his task individually, with a perfectly free, open, and unprejudiced mind, to hear, to question, and, as far as might be, to understand. He concluded with these words :

" I do not believe that with honesty and single-mindedness of purpose, on the one side, and with the willingness of the Irish people on the other, it is hopeless to look for some satisfactory solution of this terrible question. These, I believe to be the opinion and the views of my colleagues."

This remarkable speech was delivered in the presence of Lord Salisbury, who had said nothing in his own Ministerial explanations about Ireland, and had left the subject wholly to his colleague, the new Viceroy. What could the speech mean but that the subject of Home Rule had been carefully considered between the two Ministers, if not by others of their colleagues, and that Lord Carnarvon had been expressly selected for the Irish post, with the object of conciliating the opinion of Irishmen, and of endeavouring to find a solution which would concede to them a measure of self-government, more or less in accord with Colonial experience ? What more wise policy could have been adopted in view of the state of Irish opinion, and of what was then a certainty, that Parnell's followers would sweep the Irish elections, and would come back to the new Parliament with an overwhelming majority ? It may be that Salisbury and Carnarvon looked forward to the possibility of a Parliamentary alliance between the Tory Party and the Irish Party, which would redress the balance against the former in Great Britain. There would be nothing wrong in this if it were intended.

On the day after delivering this speech, Lord Carnarvon made his State entry into Dublin, and met with a most cordial reception—a great contrast to the farewell to Lord Spencer, who, though greatly respected in Ireland for his courage and honesty, had left behind him many galling memories of coercion. While Lord Spencer had always been guarded by an escort of cavalry, Lord Carnarvon walked freely about Dublin unattended.

Further evidence of a new policy of conciliation was soon forthcoming in proposals for legislation, even in the short Session preceding the Dissolution. Lord Ashbourne, in the House of Lords, introduced and carried a measure for extending very greatly the system of land purchase in Ireland, by the conversion of tenants into owners. It introduced, for the first time, the principle of advancing the whole of the purchase money by the State, repayable by equal annual instalments of interest and sinking fund, spread over forty-six years, together amounting to 4 per cent on the purchase money. Five millions were to be advanced for the purpose. The surplus fund of the Disestablished Church was to be security for the payment of interest, and one-fifth of the purchase money was to be retained, until repayment to that amount was made. At this time there was a block in the Irish land market. There were no buyers except the tenants, and the landowners, as a class, were as eager for the measure as the tenants. The average rate of purchase expected was about eighteen times the rental. At this rate the tenants, who were fortunate enough to come under the provisions of the Act, would pay 28 per cent less to the State for interest and sinking fund, than their previous rent. Lord Spencer, while not opposing the Bill, doubted the expediency of an advance by the State of the whole of the purchase money. If it were generally adopted the State would find itself in the position of being practically the landlord for forty-six years of the greater part of the land of Ireland. I maintained the same objection in the House of Commons. The Bill, however, passed, and has been the prelude to many more of the same kind, with reduced rates of interest, and extended terms of repayment. Another Irish measure, passed in this short Session, was that for extending the powers of local authorities to purchase land, and erect labourers' dwellings, a measure long asked for by the Irish Members.

But even more important, as evidence of *rapprochement* with the Irish Party, was the reception given by the Government to a motion of Parnell, in the House of Commons, censuring Lord Spencer, in relation to the administration of the law, in the cases of the Barbavilla and Maamtrasma murders, which, especially the latter, had long been the subject of great attacks on the late Government by the Irish Party. The Tory Party had supported Lord Spencer in refusing further inquiry. The new Government took a different line. The Chancellor of the Exchequer said he was authorized by Lord Carnarvon to say that he would inquire personally into any memorial which might be presented to him, on behalf of the prisoners, in these cases, with the earnest desire to do justice. In giving this undertaking, Sir M. Hicks-Beach added that, while believing Lord Spencer to be a man of honour and with a high sense of duty, " he must say very frankly that there was much in the Irish policy of the late Government, which, though in the absence of complete information, he did not condemn, he should be very sorry to make himself responsible for." A heated debate ensued, in which Sir William Harcourt said that if the experiment of governing Ireland by the ordinary law were to commence by discrediting the administration of justice, and by throwing over the judges and juries, it was foredoomed to failure. Lord Randolph Churchill replied : " I will tell you how the present Government is foredoomed to failure. They will be foredoomed to failure if they go out of their way unnecessarily to assume one jot or tittle of responsibility for the acts of the late administration. It is only by divesting ourselves of all responsibility for the acts of the late Government, that we can hope to arrive at a successful issue." [1]

In view of these declarations on behalf of the Government, Parnell withdrew the motion ; but the language used by the two Ministers, throwing discredit on the administration of the Crimes Act by Lord Spencer, while it was received with great

[1] *Hansard,* July 17th, 1885.

demonstrations of delight by the Irish Members, caused resentment and distrust on the part of the friends of Lord Spencer and the late Government, and even among many supporters of the Government. It gave rise to the suspicion that the Government had already come to secret terms with the Irish Party. A demonstration was arranged in the form of a banquet in honour of Lord Spencer. It was attended by three hundred Members of the House of Commons. Mr. Bright made a strong speech, in the course of which he alluded to the followers of Parnell as " Irish rebels." He was called to account for this in the House of Commons, but he stuck to his text. Mr. Chamberlain and Sir Charles Dilke were conspicuously absent from this banquet in honour of Lord Spencer.

The suspicions as to a compact between the Government and Parnell would have been greatly strengthened if it had been generally known, at the time, that there had been an interview between the Lord-Lieutenant of Ireland, Lord Carnarvon, and the Irish Leader, in the early days of the Tory Government, in which there was an exchange of views as to the details of a scheme of Home Rule for Ireland. The fact of such an interview was kept a profound secret. A general statement of its purport, however, was disclosed to the public by Parnell, in the course of a speech, a year later, on the second reading of Mr. Gladstone's Home Rule Bill. Parnell had been taunted with having made a speech at Wicklow, in the previous year, in which he claimed for an Irish Parliament the right of levying import duties for the protection of Irish industries. He replied that when he made that speech he had reason to believe that the Government of Lord Salisbury, if successful at the approaching General Election, would offer to Ireland a statutory legislature, with power to protect its industries. Though he declined to name his authority for this statement, it was asserted, in the Press, that it was Lord Carnarvon. Upon this Lord Carnarvon made an explanation, two days later, in the House of Lords, in which, while admitting that he was personally in favour of giving to Ireland local self-government, more or less on the Colonial plan, and that he had discussed the question with Parnell, he denied that he had spoken on behalf of the Government, or had entered into any compact with Parnell on this subject. This led to a reply

from Parnell, giving a further account of the interview.
Two years later the subject turned up again, and further
explanations were afforded by Lord Carnarvon and Parnell
as to their interview.   More revelations were later made by
Sir C. Gavan Duffy, who was in intimate relation on this
subject with Lord Carnarvon, and by Justin McCarthy, who
was also privy to the interview, and who had been in communication with Lord Randolph Churchill.   Putting all these
together, we are now able to construct a fairly succinct version
of what took place.

There can be no doubt that Lord Carnarvon had been
a convinced Home Ruler for some years past.   His views
on the subject must have been known to Lord Salisbury,
when he offered to him the post of Lord-Lieutenant, and
there must have been correspondence between them on the
subject.   Sir C. Gavan Duffy, who had strongly urged Lord
Carnarvon to propound a policy of Home Rule, arranged an
interview between him and Parnell, with the full concurrence
of Lord Salisbury, the Prime Minister.   The interview took
place in London, in an empty house of Sir Howard Vincent,
and there can be no doubt that the subject was fully discussed,
and that Lord Carnarvon explained his views as favourable
to a statutory legislature for Ireland, with power to protect
native industries.   Lord Carnarvon communicated to Lord
Salisbury what took place at the interview with Parnell, and
received from him a full approval of what he had said and
done.   It is true that no definite compact was come to at the
interview, and that the Cabinet was not informed of what had
taken place.   But it is also true that Lord Randolph Churchill
expressed himself to Mr. Justin McCarthy as favourable to the
policy of conciliation to the Irish people, without committing
himself absolutely to Home Rule.   Under these circumstances
Parnell was impressed with the belief that if the Government
survived the General Election it would entertain a scheme for
Home Rule in the new Parliament.   On the strength of this
he decided, in the course of the General Election, that the
votes of the Irish electors in Great Britain should be given to
Tory candidates—a most important reinforcement to that
party, which had the effect of securing to them from twenty to
forty Members, who would otherwise have been defeated.   As
a result, however, of the General Election, the Tory Party

was left in so small minority that, even with the addition and full support of the eighty-six Parnellites then returned (making 172 in a division), there would scarcely be a majority for the Government. It appears that immediately after the General Election, the question of their Irish policy was brought before the full Cabinet, for the first time, and the concession of Home Rule in any form was repudiated. What views Lord Salisbury expressed at this Cabinet we do not know. But we do know that Lord Carnarvon immediately tendered his resignation. It was kept back a few days, but was announced at the meeting of the new Parliament. It is obvious that the provocation to Carnarvon to resign at the moment, when the defeat of the Government was certain within a few days, must have been very great, for he was not the man to desert a sinking ship, except for some very strong political reason. The explanation afforded in the House of Lords of the resignation of Lord Carnarvon, on the opening of Parliament, was obviously incomplete, to use no stronger language.

If I have been justified in this account of these transactions, by piecing together the facts which have so far been made public, it follows that Lord Salisbury, the Premier, and some of his colleagues, were prepared, in the event of the elections being favourable to their party, to entertain, in the new Parliament, the question of Home Rule. In this he was wisely looking forward to the possibility, then not remote, of the Irish Party, eighty-six in number, holding the balance between the two main parties, and being in a position to secure to either of them the government of the country, and to dictate their terms. In such case, why should not the Tory Party be prepared to make concessions equally with the Liberals? But the rout of the Tory Party in the elections in Great Britain, completely knocked the bottom out of the scheme. A stable Government could not be formed even with the support of the Irish Party. It was obviously useless to entertain any scheme for conciliating them by the concession of anything in the shape of self-government. To do so would be to risk a schism in the Tory Party, without any equivalent advantage. The policy, therefore, was dropped, and Carnarvon was thrown over.

The only possible alternative explanation of the known facts of the case is that Carnarvon was used as a cat's-paw by Lord Salisbury ; that Home Rule was dangled before the Irish Leader, as a lure to induce him to make things easy for the Government in Ireland, in the interval before the General Election, and to secure the Irish vote in the elections in Great Britain, but without any real intention seriously to entertain it, if the elections should be favourable to the Tory Party, and with the intention of throwing over Carnarvon, when the time came for fulfilling the expectations held out to him. But this hypothesis involves such discredit to those concerned in the transaction, that it is unreasonable to entertain it. We must therefore fall back on the only alternative which is consistent with the personal honour of the statesmen concerned. The transaction, in this view, was honest, wise, and statesmanlike. The policy might have had important and far-reaching results, if the Tory Party had obtained a larger support at the elections.

At some future day, when the correspondence between Lord Salisbury and Lord Carnarvon, on the appointment of the latter as Viceroy, on his interview with Parnell, and on his resignation of office, is made public, fuller light will be thrown upon the whole transaction. That important correspondence exists on this subject is well known. There have been indications that the Carnarvon family have threatened to publish it, for the purpose of vindicating Lord Carnarvon's reputation. Till this correspondence is published we must be content to draw such inferences from the known facts of the case as are fair to Lord Carnarvon's statesmanship, and consistent with the good faith of Lord Salisbury, and some of his colleagues.

Reverting to the interval which occurred between the defeat of Mr. Gladstone's Government and the General Election, it is to be noted that the conciliatory policy of Lord Salisbury and Lord Carnarvon had most salutary results. The leading members of the Government took every opportunity of emphasizing the difference between their Irish policy and that of their predecessors. " Undoubtedly," said Lord Randolph Churchill, " we do intend to inaugurate a change of policy in Ireland. . . . The policy of the late Government so exasperated Irishmen—maddened and irritated that imaginative and warm-hearted race—that I firmly believe that had the Government remained in office no amount of bayonets or military would have prevented outbreaks."

Lord Salisbury also, speaking at Newport just before the General Election, said :

" The effect of the Crimes Act has been very much exaggerated. While it was in existence there grew up a thousand branches of the National League, and it is from them that these difficulties proceeded with which we have now to contend. The provisions in the Crimes Act against boycotting were of very small effect. It grew up under that Act because it is a crime which legislation has very great difficulty in reaching. I have seen it stated that the Crimes Act diminished outrages ; that boycotting acted through outrages ; and that the Crimes Act diminished boycotting. . . . . It is not true ; the Act did not diminish outrages. In September without the Crimes Act there were fewer outrages than in August with that Act. . . . The truth about boycotting is that it depends upon the passing humour of the population. I do not believe that in any country it has endured. I doubt whether in any community law has been able to provide a satisfactory remedy ; but I believe it contains its own Nemesis."

Meanwhile Parnell, believing that he had good expectations from Lord Salisbury and Lord Carnarvon, cried off with the Liberal Party. He had, as already shown, been willing to accept Mr. Chamberlain's scheme of a National Council for administrative purposes. He now threw this over. Mr. Chamberlain and Sir Charles Dilke had offered to go over to Ireland on a tour of inquiry, with a view to such a scheme. Their offer was now most unwisely declined, with something of contumely. It was clearly intimated to them by the Nationalist Press that their reception would not be of a friendly kind. It was, therefore, abandoned.

CHAPTER XXVII

THE GENERAL ELECTION OF 1885

PARLIAMENT was prorogued on August 11th, and though the General Election was not to take place till late in November, the leading politicians commenced the campaign in the constituencies within a few days. Parnell opened the ball by a speech at Dublin, on August 24th, in which he pledged his party to Home Rule, and little else. After boasting of the measures which had been carried for Ireland, he said : " It is admitted by all parties that you have brought the question of Irish legislative independence to the point of solution. . . . Our sole work in the new Parliament will be the restoration of our own Parliament ; and when we have obtained it, what will be its functions, what will be its powers ? We shall require our national Parliament to do those things for us which we have been asking the British Parliament to do for us."

He then proceeded to enumerate these objects—the development of the Healy Clause, the promotion of a peasant proprietary, the admission of leaseholders to the Land Courts, the extension of education on a religious basis, the improvement of the condition of labourers, the building up of industries, and so forth. There was not a trace in this of any Imperial questions. It was evident, therefore, that the Irish Parliament, he was contemplating, was to deal only with purely Irish questions. But it was to have fiscal independence, and the right to impose import duties for the protection of Irish industries. This was due to the expectations which Parnell believed to have been held out to him on behalf of Lord Salisbury.

The proposal to create an Irish Parliament with fiscal independence was ill received by the English people, including the Liberal Press.　The first prominent statesman to answer the challenge of the Irish Leader was Lord Hartington.　In a speech at Waterfoot in Lancashire, after throwing cold water on the schemes of social reform, which had been projected by Mr. Chamberlain, in his many speeches, in the previous six months, he turned to the question of Ireland, and dealt with Parnell's speech.

"I cannot believe," he said, "that there exist in this country any political leaders who will consent, either to acquire office, or to retain office, by conceding the terms by which alone Mr. Parnell says his alliance can be purchased. . . . He tells you that he will be satisfied with nothing less than a separate Parliament ; and not only a separate Parliament, but a Parliament independent of the Imperial Parliament, at least to this extent : that it is to have absolute power to deal with the land of Ireland, with the relations between landlord and tenant in Ireland, and that it is to have absolute power to protect, as it is termed, Irish industry, and Irish trade, to the exclusion of British commerce and British manufactures from Ireland.　In my opinion, Mr. Parnell, for once, has made a mistake in so openly advocating and declaring his demands, and has by that declaration ensured his own defeat. . . . If he should return to Parliament his eighty or ninety Members pledged to obey his behest, still I am convinced he will not have accomplished the object he has in view. . . . Means will be found by which a practically united Parliamentary representation will impose a firm and decided veto upon proposals which are, in their opinion, so fatal and mischievous."

Mr. Chamberlain, rather less than two months before, on July 17th, at Holloway, had made a most powerful and oft-quoted speech on the subject of Ireland, at a time when he still believed that his proposal of a National Council was acceptable to Parnell.

"The pacification of Ireland at this moment," he then said, "depends, I believe, on the concession to Ireland of the right to govern itself in the matter of purely domestic business.　Is it not discreditable to us that, even now, it is only by unconstitutional means that we are able to secure peace and order in one portion of Her Majesty's dominions ?　Its government is a system as completely centralized and bureaucratic as that by which Russia governs Poland, or that which

prevailed in Venice under the Austrian rule. . . . I say the
time has come to reform altogether the absurd and irritating
anachronism which is known as Dublin Castle. That is the
work to which the new Parliament will be called."

There was a lack of proportion between language of this
vehemence and the scheme of a National Council. When now
confronted with a scheme which seemed to be adequate to
provide a remedy for evils he had so forcibly described, he
drew back, and, speaking at Warrington a few days after
Parnell, on September 8th, he said : " If these and these alone
are the terms on which Mr. Parnell's support is to be obtained, I will not enter into the compact. This new programme of Mr. Parnell involves a great extension of anything
we have hitherto known or understood by Home Rule. . . .
If this claim were conceded we might as well abandon the
hope of maintaining a United Kingdom, and we should establish within thirty miles of our shores a new foreign country,
animated from outside with unfriendly intentions towards
ourselves. Such a policy as that I firmly believe would be
disastrous and ruinous to Ireland herself."

To this policy Mr. Chamberlain has since adhered with some
occasional aberrations. It is in my personal recollection
that, in the course of the autumn of 1885, I paid a visit to
him at Highbury, and met there Mr. Morley and Sir Charles
Dilke. We discussed many of the questions which were then
threatening to divide the Liberal Party. I need not advert
to what passed on other subjects than Ireland. Mr. Chamberlain expressed great fear that Mr. Gladstone intended to
propose a Home Rule policy. He declared, in the most
positive manner, that he would not himself go beyond his
proposal for a National Council. I said to him: "Why not
call your National Council a Parliament, and appease the
national sentiment of Ireland ? " He could not assent to
this. These were, I think, the last words which passed
between us on political topics, for shortly after this the
Home Rule question became the principal issue. There
occurred a breach, as in so many other cases of political
associates of that time, which was never mended.

In view of the prominence given to the Irish question by
Parnell, Hartington, and Chamberlain, it was expected that
the Tory leaders would deal with it. Lord Randolph Churchill,

on September 3rd, four days after Lord Hartington's speech, and less than a fortnight after that of Parnell, made an important election speech at Sheffield, but not a single word did he utter about Ireland. He was repeatedly challenged to say whether he agreed with Parnell, but he observed a discreet silence throughout the elections. It was not till October 7th that Lord Salisbury made his first pronouncement in the election campaign. It was at Newport, in Monmouthshire. His statement as to Ireland was vague and illusive. There was no emphatic challenge of Parnell's terms. It was the first principle, he said, of his party, to extend to Ireland all the institutions of England. He then went on to explain that the concession of local government to small areas would be more dangerous than to a large area (presumably the whole of Ireland). Local authorities, he said, were more exposed to the temptation of enabling the majority to be unjust to the minority, when they obtained jurisdiction over a small area, than in the case where the authority derived its sanction, and extended its jurisdiction over a wider area. In a large central authority the wisdom of several parts of the country would correct the folly and mistakes of the other parts. This seemed to point to the possibility of creating a great central authority in Ireland in the direction of a National Council, as a safer measure than the extension of local government to smaller bodies, such as County Councils. He then commented on Parnell's reference to the relations of Austria-Hungary, but merely for the purpose of showing how inapplicable such a scheme would be to Ireland. As to the larger organic question affecting Ireland, his party would never depart from its traditions. He then went on to defend his Government for not renewing the Coercion Act in Ireland. It would have been grossly inconsistent after extending the franchise in Ireland to have applied coercion—Parliament would have stultified itself by so doing. He showed how impossible it was to deal with boycotting, even with the aid of coercive measures, in a passage already quoted. The whole speech was conceived in a spirit of conciliation quite in harmony with the general attitude of Lord Carnarvon. The door was not banged against the discussion of any future scheme for giving self-government to Ireland. Tory candidates, as a rule, in the elections, were silent on the subject of Home Rule. Many expressed themselves as favourable to some scheme of Local Government in Ireland.

Meanwhile Mr. Gladstone, who had been on a yachting cruise to Norway, returned to England, at the beginning of September, invigorated in health, and eager for the fray. He had occupied himself in writing an address to the Midlothian electors. It was lengthy as a pamphlet. He had been much pressed to remain as leader of the party, in order to compose, as far as possible, the differences between its two wings, led respectively by Hartington and Chamberlain. He was willing to do so for two purposes—one to prevent a split in the party, the other to deal with the Irish question, if it should appear to be necessary and possible after the General Election. His address struck the mean line between the two rival leaders. His correspondence and conversations, however, showed that he was thinking more about Ireland, than about questions of social reform in England, which were the bones of contention between the two sections of his party. Almost alone he appears to have been conscious of the extreme gravity of the Irish question, which would come up for immediate settlement in the new Parliament.

It has already been shown, by quotations from Mr. Gladstone's speeches and correspondence, that he had, for some time past, been veering in favour of concession of self-government to Ireland, so far as was consistent with the maintenance of the unity of the Empire. He had warmly supported Mr. Chamberlain's scheme of a National Council for Ireland, and had intimated that he was prepared to go even further by giving it control over the police. He now saw looming before Parliament demands which could not be satisfied by a National Council with administrative functions only. Whatever his desire to retire from political life, he felt that it might be his duty to remain for the purpose of dealing with this question. He dealt in his address to Midlothian with the Irish question in general terms of concession, but with guarded reserve as to the scheme which he would recommend.

" In my opinion," he wrote, " not now for the first time, the limit is clear within which the desires of Ireland, constitutionally ascertained, may, and beyond which they cannot, receive the assent of Parliament. To maintain the supremacy of the Crown, the unity of the Empire, and all the authority of Parliament necessary for the conservation of that unity, is the first duty of every representative of the people. Subject to this governing principle, every grant to portions of the country of enlarged powers for the management of their own affairs is, in my view, not a source of danger, but a means of avoiding it, and it is in the nature of a new guarantee for increased cohesion, happiness, and strength. . . . I believe history and posterity will consign to disgrace the man and the memory of any man, be he who he may, that having the power to aid in an equitable settlement between Ireland and Great Britain shall use that power not to aid, but to prevent or retard it."

On September 28th, Mr. Childers, a member of the late Cabinet, and one of his most trusted supporters, who had long experience of Colonial politics in Australia, wrote to ask Mr. Gladstone's advice as to a proposed address to his constituents, in which he formulated a scheme of Home Rule in very precise terms. Mr. Gladstone replied: "I have a decided sympathy with the general scope and spirit of your proposed declaration about Ireland." This, however, was a private letter, and was not then made public. In public he would not absolutely commit himself to a scheme. On November 9th, however, in a speech at Edinburgh, he said: "What Ireland very deliberately and constitutionally demands, unless it infringes the principles connected with the maintenance of the unity of the Empire, will be a demand that we are bound, at any rate, to treat with careful attention"; and he went on to say: "It will be a vital danger to the country and to the Empire if, at a time when a demand from Ireland for larger power of self-government is to be dealt with, there is not in Parliament a party politically independent of the Irish vote." It must be admitted that this appeal to the electors of Great Britain to give a majority to the Liberal Party independent of the Irish Members was open to misconception. It gave rise to suspicion in the Irish leaders that Mr. Gladstone was playing fast and loose with the subject, and that when secure of a majority, independent of the Irish Members, he might throw them over, or insist on terms which could not be accepted. Parnell, in the absence of a definite scheme from Mr. Gladstone, came to the conclusion that it would be more to the interest of the Irish Party, that they should hold the balance in the new Parliament, and that neither Liberals nor Tories should have a majority independent of them. After vainly endeavouring to tempt Mr. Gladstone into a fuller declaration of any scheme he might have in view, he authorized, on November 21st, on the eve of the election, the issue of a manifesto by the National League of Great Britain. It called on the Irish voters in Great Britain to vote against the Liberal Party—" the party who had coerced Ireland, deluged Egypt with blood, menaced religious liberty in the schools, the freedom of speech in Parliament, and promised to the country generally a repetition of the crimes and follies of the last Liberal Administration."

The Irish voters in British constituencies were believed to number about 150,000, spread about very unequally in the constituencies. They were a very important section in the Lancashire districts, and in the larger towns in Yorkshire and elsewhere. There were very few of them in the rural districts, and in the south of England. It was variously estimated that the turnover of these voters, as compared with the General Election of 1880, caused a loss to the Liberal Party, in 1885, of from twenty to forty seats. I inclined myself to the larger figure, in part because I was one of the unexpected victims of the manifesto. I had represented the Borough of Reading for twenty-three years, and had fought successfully six elections there, generally, of late years, after very close contests. No one could have supposed that the Irish vote would affect the result in such a constituency. But there proved to be about eighty Irish Catholics, workers in the well-known biscuit factory. They had always voted for me in past elections. They now came to me with tears in their eyes, saying that they were bidden by their leaders and their priests to vote against me, and expressing their deep regret. I was defeated in the election by 129 votes. It was clear, therefore, that the eighty Irish voters turned the scale, and secured a victory to my Tory opponent. What happened at Reading doubtless occurred in many other constituencies where the two parties were evenly divided, and where the turnover of a small number of Irish voters caused the defeat of Liberal candidates.

It is now generally admitted that a very grave mistake was made by Parnell, in thus deciding to throw the weight of his influence with Irish voters in Great Britain against the Liberal Party. Not only would the twenty or forty additional Members of this party, counting double their numbers in a division, have been of the utmost importance, and have saved the Home Rule Bill from defeat in the coming Session, but the opinion of many electors in England was turned against the Irish by this interference, and by a course which had the appearance of being actuated by a want of appreciation of what had been done for Ireland by the Liberal Party in the last fifteen years. Parnell himself eventually recognized that he had made a mistake in issuing this manifesto. He more than once made this admission to Davitt.

It is not necessary to refer to the other questions which were debated and voted upon in Great Britain in the election. Little, indeed, was said upon the Irish question either for or against Home Rule. I do not think the subject was mentioned in my contest at Reading. It was the same elsewhere in England and Scotland, except in rare cases. The questions of interest there were Land Reform and the compulsory purchase of land for allotments, Free Education, the extension of Local Government, Plural Voting, the Graduation of the Income Tax, the Disestablishment of the Church. These were not only at issue between the Tories and Liberals, but many of them between the two wings of the Liberal Party. Hartington and Chamberlain fired into one another hotly on these topics.

On the Irish question Mr. John Morley was one of the few leading men who declared themselves boldly and unequivocally in favour of Home Rule. In speeches at Newcastle and elsewhere he expressed himself as favourable to a large measure of self-government for Ireland, subject to the limits imposed by the safety and the integrity of the sovereign realm as a whole. Two things, he said, had to be faced—a demoralized executive in Ireland, and a demoralized legislature at Westminster. He did not hide from himself the magnitude of the task of conceding to Ireland the great extension of self-government. It would raise deep passions, it would perhaps destroy a great party ; but those who, with himself, had the integrity of the Empire and the interests of Parliament really at heart, would not shrink from difficulties, or be deterred by dangers which beset their party.

On the other hand, Mr. Forster, in a speech to the electors of Bradford, which he had represented as a whole for many years before its division into three by the recent Act, declared against any large concession to Ireland. He would give to it local government, as he would to England and Scotland, with the exception that he could not at present give to local authorities the control of the police. He was not in favour of Chamberlain's scheme of an elective council. He believed that would be Home Rule in disguise. This was Mr. Forster's last speech. He was taken ill shortly after. He was unable to take part in the contests at Bradford. He was returned as Member for the central division, largely by the aid of Tory votes. He died a few weeks later from the effects of a malarial fever, contracted while on a tour on the Continent. There can be little doubt, however, that his death was due indirectly to the enormous strain of his two years' work as Irish Secretary. If in the above pages I have differed from Mr. Forster on a grave question of policy, that does not lessen my admiration of his splendid career as a whole, and his great public spirit.

After an unusually long campaign, the elections took place, between November 23rd and December 19th, in greatly altered constituencies, returning for the most part single Members, and with a widely extended franchise in the Counties. The Liberal Party lost heavily in the earlier contests in the English Boroughs, with the result that the representation of them was almost evenly divided. This was, in great part, due to the loss of the Irish vote. The losses, however, were made up for by successes in the Counties, where the electors, partly out of gratitude to those who had given votes to them, and partly from a desire to make use of them to better their conditions, and inspired by the election cry of " Three acres and a cow," returned Liberals in the proportion of three to two Tories. Scotland was true to its old traditions of Liberalism, and returned sixty Liberals to ten Tories.

But it was in Ireland that the greatest change took place. Up to this time there had always been a large contingent of Liberal Members from Ireland, as distinguished from Home Rulers. They were greatly reduced in 1880, but still numbered fourteen. There were also twenty-six nominal Home Rulers in the last Parliament, who could be counted on to support the Liberal Government. Both these sections were now swept away by a wave of popular feeling in favour of Parnell. Not a single Liberal was returned for Ireland. Every nominal Home Rule follower of Mr. Shaw disappeared from the scene, or was compelled to eat the leek, and to swear allegiance to the Nationalist Party, pledging himself to resign when the party called upon him to do so. Parnell all but swept the board. Out of 103 Members, eighty-five were his followers, many of them his nominees. Only eighteen Tories were returned. Ulster, the stronghold of Toryism, returned a majority of Nationalists. In Munster and Connaught, and in three-fourths of Leinster, the Parnellites carried everything before them. The votes given to opposing candidates were so few as to be negligible ; often not one-tenth, or even one-twentieth of those given for the Nationalists. Never since the birth of representative institutions was there a more conclusive, overwhelming, convincing demonstration at the polls. Ireland, in the first General Election, at which there was a really popular franchise and a fairly equal distribution of seats, pronounced by an overwhelming majority in favour of self-government. Great Britain returned a majority for the Liberals of just 100—333 Liberals to 233 Tories. For the United Kingdom, the Liberals and Parnellites together numbered 418 to 251 Tories, giving a majority of 167. If the Parnellites transferred their votes to the Tories, their joint numbers would be 336 to 334 Liberals, almost an equality.

As Mr. Gladstone had foreseen, a constitutional crisis occurred of the first magnitude, which it was the bounden duty of England to deal with. He alone of living statesmen had the authority, the knowledge, the capacity, and the force of will to cope with it. He decided, in spite of his seventy-six years, to remain in political life for the sole purpose of settling, if possible, this grave question.

CHAPTER XXVIII

FOR the first time since the Act of Union the Irish people had made their demand for self-government in their own affairs, in a constitutional form which could not be mistaken or overlooked. O'Connell had the support of only 40 of the Irish Members on his motion for the Repeal of the Union in 1835. Although, as has been shown, in 1874, 60 out of the 103 Irish Members pledged themselves on election to the policy of Home Rule, many of them were very lukewarm, and were classified as merely nominal Home Rulers. Butt was never able to bring into the lobby in favour of his proposal an actual majority of the Irish members. Now, in 1885, the recently enfranchised householders sent an overwhelming majority of 85 out of 103 Members to demand the restitution of self-government.

Mr. Gladstone was deeply interested by the result. It was evident that from that time forward he thought only of Ireland, and how best to satisfy its demands. He believed that, better than any other man, he was capable of solving it. He approached the subject with caution, and in the spirit, as he said himself, of the old Parliamentary hand. He maintained that it was no part of his duty, when not invested with the responsibility of Government, to frame a specific legislative scheme. During the few weeks which elapsed before the meeting of the new Parliament he was in constant communication, personally or by letter, with the most trusted of his late colleagues. He made no secret with them of his desire to come to terms with the Irish Party for a concession of self-government to Ireland, if their demands were compatible with the maintenance of the unity of the Empire. He found willing support in this from Lord Spencer, without whose co-operation his efforts to induce the Liberal Party, or the bulk of it, to accept his policy would most probably have failed. He met with equal support from Lord Granville, who had been his indispensable aid in promoting and defending his successive great measures in the House of Lords. With Lord Hartington it was different ; it was very soon clear that there would be a breach with him.

Mr. Gladstone's first impression was that the Irish question might, and should be, settled by co-operation between the two main political parties, in the same manner as Catholic Emancipation, the Repeal of the Corn Laws, and the recent extension of the Franchise. In this view he took the opportunity of meeting, at a neighbour's house, Mr. Arthur Balfour, a member of the Government, as Secretary for Scotland, to communicate by message, and later by letter, indirectly with the Premier. He wrote to Mr. Balfour, on December 20th, that " it would be a great public calamity if this great question were to fall into the lines of party conflict " ; that the Government of the day only could deal with it ; and that he specially desired that the existing Government should do so. If Lord Salisbury and his Cabinet would bring forward a measure for the purpose, he, Mr. Gladstone, would desire to treat it in the same spirit as he had shown in the Afghan and Balkan Peninsula questions. When he wrote this he was under the impression that Lord Salisbury, and his colleagues, were not indisposed to entertain the question of Home Rule, in some form or other. He had been fully informed of the conversation between Carnarvon and Parnell, not then generally known to the public. It appears that Mr. Gladstone's letter to Mr. Balfour was treated by the Tory Cabinet with contempt. His expressions of hope that the question should not fall into party lines were considered as mere hypocrisy. Lord Salisbury replied, through Mr. Balfour, that the Government policy would be announced to Parliament in the usual manner, at its meeting, and that it was better to avoid a departure from ordinary practice, which might be misunderstood.

In point of fact, Lord Salisbury and his Cabinet had already decided definitely against any attempt to conciliate the Irish by an advance in this direction. The correspondence between Lord Salisbury and Lord Randolph Churchill shows that as early as November 30th the Government had quarrelled with the Irish Party. The alliance between them had scarcely survived the General Election. Later, on December 8th, Lord Carnarvon, in a memorandum laid before the Cabinet, declared "that unless the Cabinet could move in the direction of Home Rule, he would not continue in office." [1] Lord Salisbury forwarded it to the principal members of his Cabinet, and asked them to express their opinion upon it. The answer of Lord Randolph Churchill, dated December 10th, is interesting. "Lord Carnarvon's memorandum was carefully considered by the Chancellor of the Exchequer, Mr. W. H. Smith, and myself. We came to the conclusion that if the Lord-Lieutenant insists on the choice being made between the adoption of his policy and resignation, the latter course becomes compulsory on us. If we go out merely on the ground of our Parliamentary position, we remain for all purposes of opposition to Home Rule as a party *totus teres atque rotundus*, but if that blessed man sets the signal of concession flying, our party will go to pieces, as it did on the Irish Land Act. The only hope for the country is to keep this present Tory Party well together; and, unfortunately, Lord Carnarvon has it once more in his power, as on two former occasions, to disintegrate, demoralize, and shatter." Lord Salisbury preferred to face the consequences of Lord Carnarvon's resignation, whatever they might be. "The Carnarvon incident," the Premier replied (December 11th), "is vexatious. I hope he will be induced to stay with us till Parliament meets. But even if he does not, I doubt if his retirement will produce any serious confusion. He will nominally retire on the ground of ill-health, or some private reason. The truth may ooze out. But we shall not mend matters by all retiring with him. The true reason will equally ooze out; and we shall have proclaimed our own impotence very loudly." [2] Carnarvon agreed to remain as Viceroy till Parliament met, and his resignation was not announced. In the interval it was decided to send Mr. W. H. Smith, the Secretary of State for War, as Chief Secretary for Ireland, in place of Sir W. Hart Dyke.

Meanwhile Mr. Gladstone, accepting the rebuff of Lord Salisbury as an intimation that the Government did not intend to make any attempt to deal with the Irish Government

[1] *Life of Lord Randolph Churchill*, II, 21.   [2] *Ibid.*, 22.

question, communicated further with his chief political friends. A statement appeared in the papers to the effect that he was prepared to concede an Irish Parliament in Dublin. It was due to the inspiration of Mr. Herbert Gladstone, but without any authority from his father. Mr. Gladstone himself informed the Press that the statement as to his views was inaccurate, and not authentic. This was rightly interpreted as not amounting to a denial, and great excitement was consequently aroused in the public mind. Lord Hartington, on reading the original statement in the Press, wrote at once to the Chairman of his Election Committee, in his Lancashire constituency, affirming his adherence to the policy he had announced, during the recent election, of deliberate hostility to anything in the nature of Home Rule for Ireland. This must be considered as the point of cleavage between him and Mr. Gladstone, which was to have such potent effect in the near future. Mr. Gladstone, on his part, on December 26th, issued a memorandum to some of his immediate supporters, on whom he could rely, in the event of his being called upon to form a Government, in which he said that, if the existing Government should be willing to deal with Ireland in a manner which could satisfy him and the Irish Nationalists, he would support them. But if not, and if he was charged with the duty of forming a Government, he would make it an indispensable condition that a scheme of duly guarded Home Rule should be prepared.

The new Parliament met, on January 21st, for the transaction of business. By this time Lord Salisbury had already determined on a policy of coercion for Ireland, and had drawn a paragraph in the Queen's Speech announcing this, but in deference to the protests of Sir M. Hicks-Beach and Lord Randolph Churchill he modified it, and referred to the subject in less positive terms. The latter had given up all idea of alliance with the Irish Members. He was engaged in casting about for an alliance with the Whigs. He suggested to Lord Salisbury that offers of office should be made to some of the leading Whigs, including Lord Hartington, Mr. Goschen, and Sir Henry James. He also pressed upon him a programme of democratic measures, such as later he became identified with. Lord Salisbury rejected these proposals with cynical scepticism as to their value.

On the meeting of Parliament, the announcement was made of the resignations of Lord Carnarvon and Sir W. Hart Dyke, and of the appointment of Mr. W. H. Smith as Irish Secretary. A correspondence was also published between Lord Salisbury and Lord Carnarvon, which made it appear that the resignation of the latter was due to an understanding arrived at when he accepted the office on the formation of the Government, that he would hold it only till the meeting of the new Parliament. It was further added that there had been no difference between the Government and Lord Carnarvon as to the policy he had pursued. We now know that the first of these statements was very far from being the whole truth. It is certain, from the published correspondence of Lord Randolph, that Carnarvon resigned because his Home Rule policy was not adopted by the Cabinet. It is only possible to explain his resignation, on the very eve of the certain defeat of the Government, by the fact that he considered that faith had not been kept with him, and that his expectations of support from Lord Salisbury and others of the Cabinet had not been fulfilled. .

The public was also led to believe that the question whether there would be a Coercion Bill was to be determined by the new Irish Secretary, after consultation with the officials in Ireland. Mr. W. H. Smith crossed the Irish Channel on the night of January 23rd, and returned on the night of the 26th. In his absence notice was given in the House of Commons by Sir M. Hicks-Beach, at the commencement of its sitting on the 26th, that on the next day the Irish Secretary would introduce a new Coercion Bill. Much merriment was caused by Mr. W. H. Smith's supposed rapid discovery, during his two days at Dublin, that coercion was necessary. But we now know from Mr. Winston Churchill's life of his father, that Mr. W. H. Smith did not come to the conclusion during this brief visit that coercion was immediately necessary, and that the notice of the introduction of a Bill was not only not authorized by him, but was distinctly opposed to his wishes. In a letter to Lord Randolph Churchill, dated from Dublin on the 25th, referring to a telegram from Lord Salisbury urging prompt action on the subject of the Coercion Bill, Mr. Smith wrote :

" There is only one opinion here—that the National League must be suppressed, and large powers obtained to protect life, property, and public order, unless the Government is prepared to treat for terms of capitulation with the Parnellites. But the Land question is at the bottom of the trouble, and gives all the force to the agitation. As at present advised, I should be unwilling to ask for large repressive powers, unless I had authority to promise a large land scheme. . . . We are at a crisis in the relations of the Imperial Government with Ireland. I may, very possibly, fail to do any good, but I will not be hurried into a positive decision on such momentous issues by the party or the papers."[1]

Lord Randolph replied by telegram on the 26th :

" Absolutely necessary for Government to state to-night their intentions with regard to Ireland, viz. suppression of National League followed by Land Bill. This is the only method of averting defeat on Jesse Collings' motion. Notice should be given to-day of introduction of Repression Bill on Thursday."

To this Mr. Smith replied :

" I think proposed action looks precipitate. There is no excessive urgency here. . . . I should prefer, if possible, to provide against the intimidation of League than denounce it by name."

Lord Randolph's answer was :

" Your telegram received half-hour after Cabinet separated. Beach has just announced introduction of Bill by you on Thursday, for suppression of National League and other dangerous associations, for the prevention of intimidation, and for the protection of life, property, and order in Ireland. Of course, great sensation. I showed your wire to Lord Salisbury. We both agreed you would not wish unanimous decision of Cabinet modified."

It appears, then, that the decision to introduce immediately a new Coercion Bill was arrived at for party purposes, with the object of defeating Mr. Jesse Collings' motion, and in the hope that many of the Whig Members would support the Government in the division on this account.

The notice of a new Coercion Bill most appropriately sealed the fate of the Government. The discussion on the Address in reply to the Speech from the Throne had already occupied three nights. On the first of these Mr. Gladstone spoke on the

---

[1] *Life of Lord Randolph Churchill*, II, 44.

Irish question, without committing himself to any scheme for dealing with the question of the government of Ireland. In a paper written some years later, and printed by Lord Morley, he gave an explanation of his position at this critical moment. He showed his extreme anxiety lest an amendment should be moved to the Address, following the example of 1833, and proposing a solemn declaration in favour of the Act of Union. He expressed the opinion that if the question of Home Rule had been prematurely raised in this way not more than two hundred Members would have voted against such an amendment.[1] In this view, Mr. Gladstone spoke in the following guarded manner :

" Responsibility lies where the means of action lie. In my opinion there could not be a greater calamity than to bring the Irish question within the lines of party conflict. If, unhappily, that shall be done, I will, so far as in me lies, take care I will not be the doer. It is the Government alone who ever act in such a matter. In my opinion, the action of a person in the position I have the honour to hold, not only is unnecessary, but would not be warrantable, and would be in the highest degree injurious and mischievous ; and I will do nothing that can tend, by making proposals, if I were prepared with proposals, to be a challenge to others to bring this question into the category of party controversies. . . .

" I do not intend, so far as lies in my power, to have it determined for me by others at what time, or in what manner, I shall make any addition to the declaration I laid before the country early in September. I stand here as a Member of the House, where there are many who have taken their seats for the first time upon these benches, and where there may be some to whom possibly I may avail myself of the privilege of old age to offer a recommendation. I would tell them of my own intention to keep my counsel and reserve my own freedom, until I see the occasion when there may be a prospect of public benefit in endeavouring to make a movement forward, and I will venture to recommend them, as an old Parliamentary hand, to do the same." [2]

Mr. Parnell had no more intention to be drawn as to the demands of the Irish Members at the moment than Mr.

---

[1] *Life of Gladstone*, III, 284.
[2] *Hansard*, January 21st, 1886.

Gladstone. For the present, he could only say he had little doubt that if the House of Commons approached the question of the government of Ireland in the same spirit, and with the same largeness of views as had characterized Mr. Gladstone's speech, such a solution could be found as would enable Ireland to be entrusted with the right of self-government, and secure those guarantees regarding the integrity of the Empire, the supremacy of the Crown, and the protection of what was called the loyal minority in Ireland, which had been required by both the political parties. He had always believed that if they could come to a decision—if they could agree upon the principle that the Irish people were entitled to some self-government, that Parliament had, to a very large extent, failed in her self-imposed task of governing Ireland during the eighty-five years since the Union—they would not find the details so very formidable. His own candid opinion was that so far from increasing the chances of separation, the concession of autonomy would undoubtedly largely diminish them.

Two more days were occupied on the Address on other topics remote from Ireland. On the 26th the motion of Mr. Jesse Collings came on, expressing regret that there was no reference in the Queen's Speech to any measure for affording facilities to agricultural labourers to obtain allotments and small holdings, on reasonable terms, and with security of tenure. His motion raised the agrarian question of "Three acres and a cow," which had filled with hope the agricultural labourers at the recent County elections in England, and had resulted in so many victories to Liberal candidates at the polls. Looking back at this question by the light of later experience, and in view of legislation for this very purpose carried by a Tory Government, it is difficult now to believe that such a motion could have involved the fate of a Government in 1886. But it was so. The subject had formed part of the unauthorized programme of Mr. Chamberlain. He had recently made a very powerful speech on its behalf at a meeting of the Allotments and Small Holdings Association. He vigorously supported his henchman, Mr. Jesse Collings. The Government had no objection to the provision of allotments, and pleaded that they had a Bill on the anvil for that purpose, but they threw cold water on the proposal to multiply small holdings of land. They were supported by Lord Hartington,

Mr. Goschen, and others of the Whig wing of the Liberal Party. Mr. Gladstone, who had not included small holdings in his election address, supported the motion.

The division took place. The Government was defeated by 331 to 252 votes—a majority of seventy-nine. Only eighteen Liberals voted with the Government, but no fewer than seventy-nine of them abstained from voting. The trick of the Government in giving notice of a coercive measure for Ireland in the name of the Irish Secretary, but without his authority, had not tempted, as was hoped, a sufficient number of Liberals to break away from their party. Seventy-nine Irish Nationalists voted in the majority. The next morning Mr. W. H. Smith returned from his brief excursion to Ireland, to find that the Government had been defeated, and to ponder over the unscrupulous use which had been made of him. The Government made haste to submit their resignation to the Queen, and Mr. Gladstone, for a third time, at the age of seventy-six, was commissioned to form a Government.

It will be seen that much, bearing on these events, has oozed out, to use Lord Salisbury's expression, even since Lord Morley's great work, especially in Mr. Churchill's life of his father. Much more will certainly ooze out when the life of Lord Carnarvon comes to be written. Indeed, there are few papers, still hidden from the historian, more important and full of interest, than the correspondence between Lord Carnarvon and Lord Salisbury. It will no doubt show how far Lord Salisbury, and others of his colleagues, were inclined to go in the direction of Lord Carnarvon's policy, and also what were Lord Carnarvon's conclusions as to his experience in Dublin in administering the law without resort to coercive powers, and what were his real reasons for resignation.

It is not to be supposed that Lord Salisbury made any distinct promise to Lord Carnarvon as to a future policy for Ireland. He more probably left it an open question, dependent on the position of things, and the attitude of his colleagues. Whatever the expectations held out may have been, it is quite certain that Lord Salisbury, after the General Election, could not possibly have carried them out, with the small number of supporters which were returned by the constituencies. To have attempted to do so, even with such support as Mr. Gladstone would have given him, would have split the Tory

Party, and have destroyed its efficacy for years to come, just as happened to the Tory Party after Catholic Emancipation and the Repeal of the Corn Laws. Lord Salisbury's best course, undoubtedly, was to abandon any inchoate schemes for reform of the Irish Government, to throw over Carnarvon, and to fall back on the main body of his party, and the old war cries. This course, at all events, was justified from a party point of view by subsequent events. It undoubtedly led to a coalition with the Whigs, and to twenty years of Tory government with their support.

It may be worth while here to refer to a conversation I had with Mr. Gladstone in 1883, showing how confidently he expected to retire from political life within a short time, and how impossible he thought it that he could ever again be Prime Minister. It fell to my lot, as First Commissioner of Works in that year, to provide an inscription to the monument erected by the vote of Parliament to the memory of Lord Beaconsfield in Westminster Abbey. I asked Lord Salisbury and Sir Stafford Northcote to write it, but neither of them would undertake it. Lord Salisbury suggested that I should write one myself, and show it to him and Northcote for their approval. In this view I went to the Abbey to see how other epitaphs of Prime Ministers had been treated. I determined on the short inscription which now appears on Lord Beaconsfield's monument. " Erected by Parliament to the Memory of the Earl of Beaconsfield, Twice Prime Minister of England." Returning to the House of Commons, I showed it to Mr. Gladstone, and asked his opinion. " Twice Prime Minister," he said ; " that is no particular distinction. I was only thinking a few days ago about the Prime Ministers since the Reform Act of 1832, and I noted that, with one exception, they had all held that post a second time. One held the post three times. You will not, I am sure, guess who that was."

I tried my hand at a guess, but failed. " It was Lord Derby," he said ; " he was three times Prime Minister, but his aggregate ministries did not extend over more than four and a half years, so they don't count for much." After some further conversation on the subject, I concluded by saying, " I hope, sir, you will beat Lord Derby's record." " Beat Lord Derby's record," he replied, in his most emphatic manner ;

" that is an absolute impossibility.   This is positively my last
Ministry, and it cannot last much longer.   A man must be mad
who thinks that I could ever again form a new Ministry.   No
one should take the post after the age of seventy."   Yet he
lived to do so twice again, and his monument in the Abbey
records the fact, rather unhappily capping the inscription
on that of Lord Beaconsfield immediately adjoining, that he
was Four Times Prime Minister.

CHAPTER XXIX

THE FIRST HOME RULE GOVERNMENT

WHEN inviting his colleagues in the last Liberal administration to join in forming a new Cabinet, Mr. Gladstone laid down, as a basis of policy, "the examination whether it was practicable to comply with the desire widely prevalent in Ireland, and testified by the return of 85 out of 103 representatives, for the establishment by statute of a legislative body to sit in Dublin, and to deal with Irish, as distinguished from Imperial affairs, in such a manner as would be calculated to support and consolidate the unity of the Empire."

Of the members of his last Cabinet, five, following the lead of Lord Hartington, refused to enter upon any such inquiry. They were opposed to Home Rule for Ireland in any shape or form. They included Lord Derby, Lord Northbrook, Lord Selborne, and Lord Carlingford. Two, Mr. Chamberlain and Mr. Trevelyan, agreed to join provisionally, but without much expectation of being able to agree to a scheme for an Irish Parliament, though willing to examine the subject. Two others were unavailable, Sir Charles Dilke, and myself who had been defeated in the General Election. Seven of the old hands accepted the new policy without reserve—Lord Granville, Lord Spencer, Lord Kimberley, Lord Ripon, Lord Rosebery, Sir William Harcourt, and Mr. Childers. Four new members were admitted to the Cabinet— Mr. Morley, Mr. Campbell-Bannerman, Mr. Mundella, and Lord Herschell (as Lord Chancellor). With few exceptions, the main body of aristocratic Whigs, who had formed such an important, if not the main, element, in successive Governments since the Reform Act of 1832, took this opportunity of severing themselves from the Liberal Party.

The most significant appointment in the new Cabinet was that of Mr. Morley as Irish Secretary. Mr. Morley had been one of the few in the General Election who boldly and unmistakably pronounced in favour of Home Rule. He had strongly and consistently opposed coercion, in 1881–2, when editor of *The Pall Mall Gazette*. His mind, at least, was made up as regards the principle of Home Rule. Lord Rosebery became Foreign Secretary, in place of Lord Granville, who took the post of Colonial Secretary, not without grievous heart-burning on finding Rosebery preferred to him for Foreign Affairs. Sir William Harcourt was appointed Chancellor of the Exchequer, the post which it was understood Mr. Chamberlain desired. This last statesman was offered, and declined, the Admiralty. He accepted the Local Government Board. It would seem that this relegation of Mr. Chamberlain to a comparatively secondary post was unfortunate. The success of the Home Rule policy was imperilled by the defection of either Lord Hartington or Mr. Chamberlain ; but it became almost impossible when both were ranged against it. In fact, there seems to have been from the first a personal antagonism between Mr. Gladstone and Mr. Chamberlain, which was one of the main causes of the defeat of the new policy.

There does not appear to have been any inquiry by a Committee representing different sections of the new Cabinet, as was indicated in the memorandum which has been quoted. A scheme for a Home Rule Bill was framed by Mr. Gladstone in consultation only with Mr. Morley. But the latter was in constant communication with Mr. Parnell. Mr. Gladstone himself had only two interviews with the Irish chief, but indirectly, through Mr. Morley, was in touch with him. The assent of Mr. Parnell was obtained to all the main features of the Bill, save only, a most important one, that of finance. Parnell was of opinion that the financial provisions were not sufficiently favourable to Ireland. He reserved the right to claim amendments in the Committee on the Bill, if it should reach that stage. But Lord Morley intimates that it was quite possible that the scheme might ultimately have broken down on this point, by the refusal of the Irish Members to agree to the financial terms.

With regard to the general features of the scheme, it was

obvious to any one who considered the subject, that there were two main alternative lines on which it might be framed. The one was based on the " Federal " principle, under which the Irish people, while having an Irish Parliament to deal with purely Irish questions, would still be represented in the Imperial Parliament. The other was based, more or less, on the Colonial principle. Ireland, under this, would have its own Parliament limited to Irish affairs, but would not be represented in the Imperial Parliament. There were merits and defects in both these schemes about equally balanced. Writing myself on the subject, in one of the monthly reviews, before the introduction of the Bill, I examined these alternatives, and ventured on the prediction that, whichever scheme was first proposed to Parliament, the other would ultimately be adopted. This prediction seems likely to be verified. The Home Rule Bill of 1886 was based on the Colonial principle, and that of 1893 on the Federal principle, and this, it may be assumed, will be the basis of the next and final scheme.

The scheme of 1886, as settled by Mr. Gladstone and Mr. Morley, and laid before the Cabinet, consisted of two Bills— one proposing a new Parliament for Ireland for purely Irish affairs, and determining its relation to the Imperial Parliament ; the other dealing with land purchase on a large scale. Under the first of these, an Irish Parliament was to be created, consisting of two orders, the one of 28 representative peers and 76 representative Members elected for ten years by electors of high qualification ; the other of 204 Members elected under the existing franchise. These two orders were to sit together for most purposes. They were to be prohibited by statute from dealing with specified Imperial subjects, 26 in number ; but otherwise they were to have complete legislative powers over Ireland, including ultimately law and police. The Irish Executive was to be responsible to them. The Irish Constabulary was for a time to be under the control of the Lord-Lieutenant.

As regards finance, Ireland was to contribute in proportion of one-fifteenth to the Imperial Debt, and to the cost of the Army and Navy, and certain Civil Services common to the Empire ; but as all the Customs duties and Excise duties collected in Ireland were to be paid over to the Irish Government, and no duties were to be levied as between England

and Ireland, and as very large quantities of spirits and beer produced in Ireland were exported to and consumed in England, Ireland would benefit by this to the extent of £1,400,000 a year. Taking this into account, the contribution of Ireland to Imperial purposes would be reduced to one-twenty-sixth, in place of one-fifteenth, and the charge per head of its population would be only 13s. 5d. a year as compared with £1 10s. 11d. in Great Britain. When Mr. Parnell complained of the proportion of one-fifteenth being too high, he did not appear to take into account the enormous gain to Ireland of the duty paid on spirits and beer, produced in Ireland, but consumed in England. The actual payment by Ireland to Imperial purposes under this arrangement would be reduced to £1,844,000 a year.

The Land Bill proposed that an option should be given to all landowners in Ireland, in respect of land let on tenancy, to be bought by the State on the terms of twenty years' purchase of the net rent, after deducting, from the judicial rent, the law charges, bad debts, and the cost of management. The tenants would have the option in such cases to become the owners of their holdings by paying 4 per cent on the purchase money in interest and sinking fund for forty-nine years. For this purpose a new 3 per cent stock was to be issued at par by the Land Commission, and it was estimated, in the first instance, by Mr. Gladstone, that an issue of £113,000,000 might be required for this purpose ; but later he reduced his estimate to £50,000,000 without any very clear explanation.

The scheme thus briefly outlined was laid before the Cabinet, and led almost at once to the resignations of Mr. Chamberlain and Mr. Trevelyan—the former because he objected in every way to the scheme of land purchase, and also to the exclusion of the Irish Members from the Imperial Parliament ; the latter mainly because he could not agree to hand over to an Irish Parliament and Irish Executive the control of the police and the administration of the law. After these resignations, the scheme was carefully examined by the Cabinet, and some important modifications were made in its details. It appeared that the land scheme was chiefly insisted upon by Lord Spencer and Mr. Morley.

Mr. Gladstone, on April 8th, introduced the main Bill in

the House. It was a memorable occasion. The House was more crowded than had ever been known. In the galleries were the Prince of Wales and all the leading peers of the other House. Not being a Member of the House of Commons, I found a place in the Gallery; and, sitting next to Davitt, was witness of the effect, on an excitable Irish temperament, of the generous phrases and appeal of Mr. Gladstone. It was one of his greatest efforts—perhaps his greatest, all things considered: the difficulty of the subject; his age; the enormous extent of the ground he had to cover; the many opponents and critics he sought to disarm. He spoke for 3½ hours with unfaltering vigour, without ever losing for a moment the rapt attention of his hearers—a speech equal in length to seven over-long sermons, and yet not a single one of his hearers left the chamber wearied by the long discourse. The speech was so densely packed with matter, and so closely reasoned, that it is impossible to condense it. Mr. Gladstone gave a history of the Act of Union, and the infamous means by which it was carried through the Irish Parliament. He referred to the promises made to the Catholics, which were broken by George III and Pitt. He showed the failure of the Act to give content: how constantly renewed Coercion Acts deprived the Irish people of constitutional liberty, and of protection from the arbitrary acts of the Executive, and how measures of reform demanded by overwhelming majorities of Irish Members were, again and again, rejected, and were only at last conceded to agitation, carried almost to the point of rebellion, and enforced by outrages and crime. He showed how disastrous had been the absence of Irish control over the expenditure of the country. It was only by a large view of the past that an adequate conception could be formed of the grave necessity for a change. He then unfolded the scheme of his two Bills with a lucidity and completeness of which he alone, of all the speakers I have heard in Parliament, was fully capable.

The debate which then followed, and that on the second reading of the Bill, were spread over sixteen days. They were worthy of the great occasion. It was notable that the main attack on the Bill came from the Dissentient Liberals. These were divided into two sections, the larger one of Whigs, led by Lord Hartington, Mr. Goschen, and Sir Henry James, who

objected *in toto* to any scheme in the direction of Home Rule ;
and a much smaller one of Radicals, led by Mr. Chamberlain,
who admitted that the existing system of Irish government
was indefensible, and was willing to amend it, but who objected to the particular scheme of the Bill.

It was not easy to understand the position of Mr. Chamberlain himself. While strongly objecting to Mr. Gladstone's
scheme, he stated in the debate, on the introduction of the
main Bill, that the true solution of the problem of Irish government was to be found, not in the position of the self-governing
colonies, but upon the lines of federation. Again, on the
second reading, he said that he was fully prepared, the very
next day, if the Government pleased, to establish between the
Imperial Parliament and Ireland the existing relations between the Dominion Parliament of Canada and the provincial
legislatures. Yet, when the offer was made later to take
the second reading of the Bill as an affirmation of the principle
of a subordinate Irish Parliament, leaving its relations to be
determined at a future stage, he showed no desire to act upon
it. The explanation of his position was probably to be found
in the conversation reported by Mr. Barry O'Brien in his
Life of Parnell. When asked whether he objected to the
exclusion of the Irish Members as a matter of detail, Mr.
Chamberlain replied: "I wanted to kill the Bill." "And you
used the question of the exclusion of the Irish for that purpose ? " Mr. Chamberlain : " I did, and I used the Land
Bill for the same purpose. I was not opposed to the reform of
the land Jaws. I was not opposed to the land purchase scheme.
It was the right way to settle the Land question, but there
were many things in the Bill to which I was opposed in principle. My main object in attacking it was to kill the Home
Rule Bill."[1]

After this frank admission, we may assume that the alternative schemes were also put forward by Mr. Chamberlain mainly
for the purpose of killing the Bill. Certain it is that when
the Bill of 1893, based on a Federal scheme, came before
Parliament, Mr. Chamberlain was just as hostile to it as to
the Bill of 1886. Mr. Gladstone clearly appreciated the
unreality of Mr. Chamberlain's alternative schemes, for in
his speech, winding up the debate on the second reading of

[1] *Life of Parnell*, II, 140.

the Bill, in reply to the assertion of Mr. Chamberlain that a Dissolution had no terrors for him, " I do not wonder at this," he retorted ; " I do not see how a Dissolution can have any terrors for him. He has trimmed his vessel, and he has touched his rudder in such a masterly way, that in whatever direction the winds of heaven may blow they will fill his sails." After describing with most telling banter the various kites which Mr. Chamberlain had set flying, he described them " as creations of the vivid imagination born of the hour, and perishing with the hour, totally unavailable for the solution of a great and difficult problem." [1]

There can be no doubt that the scheme of Land Purchase mainly contributed to the defeat of the Bill. It conciliated no one. The Irish landowners did not accept it. Looking back, we can now perceive how unwise they were not to do so ! The terms then proposed were infinitely better than those they have since been content to accept.

Three days before the introduction of the Bill the death of Mr. Forster occurred, and a few days later I was asked to become a candidate for Central Bradford in the vacancy thus occurring. It fell to my lot, therefore, to fight the first great battle for Home Rule before the electors, in one of the most influential constituencies of England, as a successor to a statesman who was vehemently opposed to the principle of the Bill. I announced myself as strongly in favour of Home Rule for Ireland, and fought the battle on that issue only, but I said that I could not support the Land Bill. I was elected, after a severe contest, by a majority of 740, about one-half that of my predecessor in the election of 1886. I returned to the House of Commons in time to speak in favour of the main Bill, and to vote for the second reading.

Of the speeches in favour of the Bill, those of Morley, Parnell, and Sexton stood out in marked superiority. I did not think that other members on the Ministerial benches, or on those behind them, showed much grasp of the subject. It was difficult for them to range over the whole historical and economic grounds, so fully explored by Mr. Gladstone. Nor did the Tory Members make much mark in the discussion. Their Leader, Sir M. Hicks-Beach, alone won much distinction by his speeches. The main attack, as already pointed out,

[1] *Hansard*, June 7th, 1886.

came from the Dissentient Liberals. Lord Hartington made
the best, the most impressive, weighty, and, indeed, most
animated speeches of his political career. It was evident that
he was profoundly stirred by the crisis. With him it was not
only a breach with the Liberal Party on the Irish question,
but along the whole line of Liberal measures. He had long
worked half-heartedly in a Liberal team. He had no longer
any sympathy with the more democratic measures in the
advanced programme, which had won popular support at
the General Election. In a letter to Mr. Gladstone, in which
he declined to join the new Cabinet, Lord Hartington said that
his adherence would be of little value. He had already, in
the Government of 1880, made concessions on other subjects,
that might be thought to have shaken public confidence in
him ; he could not go farther without destroying that confidence altogether.[1]   It would be difficult to point out any
Liberal measure, in the past ten years, with which Lord Hartington had been in sympathy. Mr. Gladstone said of him that
if he had gone into the new Cabinet, he would have had to
make up his mind to go under the Caudine Forks once a week.
His speech seemed to me to be inspired by this complete
breach with his Liberal traditions, quite as much as by hostility to the particular proposal of Home Rule. I recollect
Mr. Gladstone remarking, after Lord Hartington's speech on the
second reading, that it seemed to be the rule that ex-Ministers
spoke infinitely better against their old friends and colleagues,
after resignation and separation, than ever they had done for
them, and he illustrated this by Lord Hartington, Mr. Goschen,
and Mr. Forster.

Meanwhile the movement outside Parliament became very
pronounced and heated. A great meeting was held at Her
Majesty's Theatre, when Hartington and Salisbury met for the
first time on a public platform, and denounced the Bill. The
latter also, at Hatfield, made his celebrated and oft-quoted
speech, in which he compared the Irish people to Hottentots
and Hindoos, incapable of self-government, and suggested that
Coercion should be applied to Ireland for twenty years, at
the end of which time, she might be fit to accept any gift in
the way of Local Government, or repeal of coercion, that England might wish to give her—a speech which was delivered at

[1] *Life of Gladstone*, III, 222.

a time when the world knew nothing of the Carnarvon–Parnell incident, and which may now be considered by the light of nearly twenty years of Coercion.

Another important manœuvre of the time was that of Lord Randolph Churchill, who, flinging aside all his attempted *rapprochement* with the Irish Party, went to Ulster, and did his utmost to stir up animosity on the part of the Orange section against their Catholic compatriots, and there delivered himself of the jingling phrase, " Ulster will fight and Ulster will be right," which did much to exasperate opinion in Ireland, and to revive animosities between Orangemen and Catholics. It was directly the cause of most serious riots in Belfast.

In view of all these converging hostilities to the Bill, it became clear that some concessions must be made. The Land Bill was practically dropped. It had not been accepted by the landowners. It disarmed no opposition. It was strongly objected to by economists. It was the principal butt of Chamberlain, who insisted that it would cause the loss of millions to the English taxpayers. As regards the main Bill, it also appeared that a considerable section of the Liberal Party were averse to the exclusion of the Irish Members from the Imperial Parliament. Some concession was necessary on this point. The change of front, however, in the face of the enemy was difficult. It appeared that the Dissentient Liberals numbered about a hundred, of whom about two-thirds were followers of Lord Hartington ; the other third of Mr. Chamberlain. The first of these were irreconcilable. The others objected to the particular method of the scheme. If they could be induced to abstain from voting the Bill would be read a second time. At a meeting of the party, held at the Foreign Office, Mr. Gladstone announced that if the Bill were read a second time, it would be withdrawn, and would be reintroduced in an autumn Session, with the clause as to the representation of the Irish Members in the Imperial Parliament reconstituted. This seemed to give great satisfaction, and the hopes for the Bill rose. Mr. Chamberlain dispelled them by calling a meeting of " those Members who, being in favour of some sort of autonomy for Ireland, disapproved of the Government Bills in their present shape." Fifty-five Members were present ; many of them were hostile to Home Rule in any shape. The question for their consideration was whether they should vote against the Bill, or abstain from voting. Mr. Chamberlain presided. A letter from Mr. Bright was read, or rather the effect of it was stated, and the publication of it was promised, but was never carried out. The meeting, swayed mainly, it was said, by Mr. Bright's advice, decided to vote against the second reading of the Bill. This practically decided the fate of the Bill and the defeat of the Government. But perhaps as potent in efficacy was the offer of the Tory Leaders to those Liberals who would vote against the Government, that there would be no opposition to them, in their constituencies, from Tory candidates if a General Election should occur, and that Tory voters would be recommended to vote for them. This is said to have determined not a few waverers. This bargain had the effect of securing the return, at the General Election, of seventy-eight of the ninety-three Liberals who voted against the Government.

There came the last day of the debate—June 7th. It was a momentous one. The speeches, of very high order, were opened by Mr. Goschen. He described the Bill as a bundle of impossibilities, not the result of hasty drafting, but of difficulties inherent in the question. He said that Members were in the dark, whether the Government was, or was not, pledged to reconstruct it. Mr. Gladstone, interrupting, indignantly repudiated the statement that the Government intended to reconstruct the Bill. They had proposed to reconstruct a single clause only. Mr. Goschen affirmed that the Bill carried in it all the seeds of political, commercial, financial, and, above all, of executive friction. He raised every possible prejudice against it, and ignored altogether that any question of Irish government needed solution.

Mr. Parnell, who followed him, made what was the best speech of his Parliamentary career. It was dignified, admirably delivered, closely reasoned, and well arranged. He had already in the debate, on the introduction of the Bill, while expressing the opinion that the financial clauses were not sufficiently favourable to Ireland, said that the Bill, subject to some change in Committee in this respect, would be accepted by the Irish people as a solution of the long-standing dispute between the two countries. He now said that though he would at one time have preferred the restoration of Grattan's

Parliament, he saw advantages in an Irish legislature established for Home Government, limited and subordinated to the Imperial Parliament. The Bill, he affirmed, had been freely, cheerfully, and gladly accepted by all the leaders of national feeling both in Ireland and America. Not a single dissentient voice had been raised against it by any Irishmen holding nationalist opinions. With regard to the retention of the Irish Members, he proposed to keep his mind open. Personally he had no objection to their retention, but he believed that great difficulties would ensue, and that ultimately it would be the English Members, and not the Irish, who would object to their being retained. With respect to Ulster he absolutely declined to assent to its separation from the rest of Ireland. He then dealt with the question of protective duties, and explained his speech at Wexford, with which he had been taunted by many speakers, by the reference to the Carnarvon interview, which has already been dealt with. Though he did not give Carnarvon's name, he said that a member of the late Government had given him reason to believe that they favoured this view. The statement was at once repudiated by Sir M. Hicks-Beach. But his disclaimer merely went to this, that no such proposal had been agreed to by the late Cabinet. The debate was wound up by Mr. Gladstone, who, as we have seen, never spoke better than when he was on the verge of defeat. He dealt with all the main objections, and delivered the banter against Mr. Chamberlain, which has been quoted. His last words, delivered with entrancing dignity and pathos, were these :

" Ireland stands at your bar expectant, hopeful, almost suppliant. Her words are the words of truth and soberness. She asks a blessed oblivion of the past, and in that oblivion our interest is deeper even than hers. Mr. Goschen asks us to abide by the traditions of which we are the heirs. What traditions ? By the Irish traditions ? Go into the length and breadth of the world, ransack the literature of all countries, find, if you can, a single voice, a single book — find, I would almost say, as much as a single newspaper article, unless the product of the day, in which the conduct of England towards Ireland is anywhere treated, except with profound and bitter condemnation. Are those the traditions by which we are exhorted to stand ?

No, they are a sad exception to the glory of our country. They are a broad and black blot upon the pages of its history, and what we want to do is to stand by the traditions of which we are the heirs in all matters, except our relations with Ireland, —to make our relations with Ireland conform to the other traditions of our country. So I hail the demand of Ireland for what I call a blessed oblivion of the past. She asks also a boon for the future ; and that boon for the future, unless we are much mistaken, will be a boon to us in respect of honour, no less than a boon to her in respect of happiness, prosperity, and peace. Such, sir, is her prayer. Think, I beseech you, think well, think wisely, think, not for a moment, but for the years that are to come, before you reject the Bill."

The House, amid the greatest excitement, proceeded to a division. Never in its history did so large a number of its Members take part in it. Only 11 Members were absent, 10 of whom were Liberals. The division was 314 to 344. The Bill and the Government were defeated by a majority of 30. The full force of Nationalists, 85 in number, voted for it ; 93 Liberals voted against the Bill. A single Tory Member, Sir Robert Peel, son of the great statesman, voted for the Bill.

Mr. Bright, who had abstained from speaking out of reverence to Mr. Gladstone, finally decided, after much searching of heart, to vote against the Bill. It has been shown that his letter to the Dissentients, who were led by Mr. Chamberlain, determined the votes and caused the defeat of the Bill. It will be seen that at the General Election which followed his speech, on the eve of it, had a most potent effect upon the result. He spoke to me many times about the Bill and its policy. It appeared that what he chiefly feared was handing over Ireland to Parnell and his followers.

CHAPTER XXX

LORD SALISBURY'S SECOND MINISTRY

MR. GLADSTONE, on the defeat of his Home Rule Bill, decided at once to dissolve Parliament, and to appeal to the constituencies. The first to enter the lists in the electoral campaign was Mr. Chamberlain. In a speech at Birmingham he denounced the Government Bills, up hill and down dale, especially the Land Bill.

" Why," he asked, " of all the classes in Ireland who were going to be ruined by Home Rule, should the landlords alone be compensated ? The scheme would cost 150 millions to the British taxpayers, the most gigantic bribe ever offered to the opponents of any legislation."

As Birmingham was the Mecca of local self-government, it appeared to be necessary for him to conciliate opinion in this direction by suggesting an alternative scheme for Ireland. It did not want in boldness. He proposed a definite plan of federation founded, for the most part, on Mr. Gladstone's principles. It was a very long advance beyond the National Council scheme. When Mr. Gladstone had agreed to retain the representation of Ireland in the Imperial Parliament, there was not much difference in principle between his scheme and this new emanation from Birmingham.

Mr. Gladstone also was early on the warpath. He met with an enthusiastic reception everywhere on his way to Midlothian His election there was unopposed. He was able, therefore, to address many great meetings at Glasgow, Manchester, and elsewhere, in spite of the remonstrance of the Queen, who, Lord Morley tells us, thought that her Prime Minister should confine himself to speeches in his own constituency. He might well conclude from his personal triumph that the verdict of the constituencies generally would be favourable to his policy.

He put it before them in plain and simple language, enforced by sympathetic and eloquent passages. The plan of the Government that Ireland, under well-considered conditions, should transact her own affairs, was contrasted with that of Lord Salisbury, who asked for new repressive laws, and their resolute enforcement for twenty years. The benefits which Irish autonomy could confer were the consolidation of the Empire, an augmentation of its real strength, the extinction of ignoble feuds in Ireland, the stopping of constant and demoralizing waste of public money, the redemption of the honour of Great Britain from the stigma fastened upon her, in respect of Ireland, by the judgment of the whole of the civilized world, and the free restoration to the Imperial Parliament of its dignity and efficiency.

Lord Salisbury, on the other hand, denounced the scheme as one for disintegrating the Empire in a manner which the wildest revolutionaries had never dreamt of. Mr. Goschen, who had represented, in the last Parliament, one of the divisions of Edinburgh, was directly pitted against Mr. Gladstone. He took Ulster under his special protection. He declared that its people would never submit to Home Rule without coercion. He objected to the withdrawal of the police from the impartial hands of the Imperial executive. Justice to Ireland should not mean injustice to one-third of her population. These arguments, though put forward with great force, did not persuade the constituency. He was rejected in the election which followed, as was also Mr. Trevelyan in another Scotch constituency, the Border Boroughs.

In England the drift of public opinion was adverse to the new policy. Mr. Schnadhorst, who was then the principal agent and adviser to the Liberal Party on election matters, had given his opinion that the turnover of the Irish vote in English constituencies would counterbalance any defection of the Liberal Unionists. But it was not so. The most potent voice in the election against Mr. Gladstone was that of Mr. Bright. He was re-elected at Birmingham without opposition. On thanking the electors for his return, he declared, for the first and last time, his full opinion on the Home Rule Bill. As the result, he said, of his long study of the Irish question, and with all his sympathy for Ireland, he was entirely opposed to anything, in any shape, which should be called a Parliament in Dublin. He described Mr. Gladstone's proposed legislature as " a vestry which would be continually breaking the bars of its cage, striving to become a Parliament." The only good thing of the original scheme was the proposal to exclude the Irish Members from the Imperial Parliament. As to the proposed alternative of bringing back the Irish Members to discuss Imperial questions, what would be the result of having an intermittent Irish fever in the House of Commons ? He absolutely declined to surrender the field to the Parliamentary Party in Ireland, one-half of whom had dollars in their pockets subscribed by the enemies of England in the United States. History, he said, had no example of a monarchy or a republic submitting to a capitulation at once so unnecessary and so humiliating. He was entirely opposed to the land scheme, making England the universal absentee landlord for the whole of Ireland. The Irish patriot would be sure to say, " You have got free from the burdens of local proprietors. Will you now pay rent to a foreign Government ? " There can be no doubt that this forcible speech, delivered on the eve of the borough elections, produced a most powerful effect on the voters. The English and Welsh Boroughs which, in the previous year had been almost equally divided in their representation, returning 122 Conservatives to 120 Liberals, now sent 153 Conservatives and 20 Liberal Unionists, and only 69 Liberals. London, Liverpool, and Birmingham went almost wholly against Home Rule.

In the English Counties the result was relatively as bad. In 1885, the main success of the Liberals had been in the Counties. They returned 152 Liberals to 101 Conservatives. The defection of the Whigs was more serious here than in the Boroughs. It may be said that, with rare exceptions, all the Liberal landowners went against Mr. Gladstone. The Home Rule question did not interest the rural voters. They did not understand it.

In 1885 they had been induced to vote for Liberal candidates by promises of land reform, which would bring allotments and small holdings within their reach. By an incredible neglect, no measure with this object had been prepared by the Local Government Board and laid before Parliament. As a result of this the English and Welsh Counties returned only 85 Liberals as against 136 Conservatives and 39

Liberal Unionists. Scotland, though true in the main to the old Liberal traditions, gave a very reduced majority. In 1885 it returned 61 Liberals and only 9 Conservatives. It now sent to Parliament 42 Liberals, 12 Conservatives, and 16 Liberal Unionists. Ireland was again almost overwhelmingly in favour of Home Rule. The Nationalists lost one seat only, but speedily redressed this at a by-election.

The result for the whole country was the return of only 191 Liberals and 85 Irish Nationalists, as against 316 Conservatives and 78 Liberal Unionists. The majority, therefore, against Home Rule was 118. The verdict of the country was unmistakable. The actual majority of the electors, however, was not considerable. In the contested constituencies in England and Wales, 1,416,000 voted against Home Rule, as against 1,328,000 for it—a difference of only 5 per cent. But, as usually and, I believe fortunately, happens, the majority of voters was accentuated by the return of Members. Of the 93 Liberal Unionists who voted against the Home Rule Bill, 78 were again returned by the votes of their previous opponents, retaining just enough of their former Liberal supporters to turn the scale in their favour. This may be said to have been the determining cause of the disaster to the Liberal Party. If these 78 seats had been contested between Liberals and Conservatives in the usual manner, it is probable that a fair majority of them would have returned Home Rulers. The strategy, therefore, of the Tory Party in promising to support Liberals who voted against the Bill was equally successful in the constituencies as in Parliament. It secured, however, to the Liberal Unionists the command of the position in the House of Commons. Without their support the Tory Government could not be formed, nor could any Tory measure be carried without their approval. This was the key to the political position in the House of Commons during the next six years.

As soon as the result of the election was known, Mr. Gladstone, on July 20th, called his Cabinet together. They decided on immediate resignation without waiting for the meeting of Parliament. Lord Salisbury was again entrusted with the task of forming a Government. Two important changes were made in its personnel as compared with his last short-lived Ministry. Sir M. Hicks-Beach voluntarily gave up the leadership of the party, in the House of Commons, to Lord Randolph Churchill, whom he recognized as better fitted for the position than himself. He accepted the post of danger and difficulty, that of Irish Secretary, with, of course, a seat in the Cabinet. In other respects the new Government was much the same as the first of Lord Salisbury's ventures.

The new Parliament met on August 19th. The Irish question at once required its attention. The position was a novel one. The difference between the English and Irish elections had never before been so accentuated. Ireland, where there was an overwhelming majority of Nationalists, was to be governed and overruled on Irish questions by a majority of Tories in England, in sympathy with the small minority of Ulster Tories in Ireland. The position required statesmanship of high order and bold conception. If any lesson had been taught by the past history of Ireland, since the Act of Union, it was the danger of refusing to listen to the demands of the great majority of its Members in the House of Commons. The only constitutional alternative to Home Rule consistent with the principle of representative institutions, was concession to the majority of Irish Members on purely Irish questions.

Lord Carnarvon, apart from any expectations held out in the direction of Home Rule, during his short tenure of office, had pursued the policy of coming to agreement with the Irish leaders as to Irish questions. The question for the new Government was whether to pursue this policy still further, or to adopt the alternative of meeting Irish demands by a veto supported by English votes. The Government endeavoured to evade disclosure of its policy till the next year. No announcement was made of a new Coercion Bill. Two Royal Commissions were to be appointed, the one to report on the working of the Land Act of 1881 and the Land Purchase Acts ; the other to report on schemes for arterial drainage in Ireland. Sir Redvers Buller, an able general, was to be placed in the novel position of administrator of three or four counties in the south of Ireland, where agrarian disturbances still existed.

The Irish Members, however, would not brook this dilatory policy. The economic condition of Ireland was serious and menacing. Irish agriculture, equally with that of England, had suffered during the last two years from grave depression, due to the great fall in the prices of produce. The price of corn had fallen in 1885–6 by 30 to 40 per cent, and that of other produce from 20 to 30 per cent. Landowners in England had, almost without exception, met the losses of their tenants by generous remissions of rent, seldom less than 20 per cent, and often 30 or even 40 per cent. Some of the best landlords in Ireland followed this example ; but the greater number declined or neglected to do so. The prevalent opinion among them was that as many of the tenants had obtained judicial rents, at reduced rates for fifteen years, there was no obligation to concede any further reductions.

The Land Commission, however, was showing its appreciation of the altered position. The rents fixed by them during the last six months were 20 per cent lower than those fixed in the previous year. The question, therefore, at once arose whether the rents adjudicated, in the years 1881–5, were not too high, when measured by the generally lower prices of produce. The question also as to the 130,000 leaseholders, who had been excluded from the Land Act, and whose rack rents were now far beyond what the tenants could pay, became a most serious one.

Parnell raised this question, on behalf of the Irish Members, by an amendment to the Address and later by a Bill, in speeches of a most moderate character. He asserted that the economic condition of the Irish tenants was more serious than even in 1881, but that he and his friends did not contemplate for a moment such an agitation as was set on foot in 1880 ; but he said that neither he nor his friends would be able to hold back the wave of violence, if the Irish people were driven to desperation by the prospects of wholesale eviction. He made out an unanswerable case of falling prices and of increasing evictions of men unable to pay existing rents. His proposals were : (1) The revision of rents fixed by the Land Court up to a recent date ; (2) the inclusion of leaseholders in the Act of 1881 ; (3) power to be given to the Commission to stay eviction on payment of three-fourths of the rent (later reduced to one-half the rent) subject to the determination at a later period of the rent to be paid.

It was rumoured that the Cabinet, at the instance of Lord Randolph Churchill and Mr. Matthews, the Home Secretary, was inclined to meet the Irish Leaders in a conciliatory spirit ; but that Lord Hartington refused his consent, and made the support of his followers dependent upon a distinct refusal to make terms with the Irish Nationalists.[1] However that may have been, the Government met the Irish demand with a direct veto. The Irish Secretary said that prices were not so low in Ireland as to make the general payment of moderate rents impossible, though he admitted that in some districts they might be too high. The Government, he said, did not take the view that inability to pay was the sole ground for non-payment of rent. The unwillingness to pay was fortified by terrorism. On the other hand, the case of the Irish Members was fully admitted by Mr. Chamberlain.

" We have to deal," he said, " with a crisis which is apparently imminent, with the general inability to pay rents, with the numerous evictions and consequent suffering, and with great danger to social order. I do not think that any one will deny that there has been a great fall in the price of almost all the chief produce of Ireland, since judicial rents were fixed. The fall may be variously estimated at 20 or 30 per cent. Now if the judicial rents were fixed upon the basis of former prices and at that time they were fair, then they must necessarily be unfair now. I do not admit for a moment that there is any sanctity about judicial rents or any other rents. If rent cannot be paid and leave a fair subsistence to the tenant, no doubt the landlords must bear the loss." [2]

In spite of this very full admission of the Irish case, Mr. Chamberlain found himself compelled by party exigencies to support Lord Hartington, whom he had recently, at a meeting at Devonshire House, recognized as his leader. Most strange bedfellows in view of their recent antagonism in Mr. Gladstone's Government ! He voted against Parnell's Bill. The Irish demand was supported by the full force of the Liberal Party, and by a forcible speech of its Leader, Mr. Gladstone, without committing himself to the details of the Bill. Sir M. Hicks-Beach wound up the debate on the Bill by this emphatic, and as the sequel proved, most unwise pronouncement :

---

[1] *Annual Register*, 1886, p. 276.
[2] *Hansard*, September 21st, 1886

" The Government desires as much as any one to govern Ireland constitutionally, in accordance with the wishes of the Irish people. But we will not attempt to govern Ireland by a policy of blackmail. It is because that attempt has been made so often by the right honourable gentlemen who sit on the opposite benches, from time to time, yielding to coercion and dictation on the part of the Irish Members, in spite of what they knew was right, that we are landed to-day in the great difficulties that environ the Irish question, and that Mr. Parnell has been emboldened to place before the House a Bill which, though purporting to be a mere instalment of justice to the poor Irish tenants, is an act of gross injustice and confiscation to the landlords of Ireland."[1]

The Bill was rejected by 297 to 202—31 Liberal Unionists voting with the Government.

It was a bad beginning for the new Irish Secretary. A more unfortunate decision was never arrived at. It is impossible to condemn too strongly the refusal to negotiate with the Irish Leader. It is clear from Parnell's speeches, and from all that we have since learnt, that he was most anxious to come to terms of a reasonable character ; and that he had no wish for a renewed agitation on the Land question. If it was right to negotiate with the Irish in 1885, why not again in 1886 ? The sequel abundantly confirmed all Parnell's statements as to the fall of prices, the inability of the Irish tenants to pay existing rents, even judicial rents, and the justice of the demands for a revision of judicial rents, and for the admission of leaseholders to the Land Court. In the very next year the Government was compelled to concede these demands to the full. It did not need a Royal Commission to bring out the facts on which this concession was founded. They were notorious on Mr. Chamberlain's admission. Sir M. Hicks-Beach and his Government, backed by Lord Hartington and Mr. Chamberlain, must be held to be responsible for the grave results which followed from this denial of the claims of five-sixths of the Irish Members put forward in a constitutional form. All past experience showed that such a refusal was certain to lead to unconstitutional methods of enforcing demands. A great opportunity was lost of showing that the Imperial Parliament, when rejecting the demands of the Irish

---

[1] *Hansard*, September 21st, 1886.

people for self-government in an Irish Parliament, was able to concede the demands of the great majority of their Members on a purely Irish question, put forward in a constitutional manner free from any threats of violence—the only possible way in which the Union could be maintained with justice to Ireland.

CHAPTER XXXI

THE PLAN OF CAMPAIGN

THE results of the unfortunate action of the Government in rejecting the demands of the Irish Members, in the short autumn Session of 1886, were very soon made apparent. Parliament was prorogued on September 25th, and the Irish Secretary returned to his official work at Dublin. He found a state of things in Ireland which showed that he had been over-sanguine in the representations which he had made in the House of Commons. The agrarian position was such that he felt it his duty at once to bring all the influence of the executive Government to induce the landlords to make abatements of rent to meet the serious fall of prices of produce. The better men among them were already doing this, but large numbers were pressing their tenants for full rents, and were threatening eviction, in default of payment. One of the main centres of difficulty and disturbance was the Loughrea district of Galway, which has been described in an earlier chapter. The chief landowner there, Lord Clanricarde, had declined to make any general abatements of rent to his large body of tenants, and his example was being followed by other landlords of the district. The rents of the Clanricarde property were about 10 per cent above the average of the earlier judicial rents determined by the Land Commission between 1882 and 1885, and were fully 25 to 30 per cent above the more recent judicial rents. Very few of the tenants had applied for judicial rents, in part because Lord Clanricarde opposed in every case, and put the applicants to heavy law costs, and in part because large arrears of rent had been allowed to accumulate, and the landlord insisted on these being paid by any tenant applying to the Land Commission. Difficulties of a most serious character arose in 1885. A large body of the tenants met and signed a petition to Lord Clanricarde, asking him to make an abatement, and offering to pay their rents subject to a reduction of 25 per cent. The petition was signed by the clergy of the district, and by Dr. Healy, the coadjutor Bishop—now the Archbishop of Tuam—well known for his very moderate views on the Land question. In forwarding the petition, the agent, Mr. Joyce, strongly advised his employer to make an abatement of rent, as others of the best landlords in Galway were doing. Lord Clanricarde reprimanded him for forwarding the petition, and refused to follow his advice. " You must," he wrote, " at once, and without losing a moment of time, take full and drastic measures to secure the amount of rent due." From other letters which passed, it appeared that Lord Clanricarde looked upon the Land Act of 1881 as an invasion of his rights of property, justifying him in pressing for his rents to the fullest extreme. Living in London, never visiting his property, and knowing nothing personally about it, and incurring no personal risk himself, he left no discretion whatever to his agent.

A correspondence was later published in the Press, with respect to the management of this estate. Lord Clanricarde wrote that it was untrue that his agent had advised him to make abatements—that on the contrary, his agent had informed him that the tenants were engaged in a strike against the payment of any rent. The agent thereupon wrote to his employer complaining of this statement. " This year," he said, " is a bad one, and all landlords are making abatements. I consider it most unfair that the whole blame for your not having granted any abatement should fall upon me." After further correspondence, Mr. Joyce resigned his agency, and brought an action at law against his employer, in the course of which all the facts of the case, and the correspondence referred to, became public. The judge who tried the case made very severe comments on the treatment of the tenants, and the press of England, equally with that of Ireland, without distinction of politics, expressed the strongest sympathy for them.

The tenants of the Woodford part of the estate, finding that they could get no abatements, entered into a strict combination, binding themselves, to one another, to pay no rent at all, unless a reasonable abatement was conceded. The case was of great importance, for it was the first one, it is believed, in which the tenants of a large property entered into such a combination. It was a purely spontaneous one on their part, not promoted by the National League. It was the case of a conflict between a landowner, with immense means, unapproachable, and beyond the reach of injury or threats, and a vast body of small tenants, each of whom alone would be powerless against the remote despot. Taken singly, the tenants would certainly have to succumb to the threat of eviction, and be cleared out of their last pennies, but, united, they might be strong enough to induce or compel their landlord to come to reasonable terms.

Who could wonder that under these circumstances the tenants should combine to protect themselves ? It was an essential feature of the combination that the tenants, who were financially strongest, would stand by the weaker men, and would not, by yielding, lessen the force of the whole body against the landlord ; and further, that if some of them should be evicted, in defence of the common cause, no final arrangement would be come to by the others, unless those already evicted, who were the first victims, should be reinstated in their holdings.

The Irish judges laid down that a combination of tenants with this object was an illegal conspiracy. It may be doubted whether the English judges would hold this view. At all events, under the ordinary law, no members of such a combination could be convicted of a criminal conspiracy without the verdict of a jury ; and it is very certain that no jury in Ireland could be found to give a verdict against the Clanricarde tenants, and it is very doubtful whether any British jury would do so. The case was very analogous to that of a combination of workmen, against their employer, for an increase of wages, and should be judged of by similar considerations. A combination may be just and necessary, or the reverse, and public sympathy will be given to either side, as the equities of the case may lie. In the dispute between Lord Clanricarde and his tenants, the equities of the case were unquestionably on the side of the tenants.

Lord Clanricarde determined to break down the combination by all the power which the law would afford him. It was one of the earliest cases which Sir M. Hicks-Beach had to deal with. He authorized the employment of 500 of the constabulary to support the eviction of a selected number of the Woodford tenants. This led to a great public demonstration. Thousands of persons were present at the evictions. The farmhouses were barricaded, and were garrisoned by a number of young men of the district. Every possible resistance was made, short of using actual personal violence, against the police. Boiling water was poured from the windows and roofs ; but no actual harm was done to any one. By great efforts of the police, four or five of the tenants, with their families and defenders, were ejected from the houses.

For this resistance to the law seventy-five young men of Woodford, of good character, were committed by the magistrates for trial at the next assizes at Sligo. Bail was refused, and they remained in jail for some weeks awaiting trial. At the assizes, by packing the juries, and excluding every Catholic from them, convictions were obtained, and a large proportion of the seventy-five men were sentenced to terms of imprisonment of one year to eighteen months, with hard labour. This was but the first act in a long, protracted drama. Lord Clanricarde pressed the Irish Government to support him in a further batch of evictions. Sir M. Hicks-Beach very properly hesitated to employ the forces of the Crown in another raid of this kind, without an endeavour to arrive at a settlement. He sent for the agent of the property, and having ascertained from him that he had advised his employer to make abatements of rent, and had been refused, and that the proposed evictions were for the full rents, admitted by the agent to be excessive, he informed him that the Government would not immediately support such wholesale evictions unless abatements were made. A correspondence ensued between the Chief Secretary and Lord Clanricarde, in which the latter remonstrated against the refusal of the Government to support him, and Sir M. Hicks-Beach replied in a letter, such as had seldom, if ever, been addressed by the Irish Government to a landowner. He informed Lord Clanricarde that if he adhered to his decision to make no abatements of rent, against the advice of his agent, and contrary to the general attitude of Irish landlords, he might find that further proceedings for wholesale evictions would be costly and ineffective, and that " any application to the Government for the use of constables and military would be retarded by the pressure of other claims and duties, and would most probably be postponed, to the utmost extent permitted by the law."

After the rejection of the Tenants' Relief Bill, and the absolute refusal of the Government to admit that there was any agrarian crisis in Ireland which needed a remedy, it was certain that the Irish tenants and their supporters would not accept the position lying down. The Clanricarde case seems to have suggested to them a *modus operandi* more effective than the proceedings of the Land League in 1881–2. What has since been known as the Plan of Campaign was devised by Mr. T. Harrington, and after consultation with Mr. Dillon and Mr. O'Brien, was recommended to the main body of Clanricarde tenants by Mr. O'Brien at a meeting at Woodford, on October 17th. It was launched in *United Ireland*, on October 23rd, within a month after the rejection of the Tenants' Relief Bill. It was suggested to the tenants of every estate, where the landlords refused to make reasonable abatements of rent.

Under this scheme the tenants of any estate, where reasonable abatements were refused, were advised to combine together, after the manner of the Woodford tenants, and to offer payment of rent with a reasonable abatement. There was this important addition, that if the abatement was refused, the tenants were to pay their rents into a common fund, in the name of some friend, which was to be held in trust, till agreement should be arrived at with the landlord ; and that if evictions took place, the evicted families were to be maintained out of this fund. The importance of this addition to the more simple combination was that it was made difficult for any single tenant to break away from the combination, and to pay his rent under the threat of eviction. The scheme was settled and promulgated, without any concert with or approval of Parnell, who was at this time in England, incapacitated by serious illness. When later he became aware of it, he expressed his strong objection.

" He complained," says Davitt, " that neither Mr. Dillon nor Mr. O'Brien had communicated to him their intention to reopen in this new way the agrarian conflict. He said not a word about motives, but he severely criticized the tactical unwisdom of the whole proceeding. The plan could not possibly be justified before English public opinion, which, unfortunately, had the fate of Home Rule at its disposal. Home Rule had been beaten by tricks and lies, and this in England only. Scotland and Wales were sound, and it only needed the conversion of about one hundred thousand out of some four million English voters to enable Mr. Gladstone to win at the next General Election. Gladstone was now ' the one and only hope for Ireland.' He was seventy-six years of age. He had flung himself, in the most courageous and chivalrous manner, into the fight for an Irish Parliament, and it was nothing short of cruel, apart from the necessity of a scheme, which was a deliberate challenge to a new measure of coercion, to handicap the great Liberal Leader in his mighty task, by an agitation which would only present a sordid character to the voters of Great Britain, in comparison with the interests and welfare of Ireland embraced in the fortunes of Home Rule. . . . Parnell appeared to be in wretched health, and remarked, with a kind of foreboding spirit : ' I don't care who leads when I am gone, but I am anxious the old country should get some kind of Parliament as a result of our struggles, and unless Mr. Gladstone can do this for us, no other living Englishman can.' "[1] This advice, however, of Parnell, was too late. The Plan of Campaign had already been launched. It caught on with popular opinion in Ireland. Whatever might be urged against it from a legal point of view, it had undoubtedly most import- ant and immediate effects. Its promulgation induced a large number of landlords, who had refused to make abatements of rent, to reconsider their position, and to come to reasonable terms with their tenants. It was almost as effective as an Act of Parliament. Very great care appears to have been taken by those who were concerned in devising it, to put it in operation only in cases where rents were notoriously excessive, and where landowners had refused to negotiate with their tenants. It was put in force in the autumn and winter of 1886–7 on eighty-four estates. In no fewer than sixty of these the land- lords, after a time, gave way, and agreed to terms which, on the average, amounted to abatements of rent of 25 per cent. The scheme was adopted by the main body of tenants on the Clanricarde estate, and it speedily spread to others of the principal estates in the neighbourhood of Loughrea, those

[1] *Fall of Feudalism*, 518.

of Sir Henry Burke, Lord Dunsandle, Lord Westmeath, and Mr. Lewis.

In the meantime Sir M. Hicks-Beach had been doing his utmost to persuade landlords to make reasonable abatements of rent. He was much influenced in this by the reports and advice of Sir Redvers Buller, who, as already pointed out, had been appointed to supervise the disturbed districts of Kerry and Cork. With the experience of a generous English land-owner, Sir Redvers was startled by the indifference shown by many of the Irish landowners to the exigencies of the times, and by the extreme poverty of large numbers of the tenants, and their total incapacity to pay the existing rents. In his evidence before the Royal Commission, presided over by Lord Cowper, he expressed the opinion, as the result of his personal investigations, that the rents of many estates in his district were excessive, and more than the tenants could pay. " You have got," he said, " an ignorant poor people, and the law should look after them, instead of which the law has looked after the rich." He specified cases where numerous evictions had taken place, though the tenants were quite unable to pay. The Chief Secretary, acting on the advice of Sir Redvers Buller, endeavoured, before lending the forces of the Crown to support evictions, to discriminate whether landlords were acting reasonably or not. As above shown, he practically refused to send another force to support the wholesale evictions on the Clanricarde estate, unless the owner was willing to concede the abatements, which his agent advised to be reason-able. He called this " putting pressure within the law." For this, however, he was severely censured from the judicial bench by Chief Baron Palles, in the course of the trial of the seventy-five Woodford men. " The landlords," the Judge said, " were entitled to collect their rents, and to evict if they were not paid. The Government were bound to protect them in this course, with all the forces at their disposal, and every officer of State in Ireland, including the Chief Secretary him-self, was liable to a prosecution for a failure to perform his duty." When the Executive Government was thus warned off any intervention to prevent harshness and injustice being done, it was to be expected that the tenants themselves would devise a method, such as the Plan of Campaign, to protect themselves.

The Chief Secretary met this new movement by directing a prosecution against John Dillon, William O'Brien, and other leaders concerned in launching the Plan of Campaign, for inciting the tenants to an illegal conspiracy. At their trial the Judge directed the jury that the Plan of Campaign was *ipso facto* an illegal conspiracy, and that the advice to put it in operation was a criminal act. In spite of this, the jury, though every effort had been made by the Crown officers to pack it, did not agree in a verdict.

Whatever may be thought of the Plan of Campaign, from a purely legal point of view, it was remarkably effective for the purpose it aimed at. It did, in fact, save vast numbers of tenants from being pressed and evicted for rents, which the great ˙fall of prices had made excessive, and which most of them could not possibly pay. It undoubtedly preserved Ireland from an outbreak of agrarian crime of a grave character, which would certainly have occurred, if large numbers of tenants had been evicted. It was probably the main cause for legislation in 1887 of a remedial character for the revision of judicial rents. Parliament also has long since condoned the offence, if it were a legal offence, of those who were actually engaged in such combinations, for it unanimously passed measures, in 1903 and 1906, with the express object of reinstating many hundreds of tenants, parties to these combinations, who were selected by their landlords for eviction, and who thus suffered for the common cause of their fellow-tenants. Not only were they reinstated, but Parliament voted money for the rebuilding of their houses, and for restocking their farms.

The Plan of Campaign was furiously denounced by the Government and its supporters, and by their allies, the Liberal Unionists, in England. It was made the main excuse and justification for a new Coercion Act in 1887. Mr. Gladstone was appealed to by Lord Hartington and others to express his disapproval of such combinations. He contradicted a statement that he had approved it ; but his disavowal was given in the following cautious words, which were very remarkable, in view of the very strong current of opinion in England against the scheme. Speaking at the Memorial Hall in London, on July 29th, 1887, he said :

" The Plan of Campaign is one of those devices that cannot

be reconciled with the principles of law and order in a civilized country.   Yet we all know that such devices are the certain results of misgovernment.   With respect to this particular instance, if the plan be blameable (I cannot deny that I feel it difficult to acquit any such plan), I feel its authors are not one-tenth part so blameable as the Government, whose contemptuous refusal of what they have now granted was the parent and source of the mischief."

This speech was made after the passing of the Land Act of 1887, which practically conceded what Parnell and his followers had, in vain, asked for from the Government and Parliament, in August of the previous year, and which, if then granted, would undoubtedly have made such a scheme wholly unnecessary.   It may confidently be expected that the opinion which history will give on the scheme will be in accord with that of Mr. Gladstone.

CHAPTER XXXII

THE CRIMES ACT AND THE LAND ACT OF 1887

EARLY in 1887, before the meeting of Parliament, the Royal Commission, presided over by Lord Cowper, issued its report on the agrarian question in Ireland. It confirmed all that Parnell had alleged, on behalf of his Tenants' Relief Bill of the previous year, as to the crisis caused by the great fall of prices of agricultural produce in Ireland, the impossibility of tenants paying existing rents, and the necessity for a reduction of judicial rents adjudicated before 1886. It recommended that the term of judicial rents should be five years, and not fifteen, that rents fixed before the end of 1885 should be revised, and that leaseholders should be admitted to the benefit of judicial rents. There could not be stronger testimony to the justice of the claims made by the Irish Members, in the course of the discussion of the Act of 1881, and on Parnell's Bill of 1886. Looking at the constitution of the Royal Commission, it is difficult to believe that, in the then state of Ireland, it could have taken the responsibility of advising interference with judicial rents, unless it had obtained the approval of the then Irish Secretary to such a course.

On the meeting of Parliament at the end of January notice was given of two measures for Ireland—the one a Coercion Bill, to be introduced in the House of Commons, the other a Land Bill, in the House of Lords—the two to be proceeded with at the same time, in pursuance of a long-established, but discredited policy, known as " kicks and halfpence." The Coercion Bill, introduced in the House of Commons, proved to be the most stringent of its kind ever proposed to Parliament, not, indeed, after the fashion of Mr. Forster's Act, giving power to the Executive of Ireland to arrest and imprison any one on suspicion, but by a vast number of provisions abridging and destroying the constitutional liberties of the people in Ireland, and creating new offences. It withdrew the protection of juries, and gave full powers to resident magistrates of dealing with cases of intimidation, and of holding public meetings against the will of the Executive. It made the extraordinary proposal of enabling the Irish Government to send persons, accused of murder and other grave offences, to be tried in London. Above all, in contradiction to all precedents, it proposed that the measure should be a permanent one, and not restricted to one or a limited number of years.

It may safely be said that never, in the past history of Ireland, since the Act of Union, had a Coercion Bill been introduced with so little justification. There had practically been no increase of serious crime in Ireland, during the last two years, since the Coercion Act of 1882 had been allowed to drop by Lord Salisbury's first Government. The only new cause of complaint was the existence of combinations of tenants. These combinations did not aim at the non-payment of all rent, but only of so much of the rent as, by the admission of all the best landlords of Ireland and England, and now by that of the Royal Commission, was excessive in view of the great fall of prices. It would seem that the statesmanlike course would have been to test the effect of legislation, as proposed by the Cowper Commission, in putting an end to combinations, rather than to flout opinion in Ireland by a new and unprecedented invasion of its constitutional liberties. It is difficult to believe that Sir M. Hicks-Beach, who, we have seen, did his utmost to restrain the bad landlords from wholesale evictions for rents, which he admitted were excessive, could have assented to a policy which would compel him to support evictions with the full powers of the proposed Coercion Act. However that may be, his failing eyesight (fortunately of a temporary character) compelled his resignation. His successor, as Irish Secretary, was Mr. Arthur Balfour, who seems to have had no such compunction or misgivings as his predecessor in office. He entered upon a policy of coercion with zest and even avidity. He developed, in defence of it, debating faculties of the highest order and unexpected power, and a dexterity in meeting opponents, not merely from the overwhelming majority of the Members of the country, of which he was to be dictator, under the Coercion Act, but also from the Liberal Members for Great Britain.

There were three distinguishing features in Mr. Balfour's Coercion Policy. Never, since the Act of Union, had a Coercion Act been passed by a mere party majority, or without the consent and support of the two main political parties ; never before had such a measure been passed against the votes of a great majority of the Irish Members ; and never before had it been suggested that such a measure, infringing the constitutional liberties of the people, should be a permanent one—not even limited to Lord Salisbury's unhappy requirement of twenty years of coercion. It was not only an alternative policy to Home Rule, as Mr. Gladstone had confidently predicted, but it was based on a cynical denial and abrogation of the only alternative to Home Rule, consistent with representative institutions and the maintenance of the Union, namely, that Ireland should be treated in the Imperial Parliament, in accordance with the wishes of the majority of its Members.

At a meeting, held at Devonshire House immediately after the introduction of this Bill, it was decided by the Liberal Unionists to support this unprecedented Coercion Bill. That Lord Hartington should do so caused no surprise, for he had never in the past expressed any objection to coercion, but when Mr. Chamberlain's opposition to Mr. Forster's Act of 1881 was recollected, there was much comment, in Radical circles, on his new departure, and his consent to follow the lead of Lord Hartington in support of a perpetual coercive measure.

Mr. Gladstone threw himself with extraordinary vigour in opposition to the Bill, and made many powerful speeches against it at various stages. With respect to the proposal to send Irish prisoners across the Channel, to be tried by juries in London, he said :

" I did not believe that I should ever live to see the day when a proposal so insulting, so exasperating, so utterly in contrast with the whole lesson which Irish history teaches us, could have been submitted to a British House of Commons."

With respect to serious crime, he showed that in comparison with past years there was no justification for the measure. " What is the character, purpose, and object of such crime as exists in Ireland at the present time ? It is to obtain certain reductions of rent. It is not a movement against rent in general. I do not deny that there is intimidation. The amount of crime is small and insignificant under the circumstances. Boycotting and exclusive dealing," he said, " may be very bad things, but they are the only weapons of self-defence belonging to a poor and disheartened people." [1]

Parnell was in bad health at the time, and did not take a very active part in the opposition to the Bill, but he made more than one effective speech. He discouraged obstruction, and advised his followers to select certain important points of attack, and to disregard the other clauses. After a protracted debate, the second reading was passed on April 28th by a majority of 100. On that morning, and obviously with a view to the division, and in the hope of deterring any waverers from abstaining to vote for the Bill, *The Times*, which had been engaged in a series of attacks on the Irish Party for their agitation of the past seven years, published a facsimile letter, purporting to be signed by Parnell, and apparently addressed to one of his associates, in which he was made to explain away his reasons for denouncing the Phœnix Park murders. " You can tell all concerned," it said, " that though I regret the incident of Lord F. Cavendish's death, I cannot refuse to admit that Burke got no more than his deserts." The implication was that Parnell was a consenting party to the tragedy.

Parnell, in his place in the House of Commons, on the same night, declared this to be a barefaced forgery, and protested that he would willingly have placed his body between the bodies of Lord Frederick Cavendish and Mr. Burke and the assassin's knife. There were many, however, who would not believe that a paper like *The Times* could have been taken in by a forgery, and who did not accept the assurance of Parnell. Lord Salisbury gave a cue to doubts of this kind, in a speech delivered two days later, in which he said :

" Mr. Parnell belongs to a party, a large wing of which was worked by murder, and which has been supported by contributions from those who advocated political assassination. . . . When so grave and pressing a case of presumption exists against a man it is not sufficient to take refuge in a mere denial."

Parnell did not act on the suggestion thus made, and sup-

[1] *Hansard*, March 22nd, 1887.

ported by many others, that he should bring an action for libel against *The Times*. We now know that he was advised by eminent members of the Liberal Party that, under the conditions of public opinion in England, he would not be justified in trusting his honour to a London jury. But we also know now, beyond all question, that the letter was a forgery. It had, however, the desired effect. It undoubtedly influenced waverers, and secured for the Crimes Bill a full party majority.

On going into Committee, another great debate was raised by Mr. Reid, now Lord Loreburn, on a motion declaring " the unwillingness of the House to proceed with a measure for strengthening the law against combinations of tenants, until it had before it the full measure of their relief from excessive rents." This went to the very root of the measure, which was undoubtedly intended to break down combinations of tenants against excessive rent. The motion was rejected, after a three days' debate, by the usual party majority, the Liberal Unionists supporting the Government in full force. In the Committee stage, Mr. Morley proposed an amendment limiting the duration of the Bill to three years, and was strongly supported by Mr. Gladstone. It was rejected on a party vote.

On June 10th, when thirty-five working days had been occupied by discussions on the Bill, Mr. W. H. Smith made and carried a motion for cutting short future discussions in Committee on the Bill, by the process known as the "guillotine." He proposed that if the proceedings of the Committee were not concluded by the end of the sitting, on June 17th, the Chairman should put the remaining clauses to the vote without further discussion. The motion was carried, and by this means this comprehensive scheme of coercion was passed through Committee. The operation was repeated in the Report stage. Many of the clauses, and many proposals of the Irish Members in mitigation of them, were not discussed. Among the latter was an amendment proposing that persons convicted of certain classes of offences should be treated as political prisoners, and should not be subjected to the ordinary prison severities. The only substantial change effected in the Bill was the omission of the clause providing for the transfer to London of certain classes of Irish criminal cases.

Mr. Gladstone made a last protest against the Bill by

moving its rejection, on the third reading. He again insisted that it was the official alternative of the Tory Party to Home Rule. Lord Hartington, in reply, practically admitted this : " Mr. Gladstone's policy," he said, " will lead straight to separation. I support the Bill as a protection against organized terrorism by which that policy is presented." The Bill was passed by the House of Lords without a division, and with little discussion.

While the severest of Coercion Bills was thus wending its painful course through the House of Commons, a remedial Land Bill, of an attenuated character, was introduced by the Government in the House of Lords. It did not propose to carry out the main recommendation of the Cowper Commission for the revision of judicial rents. It proposed, however, to admit the large body of leaseholders in Ireland to the benefit of judicial rents, and it contained most complicated provisions, founded on the bankruptcy law, for dealing with arrears of rent, which had come into existence in the last two or three years of depression. It empowered the Land Commission to commute these arrears into a charge upon the tenant for a term of years. The Bill was no remedy for the emergency and agitation in Ireland, which were mainly due to the excessive rents adjudicated by the Land Commission, as measured by the recent great fall in price of agricultural produce. Lord Cadogan, who had charge of the Bill, most positively refused to deal with judicial rents. " The Government," he said, " have found it impossible to give effect to the recommendations of the Royal Commission." Lord Salisbury took the opportunity of renewing his expressions of hatred of the Land Act of 1881.

" I conceive," he said, " the Act of 1881 to be one of the most unfortunate measures ever submitted to Parliament. . . . It must inflict a blow upon all confidence in dealing with property and will require a generation to efface it. . . . A belief on the part of men that they will have to perform their promises is the very foundation of civilized society. . . . You are laying your axe to the very root of that fabric."

When, however, the Land Bill reached the House of Commons, it was soon found by the Government that two forces were impelling them to the very course which Lord Salisbury had so fiercely denounced ; the one, the Ulster tenant farmers, who, through their representatives, insisted upon an amendment, which would break the solemn compacts, and revise the judicial rents ; the other, the section of Liberal Unionists led by Mr. Chamberlain, who, having swallowed coercion, on the understanding there should be an effective remedial measure, now insisted on the bargain being carried out.   In the debate on the second reading the discussion mainly turned on this question.

" Why," said Mr. Chamberlain, " is the leaseholder to have his rent reduced, except on the ground of inability to pay ? If it is just that the leaseholder should have his rent reduced, why is the judicial renter not to have the benefit of the same relief ? "   Lord Randolph Churchill made a powerful speech in the same direction.

It may be worth while to quote from the speech of Parnell, on the same occasion, as to the effect of the Act of 1881 on the Land League.

" It was not," he said, " the Coercion Act of 1881, or that of 1882, that broke down the Land League.   I well know the truth of what I am saying.   I watched from Kilmainham Jail ninety thousand tenants going into the Land Court.   It would otherwise have been possible for us, even from our cells in Kilmainham, to have pushed the Land League movement to any extreme we chose it to work.   Mr. Gladstone saved the Irish landlords at that time by the Act of 1881."

The Government had to give way, not, indeed, to the wishes and claims of the great majority of the Irish Members, but to the importunities of the small number of Members from Ulster. The Committee, also, after prolonged discussion, struck out the bankruptcy clauses.   No one approved them.   The landlords, equally with the tenants, objected.   Unfortunately, no substitute was adopted for them.   The Government refused the claim of Parnell and the Irish Members, that the same powers should be conferred on the Land Commission of dealing with arrears of excessive rent, as had been given two years before to the Scotch Crofters Commission.   They rejected also every proposal for dealing with the case of evicted tenants, the victims of what was practically admitted to be an unjust system.   Many years were to elapse before the opposition of the House of Lords to a measure with this object was removed. It seems strange, indeed, that the Government and Parliament, when legislating in a manner which admitted so much of the claims of the Irish Party, so unwisely rejected in previous years, did not learn the lesson that the demands of the great majority of the representatives of a people on matters concerning themselves alone, are the only safe basis of legislation for them.   Before the amendments made by the House of Commons were considered by the other House, Lord Salisbury was compelled to explain to a meeting of his supporters that if he did not accept the amendment as to the revision of judicial rents, Ulster would be lost to the Unionist cause, and then Home Rule could not be resisted !

" When once," he said, in the House of Lords, in moving agreement with the amendments of the House of Commons, " the genius of an evil principle was introduced, it was impossible to get rid of it."

And thus it came about that the implacable enemy of the Act of 1881 was compelled to give the greatest possible extension to its principle, which he had so much condemned, by extending it to the large class of leaseholders, and by agreeing to revise the rents already determined by the Land Commission.

CHAPTER XXXIII

METHODS OF COERCION, 1887-9

NEVER was a graver mistake made by a Government in Ireland than that of the Chief Secretary in 1887, in not taking the Irish leaders into concert for the purpose of making his remedial measure a complete and final one. The Land Act, as passed, was indeed a very great step in advance. Compared with what it conceded, the additions required to make a settlement of the question were trifling. It was only necessary that power should be given to the Land Commission, when deciding on judicial rents, to deal with the arrears of excessive rents in the same manner as had been done in the Crofters Act for Scotland, and that clauses should be inserted to induce or compel the comparatively few landlords who had, by that time, evicted their tenants for non-payment of rents, now admitted to be excessive, to reinstate them in their holdings. The measure, defective as it was in these respects, had the effect of obviating any future combinations of tenants. For want of these small additions to it, the combinations which had been entered into in 1886-7 were not brought to an end. They continued to be a festering cause of disturbance during the next three years, and practically the main use made of the Coercion Act was to endeavour to break up these combinations, and to punish those concerned in them.

It has been already shown that the Plan of Campaign was adopted on eighty-four estates where the landlords had refused to make any abatements of rent, and that in sixty of these the landlords, when faced by this new movement, found it their best policy to give way, and after some negotiation with their tenants to concede satisfactory terms. There remained, therefore, only twenty-four unsettled cases, in which the landlords had refused to come to terms, and had begun to evict

337

their tenants. In seven of these cases agreements were later arrived at, on reasonable terms of abatement of rents, and in all of these the reinstatement of the evicted tenants was insisted upon by the tenants, and was conceded by the landlords. In most, if not in all, of the remaining seventeen cases, where these deplorable disputes continued, the ultimate question, which prevented settlement, was the refusal of the landlords to reinstate the evicted men.

It seems to be almost incredible that this small residuum of obstinate landlords were allowed to keep alive the embers of the agrarian struggle. But so it was. A very large proportion of the many hundreds of imprisonments, which took place under the Coercion Act of 1887, were in connection with these twenty-four cases, where the landlords delayed or refused to come to terms. The Plan of Campaign was, in fact, a kind of red rag to the landlord party. Its very success, in compelling so many of them to concede terms, made them fiercer against those who devised it and put it in force, and more determined to punish and make an example of all concerned in these few remaining cases. Landlord associations were founded for the purpose of defeating the Plan of Campaign, assisting those on whose properties it was in force, and finding tenants for the farms from which the tenants had been evicted. The Government, instead of trying to bring about peace, and to put an end to these troubles, by bringing pressure to bear equally on both parties, threw all the weight of its influence against the tenants, and allowed the Coercion Act to be used in support of evictions, and for crushing the combinations.

Immediately after the passing of the Coercion Act, the National League and about two hundred of its branches were proclaimed and suppressed by the Government. This did not, however, make much difference. Meetings of the League continued to be held in secret, and reports of their proceedings appeared, daily and weekly, in the Nationalist papers. The Government thereupon prosecuted several editors of these papers for reporting their proceedings. Chief among them were Mr. T. D. Sullivan, M.P., owner of *United Ireland*, then Lord Mayor of Dublin, Mr. W. O'Brien, M.P., Mr. E. Harrington, M.P., Mr. Hooper, M.P., and Mr. Walsh, editors of other papers. They were convicted, and sentenced to various terms of imprisonment, from six weeks to two months.

Mr. T. D. Sullivan had the good luck to be tried by Mr. O'Donell, the stipendiary magistrate of Dublin, who directed that he should be treated in jail as a first-class misdemeanant. No such favour was accorded to the others by the resident magistrates. They were sentenced and treated as common criminals. They resisted this to the utmost. They refused to wear the prison clothing, or to take exercise with common criminals of the baser kind, or to perform degrading menial work while in jail. Their clothes were torn from them by the warders. They were forcibly dressed in the prison garb. They were put under punishment for days and weeks, and were reduced to bread and water for food. Mr. T. Harrington, while in prison, was summoned to give evidence in the case of another prosecution at Tralee, in the centre of the constituency he represented in Parliament. He was forcibly compelled to wear the prison dress on the occasion, and was exhibited in court to his constituents in this garb. Mr. Hooper's health was most seriously injured by deprivation of food and exercise, imposed on him for refusing to perform the menial indignities of the jail.

On coming out of jail all these men announced their intention to repeat the acts for which they had been convicted and imprisoned. They continued to report in their papers the proceedings of the National League. They did so with impunity. The Government were obliged to admit that they were defeated in this class of cases. They were equally unsuccessful in their attempts to prevent the sale of these papers. After several prosecutions it was compelled to abandon them. In another class of cases the Government used what were called " the Star Chamber " clauses of the Coercion Act, for the purpose of defeating the Plan of Campaign. They summoned tenants, suspected of being parties to it, examined them in secret, and by threats of imprisonment, compelled them to turn informers, and to disclose the names of other persons engaged in the combination. They then prosecuted batches of persons so engaged. The witnesses, however, when they came into court, refused to give evidence. The prosecutions broke down, and the persons who refused to give evidence were then prosecuted and sent to jail.

Foiled in their endeavours to convict persons actually engaged in combinations, the Government prosecuted and convicted many persons for attending and speaking at public meetings held in favour of the Plan, or in sympathy with tenants who were engaged in it. The resident magistrates were ready to hold almost any public meeting, in the proclaimed districts, to be an illegal assembly, and to convict persons attending them. A marked feature of the proceedings was the strange caprice of the authorities in selecting persons for prosecution. They laid their hands upon any whom, for any other reason, they desired to punish, irrespective of the part which they had taken in meetings or in speeches. Cases occurred in which persons were prosecuted, not on account of speeches made by themselves, but for speeches made by others who were present at the meetings, but who were not themselves prosecuted.

Another very numerous class of prosecutions, under the Act, arose out of boycotting. The police, taking a boycotted person with them, applied to tradesmen, whom they selected for prosecution, for supplies of articles, which often were not really wanted, and when refused, charged these tradesmen before the resident magistrates with criminal conspiracy. Batches of publicans were convicted for refusing to supply liquor to the police, or to provide cars for them. Boycotted persons sent their servants to tradesmen selected for prosecution, with whom they never before had dealings, and when refused, charged them before the magistrates. The resident magistrates seldom failed to convict in such cases, and sentenced the accused to months of imprisonment with hard labour. They invariably refused to state a case for the Judges of the High Court. After great numbers of such cases, the Irish Party, by a clever device of Mr. Healy, were able at last to get the decision of the Judges of the High Court on a case of this kind. Four shopkeepers of Killeagh were convicted of a conspiracy to refuse supplies to the police, the only evidence against them being their bare refusal. The Judges held that the convictions were illegal, there being no evidence of a conspiracy. They threw ridicule on the decisions of the magistrates. They held that tradesmen had the right to refuse supplies to persons applying to them, and that to support a conviction there must be distinct evidence of a conspiracy. When the decision was given, several persons, in other similar cases, were in prison, undergoing sentences with hard labour. It was to be expected that the Government would at once direct their release. They refused to do so; and this course was upheld and defended in the House of Commons.

Another conspicuous use of the Coercion Act was to persecute by repeated prosecutions on trivial charges the local leaders of the people, who were concerned in combinations of tenants against landlords, who refused to make abatements of rent. Many illustrations could be given of this.

The policy was foolish and mistaken. It had exactly the opposite effect to what was intended by the Government. It tended only to raise such men in the popular estimation of the district. It gave them the status of martyrs in addition to that of popular leaders. So far from frightening or deterring others from this course, it stimulated them to follow the example, and it intensified public opinion against the authorities and the Government. It did not put an end to the boycotting of land-grabbers. Not a few of these local leaders, after treatment of this kind were elected as Members of Parliament for their districts.

I can vouch for these methods of enforcing the Crimes Act, for I personally visited, in the years 1888-9, several of the estates, where the Plan of Campaign was in operation, and made full inquiries as to the causes of the disputes, and the methods attempted by the authorities for defeating the combinations.[1] I was induced to embark on these inquiries by the fact that Mr. Wilfrid Blunt, a relative and friend, was prosecuted by the Government, under the Crimes Act, for attempting to hold a public meeting at Woodford, for the purpose of expressing sympathy with the Clanricarde tenants. Recollecting what I had seen and heard on this property in 1882, I felt strongly that the prosecution was unjust, and I went to Woodford, with many of Mr. Blunt's friends, to support him during the trial. I was again astounded by what I learned there of the treatment of his tenants by Lord Clanricarde, and of the action of the Government in support of him. I came to the conclusion that it was most necessary that public attention should be called to the wholesale evictions, which had been effected there, and were threatened. Mr. Blunt had done a public service by calling a meeting for this

---

[1] I published in 1888-9 two journals of these visits entitled *Incidents of Coercion* and *Combination and Coercion*.

purpose. He was prosecuted for so doing, and was convicted, and sentenced to two months' imprisonment as a common criminal. Never, in my opinion, was greater and more palpable injustice perpetrated.

I have already shown that, in 1887, Sir M. Hicks-Beach endeavoured to discriminate between the bad and the good landlords, and had practically refused to give the support of the forces of the Crown to the wholesale evictions by Lord Clanricarde. His successor, Mr. Balfour, seemed to have no such misgivings. He gave full support to the evictions of large batches of tenants, from time to time, on this estate, and apparently made no effort to bring this unfortunate dispute to a close by the influence of the Government. Further inquiries on the spot convinced me that the case of the tenants was overwhelmingly strong. Their combination was justifiable and necessary if ever such action could be so. The leaders were men of high principle, most anxious to prevent any acts of violence.

Later, at the invitation of the Clanricarde tenants, I presided myself at a great open-air meeting at Loughrea, for the purpose of protesting against further evictions, and of informing the public of the true nature of this dispute. The authorities, acting wisely, for once in a way, did not proclaim the meeting, and, at my suggestion, they abstained from sending any police there to risk a conflict with the people. As a result, the meeting was most orderly. It was attended by many thousands of people from all the country-side, and on the platform were many English Members, and other distinguished members of the Liberal Party.

The advantage of holding such a meeting was at once manifested. On the very morning of the meeting Lord Clanricarde's agent issued a public notice offering, for the first time, a general abatement of rents to the tenants. It was considered insufficient by the leaders of the tenants, but it afforded the hope that negotiations might lead to a settlement. It had the effect, therefore, of moderating the speeches at the meeting. By the earnest wish of the Bishop of the Diocese, Dr. Duggan, who was a strong supporter of the tenants in their combination, I did my best in my speech, while expressing a strong opinion as to the past evictions, to advise moderation and conciliation to the tenants, but I expressed the opinion that, on coming to terms with their landlord, the tenants still in possession were bound in honour to insist on the reinstatement of the evicted men.

This proved eventually to be the main stumbling-block in the way to an agreement. The first offer of abatement of rents was quite insufficient, and the landlord evicted another batch of tenants. Later, the offer was improved upon, and finally was such that the tenants were willing to accept it. If it had been made before any evictions had been carried out, there would have been no combination, and no evictions. But in the interval 170 tenants out of the 1900 had been evicted. The farms thus vacated, with rare exceptions, were at that time untenanted. No one could be found to face the odium of the district by hiring them. It was most unreasonable, therefore, to refuse reinstatement of the evicted men. But this, from first to last, Lord Clanricarde obstinately refused to do.

This miserable dispute consequently continued, and further batches of evictions were continually being carried out. It was at this stage, if not earlier, that the Government should, in my opinion, have intervened, and have brought pressure on Lord Clanricarde to induce or compel him to do an act of justice, by reinstating the men evicted for non-payment of rents, now admitted to be excessive and unjust. The Government, however, equally with Lord Clanricarde, seemed to be determined that an example should be made of the evicted men in this case.

After inquiries on the Clanricarde property, I was induced to visit others of the Plan of Campaign estates—among them the Vandeleur property in Co. Clare, that of Captain Ponsonby in Cork, the Coolgreaney Estate in Wexford, that of Lord Massereene in Co. Louth, and two or three others. There was a marked similarity in all these cases. The landlords, in all of them, had originally refused to make any abatements of rent, to meet the great fall of prices. In most of them the resident agents had advised abatements, but their employers, the landlords, had refused. The Plan of Campaign was thereupon adopted. Evictions of large batches of tenants then took place, and were supported by strong bodies of police, and by putting in force the Coercion Act for the imprisonment and punishment of any and every man connected with the movement, or sympathizing with the tenants, whom the authorities selected for this purpose.

At the time I visited these estates, the question of abatements of rent had, in nearly all of them, been practically conceded. The landlords had, at last, made offers, which the tenants were willing to agree to. The only remaining question in dispute was that of the evicted tenants, whether they should be replaced in their holdings, and have the benefit of the abatements. The combinations of tenants most justly insisted on this. The landlords refused it. There was no real difficulty in reinstating them. The vacated farms, with few exceptions, were untenanted. The fields were rank with thistles and weeds. The houses had, in many cases, been shattered by battering-rams used in the evictions. It is impossible to overstate the scenes of desolation on many of these estates. When new tenants had been induced to take the farms, they were evidently men of straw, who might easily be induced to depart. These planters, as they were called, were loathed and boycotted by the whole neighbourhood. They had taken the farms at rents much below those for which the tenants had been evicted. They were in possession of the interest of these previous tenants without paying anything for it. They were regarded as receivers of stolen property, worse than those who had deprived the tenants of it. At that stage of the movement there could be no possible doubt that the tenants were justified in morals, if not in law, in maintaining the combinations, till the evicted men were replaced on their holdings. I made speeches to this effect, in the presence of police reporters, at several of the districts where the Plan of Campaign had been adopted. I always predicted that the time would come when Parliament would interfere to insist upon the reinstatement of these evicted men.[1]

---

[1] Some years later I met Lord O'Brien, now Chief Justice in Ireland, who, at the time I refer to, was the principal law officer of the Government. He told me that on my visits to Ireland he was determined to put me in jail. He had me followed by two police reporters wherever I went. I was the only man who had beaten him. He was unable to discover cause in my speeches for arresting me. I replied that I had never said anything beyond what I had repeatedly said in England, and which I was convinced was perfectly lawful. It was satisfactory to me to find that the Irish Government had come to the conclusion that my advice to tenants on the Campaign estates, to maintain their combination till the evicted men were reinstated

The impression left on my mind, by these visits to the Campaign estates, was that a graver misconception of its duties by the Government had never occurred, even in Ireland. If it had used its influence to bring these disputes to an end, there would have been no difficulty in doing so. As a matter of fact, I was able myself to bring about settlements in two of them. On my visit to Loughrea, Sir Henry Burke sent his brother to me to ask me to endeavour to bring about an arrangement between himself and his tenants of a neighbouring estate, who had adopted the Plan of Campaign. I was able to do so, mainly through Mr. John Roche, the leader of the Clanricarde tenants in their combination. In Colonel Vandeleur's case, also, I had negotiations with his agent, which ultimately, and through Mr. Henniker Heaton, resulted in a reference of the dispute to Sir Charles Russell, and by his award, in a happy settlement. In that case the Irish Government, through its local agent, not only did not assist in a settlement, but did its very utmost to prevent it, and seemed to be bent on punishing the evicted men for having embarked in the Plan of Campaign. In both these cases of the Burke and the Vandeleur estates, the reinstatement of the evicted men was an essential condition of the settlements.

The use made of the Coercion Act to defeat and punish the tenants engaged in these combinations was made clear to me beyond question. In the Clanricarde dispute no fewer than 150 persons had been sent to prison, in connection with it, for speeches made at meetings of sympathy, often for merely attending meetings, for refusing supplies to planters, and for resisting evictions. In the case of a dispute between a Mrs. Moroney and fifty of her tenants, at Miltown Malbay, in Clare, fifty-six prosecutions and thirty-eight convictions and imprisonments had taken place. It was much the same on other Campaign estates.

All of these were, in my opinion, wholly unnecessary. It would have been easy enough for the Government to settle the disputes, if there had been the wish to do so. In the three years I refer to more than two thousand persons were convicted and sent to prison under the Coercion Act for

was not illegal. But there can be no doubt that many Irishmen, including Members of Parliament, were sent to jail, under the Coercion Act, for saying much less than this.

offences which, for the most part, were connected directly or indirectly with the twenty-four cases of combinations of tenants under the Plan of Campaign. They included twenty-two Members of Parliament, eighteen priests, a great number of journalists, tradesmen, farmers, and other men of good position. It may safely be said that very few indeed of them belonged to the criminal class, or had been guilty of what is commonly included under the term of crime. It is equally certain that hardly any of them would have been convicted, if tried by juries fairly chosen in Ireland. I doubt whether they would have been convicted by juries in England. Just as in the case of the Coercion Act of 1881 Mr. Forster found it incumbent on him to support the officials under him in Ireland in their proceedings, however arbitrary and indefensible, so Mr. Balfour never failed in the House of Commons to support, defend, and justify the same classes of officials in every case which came under discussion. Innumerable interpellations took place on the part of Irish Members. I do not recollect a single one in which Mr. Balfour admitted that even the smallest wrong had been done, or that redress was necessary. He appeared to feel no compunction when his Irish opponents in the House of Commons were subjected to the plank-bed, and other severities and indignities of the prisons. He adopted the airs of a superior person, who looked down from philosophic altitudes on the disorderly crew which Ireland sent to Parliament. His attitude in Parliament gave the cue to the Castle officials, the resident magistrates, the police, and the prison warders in Ireland in their treatment of Irish Members, and of all others representing the tenants in the agrarian disputes. He defended these subordinates with unfailing zeal, and with great dialectical powers. Under an air of indifference and nonchalance there was concealed a rapier as sharp and deadly as was ever wielded in Parliamentary contests. He never made the smallest concession to the Irish Members. The nearest approach to it was when he consented to postpone some prosecutions of them in Ireland, in order that they might remain a few days in the House of Commons to take part in some important Irish debate.

Not the least reprehensible part of this miserable policy was the treatment of the persons sent to jail, under the new Coercion Act. With the rarest exceptions, they were all treated as common criminals, and were subjected to all the harshness and indignities which are properly meted out to persons of the really criminal class. To many of them there was added the infliction of hard labour. Of the twenty-two Members of Parliament, sentenced to imprisonment, only three were treated as first-class misdemeanants. The others were subjected to the plank-bed, the prison dress, the cutting of their hair, the exercise with criminals of the baser kind, and the performance of menial jail tasks of indignity. It has been shown that many of them resisted these indignities, and submitted only to violence and constraint by the warders. Frequent discussions took place on the subject in the House of Commons. Mr. Balfour most positively refused to admit any distinction between political prisoners and others—a distinction recognized in every other civilized country. Speaking on the subject in the House of Commons on August 8th, 1888, he said :

"I state in the most positive manner, on my responsibility as a Minister of the Crown, that the one regulation which I have laid down, and which I insist upon being carried out; is this : that every person in prison shall be treated exactly alike, without any distinction as to whether he is a political prisoner or not. A political prisoner, according to my orders, is not to be treated any better or any worse than any other prisoner ; and he has not been treated any better or worse, so far as I have any control. . . . Never will I consent to draw a distinction between one class of offender against the law and another."

He took every opportunity of throwing contempt and ridicule on Mr. W. O'Brien for resisting these indignities in jail, by compelling the prison warders to deprive him forcibly of his clothes, and then lying naked, or nearly so, in his cell, rather than put on the prison dress. "I take," he said, "little interest in these histrionic performances. I took a small interest in the first representation. I take even less interest in them on the second representation."

Mr. Balfour was backed up by the Prime Minister in these sneers. Speaking at Edinburgh on December 1st, 1888, Lord Salisbury said : "I know not where this strange, maudlin, effeminate doctrine as to the treatment of political prisoners has come from. . . . So long as political prisoners are dangerous to the community, or to the State, as long as they tend to propagate blunders, and other men are likely to imitate them, so long must they be treated just as all other offenders are treated, with a view to the deterrent effect of the punishment. . . . Of course there may be some instances in which men act from a pure and undiluted patriotism. But there are also some instances in which they act for the sake of getting a maintenance which they could not get in any other way. And there are many more instances in which they act from a bastard sort of ambition—a diseased love of notoriety. At all events, to my mind, in many cases the motives which influence ordinary criminals are nobler than the motives which influence the political offenders, on whom so much sympathy is lavished."

This treatment of Irish Members made a most unfavourable impression on public opinion in England. They told their experiences at public meetings. I often heard them speak on such occasions. They deeply interested their audiences, and were heartily welcomed. They did much to change the current opinion in English constituencies in favour of Home Rule. The Government was advised that the treatment of these, and other men in Irish jails, had become odious to the people of England, and that it was necessary to change the system. Mr. Balfour had frequently maintained in his speeches that he had no power to direct how persons in jail should be treated. He now discovered that the Irish Prisons Board could insist upon what new regulations he desired. At his suggestion orders were issued by the Board to the prison authorities to dispense with some of the requirements of the prison rules, in cases where it seemed to them to be unnecessary to insist upon them, in the interest of health and cleanliness. They were also given full discretion with respect to the treatment of prisoners, but nothing was said as to how the discretion was to be exercised.

The rules appeared to be framed so as to effect the main object of avoiding the scandal of Irish Members being compelled by force to wear the prison dress, and to exercise with criminals, and at the same time to preserve for Mr. Balfour the semblance of consistency and persistency. This was effected by applying the new treatment not merely to political prisoners—for Mr. Balfour would not recognize such a distinction—but to all prisoners who belonged to the better class of society, to whom the ordinary treatment in prison would be distasteful—a distinction never hitherto made in prison rules, and one to which there are many grave objections. This treatment of men convicted under the Crimes Act was in harmony with the whole policy adopted to those engaged in the agrarian movement. It was desired to affix on them the stigma of crime, and to present them in that aspect to the people of Ireland, and also of England, and thus to ruin the cause of Home Rule. It had exactly the opposite effect. Those who were in prison became martyrs in the opinion of Irishmen. No passport to public credit and honour was so certain as that of having been imprisoned by Mr. Balfour. The Members of Parliament who suffered in this way were secure of re-election for the remainder of their lives. And no recommendation was stronger for a new candidate for election than having been in jail under the Coercion Act. Those who suffered came out of prison boasting that they would commit again the acts for which they had been convicted.

The whole policy of coercion as administered under this Coercion Act was as futile as it was unconstitutional, irritating, and vindictive. Its main object was to put down combinations by punishing those concerned in them. It was useless for this purpose. It brought the law into contempt. It showed that the Government was ranged on the side of the rich, as against the poor, of the landlords against the tenants. The immediate victims of it were the 1900 evicted men, who for years remained out of their holdings. Nothing in Irish history has been more remarkable than the tenacity with which the Irish people insisted on the restoration of these evicted men to their houses, and the absolute certainty with which these men looked forward to it. It will be shown later that they had good reason for this.

A review of the proceedings, under the Crimes Act of 1887, shows that the main provisions which led to the results above described, and which so outraged public opinion in Ireland, were those dispensing with trial by jury, and enabling the Government to relegate cases, which otherwise must have been decided by juries, to resident magistrates, who were virtually their subordinate officials. The cases which occurred are illustrations of the enormous importance of the system of trial

by jury, not only in preventing the abuse of the law by arbitrary
and dependent officials, but by virtually compelling amendment of the law when juries persistently refuse to convict.

People in England have so long been accustomed to the
safeguard of juries, that they have almost forgotten the abuses
which occurred, when the Executive Government or the
Judges could dispense with them. But high constitutional
authorities have maintained the extreme importance of the
system in its bearing on self-government, and the contentment
of the community. In his work on the Constitution, Lord
John Russell (later Earl Russell) wrote as follows :

" The verdicts of juries have operated to check the execution of cruel and oppressive laws, and in the end to repeal or
modify the laws themselves. Juries are not only the real
judges in England, but they possess a power no judge would
venture to exercise, that of refusing to put the law in force.
. . . Exercised as it has been with temper and moderation,
the discretion of juries has proved to be extremely salutary.
It has been the cause of amending many bad laws, which
judges would have administered with exact severity, and
defended with professional bigotry ; and above all it has this
important and useful consequence, that laws totally repugnant
to the feelings of the community, for which they are made, cannot long prevail in England. . . . It is to trial by jury, more
than to representation, that the people owe the share they
have in the government of the country ; it is to trial by jury
also that the Government owes the attachment of the people
to the law, a consideration which ought to make our legislature
very cautious how they take away this mode of trial by jury
by new and vexatious enactments." [1]

In Ireland, under successive Coercion Acts, since the Act
of Union, the system of trial by jury has seldom been in
full force. Sometimes it has been superseded, as in Mr.
Forster's Act of 1881, by arbitrary powers given to the Executive Government to imprison any persons whom they suspect
or distrust ; at other times, as by Mr. Balfour's Act of 1887,
power to convict and imprison has been given to inferior
judges without the safeguard of juries. The result has been
much the same in both cases. Public opinion in Ireland has

---

[1] *English Government and Constitution*, pp. 392–4.

been flouted and set aside. If Ireland had enjoyed self-government, as regards its own separate affairs, it is certain that the refusal of juries to give verdicts would have compelled the attention of its Government and its legislature to grievances, and would have led to reforms, at least a generation earlier than they were effected by the Imperial Legislature.

CHAPTER XXXIV

THE PARNELL COMMISSION

IT has already been shown that on the morning of the second reading of the Coercion Bill of 1887, *The Times*, apparently by arrangement with the Government, or, at all events, for their benefit, published the facsimile letter purporting to be signed by Parnell, and implying complicity in the Phœnix Park murders. It was set out in one of a long series of articles, entitled " Parnellism and Crime," extending over many months of 1887–8, in which the effort was made to hold the Irish Party responsible for all the agrarian outrages and crimes which had taken place in the past eight years. These letters had not, so far, produced much effect on public opinion in England. They were regarded as a belated amplification of Mr. Forster's attack at the beginning of 1883. The issue, however, of the facsimile letter gained for them a credence which they would not otherwise have attained, the more so as Parnell, acting under advice above referred to, abstained from bringing an action for libel against *The Times*.

In November, 1887, however, Mr. O'Donnell, who had long before separated himself completely from the Nationalist Party, and who was incidentally, but not prominently, named in some of the letters of *The Times*, believing himself aggrieved, brought an action for libel against Mr. Walter, the owner of the paper. The case came before Chief Justice Coleridge and a London jury in July, 1888. *The Times* pleaded that the plaintiff was not aimed at in the articles, and further that the charges contained in them were true. Mr. O'Donnell's counsel, most unwisely, as the result proved, contented himself, on opening the case, with putting in the articles complained of. He did not call his client as a witness. He reserved Mr. O'Donnell's evidence till *The Times* should present its proofs on the plea of justification. The counsel for *The Times*, Sir Richard Webster, the Attorney-General, in his reply made a speech of enormous length. He undertook to prove all that had been said in *The Times* articles on " Parnellism and Crime," including the authenticity of the facsimile letter. He produced and read in court a batch of other letters, purporting to be written by Parnell, pointing even more clearly to complicity in the Phœnix Park murders. He promised to prove the genuineness of these letters, but said that nothing would induce him to say how they had come into the possession of *The Times*. Having spent three days on these charges, he admitted that it would not be fair or just to Parnell, and his associates, to call witnesses in proof of the case, which he had thus presented, when there was no one in opposition to meet or dispute the facts, except the plaintiff, Mr. O'Donnell, against whom *The Times* did not allege complicity in these acts. He claimed that as Mr. O'Donnell had not been called as a witness, there was practically no evidence of any libel against *The Times*. The presiding Judge took this view of the case, and at once directed the jury that they would be justified in giving a verdict for *The Times*. This was done, and Mr. O'Donnell found himself completely discomfited, without having had the opportunity of meeting the charges of *The Times*. It was matter of general comment that it was somewhat beyond the privilege of counsel to make such definite and damning charges against a man, who was not a party to the suit, when it was not intended to call witnesses in proof of them. It seemed that they were not made in the interest of *The Times*, in the actual case before the jury, but as affording an opportunity of emphasizing the charges of the paper against Parnell and the Irish Party. They had, at all events, this effect, and the charges of *The Times* appeared to have the warranty of the Government, through their Attorney-General. They consequently produced a profound impression on the public.

Parnell, since the issue of the facsimile letter in *The Times*, had satisfied himself that it had been forged by a worthless and impecunious hack journalist, named Richard Pigott, formerly editor of a Nationalist paper, who was known to be ready for any blackmailing enterprise. Parnell was most anxious to bring an action for libel against *The Times*, but was dissuaded from this course by Mr. Morley. He then decided to bring the case before the House of Commons. He did so, in a speech, in which he most emphatically denied that any of the letters, quoted by the Attorney-General, had been written by himself. He pronounced them to be forgeries. He asked the House to appoint a Committee to inquire into the genuineness of them. He was willing that the Committee should consist only of English Members.

Mr. W. H. Smith, on behalf of the Government, refused to agree to a Committee, but offered to appoint a Special Commission of Judges to inquire into the charges made by *The Times* against Parnell and the other Irish Members. Mr. Parnell, he said, might either take or reject this offer. The Irish Leader, not seeing the trap that was being laid for his party, was willing to agree to the course, rather than have no inquiry at all. When the Bill for this purpose was laid before the House, it appeared that the scope of the inquiry proposed was infinitely wider than had been suggested. It was framed so as to include not only the charges against the Irish Members, but against any other persons referred to in the articles on " Parnellism and Crime." It opened out an enormous and unprecedented inquiry, covering the whole field of the agitation of the past ten years. It meant the trial by English Judges of the agrarian movement in Ireland. Parnell himself, rather than that there should be no inquiry at all, and confident that he could prove the origin of the forged letters, was not disposed to oppose the Bill on the second reading. The Liberal leaders were divided in opinion about it. Mr. Gladstone himself feared the effect of objecting to inquiry. The Bill, therefore, was read a second time without a division.

At the Committee stage, the gravity of the constitutional objections to such an inquiry was more fully perceived, and the clauses were strongly opposed. It now appeared that the Government were determined to force the Bill upon the Irish Party, and no longer gave them the option to take or reject it. The Bill was passed, through this and further stages, by the most trenchant use of the guillotine. It passed the House of Lords, in spite of a most powerful and dignified protest by Lord Herschell, in one of the ablest speeches ever delivered in that House, protesting against the danger of setting up a special tribunal to try the Irish Members and others engaged in the agrarian movement. Three Judges were appointed to hold the inquiry; they were men of well-known political views adverse to the Irish cause. The President was Sir James Hannen, a Judge of the highest reputation for impartiality. But Judges, however eminent and impartial, do not divest themselves of their instincts, and no one in his senses, sympathizing with the Irish cause, would have dreamt of submitting such a case to these three Judges.

The question submitted to them was the truth or falsehood of the charges made against the Irish Party, and all other persons in *The Times* articles, including the genuineness of the letters attributed to Parnell. This last was the only question which interested the public. It was the hinge of the whole proceeding, without which there would have been no inquiry. If these letters were genuine they threw a lurid light upon the whole cause of the Nationalist Party, which would be damned irretrievably in the opinion of the public. It was, above all, necessary that their authenticity should be cleared up at the earliest day. Immense hardship, therefore, was inflicted on Parnell, by deferring this issue, and allowing him to remain for months under the foul suspicion of being the writer of the letters, while efforts were being made to prejudice the mind of the public by taking evidence of the agrarian agitation of the past ten years. Yet this was allowed by the Judges. The Attorney-General again appeared for *The Times*. The proceedings had all the appearance, and, indeed, the substance, of a prosecution by the Government. Their aid was given in every possible way, by the ransacking of public departments in Ireland, and by the collection of witnesses, including not a few from the jails. Evidence was given of innumerable outrages committed in Ireland in the ten years. Hundreds of speeches, including those by every kind of irresponsible persons, were read and commented on. After long months spent by the Commission in this way the incriminating letters were at last reached. It then turned out that they had been sold by Richard Pigott to Mr. Houston, the Secretary of the Royal Patriotic Union of Ireland, and the writer of " Parnellism and Crime." No explanation had been given, or even asked for, by *The Times* as to the *provenance* of these letters. The manager of the paper was satisfied by a bare comparison of the handwriting of the letters with other well-authenticated letters. The letters, he said, were what might be expected of Parnell.

This was sufficient for the too credulous manager of *The Times*, Mr. Macdonald, and for the owner of the paper, Mr. Walter, who, against the advice, it was said, of the able editor, were induced to make use of these letters for the purpose of ruining the character and position of the Irish Leader, and destroying the cause which he led. It is to be feared that Mr. Walter, who honestly believed in the genuineness of the letters, suffered most grievously for this one grave error of his eminent and honourable career.[1]

The Attorney-General called witnesses to testify their belief that the letters were written by Parnell. First among them was Captain O'Shea. He then proposed to call expert evidence as to the handwriting. The Judges at last insisted on Richard Pigott being called. The cross-examination of this miserable man by Sir Charles Russell, who appeared for the Irish Members, was sensational to the highest degree. The bad spelling of the letters, illustrated by the witness in the witness-box, when called upon to write down identical words, was alone sufficient to expose him. He was compelled to admit that he had offered these letters to others by way of blackmail.

More revelations were expected at the next meeting, when the cross-examination was to be resumed, but the witness could stand it no more. He fled the country in the interval. He was followed by detectives to Madrid, where he blew his brains out with a pistol to avoid arrest. He left behind in London, in the hands of Mr. Labouchere, a full confession, to the effect that he had himself forged all the incriminating letters. It was expected and hoped that Sir Richard Webster, on behalf of *The Times*, after this terrible *exposé* and the breakdown of the main case, would, in generous terms, acknowledge the unparalleled wrong that had been done to Parnell, and express some regret for the cruel suffering inflicted on him by the long suspense. To the surprise of every one the retractation of the charge was made in guarded and frigid words : " After the evidence which has been given we are not entitled to say that the letters are genuine." Without a single generous expression of regret !

---

[1] The costs of the Irish Party in defending themselves before the Commission amounted to £42,000. The costs of *The Times* must have been many fold greater.

After the exposure of the forgery, the public interest in the Commission ceased, but the inquiry continued for seventy more days. Sir Charles Russell made a splendid defence for the Irish Party, in a speech occupying seven days, a noble vindication of his countrymen by a true patriot. Sir Henry James wound up for *The Times* in an able speech of twelve days in length, in which everything that could be urged against the Nationalist Party was put forward. Mr. Biggar, not interested in protracting the inquiry by obstruction, defended himself in a speech of twenty minutes, and ended by saying that his friend Mr. Davitt would follow him with a few words. The few words were extended over five days in a most powerful and closely reasoned speech, scarcely less effective than those of the lawyers engaged in the case.

The public meetings of the Commission came to end at last, and after some more months, the Commission issued its report in January, 1890. On the all-important new charges put forward by *The Times* the report was an acquittal. They were pronounced to be either untrue, or without foundation, or unproven. The letters were declared to be forgeries, but without reprobation of the use which had been made of them. They were dealt with in a short paragraph, referring to the evidence printed in the voluminous appendix, as though of little importance. The allegations that Parnell was intimate with the Invincibles, that he communicated with them, when released from Kilmainham on his parole, that he recognized the Phœnix Park murders as their handiwork, and that he had by a timely remittance enabled one of the murderers to escape, were pronounced to be without foundation. On the other hand, it was reported that the respondents had incited to intimidation, which was followed by crime ; that while they had denounced crime and outrage they had not denounced the system which led to crime and outrage, but persisted in it with the knowledge of its effect ; that they had entered into a conspiracy by a system of coercion and intimidation against the payment of rents for the purpose of expelling the land-lords ; and that eight of the sixty-five respondents, not including Parnell, had formed the Land League Association with the intention to bring about the independence of Ireland.

The report was accepted by the public generally as an acquittal on all the main points. The others did not interest them. They were stale. They were no more than Mr. Forster had insisted upon in 1883. They had been condoned in 1885, when the Tory leaders were in alliance with the Irish Party, and negotiated with Parnell through Lord Carnarvon. The day came at last (March 8th, 1890) when the report was considered by the House of Commons. Mr. W. H. Smith, on the part of the Government, moved a vote of thanks to the Judges for their impartial report. In conventional words, he grudgingly expressed satisfaction that the personal charges against Parnell and the Irish Members were disproved. He insisted that the other charges which were proved were of a wide and serious character. He disclaimed the intention to punish these men. Not a generous word of sympathy for Parnell fell from his lips.

Mr. Gladstone sprang to his feet in reply, and supplied everything that was wanting in Mr. Smith's address, and a good deal more. He moved as an amendment "that the House of Commons deemed it its duty to record its reprobation of the false charges of the gravest and most odious description, based on calumny and forgery, that had been brought against Members of the House ; and while declaring its satisfaction at the exposure of these calumnies, expressed its regret at the wrong inflicted, and the suffering and loss induced, through a protracted period, by reason of these charges of flagrant iniquity." He spoke on this for an hour and three-quarters. I never heard him to greater advantage. It was a marvellous performance of sustained energy for a man of eighty-one years. Indeed, I would single out the speech as a better illustration than any other I recollect of the varied oratorical powers of the veteran statesman ; his debating skill, his scornful repartees, his close reasoning, his glowing passion, his fervid appeal to the generous instincts of Members. He tore the report to pieces. He showed how incomplete, one-sided, and unfair it was ; how belated it was to inquire into matters which had occurred eight and ten years ago, which had since been condoned by the Tory leaders, in 1885 ; how the report shut out all references to the main causes of the increase of crime, the grave agricultural distress of 1879–80, the prevalence of excessive rents, and the wholesale evictions. He showed how false was the contention that the rejection of the Compensation for Disturbance Bill by the House of Lords, in

1880, had nothing to do with the increase of crime ; and that the Land Act of 1881 had not been the cause of the reduction of crime. He vindicated, as a whole, the agitation which had brought about such beneficial legislation. " As the man," he said, " responsible more than any other, for the Act of 1881— as the man whose duty it was to consider that question day and night, during the whole of that Session—I must record my firm opinion that it would not have become the law of the land if it had not been for the agitation with which Irish society was convulsed." [1]

This powerful appeal did not affect the vote of the House, which was on purely party lines. The effect, however, of such a demonstration is not to be measured by the division list. It was supported at a later stage by a passionate denunciation by Lord Randolph Churchill of the appointment of the Commission, and its method of procedure—the last speech I can recollect delivered with his full force and fire, before disease, creeping upon him, incapacitated him, without his being conscious of failure.

The two speeches together destroyed what vitality there was in the report, other than its acquittal of Parnell of the odious charge of complicity in the Phœnix Park murders. It recoiled, in fact, on those who devised the scheme of destroying their opponents in Ireland, by methods so tortuous and glaringly unfair. Parnell, as a result of it, reached the zenith of his influence in Ireland and of his reputation in England. The cause of Home Rule gained immensely. If a General Election had taken place, in the summer of 1890, there can be little doubt that the majority in England for Home Rule would have been sufficient to carry the policy to success.

[1] *Hansard*, March 8th, 1890.

CHAPTER XXXV

THE FALL OF PARNELL

AT the close of 1890 a thunderclap burst on the Irish Party. On November 15th, the suit of Captain O'Shea against his wife and Parnell, as co-respondent, was heard in the Divorce Court, and was decided in his favour. Mrs. O'Shea had originally made counter-charges against her husband, and had also pleaded connivance and condonation ; and Parnell had assured his friends and followers that he would triumphantly refute every accusation. But at the last moment the pleas in defence were withdrawn. As, however, they had charged O'Shea with acts arraigning his honour, the case was not dealt with briefly, in the usual manner of undefended suits. Evidence was gone into at length, purporting to show that Parnell, for many years past, had acted in a manner which produced a most unfavourable impression on the public.

Mr. O'Donnell, who was the personal friend of Captain O'Shea, has given an explanation of the withdrawal of the defence.

" Mrs. O'Shea," he says, " could not contemplate the possibility of continuing to bear her husband's name after her husband had dragged her into Court, and overwhelmed her reputation with charges which nothing could efface. Do you want me to be that man's wife till death ? was her question to Parnell, which left him no alternative but to bow to her decision."[1] He significantly adds : " Captain O'Shea bitterly hoped that Gladstone's Parliamentary majority would suffer like Parnell's uncrowned kingship by the event of the Divorce Court." O'Shea was a Roman Catholic, by whose Church divorce and remarriage were forbidden. The relations of the

[1] *History of the Parliamentary Party*, II, 290.

parties concerned had been well known to Parnell's supporters for some years past. It was assumed that the husband was a consenting party. In 1886, Parnell had foisted O'Shea as a candidate on the Nationalist electors of the City of Galway, at a by-election, in spite of the strongest objections on their part. Biggar, Healy, and others made speeches there, commenting in the plainest language on the relations of Parnell and Mrs. O'Shea.

Parnell was able, by a personal visit to Galway, and by threatening resignation of his leadership, to quell the revolt against his authority, and to insist on the withdrawal of opposition to his nominee. The speeches referred to were kept out of the papers, and no notice was taken of them by Parnell. O'Shea justified the suspicions of the electors of Galway, that he was not to be relied on, by voting in the same year against the Home Rule Bill. He then resigned his seat, and disappeared from politics. This was four years before he took action in the Divorce Court. In the meantime, he had given evidence before the Special Commission that the letters forged by Pigott were written by Parnell. It might seem, therefore, that O'Shea was more intent on discrediting and destroying Parnell, as his late political leader, than as the old and very intimate friend of his wife. Though the main fact of the case is not disputed, the evidence given in the divorce proceedings cannot be accepted as conclusive in relation to Parnell's conduct.

Parnell, from the first, determined to face the position, and had no intention whatever of making any concession to public opinion. He may have had in his mind cases, in the not remote past, where men in high political positions had been in the same position as himself, without any question of the [forfeiture of their claim to confidence. If so, he did not distinguish between public and private cognizance of such cases, and he overlooked the fact that the official career of one of them, then living, had been brought to an end, by the publicity of divorce proceedings.

It seemed at first that Irish opinion would stand by Parnell, and would be unaffected by the proceedings and imputations in the Divorce Court. At a meeting of the National League in Dublin, on the day after the divorce decree, and at a more public meeting at the Leinster Hall, two days later, votes of unabated confidence in him were carried unanimously, and he was assured that nothing which had occurred in the divorce proceedings would make the least difference in their political support. In England, however, it was different. At the annual meeting of the National Liberal Federation, held at Sheffield on November 20th–21st, at which Sir William Harcourt and Mr. Morley were present, though no public notice was taken of Parnell's position, it appeared that it was the almost unanimous opinion of the delegates that his continuance, as Leader of the Irish Party, in alliance with the Liberal Party, would be absolutely fatal to the prospects of the Home Rule policy, so far as Great Britain was concerned. Urgent representations to this effect were made to Mr. Gladstone, who came to the conclusion that his own leadership of the Liberal Party, which had been prolonged for the sole purpose of carrying Home Rule, would become futile if Parnell were to continue, for the time being, as Leader of the Irish Party.

There was no time to lose if a change was to be made. Parliament was to meet on November 25th, and on the same day Parnell would, in the ordinary course, be re-elected by the Irish Members as their Sessional Leader. Mr. Gladstone returned to London on the 24th, and had a consultation with three members of his late Cabinet and the Chief Whip of the Party, at which the terms of a letter, to be shown by Mr. Morley to Parnell, were agreed upon. Mr. Gladstone wrote that he had come to the conclusion that " notwithstanding the splendid service rendered by Mr. Parnell to the country, his continuance at the present moment in the leadership (of the Irish Party) would be productive of consequences disastrous in the highest degree to the cause of Ireland."

" The continuance I speak of," he added, " would not only place many hearty and effective friends of the Irish cause in a position of great embarrassment, but would render my retention of the leadership of the Liberal Party, based as it has been mainly upon the presentation of the Irish cause, almost a nullity."

Mr. Gladstone also saw Mr. Justin McCarthy, and through him sent a personal message to Mr. Parnell to the same effect. It was to be regarded as confidential, and was not to be communicated to the Irish Members, if Parnell contemplated spontaneous action, but if not, it was to be made known to the Irish Party at their meeting on the morrow. Mr. Gladstone, in sending this message, reminded Mr. McCarthy that Mr. Parnell had consulted him, after the Phœnix Park murders, as to remaining Leader of the Irish Party.

The meeting of the Irish Members took place the next day, the 25th, at 2 p.m.; fifty-nine of them were present. Mr. McCarthy was able to deliver Mr. Gladstone's message to Parnell just before the meeting. Parnell curtly replied that he would stand by his guns. Mr. McCarthy, though in the Chair at the meeting, did not carry out the further instructions of Mr. Gladstone by informing the Irish Members of his views.[1] They proceeded, on the motion of Mr. Sexton, to re-elect Parnell as their Sessional Leader, two Members only raising any objection. There must be no English dictation, it was said; we must stand by our leader.

In the meantime, Mr. Morley had made every effort to deliver Mr. Gladstone's letter to Mr. Parnell, but in vain. It was not till after the re-election by the Irish Party that he was able to do so. It was then too late. Parnell was obdurate. He said that the feeling against him was a storm in a tea-cup, and would soon pass. Morley replied that it was much more than that—that if he set British opinion at defiance, and brazened it out, it would be ruin to Home Rule at the coming election. He suggested to Parnell that if he withdrew from the actual leadership now, as a concession to public opinion in this country, this need not prevent him from again taking the position when new circumstances might demand his presence; that he might treat his re-election as a public vote of confidence by his party; that having secured this he would suffer no loss of dignity or authority by a longer or shorter period of retirement.[2] Parnell rejected this wise advice, given in a most conciliatory and tactful manner. In reply to a suggestion of Mr. Morley that the letter might be published, Parnell said, " I think Mr. Gladstone will be quite right to do so. It will set him right with his party."

Mr. Morley immediately informed Mr. Gladstone of the failure of his mission, and of the re-election of Parnell as

---

[1] Lord Morley says of this, " The gravity of the fact that Mr. McCarthy failed to deliver the message lay in this, that it magnified and distorted Mr. Gladstone's letter into a humiliating public ultimatum."

[2] *Life of Gladstone,* III, 440.

leader. Mr. Gladstone thereupon decided to publish his letter to Morley, and directed that it should be sent to the Press at once. I thought myself, at the time, that the publication of the letter to Morley at that stage was needlessly hasty, and that it might have the appearance of dictation to the Irish Party. It would have had far more serious effect, if it had not been for the subsequent action of Parnell. He drew up and issued a manifesto to the Irish people, in which he was not content with protesting against Mr. Gladstone's dictation to the Irish Party. He endeavoured to shift and widen the issue. Referring to a visit which he had paid to Hawarden, in December, 1889, he charged Mr. Gladstone with the intention to play false to the cause of Home Rule, in a variety of ways which he specified. He also charged Mr. Morley with the same intention. Both these statesmen replied in the Press, denying absolutely the versions given of their conversations. If anything more was needed to disprove these charges than these personal contradictions, it was to be found in the fact that, on the day after leaving Hawarden, Parnell spoke at a public meeting at Liverpool, on December 19th, 1889, and called on his countrymen to rejoice : " for we are on the safe path to our legitimate freedom and our future prosperity," words absolutely inconsistent with his new version of betrayal of the Irish cause by Mr. Gladstone and Mr. Morley. Before issuing his manifesto, Parnell showed it to Mr. McCarthy, who said, " I object to every word in it. It is all objectionable." It went forth, however, without change. The charges against Mr. Gladstone and Mr. Morley in this manifesto appear to have determined Mr. Dillon and Mr. O'Brien, then on a mission to the United States, to declare themselves against Parnell's leadership.

There resulted from these untoward events a serious breach in the Irish Party. About two-thirds of them favoured the temporary retirement of Parnell from the leadership. They included the most influential men of the party—McCarthy, Dillon, O'Brien, Sexton, Healy, and others—while the two Redmonds, T. Harrington, O'Kelly, Nolan, and others stood by Parnell. After eight days of discussion in a Committee Room of the House of Commons, under the presidency of Parnell, the party split into two. The larger party elected McCarthy as their leader. " No service," said Sexton to Parnell, in the course of the discussion, " rendered by any leader to any cause entitled him to effect its ruin." The smaller section continued to follow Parnell. Meanwhile, on December 8th, the Catholic Bishops of Ireland, at the instance of the papal authorities at Rome, issued a manifesto declaring that Parnell " having been convicted of the gravest offences known to religion and society was unworthy of Christian confidence."

In June, 1891, six months after the decree of the Divorce Court, Parnell married Mrs. O'Shea. This did not avail to rectify his position with Catholics, by whom the marriage of divorced persons is regarded as a sin. The Catholic Bishops issued another manifesto against him, and *The Freeman's Journal*, which up to that time had favoured the Parnellite Party, took this opportunity of going over to the other side. It brought all its great influence to bear against Parnell. The contest was now transferred from the Committee Room of the House of Commons to Ireland. Three by-elections took place in the course of the next few months: at Kilkenny, in December, 1890 ; North Sligo, in April, 1891 ; and Carlow, in July, 1891. At all three Parnell put forward candidates against those of the main body of Nationalists. They were defeated by very large majorities. The Catholic Priests of these districts made immense efforts to bring up voters to the poll. Though Parnell continued to hold his own at public meetings, especially in the larger towns, the verdict of the electors of Ireland was unmistakably against him, and in favour of maintaining the alliance of the Irish Party with Mr. Gladstone and the Liberals of Great Britain. This was confirmed at the General Election of 1892, when only nine Parnellites were elected, as compared with seventy-five of the main party.

In the ten months which followed his deposition from the leadership of the main Irish Party, Parnell made the most desperate efforts to maintain his cause in Ireland by speeches at the by-elections, and in every part of the country. His home was in England, but he crossed the Channel to Ireland every Saturday, and spoke at great meetings on the Sundays and Mondays. It was distressing to read his speeches during this period, when he was at bay before the growing opinion in Ireland against him. They became reckless and personal. His attacks on Mr. Gladstone and the Liberal leaders and his old associates were most bitter. They were replied to, or were provoked by equally bitter speeches and taunts from the opposite section of the Irish Party. He was in a miserable state of health, quite unequal to the efforts he made. It is perhaps fair to conclude that his mind was somewhat unhinged by all that he had gone through. The strain was too much for him. His constitution had been seriously undermined by illness in 1886. The consciousness that the ground was sinking beneath him, and that public opinion in Ireland was declaring, more and more, against him, must have embittered those days. The closing weeks of his life were even more mournful and hopeless than those of O'Connell and Butt. He died at Brighton on October 6th, 1891, of cardiac rheumatism, at the early age of forty-six. On the same day there died also Mr. W. H. Smith, the Leader of the Tory Party in the House of Commons, who had been so largely concerned in the appointment of the Special Commission, which it was expected would ruin Parnell and the Irish Party.

Parnell's career in the House of Commons had extended over no more than sixteen years, from 1875 to 1891. From these sixteen years, two must be deducted at the beginning, when he was silent and unnoticed, and four at the close when, from ill-health and other causes, he was seldom at his post in the House of Commons, and practically took little part in its business. His effective career, therefore, was little more than ten years. That he should have achieved the position he filled in the House and in Ireland, in so short a time, and have held it unquestioned, during these years, was most remarkable—the more so when we consider how small were his apparent equipments for it. Compared with his two predecessors in the leadership of the Irish Party, O'Connell and Butt, he had none of the qualities which might be expected to qualify him for the position. He had nothing of their sympathetic instincts, or their emotional powers of speech. He had none of their constitutional lore, or historical knowledge, or their powers of constructive legislation. Unlike them, there was nothing of fire, imagination, humour, or wit in his speeches. He had few intimate friends. He was reserved, aloof, and even frigid. He had no Celtic instincts in him. His speeches were cold, hard, and unimpressionable. But he was endowed with a dogged and imperturbable will. He knew what he wanted to say, and could say it in the fewest, clearest, and most direct words. He had a rare distinction of manner which greatly impressed his hearers. He had courage which never failed him. Above all, he had the very rare gift of instinctive command over men, and the power of compelling them to follow him.

Statesmen must be judged of by comparing their aims and objects, and their ideals at the early stages of their careers with their later achievements. When Parnell's speeches in the House of Commons, his determination to force it to listen to Irish demands, and his early speeches at Westport and other places in favour of land reform and self-government for Ireland, are compared with what was achieved during his short career, he must be placed on a high level. He succeeded where O'Connell and Butt failed. He acquired a position for himself and his party in Parliament which neither of them ever attained. He was mainly concerned in effecting a revolution in land tenure. He succeeded in inducing the Liberal Party to adopt Home Rule as their policy.

His speeches in the early stage of the agrarian movement were regarded in England as revolutionary, dangerous, and predatory. But the revolution has been successfully accomplished, or is in course of being so. Looking back at these speeches it must now be admitted that they were statesmanlike, and remarkable for their prevision. It may be doubted whether any such great reform of land tenure has been effected in any other country with less of social disturbance, and with fewer regrettable incidents. It must also be admitted that if no manifestations of discontent had occurred, there would have been no motive force to compel Parliament to listen to Irish demands. Even then, if we admit many mistakes, and all that can be urged against his action during the last year of his life, we must still recognize the great and beneficent results to Ireland of Parnell's political career.

The effect of the schism in the Irish Party, which was not healed even by the death of Parnell, was most serious to the National cause. Among other things it dried up the sources of revenue in the United States, for dissension spread there equally as in Ireland. Funds largely failed for the support of the evicted tenants. A panic occurred on those few of the Plan of Campaign estates, such as that of Lord Clanricarde, where any substantial number of tenants still remained in possession of their farms and houses; members of combinations pledged to stand by those already evicted, and not to come to terms except on the basis of their reinstatement. They gave up the combinations, accepted the terms offered them of greatly reduced rents, and abandoned the evicted men. This was notably the case in the Tipperary combination, where the town tenants of Mr. Smith Barry had combined to refuse payment of rent, not on their own account, for it was admitted they had no personal complaint, but out of sympathy for the tenants of the Ponsonby estate, where Mr. Smith Barry was backing up the owner in resisting the legitimate claims of the tenants for reduction of rents, and was carrying out wholesale evictions. The Tipperary combination was quixotic. It proved to be a great blunder. The support of the town tenants and the erection of a new Tipperary for them, which was attempted, involved great expenditure, which could not now be met. It tumbled to pieces. The Government most unwisely prosecuted W. O'Brien and Dillon and others for speeches made six months previously in connection with this affair, and sent them to prison for varying terms of four to six months. This did much to retrieve the failure of the Tipperary scheme in the estimation of public opinion in Ireland.

The Tipperary prosecutions formed the subject of a vote of censure, moved by Mr. Morley, on February 16th, 1891, in which he complained of the brutality and lawlessness indulged in by the subordinates of the Irish Government in consequence of Mr. Balfour's habit of backing them up whether right or wrong. He showed that the trial of Dillon and O'Brien was the prostitution of a legal tribunal. Mr. Balfour defended the proceedings, and was supported by a majority of 320 to 245. I was personally no more fortunate in a motion I made, in the same Session, for terminating the disputes on the Plan of Campaign estates by enforced arbitration and the reinstatement of the evicted men. Mr. Balfour opposed, on the ground that it involved a recognition of the Plan of Campaign, a movement which he said was clearly not spontaneous, but one promoted by political revolutionists. Many years were still to elapse before justice was done to the evicted tenants on these estates.

It remains to add that the last year of Mr. Balfour's tenure of office as Irish Secretary was in pleasing contrast to the earlier period. In the autumn of 1890, he paid a visit to the most distressed parts of the west and south of Ireland. As a result of this he promoted, in the following year, a scheme of light railways for these districts, which opened them out, and also provided for the employment of labour. He also carried a measure for creating a Congested Districts Board, with the object of permanently relieving these districts by enlarging inadequate holdings of land, and establishing new industries —a measure which has since been greatly developed. He was also able to extend the scheme of land purchase, by providing for an additional loan from the State of 33 millions, and by extending the period of repayment to forty-two years. These measures were well received by the Irish Members, but they did nothing to relieve the political position. The enigma of the Irish question was unsolved by six out of the twenty years of Lord Salisbury's prescription of coercion.

CHAPTER XXXVI

THE SECOND HOME RULE BILL

DURING the six years after the defeat of his first Home Rule Bill, Mr. Gladstone, in spite of his great age and increasing infirmities, devoted himself heart and soul to the Irish cause. He thought of little else in politics. In the House of Commons he lost no opportunity of backing up the Irish Members, in attacks on the Government for their methods of coercion, for breaking up public meetings in Ireland by the police, and for the treatment of Irish Members and others as common criminals. He did more for them than Parnell himself, who was very lax in his attendance in Parliament, during these years.

He also advocated Home Rule at numerous public meetings. I was present at some of them, and though there was necessarily much repetition of the main arguments for the Irish cause, there was always freshness of treatment. His speeches were delightful to listen to. The greatest of all the meetings was that at Bingley Hall, Birmingham, in the citadel of his opponents, where, in November, 1888, he spoke to an audience of over sixteen thousand. I had never heard him more effective. He spoke on this occasion for an hour and fifty minutes—an immense effort for a man of seventy-nine years, and especially so, in view of the possible risk of opposition at Birmingham. He described the fruits of the past policy of England to Ireland as unmitigated bitterness, mischief, disparagement, and dishonour. " Our opponents teach you to rely on the use of an enfeebled and superannuated weapon of coercion. We teach you to rely upon Irish affection and goodwill "—and so on. The speech was an enormous success. It seemed to carry conviction to his audience. It was, however, but another illustration that public meetings are not to be relied on as tests of the opinions of the electors of the district, for at the subsequent General Election, Birmingham returned its seven Members, in support of Chamberlain, by the accustomed immense majorities.

Mr. Gladstone was undoubtedly depressed by the set-back to his policy, caused by the unfortunate proceedings of the divorce case, and the subsequent split of the Irish Party. But later his sanguine hopes were renewed. The by-elections gradually reduced the Tory majority in the House of Commons from 115 to 67. When the General Election came at last in 1892, Mr. Gladstone still confidently expected a majority in the new Parliament of about 100. But he was over-sanguine. There was a majority for the Liberals, and the Irish Party combined, in the United Kingdom, of no more than 40. But the majority in England against him was 71. This gave rise to a new and specious argument against Home Rule. It was contended that such a great constitutional change ought not to be effected, agai st the will of the predominant partner in the Union, even if the three other partners, Ireland, Scotland, and Wales, were overwhelmingly in favour of it. Some support was given later to this view by Lord Rosebery, though it had not prevented his joining Mr. Gladstone's fourth administration. In view of the narrow majority in the United Kingdom, it was recognized that Home Rule could not be carried, without another appeal to the electors, and thenceforward it was well understood that the House of Lords would reject the new Bill, whatever form it might take. Mr. Gladstone, however, in the course of the General Election, had given his word that Parliament would not again be dissolved, at the dictation of the House of Lords, by their rejection of any Bill, even that of Home Rule.

The majority against them being only 40, Lord Salisbury's Government did not think it incumbent on them to resign before the meeting of Parliament. Mr. Gladstone, on his part, nothing daunted by the insufficiency of the majority for carrying so great a change in the constitution, at once entered the field again. A vote of want of confidence in the Government was carried at the meeting of Parliament, in August, at the instance of Mr. Asquith, by a party majority, and Mr. Gladstone, for the fourth time, undertook to form a Government. Mr. John Morley again took the post of Irish

Secretary, and Lord Rosebery again became Foreign Secretary.
Lord Granville was no longer alive to lead in the House of
Lords. His place was taken by Lord Kimberley.[1]

The new Parliament, having accomplished the task of
displacing the Tory Government, was prorogued, and met
again early in January, 1893, for a Session which lasted till
March in the following year. Mr. Gladstone, on February
13th, introduced his second Home Rule Bill. The main
change, as compared with the original Bill, was the retention
in the Imperial Parliament of the Irish Members, reduced,
however, from 103 to 80. This entailed other changes in
detail. Mr. Gladstone's speech on the occasion, though
powerful and lucid, did not compare in interest with that of
1886. There was little in it new in substance. The subject
was somewhat threadbare. His voice showed diminished
power. The debates on the introduction and second reading
were also reproductions of those of 1886, and call for no special
remark, save that Sir Edward Clarke replied impromptu to
Mr. Gladstone's speech, on introducing the Bill, in the very
best speech delivered against the Bill, in the course of these
long debates, a very remarkable performance ; and that Mr.
Chamberlain, on the same occasion, made the significant
statement that his vote against the Bill would not be a vote
against Home Rule, but the expression of an opinion that this
particular Bill did not fulfil the conditions necessary for such
a measure. The Bill passed the second reading by a majority
of forty-three.

It was in the Committee stage that the main interests of
the Bill were centred. The Tory leaders fought it, line by line
and word by word. The certainty that it would be rejected
by the House of Lords gave them an advantage in Committee ;
for it relieved them of all responsibility for improving it.
Their sole object was to destroy it in detail. Mr. Balfour announced that he would vote for any amendment, which would
injure the Bill in any way, and he kept his word by supporting any change which would make it unworkable. Through
sixty-three nights of discussion these tactics were prolonged,
and the measure was finally carried by the application of the
guillotine, which left many of its clauses undiscussed.

---

[1] I became a member of this Government as First Commissioner of Works,
and later as President of the Local Government Board.

It was in this protracted contest that Mr. Gladstone was conspicuous above all others. He met the attack with the most extraordinary vigour. In the whole course of his career there was nothing more remarkable than the way in which he met all comers, and worsted them in the fray. He was, by this time, under the infirmity of deafness,[1] but picking up, in a few words, the drift of an opponent's argument, he would draw for a reply on his wealth of knowledge and past experience. He revelled in these combats. He was completely master of the position. No one could cope with him. His exuberant spirits, his courtesy in debate, and his resources of argument, caused amazement to his opponents, and ever-increasing pleasure to his friends. It was delightful to listen to him, night after night, while in this strain. On one point only was he worsted. The Bill provided that the eighty Irish Members retained in the Imperial Parliament were to be precluded from voting on purely English and Scotch questions. This " in-and-out " clause, as it was called, gave rise to great objections, even on the Government side of the House, and Mr. Gladstone, who, it would seem, still at heart favoured his original proposal, was compelled to drop it, with the result that the Irish Members were to remain in the House of Commons. This opened up fresh difficulties and objections. The dilemma was a serious one, going to the root of the whole question.

The Bill finally passed a third reading by a majority of 34. It was rejected by the House of Lords by a majority of 419 to 41. Of the minority, thirty-eight held offices in the Government, or had been made Peers in recent years. It may be said that the hereditary Peers, almost without exception, voted against the Bill. Nothing very new was said in the debate. The Duke of Devonshire, who had carried the hostile motion in the House of Commons against the Bill of 1886, now moved the rejection of the new Bill in the House of Lords, in a speech conspicuous for its fairness and fullness of treatment. Lord Salisbury, in his powerful arraignment of the Bill, made much

---

[1] A friend of mine, an old member of the House, just before the General Election of 1892, expressed his regret to Mr. Gladstone that he was unable again to seek re-election, alleging his deafness as the cause of retirement. "Deafness," replied the old chief, " do you call that any disqualification for the House of Commons? I can assure you that for the last five years I have hardly heard anything in the House. I pick up a word or two and then I guess all the remainder."

of the point that while the majority in the House of Commons
was only thirty-four, thirty-eight of the Irish Members voting
had been condemned by the highest Judges of the land for not
denouncing the system of intimidation, which led to crime,
and for persisting in it with full knowledge of its effect.

Mr. Gladstone had been ably seconded in the House of
Commons by Mr. Morley. It may be well here to mention
that Mr. Morley, in 1892, appointed a Royal Commission,
presided over by Mr. Justice Mathew, to inquire into the
question of the tenants evicted from the Plan of Campaign
estates. The Commission reported in favour of their compulsory reinstatement as tenants, subject to a rent to be
determined by the Land Commission. A Bill founded on this
was introduced by Mr. Morley, in 1894, and was carried through
the House of Commons. He defended it on the grounds of
policy and expediency, as necessary for the peace of Ireland,
rather than on those of justice. The House of Lords contemptuously rejected the Bill. Their unwisdom and impolicy
of doing so was later abundantly made clear.

In 1903 Mr. Balfour's Government, as part of a great
scheme of land purchase for Ireland, found it expedient to
appease public opinion in Ireland by dealing with the evicted
tenants. They held out inducements to the owners not only
of the Campaign estates, but of others where tenants had been
evicted during the agrarian agitation, to reinstate the evicted
men, not as tenants, but as purchasers of their former holdings. The measure, however, was a permissive, and not a compulsory one. It did not effect a complete settlement. In 1907
the Liberal Government found it necessary to deal with the
question again. They introduced a measure for the compulsory
reinstatement of the evicted men, not as tenants, but as purchasers of their holdings. The Land Commission was empowered to advance money for the rebuilding of houses, and
for stocking the farms. Where planters were in possession of
the farms, power was given to expropriate them. The House
of Lords was now willing to pass this compulsory measure,
far more extreme than that which they had rejected in 1894.
But after a discussion, largely conducted by Peers who were
owners of Plan of Campaign estates, they inserted a clause
forbidding the compulsory purchase of farms where the
planters were *bonâ fide* farmers. In spite of this amendment,

the Act had the desired effect on the remaining Campaign estates, save only that of Lord Clanricarde, where, by further litigation, the owner succeeded in defeating the object of the Act, though the planters were willing to sell.   In 1908, an amending Bill was carried to deal with this one remaining Campaign estate.   The owner continued to resist.   At the time I write forty-three of the two hundred evicted tenants are still out in the cold.   The Congested Districts Board is negotiating for the purchase of part of the Clanricarde estate, and when this is effected the last of the surviving evicted tenants will be replaced on their holdings.   The Plan of Campaign had its origin on this property.   It will be the last in which a settlement will be arrived at.   One way or another, every one of the men evicted from these properties has been, or will be, reinstated, if not on their former holdings, in others of equivalent value.   They have been reinstated as owners.   Their annual payments for interest and sinking fund average about 40 per cent less than the rents for which they were evicted. Their houses have been rebuilt and their farms restocked at the cost of the State.   It would be difficult to conceive more ample amends to these men for the wrong done to them by eviction, and by the rejection of the Bill of 1894.   It is interesting to note that Mr. Kilbride, M.P., who was the leader of the Plan of Campaign on Lord Lansdowne's estate at Luggacurran, in Tipperary, has been reinstated in the office of the agent of the estate, his own house having been sold to a bonâ fide purchaser.

As a general result, the owners of these Campaign estates have disappeared.   The planters also, with rare exceptions, have surrendered their farms.   The evicted men have been reinstated as owners.   What persistency the whole case shows in Irish opinion, and what tenacity of purpose on the part of the evicted men !   The marvel is that such long years were necessary for giving effect to this policy, and for accomplishing an act of justice.

It remains to point out, as bearing on Parnell's programme of Land Reform laid down in his speech at Westport in 1882, that in 1893, at the instance of Mr. Morley, a Committee was appointed by the House of Commons to inquire into the working of the Land Act of 1881, especially as regards the Healy Clause and the interpretation put upon it by the Irish

Judges.   The Committee reported in favour of an amendment much in the sense demanded by Parnell twelve years previously. In 1896 Mr. Gerald Balfour carried a measure conceding in great part the Irish claim.   In 1903 a further extension was given to the scheme of converting tenants into owners by a measure proposed by Mr. George Wyndham.   It reduced the annual payments of tenant purchasers to $3\frac{1}{4}$ per cent on the purchase money, of which $\frac{1}{2}$ per cent was for the Sinking Fund.   The term of repayment of the capital sum was extended to sixty-eight years.   A large bonus was given in money to landowners to induce them to sell to their tenants.   The important feature of the scheme was its assumption that all the landowners of Ireland would be ready to come to terms with their tenants, and that tenancy would cease to exist and a universal system of peasant proprietors would be substituted. Under this and previous schemes about one-half of the Irish tenant farmers have been converted into owners, or have agreed with their landlords on terms for the purpose.   The problem, therefore, is in course of solution, and before many years are gone the scheme of conversion will be completed, and Parnell's proposal of 1882, which then seemed so revolutionary, will be accomplished.   The rents of the landowners, which form the basis of land purchase, have been greatly reduced under the operation of the Land Acts of 1881 and 1886.   It may be doubted, however, whether they have been reduced in a larger proportion than rents in England, under voluntary arrangements, between landowners and their tenants, in conformity with the great fall of prices.

CHAPTER XXXVII

THE RETIREMENT OF MR. GLADSTONE

ON the rejection of the Home Rule Bill by the House of Lords, Mr. Gladstone was precluded by his declaration already quoted from dissolving Parliament, and appealing to the electors. Later, however, in the same Session, which was prolonged till March in the following year, when the Lords had virtually rejected the Employers' Liability Bill, and had seriously mangled the Parish Councils Bill, he urged his colleagues in the Cabinet to take the opportunity, thus afforded, of appealing to the constituencies, and raising the whole question of the House of Lords. His colleagues, however, did not agree. This may have been one of the causes which determined him to resign the post of Premier, and to retire from political life. His age and growing infirmities were contributory, if not main, causes. There was also his grave objection to the great increase of naval expenditure, insisted upon by the Board of Admiralty, and agreed to by nearly all his colleagues.

I shall never forget the pathetic scene at his last Cabinet, on March 1st, 1894, so well described by Lord Morley, when the veteran chief bid farewell to his colleagues with the parting words, " God bless you all." Most affecting also was his speech in the House of Commons, on the same night, on the subject of the Lords' amendments to the Parish Councils Bill, in which, without announcing his intention to resign, he made his well-known testamentary exhortation as to the urgent necessity for dealing with the House of Lords.

" A solution," he said, " will have to be found for the tremendous and incessant conflict upon matters of high principle and importance between the representatives of the people and those who fill a nominated assembly. It is the authority of the nation which must in the last resort decide." [1]

[1] *Hansard*, March 1st, 1894.

This speech closed Mr. Gladstone's Parliamentary career. He was never seen again in the House of Commons, though he continued to be a Member of it till the General Election of 1896. He remained in fairly good health till 1897, when illness came upon him, painful and distressing. He lingered on till May, 1898, when at the age of eighty-eight he succumbed. I saw him in 1896, just before his last illness. He was greatly aged, but his memory was still wonderfully clear. In the course of conversation I asked him a question on a point which was then of public interest, whether a Prime Minister could admit a member to his Cabinet without consulting his colleagues. He replied at once : " That is a moot point. I will tell you what happened to me. When I led the House of Commons in 1866, the Prime Minister, Lord Russell, put Goschen into the Cabinet without consulting me. I thought that a very strong measure." He went on to say that a Prime Minister was certainly under no obligation to take the opinion of the whole Cabinet on the subject, but he ought to consult two or three of its leading members, as the balance of the Cabinet might be altered by a new appointment. I never saw the great man again.

His absence from the House of Commons, after the spring of 1894, caused a very great blank in that assembly. It was no longer the same. There was a magnetism in him, which had given vitality and interest to its proceedings, when he was present. He was always alert. He listened with marked attention to even the humblest Member who had anything to say. When he ceased to be there debates flagged and became dull. I can vouch for this only for the next two years, for I lost my seat at Bradford, in the General Election of 1896, and did not again return to the House of Commons. I had been in the House, as a follower of Mr. Gladstone, for thirty-three years, and had heard from the Gallery his greatest speeches for ten preceding years. I witnessed, and felt myself, during this long time, the influence of this greatest of all Parliamentarians. None of the reports in *Hansard* give an adequate impression of his speeches. They convey no idea of his resonant and penetrating voice, his graceful and impressive gestures, his luminous and sometimes hawklike eye, his earnestness and ardour, and his ever-varying moods. His speeches, as a rule, were not constructed with a view to permanent literary effect.

They were purposely diffuse. I recollect his telling me that one night, when in Sir Robert Peel's Government, he sat next his chief, during an important debate, and just before rising to speak he turned to Peel and said, " Shall I be short and concise ? " " No," was the reply ; " be long and diffuse. It is most important to present your argument in many different ways, so as to persuade men of different sections of the House." It was a characteristic of Mr. Gladstone's speeches that they were meant to persuade and convince many sections of his hearers. Though diffuse, there were passages in them of concentrated dignity and sometimes of pathos. They were wanting only in one quality—that of " humour." He could, however, deliver delightful banter. I have read many of them during the last few months. It is only by recalling the man himself that one can understand the full effect of them.

It was a feature, and in some respects a defect, of Mr. Gladstone, that any Member of the House, however obscure, could draw him in debate. He was always ready to take up a challenge, and to enter the lists against any man who ventured to attack him. Lord Randolph Churchill, in his early days, laid traps for him, and gained experience and notoriety by challenging the great chief.

No one in my recollection ever succeeded in quoting Mr. Gladstone's speeches against him. I often heard this attempted. He would prick up his ears. He seemed to have a perfect recollection of all that he had ever said on the subject, however remote. " Go on with your quotation," he would say, and the luckless assailant would find, in a sentence or two further on, that there was some qualification or reservation little noticed perhaps at the time.

While a supreme master of lucid exposition he was also an adept in the use of subtle distinctions, and of phrases, which tended to obscure rather than to throw light on the subject under discussion. There are occasions when a Minister cannot give a direct answer to an inopportune question without injury to the public service. I have known Ministers, and even Prime Ministers, who, unable to say either Yes or No, would resort to lies. To Mr. Gladstone there were infinite varieties of shades between Yes and No. He was able to make a reply such that no one could distinguish or disentangle the facts. Some people called this casuistry or sophistry. I have heard high authorities say that the art of casuistry ought not to be neglected. Call it by what name we may, the use of language in this way is at times necessary in the House of Commons in the interest of the public, or for the purpose of perplexing an unscrupulous opponent. This faculty of subtle distinction not unfrequently widened the area of discussion and drew Mr. Gladstone into unnecessary controversies.

No leader in the House of Commons was ever more generous to his opponents, or more studiously careful to avoid anything which would wound the feelings of any Member. I had an early illustration of this, in 1866, when the House of Commons was in Committee on the Reform Bill of that year. An amendment was moved by Lord Dunkellin, one of the Liberal " Cave," who were determined to defeat the Bill. It was well known that the Government would be defeated on this amendment. I recollected this story about Dunkellin : He was in the army at the siege of Sebastopol. One night he missed his way to the trenches, and being very short-sighted found himself in the lines of the enemy, and was taken prisoner. When the Russians learned that he was the son of a former Ambassador to their country, they sent him to St. Petersburg, gave him his parole, and he spent the remainder of the winter in amusing himself there. When his brother officers in the Crimea, who were undergoing the hardships of the winter in the trenches, heard of this, it was the subject of chaff among them, that it was not altogether by accident that Dunkellin had wandered into the lines of the enemy.

Sitting immediately behind Mr. Gladstone, on the occasion referred to, I reminded him of this story, and suggested that, in his reply, he should say that it was not the first time in his life that Dunkellin, with a fatal short-sightedness, had wandered into the lines of the enemy. Mr. Gladstone said, " That is excellent ; I will use it in my speech." He got up to reply shortly after, and made one of his most eloquent speeches, but without use of my suggestion as regards Dunkellin. When he sat down he turned round to me and said, " I was thinking all the time of my speech whether I could say that about Dunkellin, but I came to the conclusion that it was a little too bitter." Not one speaker in a thousand would have refrained from making use of such a retort.

The incident is an illustration of what I often observed

in Mr. Gladstone, namely, the double action of his mind when he was speaking. He would rise to reply on a subject which had arisen unexpectedly, and when he was uncertain as to what line to take. He would talk round it for some time, in the most perfectly formed sentences, while he was obviously making up his mind as to what conclusion he would adopt. Later he would state his deliberate judgment in clear and forcible words.

In these pages I have dealt with one topic only of Mr. Gladstone's long political career in the House of Commons— that relating to Ireland. But what a range it covered! What superhuman efforts he made in the twenty-six years, during which he was engaged on reforms for Ireland, and in advocating its right of self-government, and what extraordinary freshness and progressiveness of mind and purpose he showed.

It is a trite observation that the full height and grandeur of a range of mountains cannot be estimated by one who is standing near to the foot of them. The lower spurs hide the higher peaks. It is the same with great historic events, and with the careers of statesmen. They cannot be fairly judged till many years have elapsed, and till the full development of their policy comes into view. This is more true of Mr. Gladstone in relation to his Irish policy than of any other statesman of his time. The great miscarriage of his political career was his failure to carry Home Rule for Ireland in 1886 and 1893. This policy caused a breach between the great historic Whig Party, and the main body of Liberals, and threw the former into the arms of the Tory Party. It gave to the combination thus formed a tenure of office which lasted for nearly twenty years. But how different will be the verdict of history, if in the course of the next two years or even later, a Home Rule measure should be carried through Parliament. The main credit for this will undoubtedly be given to the statesman who initiated the policy, and devoted so many years of his life to the conversion of public opinion. It will then be recognized that the Whig statesmen who, by their secession, delayed the accomplishment of this policy, for so many years, did a great disservice to the State, and to no section of it more than to the Irish landlords.

Meanwhile, no final verdict can be given at present upon the policy of Mr. Gladstone. But, at least, we must all agree with the generous appreciation on his death by Mr. Balfour, that he was the greatest Member of the greatest deliberative assembly which so far the world had known.

When dealing in 1887 with the fifty years which elapsed between the Act of Union and the death of Sir Robert Peel,[1] I concluded by asking whether the expectations held out by Mr. Pitt, when presenting his measure to the British Parliament, had been realized, whether, to use his words, "mutual harmony and confidence had been established between England and Ireland." I showed that the effect of the Act had been to relegate the decision on purely Irish questions to the representatives of England and Scotland, who were ignorant of the condition and requirements of Ireland; that from time to time legislation demanded by great majorities of the Irish people was refused or rejected by majorities drawn from Great Britain; and that ultimately what was refused to the constitutional demands of the Irish people, was conceded to agitation attended by violence and outrage.

I showed that the effect of the suppression of Irish autonomy was to induce the Protestant minority in Ireland to dissociate itself from its fellow-citizens there, and to look for support in England; and to sectarianize and divide a people, who by the physical conditions of their country should be one community. I showed also that the Irish question had been the continual cause of embarrassment and disturbance in English and Imperial politics.

The events of the last half of the century recorded in the present book confirm, in a remarkable manner, the lessons drawn from the earlier period. Together they show that the only safe guide for legislation affecting Ireland is the demand of the majority of its representatives, and that Parliament has never neglected this principle without repenting later, and making concessions ultimately in advance of what would originally have satisfied the demand. It is an undeniable fact that Ireland during the last forty years passed through a period of most revolutionary changes of land tenure. They are not yet quite complete, though the principle of the expropriation of landlords, and the universal conversion of tenants into owners, has been virtually recognized by the authors of the Land Purchase Act of 1903. These great changes were forced upon

[1] *Peel and O'Connell*, 1887, p. 339.

Parliament by successive agitations attended by most regrettable outbreaks of violence.

The arguments to be drawn from these events in favour of conceding autonomy in administration and domestic legislation to Ireland, are enormously strong, and whenever such a measure is accomplished it will be recognized that to Mr. Gladstone it will have been mainly due.

INDEX